ATLAS
OF THE
CELTS

ATLAS
OF THE
CELTS

CLINT TWIST

CONSULTANT EDITOR · BARRY RAFTERY
UNIVERSITY COLLEGE DUBLIN

Philip's
ATLAS OF THE CELTS

Copyright © 2001 George Philip Limited

George Philip Limited,
an imprint of Octopus Publishing Group
2–4 Heron Quays
Docklands
London
E14 4JP

Commissioning Editor *Christian Humphries*

Executive Art Editor *Mike Brown*

Text Editors *Christian Humphries*
Rachel Lawrence

Consultant Editors *Dr Barry Raftery*
Dr Jane McIntosh

Picture Research *Christian Humphries*
Clint Twist
Rachel Lawrence

Page Layout *Ivan Dodd Designers*

Mapping *Andrew Thompson*

Production *Sally Banner*

ISBN 0 540 07880 8

Printed by Cayfosa-Quebecor, Spain

Details of other Philip's titles and services can be
found on our website at
www.philips-maps.co.uk

HALF-TITLE PAGE: Bronze and wooden bucket (1st
century BC) found at Aylesford, southern England.

OPPOSITE TITLE-PAGE: Detail of a cult wagon (7th
century BC) found at Strettweg, south-east Austria.

OPPOSITE FOREWORD: Crucifixion plaque (8th century
AD) from Ireland.

CONTENTS

FOREWORD

South of Ireland is the Celtic Sea, a sea lacking the oil for which Ireland had hoped. Even without that oil, Ireland's economy is currently booming and has been named after that unlikely beast the 'Celtic Tiger'. But it is not just in Ireland that the 'Celts' loom large. Archæologists, historians, philologists, anthropologists, art historians, artists, politicians, journalists, book publishers, football teams, druids and witches have all, in varying ways, concerned themselves with 'Celts' or with perceptions of 'Celts'. For many people in parts of northern and western Britain, but in Ireland especially, Celts are today a potent reality, an ancient people who invaded and settled.

In Ireland, priding itself as the last bastion of European 'Celticity', Celts are accepted by all but a few scholars as the immediate ancestors of the Irish. People 'feel' themselves to be Celtic, instinctively and without reservation. In daily life, the Celtic ethos is all pervading. A full page of the commercial section of the Dublin telephone directory lists businesses proudly proclaiming their 'Celticness': Celtic Bookmakers, Celtic Cabs, Celtic Computers, Celtic Corporate Hampers, Celtic Sun Lounges to take a random selection. Celtic is thus a badge of Irishness.

The rigorous scrutiny of modern scholarship, however, has looked askance at such nostalgic oversimplification. Today, there is discussion on the meaning of 'Celticity', especially among specialists in Britain and Ireland. The debate involves three distinct but interrelated components: archæology, language and the written sources. Each can be studied independent of the other, but only by bringing together the three strands can we aspire to a fuller picture.

The classical sources are quite specific. Greeks, in the 6th century make passing references to *Keltoi*, a people who existed north of Massilia (modern Marseilles). Romans, some time later, speak of *Galli* and *Gallatae* but also *Celtae* which, as Caesar tells us, was the name by which some of the tribes of Gaul described themselves.

The veracity of the Roman texts, documenting great migrations led by fighting men, is scarcely in doubt. The disastrous attack on Rome, which left a lasting scar on the Roman psyche, and later the attack on Delphi, are not the stuff of fantasy. The thousands of flat cemeteries, spreading from Gaul to the Carpathians, dominated by the burials of heavily armed warriors, cannot be seen as other than the graves of these migrating peoples. So the historically attested folk movements across Europe find confirmation in the material record and conventional archaeological dating is in keeping with what we may accept as historical reality.

Thus, two of the three key elements – history and archæology – are seen to coalesce. But what of language? It is surely axiomatic that ultimately, by our own definition, Celts are those who spoke a Celtic language. And here is the kernel of the 'Celtic' problem: even though we can identify migrating peoples both archaeologically and historically we cannot know to what extent the people in question spoke Celtic. Caesar tells us that some of the inhabitants of Gaul *called* themselves "Celtae", but we cannot be certain what language they spoke. The use of the term in ancient times is quite different from its usage today.

For the term is a modern construct, referring to a family of languages, first recognised by the Scot George Buchanan in the late 16th century. It was purely a linguistic concept, devoid of cultural implications.

We cannot say, therefore, that all those peoples involved in the mass movements were Celts. We can take it that these movements consisted of heterogeneous population, and indeed linguistic, groupings, drawn together from the melting pot of Europe, in pursuit of the common aims of land and plunder. But we do have tribal names and we do have the names of tribal leaders, which can only be seen as Celtic in the linguistic sense. The nature of the evidence is such, however, that often there will be doubt and uncertainty, and it is wrong to regard 'La Tène' and 'Celt' as synonymous just as it is wrong to regard La Tène art as diagnostically Celtic. By the same token, however, those who buried their dead in large, flat cemeteries, who had distinctive weapons and personal ornament and whose high status metalwork was adorned with versions of the pan-European La Tène style of ornamentation, included in their number those who may be termed Celts.

In 1946, T.F. O'Rahilly, a distinguished Irish historian, wrote

> "No archæologist by examining an archæological
> object – whether a bone or a brooch, a sword or a
> sickle – can possibly tell us that the object in
> question belonged to one who spoke a particular
> variety of Celtic".

A mere eight years later, in 1954, an iron sword of Middle La Tène character from Port in Switzerland was found to have the name "KORISOS" in Greek letters stamped on its blade. The name, which we can take as linguistically Celtic, must refer to the owner or, more likely, the sword smith. With this weapon – a Celtic name on a La Tène sword of the type found widely in Europe, in the graves of the migrating tribes – archæology, language and history are in complete harmony.

In Britain and Ireland, Celts are more elusive even though, in certain parts, Celtic dialects survive. In Ireland, indeed, Celtic is the first official language of the State, a compulsory subject in every school, yet at no time, before the first stirrings of 19th-century nationalism, did anybody ever call themselves Celtic.

There is today no convincing archaeological evidence that either island was invaded by Celtic peoples. By contrast, all indications point to continuity from earlier times. But the problem of language persists. Philologists are uncomfortable with the static picture presented by archaeology. The view has been proffered that babies learn from their mothers. According to this thesis, a new language presupposes women, and women must be taken as evidence for the immigration of tribal groupings, not merely armed male freebooters. Thus there is conflict between archaeology and the linguistic evidence, centring critically on the means by which languages spread. This conflict remains to be resolved but might, perhaps, with profit focus on the earliest dating of insular Celtic.

In Ireland and Britain, at any rate, Celts remain, as yet, in the shadows. On the European mainland, however, Celts emerge in the full light of history, as larger-than-life figures of flesh and blood, the first to escape the darkness of the unlettered past. We can picture them readily, from haughty Brennus to doomed Vercingetorix, both of whom entered Rome under very different circumstances. We can see them, uncowed by the great Alexander and hear the sound of trumpets and the clashing of swords at Telamon. These were no mean people who left behind a noble legacy.

The story of the Celts is a story worth telling and this book is such a story.

BARRY RAFTERY
UNIVERSITY COLLEGE DUBLIN

CHAPTER
ONE

▲ Detail on a bronze flagon from Dürrnberg, west-central Austria (late 5th century BC).

WHO WERE THE CELTS?

Many people can conjure up a surprisingly clear picture of the ancient Celts: proud, fiercely independent people, heroically represented by Vercingetorix (d. 46 BC) and Boudicca (d. AD 60). The ancient Celts are viewed as ferocious enemies when roused by the threat of foreign oppression – their warriors charging, in chariots and on foot, fearlessly into battle. When not at war, the ancient Celts are popularly seen as unsophisticated farming folk, ruled by clan chiefs and kings much given to feasting, personal adornment and barbarian splendour. In arts and crafts, the ancient Celts are considered skilled and inspired metalworkers, as well as poets and musicians of great renown. The druids loom in the shadowy edges of the picture – the mystical seers and keepers of ancient knowledge.

This picture, though useful as an *aide-memoire*, is far from complete. The heroic struggle against the Romans dates back to the Celts' defeat at the Battle of Telamon (225 BC). Before Telamon, the Celts were an ever-present threat to Rome. The struggles of Vercingetorix and Boudicca represent the swan song of the ancient Celts, a last snapshot before they were submerged (and largely assimilated) into the Roman Empire.

Celtic supremacy in the Iron Age

A more 'modern' picture of the ancient Celts sees them as either the first masters of Europe or the first pan-European civilisation. This picture covers a wider period:

extending back to *c.*750 BC and, although it covers the whole of Europe from Spain to the Black Sea, the focus is on central Europe, and the British Isles are relegated to the fringes of the Celtic world. These Celts emerge at the dawn of the Iron Age and spread vigorously, dominating much of Europe north of the Alps by *c.*200 BC.

The myth of migration?

An even more recent approach questions many of the assumptions made about the ancient Celts. It interrogates the nature of Celtic identity, and attempts to deconstruct and demythologise some of the history that built up around the Celts through the centuries. This picture has gained limited support. It sees no great folk-movements – apart from a few migrations for which there is definite historical evidence – but detects instead innovations and fashions travelling along ancient and sophisticated networks of trade between historically related groups of people. This approach challenges some firmly established beliefs about history and ethnicity, archæology and language. Yet, while this proposal provides a healthy counter-balance to the traditional tendency to explain everything by migrations, the history of migrations cannot be entirely ignored.

What exactly do we mean by the term 'Celts'?

When we refer to the Celts, do we mean people speaking a Celtic language as defined by those who

◄ **The Gundestrup cauldron** highlights the difficulty of determining and interpreting Celtic art. The silver cauldron was found at Gundestrup, West Himmerland, north Jutland, Denmark. It is generally thought to be of Celtic origin, and was perhaps brought to Denmark as plunder. Perhaps the most famous of all 'Celtic' finds, the cauldron is commonly dated to the 1st century BC, since the 'thorn' spurs worn by the first rider on this panel are rare before this date. Some argue that the panel shows a human sacrifice while armed men prepare for war. Others believe that the scene is a depiction of the warriors' initiation rite. The panel is divided by a 'tree of life'. Beneath the tree, are the infantry with caps, knee-length tunics, spears and shields. Through the initiation rite, conducted by the priest or god with braided hair on left, the foot soldiers become cavalrymen with crested helmets, short jerkins and hoses. In this latter account, the warrior is being placed in a pit (rather than a cauldron), covered with a piece of turf.

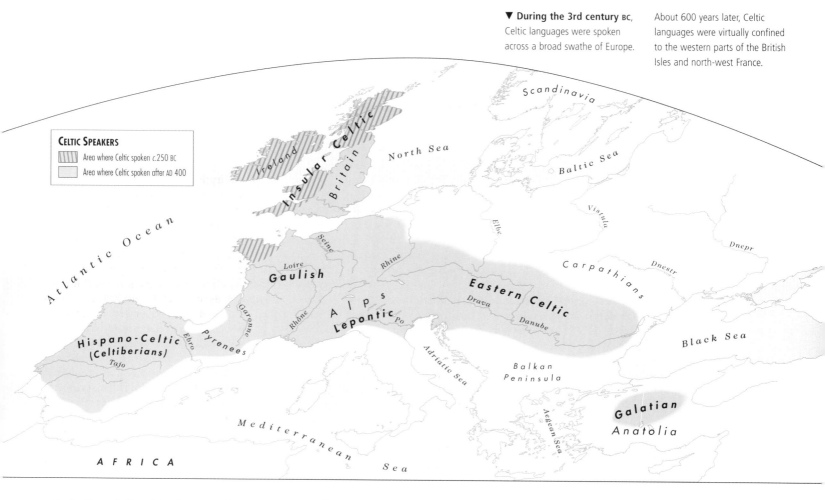

▼ **During the 3rd century** BC, Celtic languages were spoken across a broad swathe of Europe.

About 600 years later, Celtic languages were virtually confined to the western parts of the British Isles and north-west France.

CELTIC SPEAKERS
Area where Celtic spoken *c.*250 BC
Area where Celtic spoken after AD 400

study the relationships between languages; not only present-day languages, but also those known only from inscriptions and inference? Or do we mean people of Iron Age Europe as defined by archæologists who study the similarities and differences between art styles and manufacturing techniques?

For our first glimpse of the ancient Celts, and for the first use of the word 'Celtic', we have no option but to start with history. Physical archaeology rarely provides us with written records, and the archæology of language is nothing but words.

The first histories of the Celts

The Celts emerge into history, and then only fleetingly, in the writings of Greek historians. At the end of the 6th century BC, Hecataeus of Miletus places the *Keltoi* (Celts) some distance north of present-day Marseilles in southern France. A little later, Herodotus (484?–420? BC), the 'father of history', has them living in Spain and the upper Danube region. Most contact between Greeks and Celts took the form of indirect trade across the adjacent fringes of their respective worlds. However, it is highly likely that there were many direct encounters between Greeks and Celts. We know that Celts were mercenaries in the war between Sparta and Thebes (367 BC), and that Alexander the Great (356–323 BC) met the Celts in 335 BC. By 279 BC, when a band of Celts sacked the sacred treasuries at Delphi, Greek power was on the wane and the Celts were engaged in struggles with Germanic tribes and the emerging might of Rome.

We know most about the ancient Celts from the Romans, who called them Gauls. Caesar tells us that some of those living in Gaul called themselves *"Celtae"*. Only a few Celtic inscriptions have been found in Gaul. Most of the Celtic words that we have from the period are contained in reports by various Roman generals and historians, who use them to refer to their barbarian enemies, their weapons and their places of settlement.

We can be fairly certain that during the period of the Roman conquests in western Europe, many (if not most) of the inhabitants of Gaul and Britain spoke one of a number of related languages we now describe as belonging to the Celtic language group. Other related languages were spoken across a much wider area extending from Spain to the Balkans but, then as now, the fact that a language is spoken in an area does not mean that it is spoken by everybody all of the time.

▶ **Human head** on a bronze handle mount of the so-called 'Aylesford bucket', discovered in Kent, southern England. The bronze and wooden bucket dates from the 1st century BC. The swim-bladder protuberance on the head is typical of Celtic art from the La Tène period. It has been suggested that this is a depiction of a helmet and head-dress.

LANGUAGES AND THE PAST

▶ **Linear B** script inscribed on a clay tablet from Knossos, Crete, dating from *c.*1450 BC. In AD 1952, Michael Ventris deciphered the language as Mycenaean Greek, the oldest known dialect of Greek and, as such, the oldest written example of an Indo-European language. The script, read from left to right, has 90 syllabic signs, but cannot express groups of consonants. It was exclusively used to record the administration of the Mycenaean palaces.

▲ **Cathedral at Monreale**, near Palermo, Sicily. The cathedral (begun 1174) is a splendid example of the cross-fertilisation of different cultures and languages. It was built at the behest of the Norman king William II. The cathedral is a dazzling mix of Norman, Byzantine and Islamic artistic styles. Most of the mosaics are accompanied by inscriptions written in Latin or Greek.

▶ **Indo-European languages**
The Indo-European group of languages subdivides into nine branches. The Greek, Italic, Germanic, Slavic, Baltic, Celtic, Albanian and Armenian branches are spoken in modern-day Europe, while the Indo-Iranian branch is found in India, Nepal and the neighbouring countries.

Language is fundamental to human culture, indeed in many respects language is human culture. Speech is our primary means of communication and words are the units with which we construct sense. Language is also an enormously powerful social force. A shared language is both unifying and defining, and forms a barrier that excludes non-speakers.

Origins of humans and language

There is a lot more to language than mere words. The appropriate words must be used in an agreed sequence, and usually according to complicated rules of grammar. Languages are so complex, and yet so easily learned by children, that some experts have argued that humans must have an innate language-ability 'hard-wired' into their highly evolved brains.

Many scientists believe that modern humans (*Homo sapiens sapiens*) evolved *c.*130,000 years ago in East Africa. By analysing changes in mitochondrial DNA, geneticists can trace the human population back to a single ancestral 'Eve' figure. In much the same way, many philologists believe that there must once have been a single ancestral language, from which all other languages have evolved. The current theory is that humans began using a fully developed language *c.*50,000–40,000 years ago.

Language and writing

The study of language is a library-bound occupation. The languages of today merely provide a snapshot of contemporary language usage. To trace the development of languages, philologists must study not only earlier versions of present-day languages, but also those languages that were once spoken and are now 'dead'.

The study of past languages depends on stored language in the form of writing. Consequently, there is no material available for study before the invention of writing in Mesopotamia in *c.*3300 BC, but obviously there was language long before that date. It must be stressed that writing is not language, but a technology for recording language, and the two should not be confused. Modern English, French and Swedish are patently different languages, but they are written using the same basic Roman alphabet.

More than two centuries of study have enabled philologists to establish the relationships between most of the world's known languages, both living and dead, and group them into families and 'super-families'. These are often presented as a tree-diagram, with the living languages at the top and the ancestral languages at the bottom. The Celtic languages belong to the Indo-European language group.

Indo-European languages

Since the Renaissance period, European scholars have been aware of close links between their languages, links that seemed to be closer than could be explained by coincidence. During the 17th and 18th centuries, the comparative study of languages intensified and extended to include ancient languages. For example, scholars associated contemporary Welsh and Breton with ancient Celtic, and began to examine other links with ancient languages.

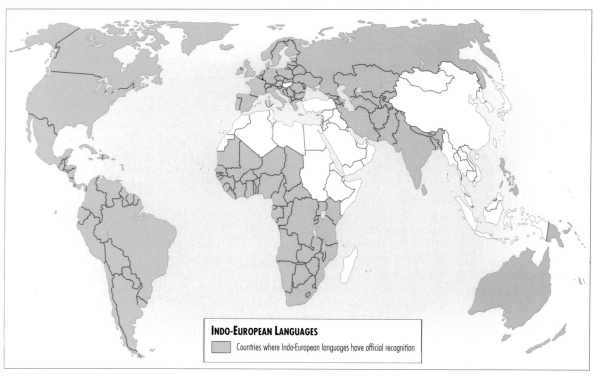

INDO-EUROPEAN LANGUAGES
Countries where Indo-European languages have official recognition

In 1786, Sir William Jones (1746–94), a British judge at the Calcutta Supreme Court, gave his presidential lecture to the Asiatic Society of Bengal. In this speech, he highlighted the close similarities between three (apparently separate) 'dead' languages: ancient Greek (which is quite different from modern Greek), Latin (the language of the Roman Empire) and Sanskrit (the sacred language of ancient India). One striking example of the similarities is the phrase 'sky father', which in Greek, Latin and Sanskrit is: '*zeu pater*', '*ju piter*' and '*dyaus pita*' respectively.

In 1813, the term 'Indo-European' was coined to describe the language group that Jones had identified. Since then, the discovery and translation of other ancient languages has added to the Indo-European group, and revealed a network of ancient Indo-European languages. This network stretches from central Asia (Tocharian) to western Europe (Celtic).

The Indo-European languages, some of which are known only from a handful of words, can be divided (according to relationships between them) into a number of branches. While most of these sub-groupings are generally accepted, some of the linguistic relationships remain controversial, as does their dating. The English language, for example, developed from the Germanic branch sometime after AD 500, but the origins of the Celtic languages are more obscure. Some authorities link Celtic with the Italic languages, and most are agreed that Celtic languages were first spoken around 1000 BC.

Indo-European domination

During the last 500 years, some Indo-European languages have spread all over the world and, in terms of official usage, the Indo-European language family now dominates the globe. This recent expansion, and the consequent decline – both in status and popular usage – of other languages can be traced back to population movements, which symbolically began with Christopher Columbus' voyage to America in 1492.

Tocharian has not been used for many centuries, but Celtic languages are still spoken in a few areas of Europe. To explain fully this enduring Celtic presence in Europe, and to appreciate the full extent of the Celtic heritage, it is necessary to examine the origins of the first Indo-European speakers.

▲ **Archaic Sumerian** script on a clay tablet from Jamdat Nasr, central Iraq, dating from *c.*3200–3000 BC. The tablet is one of the earliest examples of a written language. Archaic Sumerian remains poorly understood, but the tablet is believed to list quantities of various commodities.

▶ **Family tree** of Indo-European languages. Languages that are dead in the vernacular, such as Thracian or Lepontic, appear in italics. 'N' stands for North European Area, and 'S' for South European Area – as determined by reconstruction from indigenous substratal languages. 'W' stands for West Indo-European, and 'E' for East Indo-Euopean – as reflected in ancient dialectical groupings. Cimmerian is a hypothesised language in the proto-Baltic and Slavic area. Prehellenic is sometimes called Pelasgian. The tree shows the interrelationship of all the modern languages of western Europe (Celtic, Germanic and Romance) as well as many of the languages used in the Baltic states, Russia and northern India. There are *c.*2000 million speakers of Indo-European languages. Proto-Indo-European (PIE) is the hypothesised parent language of the family.

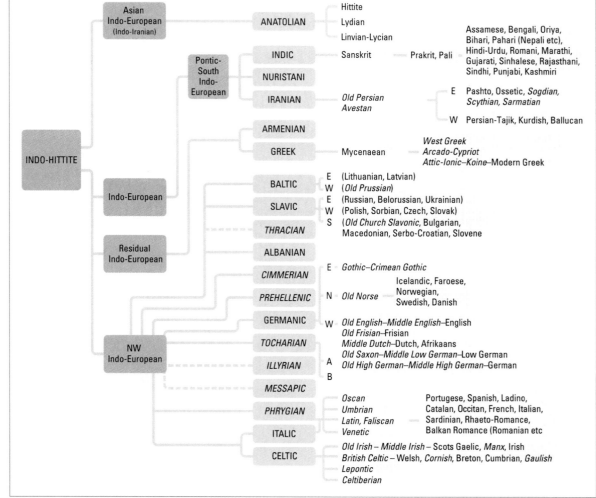

EARLY INDO-EUROPEAN EXPANSION

One of the main strands of Indo-European studies is the reconstruction of the ancestral language, known as Proto-Indo-European (PIE), from which the other languages in the group subsequently evolved. If there was a PIE language, then there must have been an ancestral group of PIE speakers who lived somewhere at some time. Academics vie for the prestige of establishing the location of the PIE 'homeland', and archaeologists search for artefacts that could bear a PIE label.

Language and politics

This would have been fine if it had remained merely a matter of dispassionate academic concern but, especially between the 18th- and 20th-centuries, language became inextricably and overtly linked with political nationalism. Language turned into a rallying cry, not just for oppressed peoples to justify their demands for independence, but also for their oppressors to validate their authority. Linguistic theory became tragically entwined with theories of national and racial supremacy.

The wholesale consequences of the pseudo-science that produced the Aryan ideal were Adolf Hitler's (1889–1945) racist polemic *Mein Kampf* (1925), and the obscenity of the Nazi extermination camps – images of which have burnt an ugly scar across our collective memory of the 20th century. In the post-World War II (1939–45) and post-colonial era of the United Nations (UN), Indo-European studies became distinctly unfashionable, tainted by its associations with racism.

The invasion theory

Nevertheless, a basic problem remains – not all the languages of modern Europe are Indo-European. Some, such as Hungarian, can be explained as later intrusions; but others, such as Basque and Finnish, are best explained by seeing the Indo-European languages themselves as intrusive. This prompts further questions: if these languages are not native to Europe, then where did they come from and when?

The most popular explanation is the 'invasion theory', which argues that the Indo-European languages were carried into Europe by a series of mass migrations. One version of this theory places the PIE homeland in southern Russia, with PIE speakers characterised as fierce cavalrymen and pastoral farmers. According to this theory, they spread in a series of waves after c.3500 BC. The wave that included the Celts arrived in central Europe in c.1000 BC. Further Indo-European expansion within Europe squeezed out all the other languages except for Basque, spoken today by the people of the western Pyrenees in north Spain and south-west France.

This theory concurs with Europe's history of mass human migration, such as the Germanic invasions of the 5th century AD, and a number of archaeologically defined cultures have been associated with PIE speakers, especially in southern Russia. Elsewhere the archaeological evidence is less convincing. According to the rules of language, the ancestral Celtic language cannot have developed much earlier than c.1000 BC. Yet in places such as Britain and Ireland, where Celtic traditions linger strongest, there is no sign of any significant immigration during the first millennium BC.

Turkish homelands?

A second theory places the PIE homeland in Anatolia, and a few thousand years earlier, c.6500 BC. From this

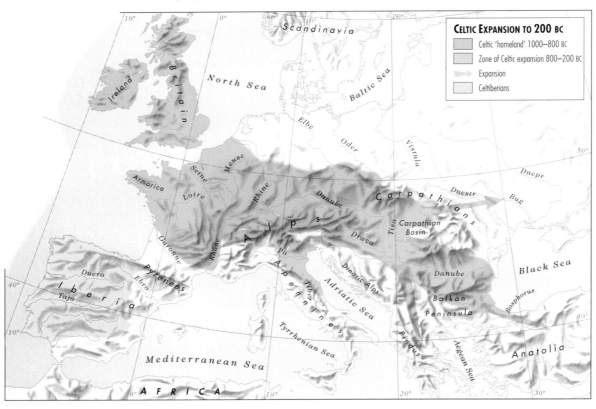

CELTIC EXPANSION TO 200 BC
- Celtic 'homeland' 1000–800 BC
- Zone of Celtic expansion 800–200 BC
- Expansion
- Celtiberians

◄ **Celtic expansion to 200 BC**
By 1000 BC, the Celts had settled in areas of modern-day France and Germany. Following the growth of the La Tène culture, the Celts dispersed throughout Europe. From the 5th century BC, they migrated throughout central and western Europe, reaching the British Isles in c.5th century BC. The Celts spread southwards, invading Italy in c.400 BC and sacking Rome in 390 BC. In 279 BC, Celtic tribes sacked Delphi in Greece and by 278 BC, they had crossed the Bosphorus into Anatolia. Also in the 3rd century BC, Celtic tribes expanded into northern Spain and became integrated with the Iberian peoples already living there; the area became known as Celtiberia.

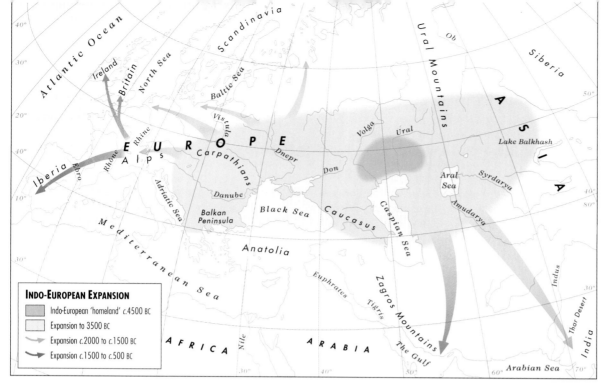

INDO-EUROPEAN EXPANSION

- Indo-European 'homeland' c.4500 BC
- Expansion to 3500 BC
- Expansion c.2000 to c.1500 BC
- Expansion c.1500 to c.500 BC

◄ **Indo-European expansion**
This map illustrates the invasion theory of Indo-European expansion, which identifies an Indo-European homeland in southern Russia. From here, Indo-Europeans migrated westwards into central Europe, reaching the British Isles in 1000 BC.

Anatolian homeland, the Indo-European languages spread throughout Europe and beyond with (and as a direct consequence of) the expansion of farming. By c.4250 BC, the two, interrelated phenomena had arrived in Britain and Ireland. Although this theory may fit more closely with the archæological evidence (though it should be noted that it runs counter to historical evidence in Asia), and avoids discredited ideas of 'racial' superiority based on military prowess, it has failed to convince most philologists and historians. The implication for Celtic studies of this second theory is that Celtic languages have been spoken in western Europe since at least 4000 BC, a date that philologists claim is unsustainable.

Interestingly, both theories can draw on support from genetics – it all depends on how one looks at the evidence. Scientists have analysed the geographical distribution of genetically influenced factors in human blood. Plotting the distribution of one factor produces a pattern that strongly suggests that Europe's population arrived from Anatolia. Plotting the distribution of another blood-factor produces a different pattern, one that conforms to the theory of invaders from southern Russia.

What is certain is that linguistic change is a complex phenomenon, of which large-scale migration may be only one cause out of many possibilities. The replacement of Europe's earlier languages by Indo-European counterparts need not have been due to mass migration.

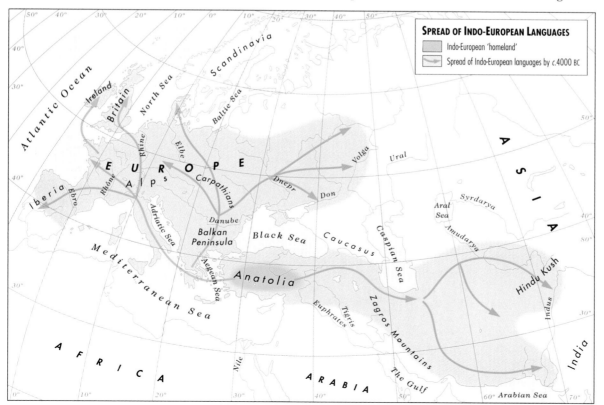

SPREAD OF INDO-EUROPEAN LANGUAGES

- Indo-European 'homeland'
- Spread of Indo-European languages by c.4000 BC

◄ **Spread of Indo-European languages** Some archæologists suggest an alternative hypothesis to the invasion theory. They argue that Indo-European expansion took place much earlier from a homeland in Anatolia.

LABELS AND MATERIAL CULTURE

It is human instinct to label things. To give objects a mutually acknowledged identity is one of the roots of language, and labels were coincidentally among the earliest uses of writing in pre-dynastic Egypt. The Celts are, and always have been, a linguistic entity – 'Celts' is a convenient label for people who speak Celtic languages, or who are descended from Celtic speakers. In historical accounts, Celts are most frequently encountered with another label affixed, one which locates them in a particular time and place. The labels most frequently appended to the Celts are 'Iron Age', 'Hallstatt' and 'La Tène'. These terms have nothing to do with language, instead they originate in archæology and represent an extremely compressed and 'shorthand' form of description.

Archæology and the 'Three-Age' theory

Aside from some specialised areas of study and methodology, archæology proceeds by digging objects out of the ground and labelling them. Properly speaking, every object excavated, whether human remains or artefact, is a fossil (evidence of past life) but this terminology is not widely accepted.

The basic principle of scientific archæology (as opposed to the rapacious kind that seeks only objects of value) is stratigraphy: if one object is discovered below another object, the lower object is considered older. This principle was developed from the experience of excavating tells (large mounds) formed by the accumulated debris of successive human settlements. Tells are common in the Middle East and some occur in the Balkan region, but they are absent from most of Europe.

The 'Three-Age' theory of western Eurasian cultural development in pre-history – that people proceeded from stone to bronze and then to iron tools – was devised by Christian Jürgensen Thomsen (1788–1865), curator of the National Museum of Denmark, as a means of classifying and arranging the various local antiquities in his care. Intuitively correct, the Three-Age system has become accepted as the backbone of archæological chronology in Europe and Western Asia, although it has little currency in other regions where material culture and technology developed differently.

► **Bronze shield** found in the River Thames at Battersea, southwest London. The Battersea shield is probably the most famous example of Insular La Tène art, if not of British Iron-Age art as a whole. The red glass inlay bears great similarity with that on the flagons found at Basse-Yutz, Mosel, north-east France (*see* page 47). The 'enamelled' sections with swastika motifs form the eyes of a fantastic beast. The shield probably dates from the 2nd or 1st century BC.

Subsequent research has shown that the Stone Age lasted for at least a million years, and did not end until well after the development of farming. Studies have also revealed that the Bronze Age was preceded by a less widespread Copper (or Chalcolithic) Age. The Iron Age, however, remains largely as originally conceived – that period when iron tools were used. As such, it is a useful but imprecise term.

There is fuzziness around the chronological and geographical edges of the Iron Age. The onset of iron tools was neither a sudden nor simultaneous event, but like other cultural phenomena, it began in some locations before others. The European Iron Age began in Greece and Italy long before it started in Britain or Denmark. Furthermore, the end of the Iron Age is usually defined as the beginning of the Roman period, which is also given various dates, dictated by the advance of the legions across the continent over a period of some 300 years. In Denmark, which escaped Roman invasion, the Iron Age ends in the gloom of the Dark Ages. In Ireland, which also escaped Roman subjugation, the Iron Age is followed by a great cultural flowering.

Material cultures of Hallstatt and La Tène

In the archæological time-scale of western Europe, Hallstatt and La Tène are subdivisions of the Iron Age – first the Hallstatt period, then the La Tène period - but they signify much more than this. Archæology has its own rules about the precedence of names, and cultures are usually named after the site where they were discovered and identified.

In this context, 'Hallstatt' may be defined as "closely associated with a distinctive style of material culture that is typified by artefacts found in a cemetery at Hallstatt in west-central Austria that dates from the start of the Iron Age to c.480 BC." The 'La Tène' label has a similar meaning, but the end of the definition might read "...artefacts found on the bed of Lake Neuchâtel in east Switzerland, and dating from c.480 BC to the end of the Iron Age."

Neither Hallstatt nor La Tène 'means' Celtic. Some Celtic-speaking peoples undoubtedly made and used objects that can be categorised as Hallstatt or La Tène.

These particular styles of material culture may even be exclusively Celtic, but that is all – they are not synonyms.

Material culture is in many ways the most transient of ethnic indicators. For instance, office workers in Tokyo, Mumbai, and Mexico City may share an almost identical material culture – they use artefacts such as telephones and computers that are manufactured by global corporations, and they may wear clothes that conform to international standards of business dress. They may even communicate with each other using an internationally understood 'business' language, most probably English. At home, however, they speak entirely different languages and, although these languages can be translated, their cultures and ethnicity remain distinct.

▲ **Bronze axe with horse** found at Hallstatt, west-central Austria. This ornamental axe dates from the 7th century BC. The 'primitive', stylised and plastic quality of the depiction of animals, coupled with the use of geometic designs such as zig-zags, are hallmarks of Hallstatt culture.

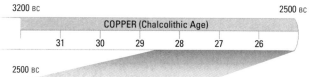

3200 BC						2500 BC
COPPER (Chalcolithic Age)						
31	30	29	28	27	26	

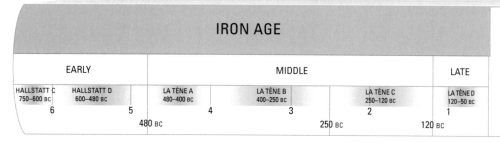

2500 BC																			750 BC
BRONZE AGE																			
EARLY (Unětician culture)					MIDDLE (Tumulus culture)				LATE (Urnfield culture)										
												HALLSTATT A 1200–1000 BC			HALLSTATT B 1000–750 BC				
24	23	22	21	2000	19	18	17	1600	15	14	13	12	11	10	9	8	7		

750 BC						50 BC	
IRON AGE							
EARLY			MIDDLE			LATE	
HALLSTATT C 750–600 BC	HALLSTATT D 600–480 BC	LA TÈNE A 480–400 BC	LA TÈNE B 400–250 BC	LA TÈNE C 250–120 BC	LA TÈNE D 120–50 BC		
6	5	4	3	2	1		
	480 BC			250 BC	120 BC		

◄ **Chronology of the Metal Ages** in Europe. The period from the 3rd to the 1st millennium BC has been classified into three ages (Copper, Bronze and Iron). The timeline also shows the various sub-divisions within each age.

CELTIC LANGUAGES TODAY

Putting languages on a map is not a once and for ever activity. In just about every habitable location on Earth, language use has changed dramatically over the previous 2000 years and uncontaminated patterns of language use are now found only among 'primitive' peoples in the remotest regions. Overall, the number of 'living' languages has declined, largely because of population movements. At the end of the 20th century, this trend accelerated with the advent of satellite telecommunications and the Internet.

Q-Celtic and P-Celtic
Today, Celtic languages are confined to the maritime fringes – the peninsulas and islands – of north-west Europe. Modern 'Celtic' Europe is divided into six regions, each with its own language, but in none of these regions is a Celtic language spoken predominantly; and in only three of these regions (Ireland, Wales and the Isle of Man) does the Celtic language have any official status.

In total, there are c.3.5 million Celtic speakers across the six regions. However, there is now probably nobody whose spoken and written communications are

entirely restricted to a Celtic language. During the last quarter of the 20th century (1981 census), c.5,000 people claimed to be monolingual in Irish. As "mother tongues" two of the six languages have already become extinct, and survive only as historical curiosities, known only to academics and enthusiasts.

Philologists are inclined to divide the present-day Celtic languages into two branches. Irish, and its dialect derivatives Scots Gaelic and Manx form one branch known as Gaelic (Goidelic), or Q-Celtic. Welsh, Breton and Cornish form the other branch, which is known as Brythonic, or P-Celtic.

The division is based on a sound shift that occurred during the development of the Celtic languages. The Gaelic branch retained the hard Proto-Indo-European 'kw' sound, written as 'q' and later as 'c', while the Brythonic branch changed 'kw' to 'p'. Such sound shifts are quite common in the development of languages, especially in the period before language became 'frozen' by writing. A similar shift occurred during the development of Greek, which is why only the earliest Greek alphabets have the letter 'digamma'.

Opinion is divided both as to the timing and significance of the *Q-P* sound shift in the Celtic languages. Linguistic evidence suggests that the shift occurred sometime around the 5th century BC, which supports the idea that Ireland was 'celticised' by a separate and earlier wave of Celtic invaders than those who occupied the rest of the British Isles. The change from 'kw' to 'p' was adopted in England, but not in remoter Ireland. However, it can be argued that the linguistic evidence is based more on theory than on fact – examples of early Celtic writing are fragmentary and very rare, and most written evidence dates from after AD 500. Furthermore, archæologists have found no evidence for Celtic invasions of the British Isles at any time during the 1st millennium BC. On the other hand, linguistic change can occur without invasion, so the lack of supporting evidence for the 'invasion theory' does not discount the linguistic argument.

Celtic – an uncertain future
At the beginning of the 21st century, the Celtic languages face uncertain futures. In Ireland, the use of Irish has declined steadily since the 16th century. There was a literary Gaelic revival at the end of the 19th century as an adjunct of the nationalist movement, and Irish is now officially the first language of the Republic of Ireland, although it is used rarely in everyday life. Indeed, less than one-third of the population claim to be able to speak any Gaelic, and as a spoken language it is restricted to parts of the extreme west.

Gaelic was introduced to Scotland from Ireland and, although once widespread, it is now spoken by only

▶ **Isle of Man flag** The *triskele* symbol (three legs) is similar to the swastika, which was debased by its association with Nazism. The legs of the Isle of Man flag have armour and spurs. The symbol was popular among the ancient Celts and Norseman of north-west Europe. The last native speaker of 'traditional' Manx died in 1974. In 1985, the Tynwald (the Manx Parliament established by the Vikings more than 1000 years ago) established the Manx Gaelic Advisory Service to assist in the revival of the language.

▶ **Frontispiece** to *The Emigrant's Guide to North America* (1841) by Robert McDougall. This Gaelic book provided a practical background for Highland Scots emigrating to Canada, as well as serving as a form of travelogue, describing particular sights and sounds on McDougall's journey to Goderich, south Ontario. The Gaelic text reads, "He who sets out in good time/Will produce food and a crop of substance/While hopeless weak people/Are dying of famine:/His wife and children/Will be prosperous and good-looking/While poor souls without drive/Are oppressed under the Lowlanders."

CEANN-IÙIL AN FHIR-IMRICH DO DH'AMERICA MU-THUATH; OR, THE EMIGRANT'S GUIDE TO NORTH AMERICA. BY ROBERT M'DOUGALL, ESQ.

GLASGOW: J. & P. CAMPBELL, 24, GLASSFORD STREET. OBAN: J. MILLER.—INVERNESS: J. BAIN & CO. DINGWALL: A. KEITH. MDCCCXLI.

about two per cent of the population, mostly in the Western Isles. In the early 20th century, there was a deliberate attempt to stamp out Scots Gaelic. Recently, nationalist sentiment following devolution and the establishment of a separate Parliament has boosted interest in the language. The Manx language of the Isle of Man was also introduced from Ireland. Although it still has some formal usage in the island's Parliament (the Tynwald), Manx is, apart from learned interest, dead.

The Welsh language is the closest survivor of the ancient British language spoken before the Roman invasion. The use of Welsh declined from the Act of Union (1536) until the 18th century, since when it has been steadily revived. During the 1960s, the Welsh language was politicised by Welsh nationalists, and the painting out of road signs in English became a widespread form of political protest. Within the Principality of Wales, all official documents now must be bilingual (Welsh and English), and there is a separate Welsh-language television channel. As a spoken language, however, Welsh is mainly confined to rural areas.

The Cornish language died out in the late 18th century, but has since been revived by enthusiasts. The Breton language of Brittany in north-west France, probably originated with the language of the ancient Gauls, but was later influenced by Welsh and Cornish settlers. Breton was revived from near extinction during the 17th century, but has now declined to c.800,000 speakers.

It remains to be seen what becomes of the Celtic languages in the 21st century, but one thing is already clear: in the modern world, Celtic identity cannot be confined to those who speak a Celtic language.

▲ **Bilingual road sign** in Llangollen, east Wales. Welsh has probably the largest number of speakers of any Celtic language today. A survey published (1995) by the Welsh Office estimated that about 22% of the population of Wales speak Welsh.

◄ **Dorothy Pentreath** of Mousehole, Cornwall, south-west England, was the last native speaker of the Cornish language. She died in 1777. In 1860, a memorial to her was erected by Prince Louis-Lucien Bonaparte (1813–91), nephew of Napoleon I and an expert on the Basque language and English dialects.

► **Celtic language today** The main difference between modern Irish and Scottish Gaelic is the occurrence of many Norse loanwords in Scottish. Whilst Irish and Scottish are still spoken in western Ireland and Scotland, Manx became extinct on the Isle of Man in the 19th century when it was displaced by English. There are structural and grammatical similarities between Goidelic and Brythonic languages, but significant differences lie in pronunciation.

CELTIC LANGUAGES TODAY
Goidelic – Q-Celtic
Brythonic – P-Celtic

CHAPTER
TWO

▲ Unicyclist support for a couch found in a 'prince's' tomb at Hochdorf, south Germany (6th century BC).

PREHISTORIC EUROPE

▼ **The Copper Age** preceded the Bronze Age in Europe. The Millaran culture in south-east Spain was one of earliest societies to use copper. The later Corded Ware culture in northern and eastern Europe marked the beginnings of a shift from communal to individual burial. The Beaker folk probably originated in Spain, but they soon spread into central and western Europe in their search for copper and gold. In central Europe, the Beaker folk came into contact with the Battle-Axe culture. The Beaker culture are often credited with introducing copperwork to the British Isles.

To see the Celts of 500 BC as barbarians, is to see them from the south, from the urbanised perspective of the Mediterranean city-states. From a 'north-of-the-Alps' perspective, the Celts preserved and developed a 4000-year-old tradition of mixed farming, and a 2000-year-old expertise in bronzeworking. The existence and nature of these two technologies, agriculture and metalworking, has been verified through archaeological evidence; and their developmental stages are used to mark the opening 'chapters' in the story of Europe.

The early settlement of Europe has been studied intensively, but remains imperfectly understood. There is an accumulated mass of archaeological detail, but a comprehensive picture still eludes us. The outlines can, however, be sketched in broad strokes with some confidence.

During the Neolithic and Bronze Age periods, Europe as a whole was sparsely populated by comparison with today. Yet from time to time, and in numerous localities, population may have exceeded levels found in some parts of modern rural Europe. Some of these population groups flourished over time, and evolved distinctive styles of technology and decoration. These groups are the 'characters' who inhabit the early chapters of our story.

Early agriculture

Early farming techniques, originating in the Near East and Anatolia, were practised in parts of the southern Balkans and Greece by 7000 BC, and spread in a broadly north-westerly direction across Europe during the next 3000 years. The expansion of farming can be traced by related pottery styles, since vessels were required for such purposes as the storage of grain and the transport of water. One major route of growth, taken by groups identified with linear band pottery (vessels decorated with pairs of parallel lines arranged in spiral or meander patterns), was along the River Danube into central Europe and along other rivers into the Netherlands and northern France. The other main route, associated with impressed pottery (vessels decorated with incised marks), followed the coastline from Greece to Italy to southern France and into Spain. By c.4000 BC, farming had been established among scattered communities across most of Europe.

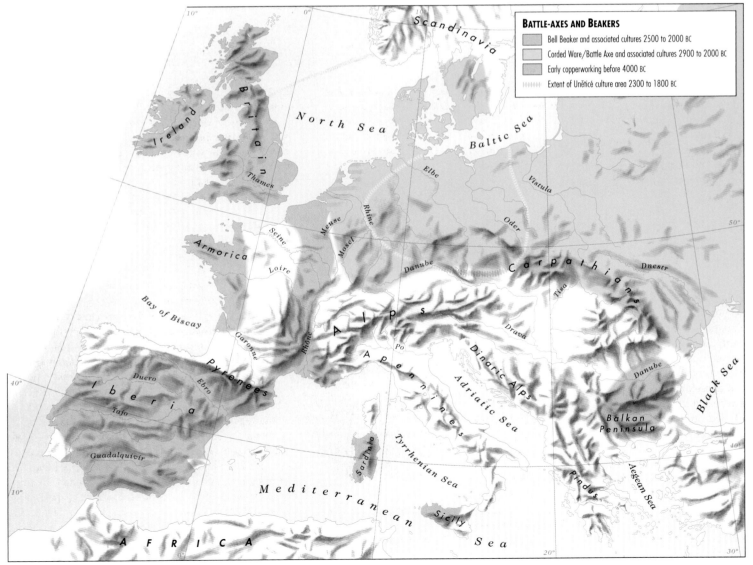

BATTLE-AXES AND BEAKERS

- Bell Beaker and associated cultures 2500 to 2000 BC
- Corded Ware/Battle Axe and associated cultures 2900 to 2000 BC
- Early copperworking before 4000 BC
- Extent of Unětičé culture area 2300 to 1800 BC

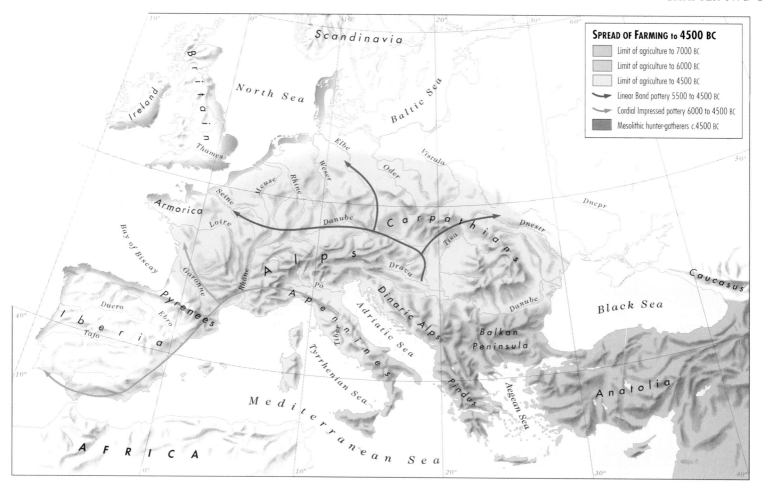

SPREAD OF FARMING to 4500 BC

Limit of agriculture to 7000 BC
Limit of agriculture to 6000 BC
Limit of agriculture to 4500 BC
Linear Band pottery 5500 to 4500 BC
Cordial Impressed pottery 6000 to 4500 BC
Mesolithic hunter-gatherers c.4500 BC

The nature of this transformation is uncertain. Older theories often emphasise the rapid advance of pioneer farmers 'leap-frogging' to the next patch of fertile soil. Other theories have noted that a gradual advance of less than one kilometre (0.6 miles) per year would be enough to account for the expansion. More recently, attention has focused on the acquisition of farming techniques – and associated technologies such as decorated pottery – by Mesolithic hunter-gatherers.

Whatever the nature and speed of the event, its effects were dramatic. By 4000 BC, the destruction of Europe's forests was well under way. Using polished stone axes and fire, the early cultivators cleared tracts of woodland for their fields and pastures. Sustained grazing of drier, upland areas produced large areas of virtually treeless landscape. Fertile land was 'ploughed' using crude devices, dragged by humans, which did little more than scratch the soil. In the far west of Europe, great megalithic tombs were constructed, perhaps to symbolise this new relationship with ancestors and the land. Later innovations, such as wheeled vehicles in northern Germany (by c.3000 BC), led to greater productivity and increased the cultivators' potential for accumulating a surplus.

Metals and trade

Trade in Europe long predates agriculture, and during the Mesolithic period, from c.12,000 BC, hunter-gatherers distributed stone tools over considerable distances, as did the Neolithic farmers who gradually replaced them. Settlement is a prerequisite for crop farming, and settlements, no matter how well situated, can have a

▲ **The spread of farming** in Europe is marked by the use of Linear Band pottery in central and northern Europe, and Cordial Impressed pottery in southern and western Europe.

▲ **Bell Beaker** from the Early Bronze Age, discovered at Seahouses, Northumberland, north-east England.

restricting effect on human access to resources. Trade and exchange between agricultural groups were essential, because few (if any) settlements were able to achieve complete self-sufficiency. Surplus harvest, livestock and perhaps humans were traded and exchanged along with other items, such as pigments for pottery. After c.3000 BC, a new form of wealth – metal – made its appearance.

The spread of metalworking in Europe is broadly associated with two related cultural groups: the Corded Ware (c.3000–2400 BC) cultures in the east, and the Bell Beaker (c.2600–2000 BC) cultures in the west. Among the Corded Ware cultures was a group of south Russian farmers who had domesticated the horse and learned to ride. The apparent spread into Europe of their distinctive burial mounds (kurgans) has been interpreted as the first incursion of Indo-Europeans (possibly including proto-Celts) into central Europe. Older theories envisaged similar events in the west – a 'Beaker Folk' actively colonising and gaining local supremacy. More recent ideas tend to play down the role of human migration, and are inclined to interpret Bell Beakers as a fashionable status symbol used by various unrelated peoples.

What is certain is that, along with the spread of metalworking, the Corded Ware and Bell Beaker cultures are associated with a move from communal to individual burial, and an increased emphasis on pastoralism. In Europe, bronze was probably first produced (c.2500 BC) in what is now the Czech Republic. Within a few centuries, a bronzeworking culture (named Unětice after a cemetery site in the Czech Republic) extended from the Alps to the North Sea.

COPPER AND BRONZE

The development of bronze technology was not a single event, but part of a European metalworking tradition that stretches back nearly 7000 years. At first, lumps of naturally occurring metals – mainly native copper from outcrops, but also alluvial (placer) gold – were cold-hammered into attractive or ritual shapes. The manufacture of these items probably involved the basic technique of using heat to alter the physical properties of metals. This was not a great advance – the earlier production of pottery had also involved the controlled application of heat.

By c.4000 BC, copperworking (the smelting of ore and fabrication of objects) was developed independently in the Balkans and southern Spain, where there were rich deposits of copper ores. Similar technologies had been developed earlier in parts of the Middle East, from Anatolia to Iran, and were later (c.3000 BC) developed in northern Italy.

Initially, hammering was the main technique, with heat being used to soften the metal while working, and perhaps harden it afterwards during the process of tempering. The first castings were made in simple one-piece, open moulds carved from stone. Sometimes the copper extracted by smelting was naturally alloyed with arsenic or antimony, which made the finished metal harder and gave it an attractive, silvery sheen. Copperworking skills spread throughout most of Europe between 3000 and 2000 BC, and, while it did not radically affect society because copper was of limited use for tools and weapons, it had some importance in enhancing prestige.

The importance of bronze

The alloy of tin and copper, usually called bronze, was introduced into central Europe in c.2500 BC, and by 2000 BC bronzeworking was a fledgling industry at several sites in Switzerland and Germany. Bronze is harder and stronger than copper and makes a better edge for cutting implements. However, because tin is much rarer in the Earth's crust and accessible deposits are few and far between, bronze is also much more difficult to produce than copper.

Despite, or indeed because of, the effort and expense involved in its production, bronze, unlike copper, did have a major impact on society. The desire for bronze and the quest for tin deposits were a tremendous spur to trade and exploration. Bronze was also a major factor in the development of

◀ **Bronze flask** found at Dürrnberg, near Hallein, west-central Austria. It dates from the 4th century BC. The flask is 60 centimetres (24 inches) high and can hold 17.5 litres (nearly four gallons) of liquid. To the left of the flask sits a 'Berru-style' bronze helmet (also from the 4th century BC) that was found in the same grave at Dürrnberg.

warrior-élites who controlled the supply of metals and used them to demonstrate their personal wealth and status. Bronze even conveyed status at one remove. The bronze vessels used by the élites were sometimes imitated in clay by potters serving the aspirations of those on the fringes of the bronze-using zones, and by Scandinavian stoneworkers who painstakingly made flint copies of bronze daggers.

Advances in metalwork

During the Bronze Age in Europe (*c*.2500–800 BC), various improvements in metalworking techniques were made and these spread, with varying degrees of speed and direction, across the continent. In *c*.2400 BC, two-piece moulds, which produce objects with completely moulded surfaces, were introduced into the Carpathians, eastern Europe. In *c*.2000 BC, the Unĕticé culture (in what is now the Czech Republic) developed a method of casting bronze handles to separate bronze blades, and the first metal vessels (made of hammered gold) were produced in the Balkans *c*.200 years later.

After *c*.1300 BC, hammering became a popular method of shaping bronze. The hammered sheets were fastened with rivets or by overcasting, and surfaces were decorated by engraving or *repoussé* (hammered into relief). The lost-wax (*cire perdue*) process of casting was adopted from about the same date, enabling the production of small and intricate bronze items. Alloying skills also developed, and lead was added to casting bronze to increase its fluidity when molten.

Bronze rapidly replaced stone and copper for tools, such as sickles, axes, adzes and chisels, and weapons such as daggers, although chipped stone continued to be used for everyday cutting tasks in many areas. Bronze also enabled the development of a new weapon – the sword. With the development and spread of swords came the whole panoply of warrior display made in bronze – chest protectors, helmets, leg and arm guards. These were of limited practical use, and were primarily for display. Although military applications appear to have taken priority, there was enough metal in circulation by the Late Bronze Age to produce a wide range of jewellery, tableware and personal accoutrements such as mirrors and razors. Bronze remained in common use throughout the Iron Age and, if anything, its social and economic significance as the material of prestige objects increased after the introduction of iron.

After *c*.1000 BC, the skills of central and northern European bronzeworkers were in every way comparable with those of their southeastern Mediterranean counterparts, the differences were ones of scale and organisation. The aristocracies of the Middle Eastern, Greek and Roman empires could command considerable resources to produce massive bronze objects – such as life-size statues and enormous wine vessels. North of the Alps, where resources and populations were smaller and less concentrated, organised 'industrial' activity was confined to workshops mass-producing small items such as axe-heads or harness fittings. Some of the bronze axe-heads produced were of such poor quality alloy, that they were probably intended for use as a medium of exchange rather than as axes.

▲ **Bronze spear and mould** found in Britain, and dating from the pre-Celtic period. They illustrate the sophisticated early techniques used to produce bronze weapons.

▼ **Two bronze axe-heads** found in Britain. Bronze is an alloy of copper and tin. In order to produce these axe-heads, copper was smelted and combined with smelted tin, probably in a

proportion of nine to one, in a charcoal-burning furnace. The molten bronze was cooled in a clay channel and divided into ingots which were then remelted and poured into a clay mould.

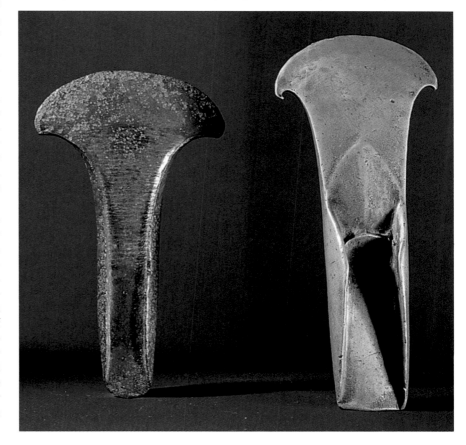

MIDDLE BRONZE AGE (2000–1600 BC)

The increase in the numbers and variety of bronze objects that characterised the Unětiće culture, in what is now the Czech Republic, soon spread to adjoining regions (including Silesia in Poland) and thence to other parts of Europe. Even those regions, such as Scandinavia, that lacked raw materials became involved in metallurgy by trading metals for amber and fur. Other economic factors also began to influence European society at this time. Woolly sheep, for example, were introduced, which could be sheared annually to produce large amounts of valuable fibres for clothing. Pastoral farming, especially cattle rearing, became more widespread in western Europe, and horses spread to the Atlantic coast region. The horse, probably domesticated, is also found in Beaker levels at Newgrange, County Meath, Ireland. The most energetic and innovative area at this time was Carpathia in eastern Europe, where two-piece moulds with clay cores were used to make shaft-hole axes, and an advanced form of prestige weaponry – the chariot – was introduced from farther east.

These factors further encouraged the development of warrior élites who, by accumulating and controlling wealth in the form of metals, livestock and woollen cloth (and employing skilled workers such as smiths and weavers), were able to establish themselves in a socially dominant position. In the early centuries of the 2nd millennium BC, fortified hilltops became an increasingly common feature of the European landscape, and many rich warrior graves attest to the wealth and ostentation of the new élites.

Trade in metals

Another result of these economic developments was an explosion in the volume and complexity of metal trade, mainly in copper, tin and bronze. Traditional trade routes developed into a series of regional trading networks that stretched right across Europe. The élite centres traded and exchanged raw materials and finished goods, both locally and over long distances. The commodities traded were not restricted to metals. For instance, amber from the Baltic coast was available at this time both in Britain and Ireland to the west, and in Greece further east. Trade in fur was also significant.

The trade routes themselves generally followed water – either by sea (following coasts and crossing to islands), or along Europe's great rivers such as the Danube and Rhine, natural highways to be travelled by boat or followed on foot. In the south-east, the trade network centred on Greece and under the control of the Mycenaeans, was in direct contact with the civilisations of the eastern Mediterranean, and therefore its history is

▼ **Urnfield culture** first emerged in c.1300 BC in eastern Europe. During the 12th century BC, it spread into what is now Italy and northern Europe. By 850 BC, it had been adopted by Celtic tribes throughout Europe. In the Atlantic regions, however, the burial tradition remained.

▼▶ **Urnfield culture** This Late Bronze Age urn (c.1250–850 BC) was found at the Celtic *oppidum* of Mont Lassois, north-east France. The geometric pattern is typical of the period.

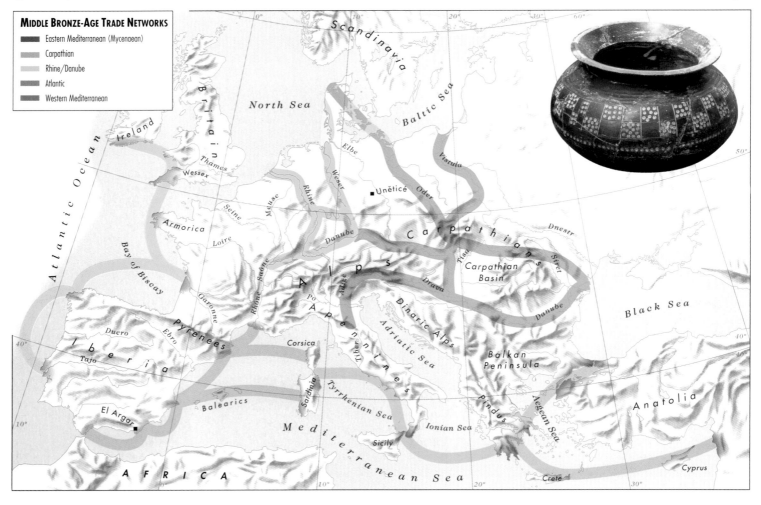

MIDDLE BRONZE-AGE TRADE NETWORKS
- Eastern Mediterranean (Mycenaean)
- Carpathian
- Rhine/Danube
- Atlantic
- Western Mediterranean

well documented. The other European trade networks were excluded from direct contact with Mycenae, and consequently have no clear identification with a named group. At best, we can say that the trade network in the extreme west of the Mediterranean was centred on El Argar in south-east Spain, or that the ranchers of the Wessex culture in southern England were part of the Atlantic trade network.

Although they cannot be ethnically identified like the Mycenaeans, the peoples of other regional networks certainly fostered the development of regional styles of manufacture and decoration. Some of these styles, both technical and 'artistic', entered the trade network and became adapted, altered and dispersed. Although 'civilian' artefacts such as jewellery are present, the archaeological record of the Middle Bronze Age has a strong 'military' bias.

Urnfield culture

About 1300 BC, at the beginning of the Late Bronze Age, a social revolution known as the Urnfield phenomenon began to transform Europe. In the course of the next 500 years, a remarkably unified culture was progressively established over much of central and western Europe. Emerging initially in western Carpathia, the phenomenon spread first, not to adjacent territory, but to the hubs of the nearby trading networks.

The distinguishing feature of the transformed societies, is a change in 'funeral' practice. From a tradition of inhumation (burial), or other means of disposing of the dead – for long periods in Britain, for example – there is no readily detectable archaeological record for the practice of burial – there was a shift to cremation, with the ashes of the deceased placed in pottery 'urns' that were buried in large cemeteries (urnfields). This change, generally interpreted as evidence of a revolution in belief systems, was by no means complete and most urnfields contain a mixture of inhumation and cremation. The significance of these differences is a matter for fierce debate and issues of ethnicity and migration remain unresolved, although it seems generally agreed that, in eastern Europe at least, the early Urnfield period was marked by major social upheaval involving significant population movements.

▼ **This bronze cuirass** from St-Germain-du-Plain, east France, dates from the Late Bronze Age (c.1250–850 BC). About 50 cm (20 in) high, it was crafted from an embossed bronze sheet.

▼▼ **During the Middle Bronze Age**, trade routes used by the Mycenaeans expanded further west to mainland Italy. In central Europe, the River Danube opened up trade routes to the north and west.

URNFIELD CULTURE

- Urnfield culture 1350 to 1250 BC
- Urnfield culture 1250 to 1000 BC
- Urnfield culture 1000 to c.850 BC
- Atlantic culture c.900 BC

HALLSTATT A and B (1200–750 BC)

It has been argued that the Celts emerge as an identifiable linguistic group in Europe during the Hallstatt period (c.1200–480 BC), which is named after a prehistoric salt-mining site in west-central Austria. The name 'Hallstatt' can be broken down into 'Hall', the Celtic word for 'Salt', and 'statt', Celtic for 'place'.

The period is subdivided into four phases: Hallstatt A (c.1200–1000 BC) and B (c.1000–750 BC) are assigned to the Late Bronze Age; and Hallstatt C (c.750–600 BC) and D (c.600–480 BC) are reserved for the Early Iron Age. It has become common practice to use the term Hallstatt to refer just to phases C and D, with phases A and B absorbed under the umbrella of the Urnfield period.

Salt-mining began at Hallstatt in c.1000 BC, and was probably initiated by miners from nearby copper mines. Salt was an essential, and therefore valuable, commodity for agricultural communities (both as flavouring and as a preservative) and away from evaporation sources along seacoasts was scarce. The huge deposit of rock-salt at Hallstatt offered a source of ready wealth for those with the expertise to extract it.

Tunnelling diagonally into sloping ground, a process known as 'adit-mining', the Hallstatt miners excavated a labyrinthine network of underground passages. Because salt is such a good preservative, many organic items, such as antler picks, wooden axe-handles and leather rucksacks, lost or abandoned by the ancient miners, have survived for thousands of years in almost perfect condition.

Settlement at Hallstatt

For the first century or so, salt extraction was carried out as an isolated industry – no traces of permanent habitation have been found – perhaps by gangs of miners working seasonally. The salt mines provided a source of additional wealth for those who controlled the metal resources of the region. Shortly after 900 BC, a settlement was established, based entirely on mining and exporting salt. Hallstatt quickly grew to around 300–400 inhabitants, much larger than most settlements in Late Bronze Age Europe. The inhabitants buried their dead in a nearby cemetery and, although they initially followed the prevailing practice of cremation, the Hallstatt graves included a greater than average number and variety of goods, thus standing out from the general Urnfield culture. These goods reflect the wealth and the long-distance trade links of the inhabitants. More than a thousand of the graves have been excavated and studied, and an analysis of their contents led to the chronological subdivision of the Hallstatt period into A, B, C and D.

Although it has become the defining site, determining both the dating of the period and the technological and decorative styles identifiable in grave goods, Hallstatt itself was atypical in many respects. It was a large commercial production centre with little or no agricultural base, at a time when most settlements were small and agricultural. Even the few settlements that rivalled or exceeded Hallstatt in size were predominantly inhabited by farmers.

Nevertheless, the burials and presumed lifestyles of Hallstatt's inhabitants would seem on the face of the archaeological evidence to have been very similar to those of other élite groups in south-central Europe at this time. Of particular note is the large number of

▶ **Miner's knapsack** from a salt mine at Hallstatt, west-central Austria. The sack, 90 centimetres (35 inches) high, dates from the 10th or 9th century BC. It is made of cowhide, strengthened with strips of wood. An attached wooden stick was used to help empty salt from the sack.

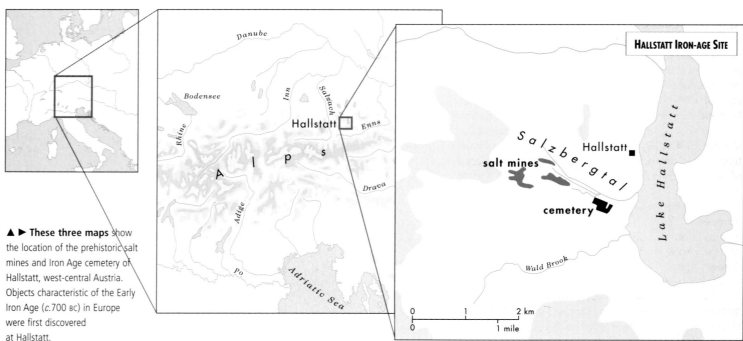

▲ ▶ **These three maps** show the location of the prehistoric salt mines and Iron Age cemetery of Hallstatt, west-central Austria. Objects characteristic of the Early Iron Age (c.700 BC) in Europe were first discovered at Hallstatt.

HALLSTATT IRON-AGE SITE

◄ **Miner's pick-axe and scoop** made of maple wood, discovered in the salt mines at Hallstatt, west-central Austria. The axe and scoop date from between the 10th century and 6th century BC. Salt mining began at Hallstatt in the 10th century BC, and continued until the 1st century AD. Mining resumed in the 12th century.

▼ **Watercolour (1878) by Isidor Engel** from Johann Georg Ramsauer's account of his excavations (1846–63) of 980 graves at Hallstatt, west-central Austria. The drawing shows the graves that were exposed when Emperor Franz Joseph visited on October 19, 1856.

weapons and armour found in the graves – not the normal accoutrements of a miner, but a reflection of the warrior-élite ethos that had been developing in Europe throughout the Bronze Age.

The Hallstatt style

Across south-west Germany, Austria and Slovakia there was a distinctive Hallstatt style of material culture. During the earliest period of the Hallstatt burials (the latter part of Hallstatt A), when Urnfield influence was at its strongest, there were swords and tableware in Italian styles, and items decorated with traditional Bronze Age motifs such as birds. A few items made of iron may be evidence of contact with early iron-producing communities in northern Italy.

During the subsequent Hallstatt B phase, Urnfield cultural influence appears to have declined somewhat, and there is an increase in the number of élite-style burials beneath mounds. This has been interpreted as a sign of a resurgence of 'native' populations against Urnfield invaders, but this is questionable. Of particular note during this period is the development of the slender Hallstatt-type bronze sword, with a scabbard tipped by a distinctively 'winged' shape, the presence of which, archaeologically speaking, is considered to be an indicator of Hallstatt influence.

If there has to be a 'historical' point of origin for the European Celts, defined both in time and place, then it is most conveniently located here: in south-central Europe during the Hallstatt A and B phases of the Late Bronze Age. It follows (and perhaps in some way results) from the upheavals of the Early Urnfield period. The linguists are unhappy with the presence of 'proto-Celts' before the Late Bronze Age, and the later Hallstatt peoples of this region (during phases C and D) undoubtedly contained Celtic-speaking groups.

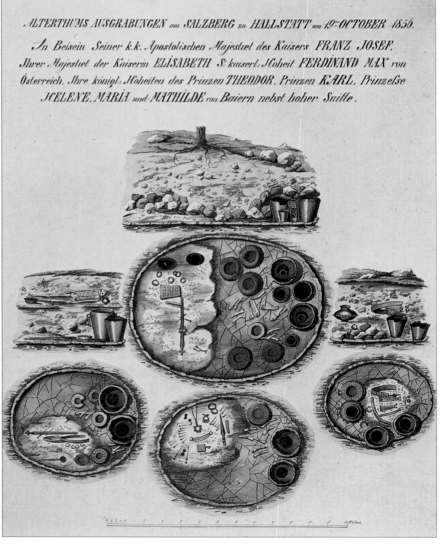

HALLSTATT C (750–600 BC)

The start of the Hallstatt C period almost coincides with the start of the Iron Age in central Europe. During the 8th and 7th centuries BC, ironworking (not unknown beforehand) spread rapidly throughout the Urnfield region (*see* map, page 26). By 600 BC, iron tools and weapons were in common use in some areas, largely replacing bronze except for some prestige objects such as parade armour. Archaeological evidence for the earliest stages of European ironworking is extremely rare. The remains of even a small forge or furnace are enough to include a region in the 'iron-using area', but it is no guarantee of a continuous tradition of ironworking. Initially, ironworking skills may have been acquired and lost several times before becoming established.

Consequently there was no rapid transformation of society resulting from the onset of the Iron Age, rather an acceleration of existing trends. Fortified hilltops became more numerous, and the leading members of élites were afforded 'chieftain's' burials – richly furnished inhumations, sometimes accompanied by elaborate funerary carts or wagons. These vehicle burials were obviously reserved for the most important members of the emerging aristocracies. During the C phase, Hallstatt culture became more clearly defined, both stylistically and in terms of social organisation.

Hallstatt C culture

During Hallstatt C, a core area emerged, marked by clusters of wagon burials, perhaps indicating settled lineages. Significantly, these early potential 'centres' are situated adjacent to the rivers that formed the main trade routes. There were other isolated wagon burials, mainly inside the core area, but also further west.

GRAVE GOODS

The Strettweg cult wagon (shown restored below) was recovered from a barrow in Styria, south-east Austria. It is thought to have been a funerary gift for a prince whose ashes were also discovered in the barrow. Perhaps dating from the 7th century BC, the four-wheeled bronze wagon is 33cm (13in) high and 48cm (122in) long. It features warriors on horseback, standing axe-bearers, and stags, all surrounding a tall, nude female figure carrying a dish upon her head. Some experts argue that the chariot depicts a sacrificial procession. An ithyphallic male figure is killing a stag for the central female deity. The spiritual intensity of the scene is enhanced by the figures, who are mainly gazing up with sombre expressions.

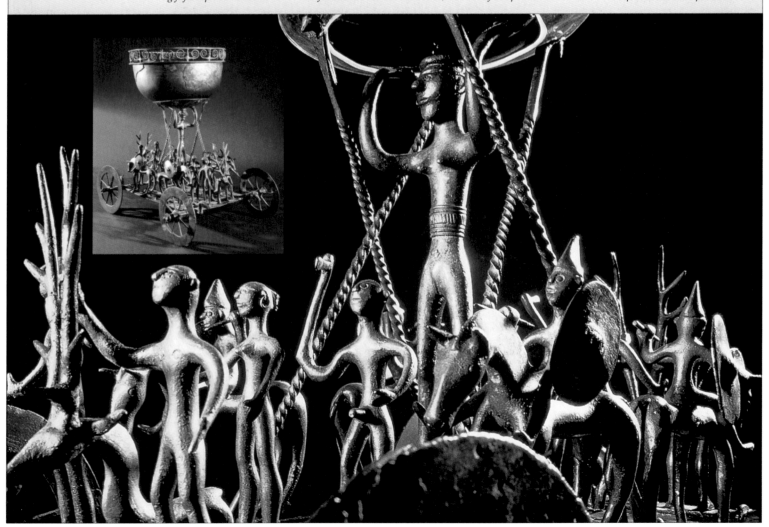

Multiple finds of Hallstatt C-type iron swords have also been made to the west of the core area, and these help to define a secondary area, where the Hallstatt culture was less well established. This evidence might be indicative of pioneers claiming new territories in the west, or may merely represent the time lag of cultural transmission and assimilation in more sparsely populated and economically less developed regions.

Wagon burials were not a new element in European ritual, but certain details – notably nailed-on iron tyres – appear to be an innovation confined to Hallstatt C peoples. Although the issue is still debated, it is widely believed that the Hallstatt wagons (and a few carts) were not specially constructed hearses, but were adaptations of vehicles in daily use. The use of iron tyres to protect the wooden wheels indicates a concern for the reliability of wheeled transport, rather than having any ritual significance. Accompanying the vehicles in some of the burials, and also buried separately on their own, were spectacular wooden yokes, covered with imported leather and decorated with bronze fittings. Elaborate bronze bits and harness decorations were also included in graves, especially in Bohemia and Bavaria. Hallstatt C burials are often closely associated with the horse, but unlike many of the 'chieftains'' tombs found to the east on the Eurasian steppes, neither the Hallstatt peoples, nor the historical Celts after them, buried horses along with wagons.

Other features of Hallstatt C culture include large numbers of bronze and iron swords, and in the eastern part of the region, where axes were preferred to swords, distinctive bronze axes with winged and cast-on decoration are representative. A few items of Etruscan origin have also been found in Hallstatt C graves, but their significance remains unclear.

Emergence of 'princely centres'

The changes in south-central European society during Hallstatt C should not be overestimated. Settlements such as Hallstatt were still rare and atypical. Wealth was accumulated in the hands of individuals and families, but no other settlements, even important centres of metal production, grew to the size of Hallstatt.

Towards the very end of the C phase, there was a significant development in Hallstatt society. Large 'princely' and commercial centres emerged in the far west of the region, and here were discovered the first Greek imports into central Europe – flagons made in Rhodes that probably once contained wine. These new centres were one of the principal features of the final, Hallstatt D period that emerged after 600 BC. Coincidentally, a new salt mine opened in c.600 BC, at Hallein, near Hallstatt. Hallein offered traders much easier access than the old mines at Hallstatt, and the Hallstatt settlement thereafter gradually declined in size and importance.

▲ **Bronze axe** (palstave) found at Dürrnberg, near Hallein, west-central Austria. The geometric design is typical of Hallstatt style.

▼ **Hallstatt C** The remains of Hallstatt C vehicle burials and weapons tell us much about the growth in size and commercial status of Bronze Age settlements between 750 and 600 BC.

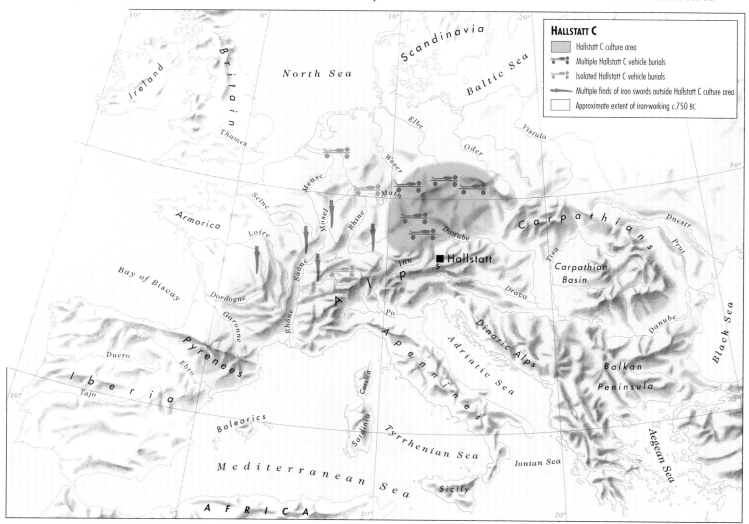

IRON TECHNOLOGY

The secrets of ironworking were developed in roughly the same place, and at roughly the same time as the chariot – that is, from eastern Anatolia to the Caucasus between *c.*2000 and 1800 BC. Use of the chariot spread rapidly, and by 1300 BC, chariots were in use from Denmark to China. Ironworking, however, did not spread at the same rate, and for *c.*200–300 years, it remained a virtual monopoly of the Hittite Empire in Anatolia.

Iron was known elsewhere during this period, but it was extremely rare. Limited supplies were exported by the Hittites, or were captured from them, and sometimes these became traded commodities. Small bits of iron were found in Europe during the Late Bronze Age, but only as a decorative and novelty substance. Some of this very small quantity of metal may have been produced locally.

Not until after the collapse of the Hittite Empire, in *c.*1200 BC, did iron production become more widespread. Ironworking, for example, began in Greece in *c.*1000 BC, and in northern Italy in 900 BC. North of the Alps, in 'Celtic' Europe, the Iron Age began in *c.*750 BC.

The spread of iron

Once released from the Near East, ironworking spread very rapidly – 'travelling' from the Po Valley to Britain and Ireland in less than two centuries. Old-fashioned ideas of a transforming technology being spread by immigrants, invaders or travelling smiths, can, however, be discounted. The nature of the archæological evidence argues against ironworking being transmitted by mobile groups or individuals. What seems to have arrived first was the information that iron ore could be used to make metal. The first ironworkers appear sometimes to have used what were essentially bronzeworking techniques, increasing the temperature to smelt iron, to make artefacts that were close copies of bronze originals.

Furthermore, ironworking was not in itself a transforming technology, and there was no immediate social revolution associated with its early spread. In most parts of Europe, ironworking initially occurred on a very small scale, and over widely scattered locations. Consequently, the early use of iron was relatively restricted, although the superior malleability and strength of the metal were exploited for some weapons, some tools and a few prestige objects, such as drinking vessels or bridle-bits. It was not until well into the Roman period that Western Europe can be said to have properly entered the Iron Age, and even then, iron was not as ubiquitous as bronze had once been.

At this time in history, the transforming power of iron lay not only in the actual metal, but in its abundance in the Earth's crust. Bronzeworking required the extraction and co-ordination of two metals, one of which, tin, was rare, and consequently long-distance trade was a prerequisite of the Bronze Age. Iron, however, only required deposits of iron ore, which were to be found in almost every region of Europe.

Techniques of ironworking

Iron is harder, stronger and, if treated correctly, much more elastic than bronze. However, in the Western world there was only one known way to shape iron, by

▲ **Iron dagger** with bronze handle and incised bronze scabbard, dating from the 6th century BC, found at the Hallstatt cemetery, west-central Austria, The handle features two human figures.

▶ **Blacksmith's tools** and iron ingot found in the Byci scala cave, Moravia. The items date from the 6th or 5th century BC, and are linked to the Hallstatt culture. The technique of smelting iron, probably discovered in Anatolia, had a profound impact on European society and ushered in the classical civilisations of Greece and Rome. Iron ore was an abundant resource and, after being heated in a furnace, produced the hardest and strongest metal then known to man. Before the introduction of coinage in Europe, ingots were used as a medium of exchange.

hammering. Techniques for casting iron were not present in Europe until the Late Middle Ages. In fact, hammering was intrinsic to the production of iron. In smelting, the ore produced a honeycombed bloom of iron metal that contained considerable amounts of slag (impurities). The slag was removed by repeated heating and hammering of the bloom, until only a solid mass of iron remained. Because charcoal was used in iron smelting (to support the high temperature required), the products of the early smiths were actually steels (iron alloyed with carbon) of greatly varying quality.

The first iron implements, such as axes, knives, chisels, swords and sickles, had simple shapes. As skills developed, the implements became larger and more complex. By *c.*200 BC, scythes, with blades up to 120 centimetres (3.4 feet) long, were being made and were used in large numbers for harvesting grain. Another, often overlooked, use of iron is nails. Copper and bronze are too flexible for practical and effective nails. In these materials, rigidity is only achieved through impractical size. On the other hand, iron, despite being prone to rust, is an ideal material for nails. The so-called '*murus gallicus*' (literally 'Gallic wall'), which resisted Roman siege machines, was interlaced with timber beams that were nailed. The wall surrounding even a small *oppidum* (town) must have required millions of iron nails.

All iron products had to be actively shaped, as opposed to passive casting, and the smiths' skill became paramount. Using acquired or inherited skills, the best smiths were able to pattern-weld laminated sword blades that held extremely sharp edges, and then temper the blades by controlled heating and cooling (quenching) to produce extraordinary strength and flexibility. By the middle Iron Age, some European smiths were stamping their blades with a maker's mark.

◄ **Wrought-iron fire-dog** discovered at Welwyn, south-east England. The upper end of the fire-dog, shown here in detail, is wrought in the shape of a stylised bovine animal with balled horns. It dates from the 1st century BC.

► **Forge** at Asparn an der Zaya, north-west Austria. This is a detailed reconstruction of the interior of a forge from the La Tène period (*c.*480–50 BC). The tools on display are copies of items from *c.*200 BC.

SWORDS

The latter part of the 20th century saw many archæologists dismiss the significance of swords as archæological indicators. This treatment of swords was part of a wider trend that rejected militaristic explanations of prehistory, and was especially harsh on 'invasion hypotheses'. However, it seems hardly sensible to ignore or dismiss artefacts that have maintained a continuous existence as prestige symbols among European élites for the last 4000 years.

That said, care must be taken not to place undue emphasis on swords, or assign qualities to them that are the result of more recent imagination. Despite the best attempts of fiction-writers to convince the public otherwise, there is no evidence for swords being imbued with mystical significance in Iron-Age Europe. Named swords, such as Excalibur, are rooted in medieval romance, and swords appear to have been buried with their owners or deposited in rivers or lakes, rather than handed down from generation to generation.

What is perhaps most repellent about a fascination with swords, is that a sword is fundamentally the most efficient and convenient method of slaughtering human beings by hand. Although swords were used by societies as prestige items, badges of rank, or symbols of authority, they were rooted in this bloody reality.

Birth of the sword

The sword first appeared in the Bronze Age. Older materials such as stone and copper were not strong enough to make a practical sword, although the idea is prefigured in the 30-centimetre (12-inch) flint blade found in a 6000-year-old cemetery at Varna, eastern Bulgaria.

Swords developed out of short, bronze daggers that were initially made with a separate blade attached to a handgrip with rivets. The same blades could also be attached at right angles to a longer handle to make a halberd (a fighting pick). Early swords were made in the same way, the extended blades could be strengthened with folds and ribs but the weakness of the riveted attachment to the handgrip was a serious limitation upon the fighting qualities of the weapons. Subsequent innovations produced tanged blades, where the grips are fitted onto a continuous length of metal. Organic materials, such as antler and horn, seem to have been favoured as handles for fighting swords, while those intended primarily for display had elaborate metal hilts. However, functionality was never entirely sacrificed to demands of decoration, and no purely ornamental swords have been found.

Sword fighting

Against poorly armed opponents, such as recalcitrant farmers, the sword is a simple tool of butchery. Against equally matched opposition, such as fellow members of the élite, it was a weapon admirably suited to contests of a more 'sporting' nature. The type of sword dictated both the style of this sport and its accompanying ritual code.

For the early smiths, making a sword was a compromise between length, which increased the user's reach, strength, which dictated how the weapon would behave in battle, and weight, which affected the ability of the user to wield the sword. Early long swords, such as those used by the Mycenaeans, were fairly weak and narrow. Such swords dictated a certain style of fighting because their lethality lay in the point, and they were unsuited to a swinging, slashing style of fighting. Later European swords were wider and stronger, with two sharp edges to supplement the point. The subsequent history of sword-fighting, either in war or sport, has essentially been one of changing fashions in the emphasis placed on either the edges or the point.

Swords were by no means the only weapons used by European warriors, and they never dominated the battlefields. Spears were used in much greater numbers, while axes, particularly in the east of the Hallstatt area, retained their traditional status, and were often carried in preference to swords. Neither the spear nor the axe, however, offered the user such a wealth of opportunities for demonstrating both individual skill and personal courage – two of the most highly esteemed qualities among groups of warrior-élites.

It is generally accepted that the adoption of longer swords by central European peoples near the start of the Iron Age is linked to the introduction of cavalry onto the battlefield, because a mounted warrior can wield a longer sword to greater effect than his comrades (or enemies) fighting on foot. However, the link between long swords and cavalry is by no means proven, and during the

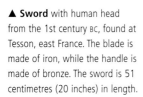

▲ **Sword** with human head from the 1st century BC, found at Tesson, east France. The blade is made of iron, while the handle is made of bronze. The sword is 51 centimetres (20 inches) in length.

▶ **Human figure** on a bronze sword handle. It probably dates from the 1st century BC. Although it was found in County Donegal, north-west Ireland, it was undoubtedly of Continental origin. The fact that it is a figurative piece suggests a Roman influence.

subsequent Hallstatt D period, swords became shorter, only to become longer again in the La Tène period, with blades reaching 90 centimetres (36 inches) in length. These changing styles, and the elaborate decoration of the sword hilts, reflect the individuality and prestige of their owners, whether mounted or not.

The Romans, methodical in all things, eventually settled on the very antithesis of the long La Tène sword – the short, broad-bladed *gladius*. The *gladius* was perfectly suited to the closely drilled tactics of the Roman legions, who advanced en masse, shield to shield, hacking and stabbing with their swords. The swords carried by their Celtic foes suggest more expansive and individualistic behaviour.

▶ **Ivory handle** with rich amber inlay, dating from the 7th century BC, found at Hallstatt, west-central Austria. The handle, maximum diameter 9.5 centimetres (3.7 inches), was part of an iron sword.

◀ **These four swords** are a good example of the variety of swords produced in the Late Bronze Age (1250–850 BC). Working from right to left, the longest weapon is a Liptau-type sword; next is the tongue-shaped sword; then the so-called antenna-type sword; finally, the shortest sword is almost dagger length. All four are made entirely of bronze.

35

HALLSTATT D (600-480 BC)

The Hallstatt D period is marked by geographical and economic changes that inextricably (and ultimately fatally) linked the Celts with the Mediterranean world. Western Europe ceased to be a largely self-contained and independent entity, and became part of the economic 'machine', driven by the Mediterranean civilisations. These links were forged by the Etruscans and Greeks, and were later forcibly strengthened by the Romans.

The most striking feature of the Hallstatt D period is a proliferation of the fortified residences (princely centres) that had begun to emerge at the end of the Hallstatt C period. These new centres were all established in a zone that extended westwards from the Hallstatt C culture area into central France. The westward shift of Hallstatt culture appears to have been the result of Greek commercial enterprise along the Rhône Valley trading route. This new, western route was in direct competition with the Etruscan-dominated trade routes from north Italy via the Alpine passes. We know that some Hallstatt peoples went west with the Greeks because Hallstatt D material is not found in eastern Austria.

The 'aristocracy' who occupied these fortified residences were given rich inhumations that followed earlier traditions, but with a shift in emphasis. Compared with Hallstatt C burials, those of the D phase are less closely associated with the horse. Vehicles still accompanied the most prestigious burials, but there was a decline in the numbers of yokes, bits and harness decorations.

Growth of princely centres

Some of the princely centres developed into much more than fortified residences. Their walls and ramparts enclosed considerable areas – 3.2 hectares (8 acres) in the case of Heuneburg, south Germany – and contained workshops, storerooms and neat rows of dwellings. As centres of trade, production and population, it has been argued that these princely centres were the first 'towns' in Europe north of the Alps.

The largest and most important of the centres – Heuneburg, Mont Lassois in north-east France, and Hohenasperg in south Germany – were situated on commanding positions overlooking strategic trade routes. Lesser centres, such as those at Bourges, Château-sur-Salins, Britzgyberd and Chatillon-sur-Glane in France, and Zürich and Bern in Switzerland, were significant at a local level and might also have developed into 'towns', if economic growth had continued.

One indication of the extent of trade contacts, especially among the super-élite, is found in the Hohmichele burial mound near Heuneburg. In c.550 BC, a local 'prince' died, and his wife was buried alongside him. Among her funerary regalia was some Chinese silk fabric, which must have been produced more than 10,000 kilometres (6000 miles) away.

As well as provoking economic development, the shift in trade patterns gave the Hallstatt peoples their first direct contact with Greek artefacts and art styles, rather than the Greek-inspired products of north Italian artisans. The flow of such artworks in the Hallstatt zone was never more than a trickle, and may have consisted

▲ **Chased gold belt** with hook from grave 505 at Hallstatt, west-central Austria. It dates from the 6th to 5th century BC. The fine quality of the engraving is testament to the skill of the craftworkers.

▶ **Main princely centres**
c.500 BC The growth of princely centres to the west of the Hallstatt C area was a direct result of the expansion of Greek trade routes.

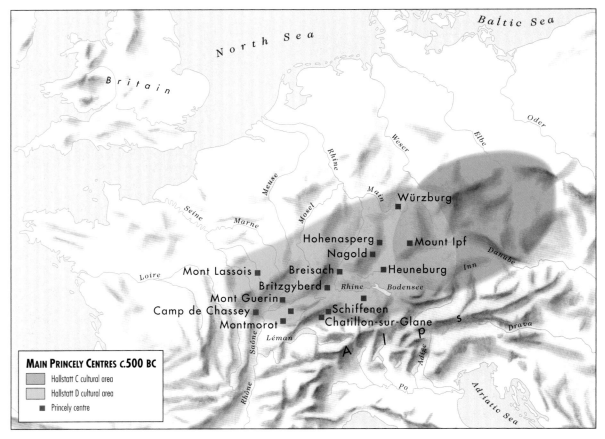

MAIN PRINCELY CENTRES c.500 BC
- Hallstatt C cultural area
- Hallstatt D cultural area
- ■ Princely centre

◄ **Detail on the Kuffern situla**
The frieze is an outstanding example of the late situla style (5th century BC). The detail shows a seated man in a large hat carousing. Behind him is a rack of situlas. Situlas were pails filled with alcoholic drink. Drinking and feasting appears to have been an important Celtic ritual. The embossed decoration on the situla reveals the hierarchical structure of Venetic society. Women are depicted as servants, bringing food and drink in a type of ladle.

entirely of 'gifts' given to various members of the local aristocracy in order to encourage and facilitate trade in more mundane commodities such as grain, hides and slaves. In turn, some of these gifts might have been redistributed among the princes' favourite retainers. These artworks included fine quality decorative pottery from Attica (the region around Athens) and south Italy. Although few in number, these imports appear to have made a lasting impact, and stimulated the transfer of technology. During the Hallstatt D period, wheel-turned pottery (shaped or 'thrown' on a rapidly rotating turntable) was produced north of the Alps for the first time.

A further example of Greek involvement is provided by the fortifications of Heuneburg, dated to *c*.580 BC. Some of the bottom parts of the walls were constructed using stone, neatly topped with courses of mudbricks. Mudbricks were not a traditional building material in southern Germany, but they were exactly what would have been specified by a Greek military engineer of the early 6th century BC.

The Hallstatt period ended with the collapse of the phase D centres, and the political and economic structures that they represented. Mont Lassois, for example, was abandoned shortly after the burial of the Vix princess (*see* page 39), and the Heuneburg settlement experienced a similar fate. The nature of this transition also remains a matter for speculation. Greek traders in the western Mediterranean may have shifted their attention to Spain, neglecting the Rhone Valley and depriving the Hallstatt D princes of the exotic goods they needed to maintain their prestige and power. Alternatively, the inhabitants of the peripheral zone to the north of the princely centres, may have decided to gain direct access to Mediterranean goods by either circumventing or eliminating the Hallstatt D princes.

There may have been a period of co-existence between Late Hallstatt D and the new culture of La Tène, or the Hallstatt culture may have collapsed first. Whatever the reasons for and nature of the transition, power and wealth shifted northwards and a new culture emerged on the fringes of the Hallstatt C and D zones.

ETRUSCAN INFLUENCES

The 'Kuffern situla' shown here dates from the 5th century BC. It is made of sheet bronze, and is 25 centimetres (9.8 inches) high. The situla was discovered at Kuffern, north-east Austria. Situlae are bronze wine-buckets. They were first made in the Middle Urnfield period, initially in the area around the head of the Adriatic. While the technique and shape of the Kuffern situla is rooted in the Early Iron Age, the design of its engraved and repoussé frieze was probably inspired by Etruscan art, and shows elements of the emerging La Tène style.

BURIAL MOUNDS

The disposal of the dead is of the utmost interest to archaeologists and pre-historians. The customs and practices associated with the recently deceased are rightly considered a vital cultural marker, and changes in these practices are considered especially significant. Furthermore, the goods deposited with some human remains constitute a large part of the archaeological record. One of the defining characteristics of the Early Iron Age in temperate and northern Europe is that the most powerful members of the developing Celtic élites were buried with rich grave goods beneath great mounds of earth.

Burial mounds were not a Hallstatt innovation. The concept of burying an important individual beneath a raised mound has been a feature of many societies – as far apart in time and space as the pyramids of Egypt (from *c*.2700 BC) and the tomb of Qin Shihuangdi (259–210 BC), first Emperor of all China. In Europe, mound burials of individuals first appeared during the social transformation associated with the Corded Ware and Bell Beaker cultures (*see* pages 22–23), when they began to replace the communal burials and ossuaries (containers of bones) of the megalith builders. Among the earliest mounds in western Europe, are those at Helmsdorf and Leubingen in east Germany, which were constructed in *c*.2000 BC. A few hundred years later, mound (barrow) burials were adopted by the Wessex culture in southern England. The continuing significance of these mounds is demonstrated by the presence of other inhumations that were later inserted into some mounds.

The mounds may have had social functions other than as an indication of status. Burial mounds, and the grave goods deposited in them, may have served as a method of disposing of excess wealth (in the form of labour and goods) within the local economic system. A similar function has also been suggested for the votive hoards, in which metal objects were cast into

▶ **Burial mounds** The wealth of objects found in the burial sites at Hochdorf and Vix tell us much about the affluence of the Hallstatt D period.

▼ **Burial mound at Kilchberg**, near Tübingen, south-west Germany. The barrow (partially reconstructed) dates from the 6th century BC, and contains the grave of a Celtic 'prince'. It is 13 metres (43 feet) in diameter.

BURIAL MOUNDS
Hallstatt D cultural area

watery places such as rivers and bogs. The fact that many of the mounds were broken into and robbed, sometimes within a few years of the burial, indicates that robbers and thieves existed then as now.

'Royal' burials

The Urnfield revolution of the Late Bronze Age never completely replaced inhumation rites, and there has been considerable debate about the significance of burial customs, particularly over the differentiation (ethnic or religious) that archaeologists observe in cemeteries of the time. During the Hallstatt C phase, there was an increase in the number of mound burials, especially those that included vehicles, decorated yokes, and other elements closely associated with the horse. Similar burials continued during the Hallstatt D phase, many of which also contained vehicles. Those that escaped plunder provide an incredible

▲ **Pure gold torque** from the tomb of the 'Princess of Vix', north-east France, dating from *c*.500 BC. The ends of the neck-ring are finely decorated with winged horses (Pegasus) and lion's paws.

glimpse of the wealth and ostentation of the 'aristocracy' in Europe during the Early Iron Age.

The Hochdorf mound, which is located near the princely centre at Hohenasperg in south Germany, is 60 metres (200 feet) across, and originally stood about six metres (20 feet) high. It covers the grave of a 40-year-old male, who was buried with a considerable amount of personal gold jewellery (belt plate, torque and brooches) and was even provided with decorated gold boot plates. The body lay on a 2.75 metres (nine feet) -long, sheet-bronze couch (probably upholstered in rich fabrics) held up by eight female figurines, supported by wheels, lending them the appearance of a monocyclist. A bronze cauldron, made by Greek artisans in Italy, contained traces of mead, which may have been used for a funeral toast – nine metal drinking horns (including one made of iron) were also included. Alongside the body was an intact 4-wheeled wagon with iron fittings, on which had been piled tools and tableware. Taken together, the grave goods undoubtedly represent the full panoply of a powerful chieftain.

Near Mont Lassois, north-east France, is the Vix mound, which covered the grave of a 35-year-old woman. Her body had been laid on the chassis of a four-wheel cart (the wheels were removed and stacked separately) and around her neck was a gold torque weighing nearly 500 grammes (18 ounces). Among other grave goods was a complete set of wine-drinking gear, including the largest-known bronze krater (a vessel used for blending wine). The exact origin of this piece (shown left) is uncertain, but it was probably purpose-made in Sparta, Greece, and assembled in France. The placement in a grave of such a spectacular and ostentatious item must be testament to the importance of the woman who has become known as the 'Princess of Vix'.

In the post-Hallstatt period, burials became less lavish. Eventually cremation was to replace inhumation, and finally spread to Britain by c.50 BC. In some places (notably the Champagne district of north-east

◀ **Bronze krater** from the 'Princess of Vix' tomb in north-east France. The Vix krater, dating from c.500 BC, is 1.64 metres (5.4 feet) high and weighs 208 kilogrammes (468 pounds). It is decorated with a low-relief frieze of infantrymen and charioteers driving quadrigas (four-horse chariots). The voluted handles are adorned with gorgons.

France, and in Yorkshire, north England), vehicle burials continued, but with chariots rather than wagons or carts. The chariots were usually dismantled and placed over the corpse, rather than the body being laid out on the chariot (as is the case with the burial in the Champagne). The circular mounds raised over the graves were much smaller and surrounded by rectangular enclosures. After c.100 BC, burials disappear almost entirely from the archaeological record in continental western Europe. Other practises, such as the scattering of ashes or the exposure of corpses, are likely to have been adopted.

▶ **Gold cup** and gold-plated iron antenna-style dagger with scabbard from the tomb of a chieftain at Hochdorf, near Stuttgart, south Germany. The items date from the 6th century BC.

GREEK AND ETRUSCAN TRADE

There are different ways of seeing the trade between the emerging Celtic world and the Mediterranean. From a Celtic perspective, atop Mont Lassois for example, this trade was absolutely central to the princely existence. Trade was the essential source of wealth, power and prestige. Involvement in trade set the Hallstatt D princes apart from their fellows. In another sense, however, this trade amounted to no more than a fairly minor and local action in a full-blown trade war that ranged across almost the entire Mediterranean region. The main protagonists in this often bloody conflict were Greek and Phoenician seafarers.

The changing fortunes of the two sides, and their temporary achievement of local supremacies, can be linked to developments in the 'Celtic' world. What is unclear, however, is the nature of any cause and effect. Did the swings in trade follow the market, or, as seems more likely, did changes in trade patterns dictate the location of economic centres in the Celtic world?

Greek expansion

The early phases of Hallstatt culture inherited from the Urnfield period a fundamentally eastern and southern orientation. To the east, the River Danube provided a route for the importation of horses and advanced technologies. To the south, routes across the Alps offered links with the Villanovan and Etruscan cultures of north Italy.

The pronounced westward shift during Hallstatt D has been closely linked to a period of aggressive commercial expansion by the Greeks, who had already colonised much of southern Italy and were vying with the Phoenicians for Etruscan trade. In c.600 BC, Greeks from Phocaea established the colony of Massilia (now Marseilles) on the south coast of France at the mouth of the River Rhône. The new colony not only gave the Greeks a direct route into western Europe, completely bypassing northern Italy, but was also a useful transit centre for trade with metal-rich Spain.

▲ **Gold drinking horn** with bronze core, made in the 6th century BC. The horn is 15 centimetres (5.9 inches) long. Such horns were used for the consumption of wine.

▶ **Trade with the Mediterranean** The Hallstatt C period saw the growth of trade routes from Etruria (northern Italy) which brought bronze drinking vessels. Greek expansion during the Hallstatt D period presented a threat to Etruscan trade as Greeks who had settled in southern France established trade routes up the Rhône Valley bringing amphorae (jars for oil and wine).

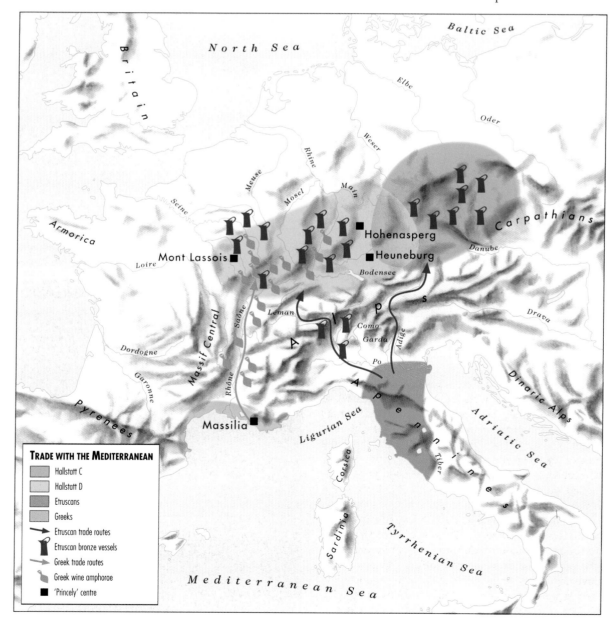

TRADE WITH THE MEDITERRANEAN
- Hallstatt C
- Hallstatt D
- Etruscans
- Greeks
- Etruscan trade routes
- Etruscan bronze vessels
- Greek trade routes
- Greek wine amphorae
- 'Princely' centre

Greek enterprise was rewarded. Massilia flourished, carrying not only all trade with Greece but also large quantities of Etruscan goods, while the routes across the Alps declined almost to the point of extinction. In *c.*535 BC, this Greek stranglehold was reinforced by their naval victory over a combined Etruscan and Phoenician fleet off the coast of Corsica. Following this defeat, the Etruscans again shifted their trading network, re-establishing routes through the Po Valley in an attempt to outflank the Greeks to the east. For this reason, the earliest Mediterranean goods to reach the emergent La Tène cultures in the Marne and Moselle regions were Etruscan bronze flasks that had been exported along these revitalised routes.

The wine trade

The Hallstatt D princes (and princesses) would not have been concerned with such wider issues, nor will they have been much concerned about the importation of Mediterranean artefacts. Bronze jugs, jewellery and painted pottery were desirable objects that conveyed status upon their owners. Such artefacts, however, were hardly a basis for long-term trade, especially given the skills of European smiths. Instead, wine seems to have been the spur to trade.

Hallstatt peoples were by no means ignorant of alcohol – they had mead, and probably versions of beer and cider – but they had nothing to compare with rich, potent, Mediterranean wine. Quite apart from the intrinsic qualities of wine, it enabled the princes and their retinues to copy the fashions of the dimly apprehended world of the urbanised south. The paraphernalia of wine drinking was avidly collected and displayed, although the Celts famously did not water their wine as the Greeks did. Nine drinking horns found in the Hochdorf mound, south Germany, may represent a faint echo of a Greek drinking symposium. Wine was not, however, an everyday drink and, far from spreading Greek enlightenment among the barbarians, it served to reinforce the hegemony of the existing warrior-élites.

Wine remained a rare commodity outside the growing zone that then fringed the Mediterranean. It seems likely that by establishing a monopoly over this exotic substance, and carefully controlling its distribution and consumption, the Hallstatt D élite were able to command considerable local resources and build (literally) positions of great power.

The trade was inspired and run by the Greeks and prestige items such as the Vix krater were probably diplomatic gifts to encourage the establishment of trade. In exchange for wine, local chiefs had to supply what the Greeks wanted. Several commodities have been suggested, ranging from furs and hides to metals such as gold and tin. In later periods, we know that human slaves were one of the major exports from Celtic lands, and a similar situation probably existed at this time.

While some of the commodities traded to the Greeks may have been produced within the Hallstatt D zone, it seems likely that others, such as gold and tin, were obtained from areas further north and east. This extension of trade may have stimulated the hunger for Mediterranean goods that supposedly led to the great migrations of the La Tène Celts.

◄ **Etruscan bronze situla** with two ribbon handles, found in the tomb of the 'Princess of Vix', north-east France. The situla is 55.5 centimetres (21.7 inches) high. The bronze, fluted bowl at the base of the situla is also an Etruscan import. Its diameter measures 16.8 centimetres (6.6 inches).

▲ **Fighting warriors** on an Attic cup discovered in the tomb of the 'Princess of Vix', north-east France. The cup, which dates from the 6th century BC, was imported from Athens. The stylised black figures are typical of Greek pottery from this period.

◄ **Bronze gorgon (Medusa)** on the voluted handle of the Vix krater unearthed in north-east France. The krater dates from *c.*500 BC. In Greek mythology, if humans looked at the three gorgon sisters (Stheno, Euryale and Medusa) they were instantly turned to stone. Medusa, the only mortal sister, was transformed by Athena into a winged monster after she slept with Poseidon.

EASTERN INFLUENCES

Since the beginnings of 'Celtic studies', several commentators have detected strong similarities between elements of Celtic art and the 'animal art' style associated with the Eurasian steppes. Recently, art historians appear to have convinced themselves that all the main elements of Celtic art can be traced back to Greek prototypes, and that the similarities with steppe art are superficial and have no real significance. This accords well with those who ardently reject hypotheses of 'invasions from the east', and with those who view ancient Greece as the sole fountainhead of European civilisation.

later from the Caucasus via the Carpathian basin. All of these components are intrinsic to Celtic culture, and may be accepted as such without the implication that the Celts originated with any population movement associated with these innovations. Nevertheless, cultural transmission cannot happen without contact, and the nature of this transmission escapes definition.

The Scythians

The Carpathian basin can be considered the westernmost island of a steppe region that extends almost to the Sea of Japan. Life on the steppe, where pastoral nomadism was

▶ **Eastern influences** The nature of archæological finds in Poland, Transylvannia and Romania suggest the possibility of contact between Celts and peoples from the east, most likely from the Black Sea region.

▼ **Bronze bird's head** dating from the early 3rd century BC. It was discovered in a grave at Brno-Malomeriče, Moravia. Probably forming the handle for a wooden jug (now lost), the openwork mount with lateral tendrils is 18 centimetres (seven inches) high. It was made in the lands of the Boii in central Europe.

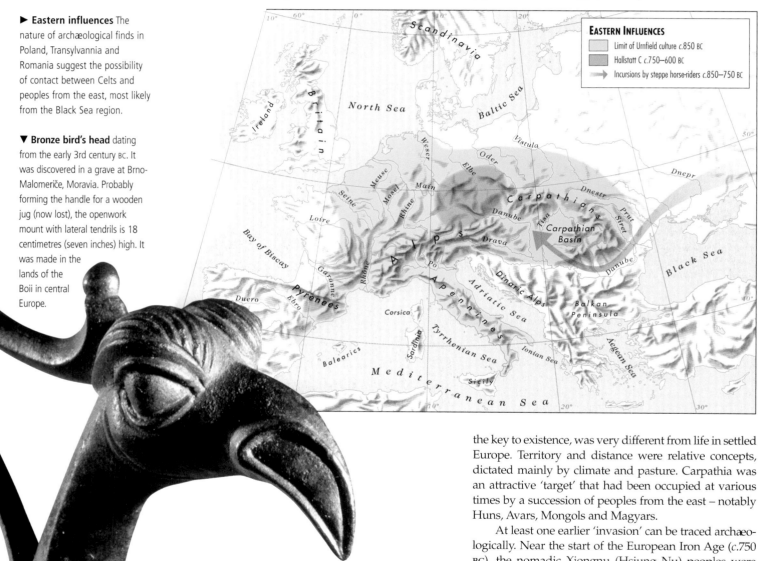

EASTERN INFLUENCES
- Limit of Urnfield culture c.850 BC
- Hallstatt C c.750–600 BC
- Incursions by steppe horse-riders c.850–750 BC

In a broader view of European prehistory, however, it seems unlikely that the peoples of Hallstatt Europe, who included the Celts, were not subject to some form of eastern influence. However strong the native traditions stretching back to the Neolithic period, several important cultural components had already intruded into central and western Europe from the east. For example, pastoralism and horses arrived during the Corded Ware/Bell Beaker transformation (*see* pages 22–23); and chariots and advanced metallurgy arrived

the key to existence, was very different from life in settled Europe. Territory and distance were relative concepts, dictated mainly by climate and pasture. Carpathia was an attractive 'target' that had been occupied at various times by a succession of peoples from the east – notably Huns, Avars, Mongols and Magyars.

At least one earlier 'invasion' can be traced archæologically. Near the start of the European Iron Age (*c*.750 BC), the nomadic Xiongnu (Hsiung Nu) peoples were ejected from north-west China. Their abrupt emergence onto the steppe created a series of displacements as the other steppe peoples adapted (often by migration) to the new situation. The effects of these displacements were eventually felt around the northern shores of the Black Sea, where Cimmerians and Scythians were pushed south and west. The Cimmerians remain rather obscure, but their attacks are mentioned in Assyrian records. The Scythians, however, are clearer historically, thanks largely to Greek writers, who provided a very detailed, if

ANIMAL ART STYLE

This electrum (gold and silver alloy) ornament in the form of a reclining stag was found at Tapioszentmarton, Hungary. Produced in the 6th or 5th centuries BC, it is 22 centimetres (8.7 inches) long. The piece is a good example of the so-called 'animal art' style of the Scythians. It has been argued that the influence of Scythian art was responsible for the widespread use of 'eastern' elements in Early Style Celtic art. The depiction of animals, such as ibex or stags, looking backwards and with their legs folded is typical of Scythian art. Similar motifs are found in Early Celtic art, and an emphasis on masks and animals is often seen as typical of this Early Style.

somewhat confused, description. By the time of these reports, the Scythians were already subject to strong Greek influence, at least around the shores of the Black Sea. Some had taken up crop farming to produce grain for export, and they commissioned Greek artisans to produce jewellery. Others still followed a more traditional warrior lifestyle: their enemies reporting that they drank wine from the skulls of the vanquished. This lifestyle was by no means exclusively male, and several women-warrior graves have been found in southern Russia.

Farther west, at least one sizeable group of Cimmerians or Scythians entered Carpathia. Here, probably while intermingling with the local population, they formed what is known as the Vekerzug group, which is characterised by harness equipment typical of the steppes. Other Scythian-related material has been discovered at Mures-Tirnave in Transylvannia, western Romania, and at Witaszkowo (Vettersfeld), east Poland.

According to the findings, there was at least one group of recent steppe origin living in Carpathia during the early part of the Hallstatt C phase. Some members of this group (or others) may have ventured even farther north and west. Whilst the evidence is not conclusive, it suggests that direct contact between the early Celts and steppe peoples was at least possible. It follows, therefore, that Celtic art may have drawn from influences other than those of Greece.

◄ **Head of mythical animal** found in Brno, Moravia. The head is 4.5 centimetres (1.77 inches) high, and forms part of the bronze decoration of a wooden jug. It dates from the 3rd century BC.

LA TÈNE

The name La Tène looms large in the study of the Celts. Like Hallstatt, La Tène refers directly to a particular site and, by association, to a period of European history and to a distinctive art style – which together define a cultural area in time and space.

The leading inhabitants (and doubtless many, if not all, of their 'dependants') of La Tène were unequivocally and undeniably Celtic, but they did not have exclusive rights to that term. There were many Europeans who spoke a Celtic language, but who did not take part in the first great flowering of Celtic culture that was La Tène.

Place

During the Iron Age, the area that was to become Switzerland was inhabited by Celts in the west and Rhaetians in the east. La Tène is situated on the shore of Lake Neuchâtel, north-west Switzerland. It was a ritual and ceremonial centre. Some of the wooden structures were built on piles driven into the lake-bed, and the emergence of these from the mud

prompted the site's discovery. The real value of the La Tène encampment is in the large amount of artefacts (both organic and inorganic) that have been recovered. These included a number of bronze items that appear to have been ritually deposited in the lake.

As with the Hallstatt cemetery goods, an analysis of the manufacturing and decorative techniques employed for these items enabled the establishment of a La Tène chronology and the identification of the La Tène style. The dating of some of the timbers from the site indicates that they were felled in c.250 BC, but use of the site undoubtedly ranged either side of that date.

Time

The La Tène period (from c.480 to 50 BC) coincides with the Middle and Late Iron Age in continental Europe. It is usually subdivided into four phases: A, B, C and D. The La Tène period lies well within the range of written European history and,

▶ **Gold torque** and bracelet, found (1956) in a tomb at Reinheim, near Sankt Ingbert, Saarland, south-west Germany. The tomb, a wood-lined chamber covered by an earth mound, contained more than 200 pieces of jewellery dating from the early 4th century BC. The balusters and beading are typical of Early La Tène art. The style of the torque is known as a *Wendelring*, a twisted, spiral ring. (For a close-up of the end of the torque, *see* photograph far right). The bracelet is also richly decorated, featuring shortened (possibly female) figures with their arms crossed over their stomachs.

◀ **La Tène,** north-west Switzerland, gave its name to one of the most important periods in the cultural history of the Celts. The site lay on the shore of Lake Neuchâtel. The photograph shows Marin-Epagnier, the west bank of Lake Neuchâtel, and the Jura Mountains on the horizon.

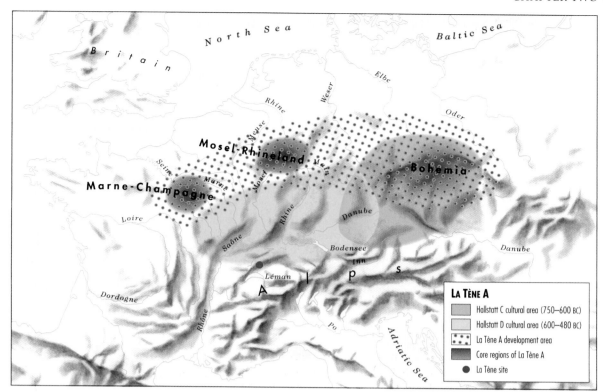

▶ **La Tène A** During the La Tène A period, the core Celtic areas shifted northwards into modern-day Switzerland and the surrounding areas. La Tène culture became less unified during the La Tène B period as Celts migrated west towards Britain and eastern Europe. Repeated German and Roman invasions from the north and south during the La Tène D period brought an end to the power and prosperity of the La Tène peoples. By c.50 BC, the La Tène regions had been completely absorbed into the Roman Empire.

LA TÈNE A
- Hallstatt C cultural area (750–600 BC)
- Hallstatt D cultural area (600–480 BC)
- La Tène A development area
- Core regions of La Tène A
- ● La Tène site

although there is initially no direct connection, it is interesting to measure the La Tène chronology against that of classical studies.

La Tène A (c.480–400 BC) roughly coincides with Athens' period of greatness – from the reforms of Cleisthenes (c.570–c.508 BC) to eventual defeat (405 BC) by Sparta at the end of the Peloponnesian War (470–404 BC). La Tène B (400–250 BC) is the period of the historically documented Celtic migrations, and coincides approximately with the Hellenistic period. La Tène C (250–120 BC) witnessed the emergence of Rome as a European power, and La Tène D (120–50 BC) ends with the Roman conquest of Gaul.

Culture

At about the same time as Athens and Sparta were jointly repelling the Persians (480 BC), the Celts abandoned the princely centres of Hallstatt D. A new élite culture emerged around the north of the former Hallstatt C and D zones. This La Tène culture is first identified in vehicle burials found in the Marne and Mosel districts, and in Bohemia. The most notable feature of these burials is that they contained a two-wheeled chariot (usually assembled) as opposed to the four-wheeled, disassembled funerary carts favoured by the Hallstatt cultures. Chariots were not a La Tène innovation, but it was during the La Tène period that Celtic chariotry had its day in the field.

Another distinctive feature of the La Tène burials, is their overtly militaristic character compared to Hallstatt graves, with many more swords and spears being buried alongside the dead. The gradual lengthening of swords during the La Tène period may be related to the adoption of chariots and an increase in fighting from horseback, although it might also have resulted entirely from the dictates of aristocratic fashion.

Some of the chariot graves contained other high-status objects, but nothing on the scale of the Vix krater or the Hochdorf couch. Sets of Mediterranean-style drinking utensils (either imported or copied locally) were popular, an affectation that the La Tène élites either inherited or adopted from their Hallstatt predecessors. Although Early La Tène culture was undoubtedly well organised, and its leading members could comand considerable resources of materials and skilled artisans, it did not initially give rise to any commercial centres to replace those of the Hallstatt princes.

During the La Tène A phase, this new culture spread rapidly across central Europe, forming a cultural continuum from northern France to Austria. There is every indication that this culture was remarkably successful and energetic. Towards the end of La Tène A, at about the same time as Athens was attempting to capture Syracuse, groups of well-equipped Celts began streaming southwards and eastwards from the newly established La Tène heartland. The great Celtic migrations had begun.

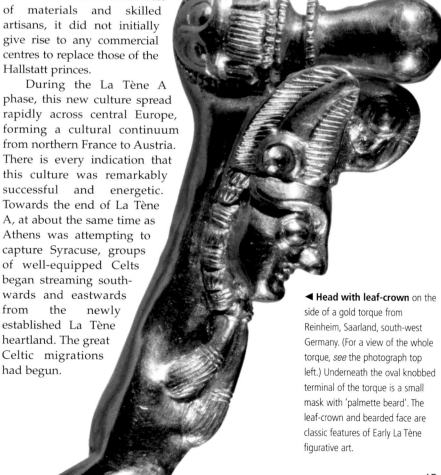

◀ **Head with leaf-crown** on the side of a gold torque from Reinheim, Saarland, south-west Germany. (For a view of the whole torque, *see* the photograph top left.) Underneath the oval knobbed terminal of the torque is a small mask with 'palmette beard'. The leaf-crown and bearded face are classic features of Early La Tène figurative art.

EARLY LA TÈNE ART

The art of the La Tène Celts is one of the outstanding achievements of pre-Roman Europe. Although the original seeds of the style may be detected in Greek and Etruscan imports, the subsequent flowering of the La Tène style owed nothing to the classical tradition, and was a clearly unique development.

Imaginative and distinctive, with its flowing curves and trumpet voids, La Tène art has a strong appeal to the 'modern' aesthetic that emerged after the 19th-century development of photography. La Tène artists had their own reasons for rejecting realism in favour of the abstract, the fantastic and the symbolic; and the artefacts they produced have a strong 'primitive' flavour that transcends the millennia and still appeals to contemporary tastes. While the appreciation of La Tène art is certainly to be encouraged, a preoccupation with form is in danger of obscuring the fine details of the content. For all their gaudy barbarian splendour and heightened sense of 'style', La Tène artworks represent levels of skill and sophistication that matched those of the great Mediterranean civilizations.

With regard to the dating of La Tène artefacts, it is important to bear in mind that, as with Hallstatt, it was the 'internal' sequencing of artistic developments that provided the framework for the chronological subdivision of the whole period, rather than 'external' factors. Most authorities accept a broad subdivision of La Tène art into successive periods (corresponding approximately to Early, Mature and Late) but there is no exact correlation between the art periods and geopolitical events in the Celtic world.

La Tène art is fundamentally a metalworker's art. Although some of the styles and motifs were sometimes applied to pottery, it was the surfaces of gold and bronze objects that provided the La Tène artists with their blank 'canvas'. The two main techniques used, apart from cast-in shapes, were deforming the surface by hammering (*repoussé*), or engraving the surface with a variety of iron tools. *Repoussé* designs were usually hammered freehand against a leather backing; although some repetitive designs made use of pre-shaped 'templates' which carried the design in reverse. Engraved designs were often worked out beforehand on pieces of wood or bone.

Although the Celts are not usually considered great sculptors, it should be noted that all of the human heads and grotesquely distorted animals that decorate the handles, lids, and spouts of metal utensils,

▼ **Bronze bearded head** wearing a leaf crown, forming part of the handle of a jug, dating from the mid-4th century BC. The jug was found in a princess' grave at Waldalgesheim, west Germany. This piece is often cited as marking the start of a second, 'classic' phase of Early Celtic art.

► **Bronze phalera** (disc) found at St-Jean-sur-Tourbe, Marne, north France. The phalera, which is 24.5 centimetres (9.5 inches) in diameter, dates from the early 4th century BC. The filigree border features lyre scrolls and a 'running dog' pattern. The concentric circles give an impression of movement.

►► **The 'Dürrnberg flagon'** (far right) was found in a tomb at Dürrnberg, near Hallein, west-central Austria. The fluted bronze flagon, dating from the late 5th century BC, is 47 centimetres (18.5 inches) high. The main body of the flask features ribbed, sunken *repoussé* panels. On the handle is an animal resting on a human head. The rim has two smaller animals, from whose jaws protude their victim's tails.

had to be painstakingly carved or modelled in wax before they could be cast in bronze. Metal artefacts, were sometimes further decorated with coloured inlays of coral or glass, and later by enamelling.

Early La Tène

Between the 5th century and the mid-4th century BC, Early La Tène craftworkers were partly reliant on Hallstatt traditions of repetitive geometric designs (such as cross-hatched triangles and lozenges), but they also selectively incorporated motifs (such as palmettes and lotuses) taken from imported metalwork.

Subsequently, as classical influence reached its height and Celtic art became 'orientalised' – just as Greek art had been a few centuries earlier – regional styles began to emerge. In Austria and Bohemia, human faces – often distorted and half concealed – became popular motifs, as did patterns incorporating animals. A La Tène-style sword scabbard from one of the latest graves in the Hallstatt cemetery is engraved with a line of soldiers (infantry and cavalry) that are strongly reminiscent of similar images on Greek arte-facts. However, the depiction of whole human figures is so rare in Celtic art that some commentators have spec-ulated that religious taboos may have forbidden the representation of the entire human form, hence the popularity of heads and animals.

In Germany and France, patterns derived from vegetation predominated, with the same motifs being endlessly repeated. However, geometry was not abandoned altogether, and some artisans produced elegant and vegetal designs with very precise and complex compass work. Their apparent simplicity belies a high degree of mathematical understanding and skill.

During the latter half of the 5th century BC, these various styles became current throughout the whole of the La Tène culture area through trade and cross-fertil-isation. The Celtic migrations of the 4th and 3rd cen-turies BC would carry these styles into other parts of Europe, and divergent trends would produce artworks that were radically different from the Hellenistic style then prevalent in the Mediterranean region.

▲ **Gold openwork** on a varnished bowl from Schwarzenbach, Hunsrück-Eifel, east Germany. The bowl (5th century BC) is a good example of the Early La Tène adoption and adaption of motifs from eastern Mediterranean art

◄ **Beaked flagon** found (1927) at Basse-Yutz, Mosel, north-east France. One of a pair of near identical flagons, the rich ornamentation on this jug is among the finest surviving work from the so-called 'grotesque' transitional phase at the end of the early phase of La Tène art (early 4th century BC). The beautiful coral and enamel inlay is similar to that found on the Battersea shield. The delicately crafted animals, such as the duck on the spout and the dog on the handle, are composed of spiralled geometric elements. The elegant shape of the jug shows a strong Etruscan influence. The flagon itself is 40.6 centimetres (16 inches) high. It was probably designed to impress important guests at banquets.

CELTIBERIANS

▶ *La Dama de Elche* (Alicante) found (1897) in south-east Spain. Perhaps the most famous piece of Celtiberian sculpture, the 'Lady of Elche' is a painted limestone bust with a spectacular head-dress. While some experts date the sculpture to the 4th century BC, others believe it belongs either to the Hellenistic or Roman periods. The bust is 56 centimetres (22 inches) high.

▼ **Celtiberians (right)** and Asturians (left) from a 19th-century lithograph by Villegas. The culture of Celtiberia was strongly influenced by the Iberian people of the Ebro valley. The Celtiberians were fearsome warriors, and one of their inventions, the two-edged Spanish sword, was later adopted by the Romans.

There is no doubt that Celts inhabited areas of the Iberian Peninsula; modern archaeology has confirmed their presence as reported by the classical authors. However, the relationship of these Celtiberians to the rest of the Celtic world is far from clear, especially as they were seemingly little affected by La Tène culture. Even more than with other groups of early Celts, our knowledge of the Celtiberians is plagued by uncertainties.

Situated in the extreme west of Europe, the Iberian Peninsula is geographically distinct from the rest of the continent. Surrounded on three sides by sea and bordered by the Pyrenees on the fourth, Iberia has a decidedly self-contained and insular aspect. It is a part of Europe, but is in some ways closer to Africa, from which it is separated by a stretch of sea much narrower than that between Britain and France. By *c*.400 BC, Celtic languages were spoken widely (but not exclusively) throughout much of Iberia.

The Celts and the Phoenicians

In later Hallstatt times, at least four unrelated languages – Iberian, Phoenician, Basque and Celtic – were spoken in Iberia. Of these only Celtic is a member of the Indo-European language family. Iberian was the language of the metal-rich kingdom of Tartessos in the south-west, and was also spoken extensively across the southern half of the Peninsula. Tartessos formed close trade links with the Greeks and Phoenicians, the latter founding the city of Gades (now Cádiz) in *c*.800 BC. Gades became a vital link in the Phoenician metal trade that extended along the Atlantic seaways as far north as Cornwall.

Other Phoenician cities were later founded along the south-east coast, but their relationships with the native Iberian-speakers were not as cordial as in Tartessos. The Iberians retreated to their inland hillforts and resisted Phoenician attempts at expansion. Southern Iberia was drawn farther into the Mediterranean economic zone (and made linguistically more complex) by the arrival of Greek traders, who founded their own cities to compete with those of the Phoenicians.

In the far north of the Peninsula, Basque, which has no known linguistic affiliations, was spoken over a much wider range than at present. In the north-central region of Iberia, Celtic was spoken; and this was the Celtiberian heartland.

Celtic expansion

Information on the extent of Celtic speaking comes largely from place-names. According to this evidence, which is broadly supported by archæology, there was

a Celtic expansion out of the Celtiberian heartland that began in the 5th century BC, and which may have continued until the 3rd century BC. The main thrust of this expansion was southwards and westwards, especially into the far north-west, the region of Spain known today as Galicia.

Outside the heartland, the Celtic tribes all have ethnic names, such as *Gallaeci* and *Gallaecia* in present-day Portugal and *Celtici* in Andalucia, rather than ones based on personal names. It has been suggested that these self-conscious 'ethnyms' support the idea of small groups of Celts intruding into ethnically different territories. Archæology is inconclusive in this matter, and it therefore seems reasonable to suppose that the internal spread of Celtic within the Iberian Peninsula between 500 and 300 BC was due to small warrior-groups of Celtiberians establishing local supremacy away from their heartland. The question of how Celts were in Iberia in the first place, however, has no such simple or plausible explanation.

If one accepts the invasionist hypothesis, the key to understanding how the Celts 'arrived' lies in determining when they arrived. There are good linguistic and archaeological grounds for rejecting either a very early or indeed a very late arrival. The idea that Celtic languages had been developing in Spain since the Neolithic period does not correspond with linguistic theory, and an arrival as part of the La Tène migrations can be discounted due to a scarcity of relevant archæological evidence.

It was once widely believed that the Celts arrived in Iberia with the Urnfield culture, which extended into Languedoc in southern France, and led to a closely related culture along the north-east coast of Iberia. Although the Celtiberians did follow a cremation burial rite,

archaeology has shown that the Urnfield and Celtiberian areas of Iberia were quite distinct with no overlap.

Spanish pre-historians now tend to play down the notion of an 'arrival' or invasion, and stress local developments. They point to links between the Celtiberians and the Atlantic culture of the Late Bronze Age, which had trading contacts with other parts of Europe. They argue that some proto-Celtic elements were adopted as a result of these contacts, and that these then developed separately in Iberia, modified by Mediterranean influence.

▲ **Boar-hunting** on a bronze cult-chariot discovered at Mérida, west Spain. From the Hallstatt period on, hunting was a popular sport among the Celtic nobility. This piece dates from the 9th to 5th century BC. Note the tight-fitting jersey like garment of the hunter and his short spear.

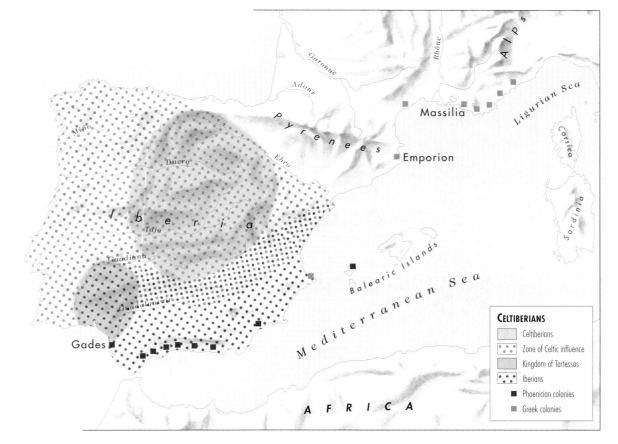

CELTIBERIANS
Celtiberians
Zone of Celtic influence
Kingdom of Tartessos
Iberians
■ Phoenician colonies
■ Greek colonies

◀ **Celtiberians** Whilst it is uncertain exactly how the Celtiberians came to inhabit the Iberian Peninsula, archæological evidence suggests that Celtiberian tribes had dispersed throughout the peninsula by the 5th century BC.

CELTS IN NORTH ITALY

Although the Italian peninsula is more centrally located than the Iberian, it has a similar insular aspect, being isolated from the rest of Europe by seas and mountains. The snow-covered peaks of the Alps collectively form a formidable geographical barrier that neatly separates central Europe from the Mediterranean world. It has long been held that the Alps remained the southern boundary of the Celtic world throughout the Hallstatt period. There is some evidence, however, that Celts were living south of the Alps for at least 200 years before the La Tène migrations.

Like most geographical barriers, for thousands of years people have been searching for ways to cross the Alps. The discovery in the 1990s of the so-called 'Iceman' provided dramatic evidence of this quest from an exceptionally early date. The body that thawed out of a glacier proved to be a 35-year-old man who had died in c.3200 BC.

Italy

South of the Alps, although the Italian peninsula benefitted from a geographical unity, this did not manifest itself in any cultural unity. By 500 BC, there were many distinct cultures and several civilisations competing for control of local resources. In the south and on the island of Sicily, Greek and Phoenician colonists and traders were engaged in a long, slow war of commercial and military attrition. Northern Italy, from the Po Valley almost to the Bay of Naples was under Etruscan influence.

South of the Alps, the Iron Age started in c.900 BC with the Villanovan culture in the Po Valley, which was firmly rooted in Late Bronze Age and Urnfield traditions. In the southern part of the Villanovan culture area, perhaps through contact with Mediterranean peoples, Etruscan civilisation emerged in c.750 BC. The Etruscans spoke a non-Indo-European language, and under Phoenician and Greek influence developed city-states that traded local metal ores for imported luxuries. In central Italy, sandwiched between Greeks and Etruscans, were a few small Latin-speaking communities, one of which was Rome.

Although the main focus of Etruscan enterprise was directed towards the Greeks and Phoenicians to the south and west, they also maintained links with the head of the Adriatic, where thoroughbred horses were exchanged for elaborate metalware. Some of these Etruscan metalwares, like those of the Villanovans before them, found their way via transalpine routes to Hallstatt communities.

To the north of the Etruscans, were several other northern Italian cultures. In the west, centred around the Bay of Genoa, were the Ligurians – traders and seafarers, who spoke an Indo-European language similar to Celtic. To the east were the Veneti. They also spoke an Indo-European language and shared their name with a later tribe in Brittany that engaged in similar trading activities. Although both the Ligurians and the Veneti shared a language similar to that of the Celts, ethnically they are not considered Celts. In the central region of Italy, however, were two cultures about whose ethnicity we are less certain – the Este in the east, and Golasecca in the west.

Este and Golasecca

Este culture flourished in a few metalworking centres from c.600 BC to 500 BC. The most distinctive products

▲ **Etruscan bronze sculpture** of a girl acrobat. The piece once formed the handle of a lid on a *cista* (toilet box), usually found in tombs. The sculpture measures 6 × 15 centimetres (2.5 × 6 inches). The figurine dates from the 3rd or 2nd century BC.

▶ **Grazing stag** on the 'Este situla' found in grave 126 at Villa Benvenuti, Veneto, north Italy. The situla was made in c.600 BC. This engraved and embossed detail appears on the middle frieze of the situla. Such depictions of processions of animals are typical in Greek and Etruscan art.

were decorated bronze buckets (situlae), some of which have been found in graves at Hallstatt itself, and also at nearby Hallein. Although the art style of the situlae is definitely non-Celtic, bronze buckets subsequently became part of the Celtic repertoire. One of the earliest depictions of a Celt (the Bologna stele depicting an Etruscan cavalryman attacking a naked Celtic infantry-man) is from what was nominally Este territory.

Golasecca culture was centred on Lake Como, and there is some evidence that it may have contained Celtic-speaking elements from about the end of the Hallstatt C period. Some commentators have suggested the existence of entirely Celtic settlements on the southern fringes of the Golasecca culture area. A number of Golaseccan vehicle burials, dating from between 700 and 500 BC, stand out as being markedly different from contemporary Etruscan chariot burials. Although there are many differences, the Golaseccan vehicles seem to have a number of stylistic similarities to Hallstatt C and D burial wagons, and we can state that overall they are more Celtic than Etruscan. The language of the Golaseccans – Lepontic – is known from just a few inscriptions. Linguists have declared Lepontic to be basically Ligurian with Celtic affinities.

During the final stages of Hallstatt D and the Early La Tène period, the Golaseccans became middlemen in the Etruscan trade with the emerging Marne and

Mosel regions. This link with the new centres of Celtic power may have led to increasing 'celticisation'. When the great Celtic migrations began, there is every reason to believe that the newcomers who poured through the Alpine passes into the Po Valley did not find themselves among complete strangers.

▲ **Greek vase** This red-figure (oenochoe) vase from Etruria dates from the late 5th century BC, and depicts a sacrificial scene. The colonisation of southern Italy by the Greeks and the trade links they established had a significant impact on Etrurian art and culture.

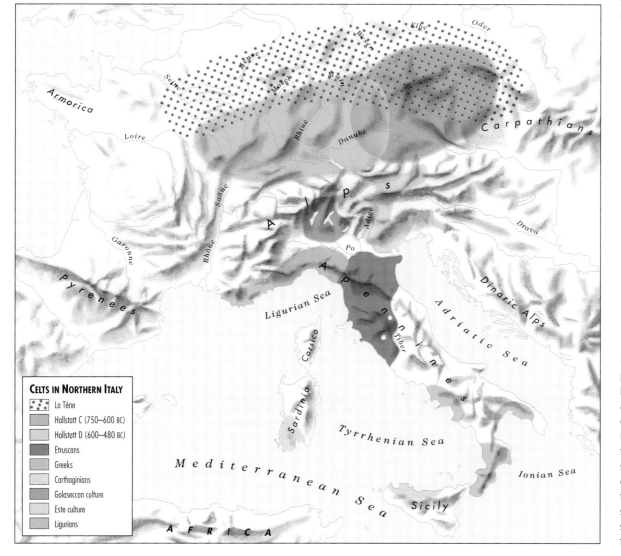

CELTS IN NORTHERN ITALY

⣿	La Tène
	Hallstatt C (750–600 BC)
	Hallstatt D (600–480 BC)
	Etruscans
	Greeks
	Carthaginians
	Golaseccan culture
	Este culture
	Ligurians

◄ **Sub-Alpine Celts** Alpine passes allowed limited contact between the early Celtic cultures and the emergent Mediterranean civilisations active in Italy. Northern Italy was dominated by the native Etruscans, while the south was largely under the control of Greek colonists. In the far north of the peninsula, the sub-Alpine Golaseccan culture shows signs of Celtic influence from c.700 BC.

CELTIC EUROPE IN 400 BC

By 400 BC, Celtic-speaking societies had been developing in Europe for several hundred years. Taken as a whole, this early period can be characterised as one of gradual economic intensification and geographic expansion. On the continent of Europe, the Hallstatt B élites had been superseded by their more westerly phase D counterparts, who benefitted from Greek commercial enterprise. After 500 BC, these groups had, in turn, been replaced by a more widely dispersed group of La Tène élites who, over the succeeding century, developed a remarkably homogenised culture with a very distinctive art style.

While recognising this early manifestation of Celtic unity, it must be emphasized that, in 400 BC, La Tène culture and Celtic-speaking Europe were by no means co-extensive. There were, in fact, two Celtic zones: the La Tène zone across central Europe, and a peripheral zone (including northern Italy, the Iberian Peninsula and the British Isles) where Celtic languages were spoken, but where La Tène culture had little impact at this time.

A literate culture?

By no means all of the inhabitants of the peripheral zone spoke Celtic, and within the La Tène heartland linguistic homogeneity is by no means certain. The only proof of language is writing, and Celtic inscriptions are very scarce, particularly before 400 BC.

Those few inscriptions that survive are sparse, and leave many questions unanswered. For example, what proportion of the population could read? How many could read the language of the inscription, or were

▶ **Vase** from Saint-Pol-de-Léon, Finistère, north-west France. The spiral decoration is in the Waldalgesheim style, and derives from metal engravings of the 4th century BC. Today, Saint-Pol-de-Léon lies in the Breton-speaking area of France.

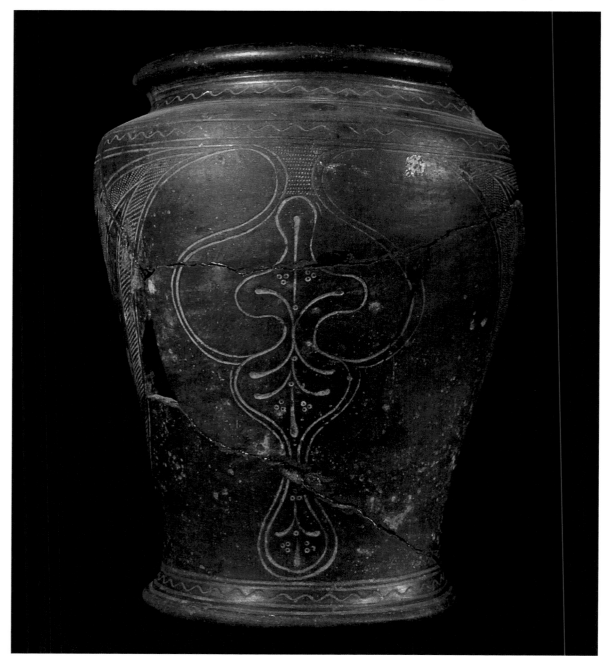

intended to read it? Was the language that they read the same as the language they spoke at home? Even in exclusively Celtic-speaking areas, there are bound to have been differences of accent, dialect, and other characteristics, such as 'educated' speech ('correct' pronunciation), and perhaps even the reserved use of specific 'royal' or sacred vocabularies.

One perspective on the spread of Celtic languages in Europe, is to view 'Celtic' as a *lingua franca* that developed after *c.*1000 BC among warrior élites who, through a variety of military and economic strategies, were able to establish local dominance. While sidestepping issues of ethnic origin and precise chronology, this view does provide a framework for understanding what Early Celtic Europe was like.

Farming and rituals of war

Celtic society was mainly composed of small-scale farmers who grew cereals such as barley and wheat as staples, and raised large numbers of pigs, sheep and cattle. Horses were used as work animals as well as for transport. These farmers collectively supported (or were dominated by) élite male groups, for whom an ideal life consisted of war, sport and hospitality. The distinctions between war and sport were likely to have been somewhat blurred as both took place mainly within the Celtic communities. Warfare between Celts – to restore hurt pride, score points off neighbours or just for sheer entertainment – may well have developed into fairly ritualised affairs intended to minimise casualties among the élite. The concept of any form of 'national' warfare would have been entirely alien to Celts at the end of the 5th century BC. Such concepts could only arise when the élites came into military conflict with a significant other (as opposed to peoples less well organised than themselves), in the form of highly disciplined Mediterranean armies.

Feasting and gift-giving

Within the élites there seems to have been the same pyramid structure as in Celtic society as a whole. Social and political power rested in the hands of single individuals or families who, either through inheritance or by right of force, had established monopolistic control over the available 'wealth' of a district or region. Power was maintained through traditional aristocratic means, by 'purchasing' allegiance with largess. 'Celtic' institutions, such as feasting, not only allowed a 'prince' to dispense lavish hospitality, but also provided a specific peer-arena within which the upper echelons of the élite (barons/senior courtiers) could compete with each other in a variety of ways that avoided bloodshed.

The other arena for competition and the purchase of allegiance within the élites, was in the giving and receiving of prestigious gifts, especially those, such as swords and jewellery, that could serve as badges of rank and status. Apart from a trickle of Mediterranean goods, which largely dried up after 400 BC, there was no source of such gifts other than local craftworkers. If we seek an explanation for the development of La Tène art, we need look no further than the dictates of fashion and social climbing among the Celtic aristocracy.

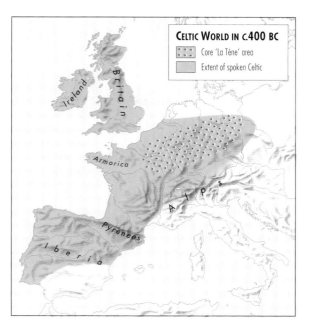

◀ **Celtic world in *c.*400 BC**
While Celtic languages may have been spoken across most of western Europe by the end of the 5th century BC, the distinctive La Tène culture was confined to a relatively small area. During the following century, as the Celts pushed southwards and eastwards, both their language and their material culture became much more widespread.

During the Early La Tène period, some of these Celtic élites consolidated into larger tribal groupings that became associated with a geographical area, the Boii in Bohemia, for example. In 400 BC, these 'tribes' were the largest ethnic units to which any of the Celtic-speaking inhabitants of Europe would have admitted belonging; and the vast majority would have had no greater sense of belonging than to their own dispersed village.

▼ **Celtic helmet** found at Agris, Charente, west France. This beautiful helmet is made of iron and bronze, and is covered with gold and inlaid with coral. It dates from the 4th century BC.

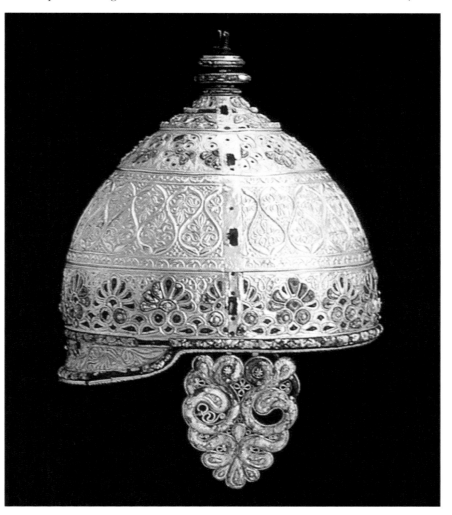

CHAPTER
THREE

▲ Detail from a panel of a silver cauldron (probably 1st century BC), found at Gundestrup, north Jutland, Denmark.

THE ROMAN EMPIRE

While ancient Greece, considered by many to be the birthplace and cradle of western civilisation, had a considerable influence on the arts and behaviour of the Celtic élites, it had, apart from a few scattered military encounters, little political impact on the early Celts.

By 400 BC, the Greeks were on the decline in western Europe. War with Persia (492–479 BC), swiftly followed by the devastating Pelopennesian Wars (431–404 BC), had taken their toll. In contrast to the precocious and heroic conquests of Alexander the Great (c.356–323 BC) in the east, Greek power in the west was first truncated, then eradicated. Initially their rivals in trade and colonisation, the Phoenician-speaking Carthaginians from North Africa, opposed them. Subsequently, the Greek territories in the west, Greece itself, the Carthaginians and their territories, and a good portion of Alexander's conquests in the east, were all to be absorbed into the Roman Empire. Almost as an afterthought, the Roman Empire also swallowed virtually the whole of La Tène Europe, and most of the other Celtic-speaking areas.

The founding of Rome

According to tradition, the city of Rome was founded in 753 BC, approximately coincidental with the beginning of the Hallstatt Iron Age. A Roman state endured for almost a millennium, from the expulsion of the last Etruscan king in 509 BC to its eventual conquest (at least in the west) by the Ostrogoths in AD 478 (see pages 108–109). The history of the Romans is also the history of the transition from the ancient to the medieval worlds.

Romans and Celts first encountered each other early in the 4th century BC, at a very sensitive time in Rome's history. The city was just beginning to expand at a local level, and was basking in the glow of victory after capturing (396 BC) the Etruscan city of Veii (now Veio), when it was attacked by Celts. Raiding deep into Italy, the Celts smashed through the Roman army, sacked most of Rome and then extracted a huge bribe in return for peaceable departure.

Defeat by the Celts was a massive blow to Roman power and prestige, but the city soon recovered and within 50 years Roman armies and diplomats were back about their business of extending Roman influence. However the psychological blow to Roman pride and self-confidence was much greater, and out of all proportion to the actual military threat posed by the Celts. The intrusion of an unruly mass of armed barbarians into the familiar and neatly defined Mediterranean landscape of cities and states left a scar that lasted long after the actual injury had healed.

Although avarice and ambition played their part, the growth of the Roman Empire was not wholly the result of rapacious greed and an unquenchable thirst for expansion. In many respects Roman policy was preoccupied with the search for secure frontiers – frontiers that would protect them from the barbarians beyond, who were represented in the collective Roman imagination by naked and bloodthirsty Celts. If we had to rely solely on the Greeks for our

▶ **Roman eagle** from the 2nd or 3rd century AD. The eagle was the Roman army standard, symbol of the legion and object of veneration. In AD 312, Constantine replaced the eagle with the cross. The power, speed, courage and nobility of the eagle made it a perfect symbol for an army. The Romans called it Jupiter's 'storm-bird'.

▼ **The Roman Empire** was the first state to bring unity to much of Europe. From the cold hills of southern Scotland to the deserts of North Africa, Rome introduced a common culture, language and script, and a political system that gave equal rights to all citizens. Roman culture also spread to lands beyond the imperial frontier, influencing among others the Germanic barbarians who later overran the Empire – but who also perpetuated many of its traditions and institutions. Roman expansion was curtailed early in the 1st century AD and the empire adopted an essentially defensive posture. Although the internal divisions of the empire were reorganised several times, the external frontiers were subject to little change until the final collapse.

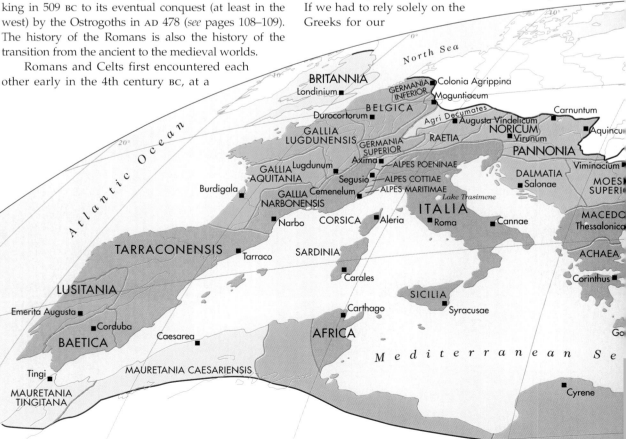

THE ROMAN EMPIRE AD 106	
———	Imperial frontier AD 106
▨	Roman expansion 201–100 BC
▨	Roman expansion 100–44 BC
▨	Roman expansion 44 BC– AD 106
BAETICA	Roman province
Agri	Roman region
■	Roman provincial capital

information on the Celts we would know as much about them as we do of the Scythians. However, the Romans had 400 years of trade and intermittent warfare with the Celts, and their historians have provided numerous accounts with a considerable amount of detail, much of which has been borne out by subsequent archaeological investigation.

Roman expansion

Once they regained their composure and momentum, Rome's diplomatic and military forces became virtually unstoppable. Until the mid-3rd century BC, Roman power was confined to central and southern Italy, where it overcame Greek and Etruscan opposition. In 264 BC, Rome entered the international arena when it embarked on the first of the Punic Wars with Carthage. In 241 BC, despite having to build a navy from scratch, Rome emerged victorious and gained control of Sicily.

The Second Punic War (218–202 BC), provoked by Hannibal's (247–c.181 BC) invasion of Italy in 218 BC, ended in Carthaginian defeat and the Roman annexation of northern Italy and southern Spain. A third war (149–146 BC) extinguished the Carthaginian threat and added their North African territories to the Roman Empire. Greece, which had supported the Carthaginians, also became part of the Empire.

Rome now had extensive, but very vulnerable frontiers. In the course of the next three centuries, these borders were consolidated through a combination of conquest, peaceful annexation and inheritance. Anatolia (Asia Minor), the Levant (Middle East) and Gaul were successively occupied, and when Egypt was acquired in 31 BC the Mediterranean Sea became a 'Roman lake' surrounded on all sides by the Empire.

◀ **Top of a Roman standard** found at Kömlöd, Hungary. The Roman army marched into battle under standards such as this. The top panel contains an eagle. The central panel shows Jupiter Dolichenus standing on a bull and Juno standing on a hind. The bronze triangle dates from the 1st to 3rd century AD, and is 36 centimetres (14.1 inches) high.

Further Roman expansion added most of Britain in AD 43, and established the Rhine and the upper Danube as the Empire's north-east frontier. A final expansive thrust added Dacia (roughly modern Romania) and Arabia in AD 106. Although the situation in the east remained somewhat fluid, the frontiers of the Roman Empire in AD 106 were doggedly maintained for another three centuries, during which time Celtic Europe was largely Romanised out of existence.

▼ **Roman legionary** The expansion of the Roman Empire was achieved by the flexibility and discipline of its army. The legions formed the backbone of the Roman army. Each legion consisted of c.6000 soldiers divided into ten cohorts. The legionary shown here has short body armour (*cuirass*), braced helmet, short sword (*gladium*) and large shield (*scutum*).

WARRIOR MIGRANTS

The great Celtic migrations of the 4th and 3rd centuries BC spread La Tène culture far and wide, and brought the Celts into close contact with a variety of peoples, both more and less 'civilised' than themselves. The archæological recovery of La Tène material from sites across Europe has helped historians chart the progress of Celtic expansion. In many cases, it has provided concrete evidence to support the surviving historical accounts.

The main axes of this expansion were to the south and east, in contrast to the earlier westward and northward shifts apparent in the transitions from Hallstatt C to D, and from Hallstatt D to Early La Tène. The scale of the movement was also much greater. If the Mosel region of north-east France is taken as the geographical centre of the La Tène culture area in c.420 BC, then within 150 years the furthest outposts of Celtic migrants were c.2200 kilometres (1400 miles) to the south-east, in Anatolia.

Unlike many other migrations, such as the series of such events following the Chinese expulsion of the Hsiung Nu in c.180 BC, the movement of the Celts does not seem to have had any external cause: there was no enemy looming to the north or west to push them south-eastwards. Admittedly, the Celts were well equipped for mobility with horses, wagons, carts and chariots, but they were not nomadic – they were farmers who lived in settled communities. Why then did large numbers of them undertake such long and often perilous journeys? The root causes of the great migrations seem to lie within the nature of Celtic society.

Raiding

Celtic farming methods, which closely combined crops and livestock, were sufficiently productive to support an élite of predominantly young men, who were surplus to the requirements of food production and were therefore free to assume a full-time warrior/aristocrat lifestyle. Within and between these élite groups, peer-relations were mediated by a number of semi-ritualised activities that provided opportunity for the acquisition, display and appreciation of personal status and prestige.

One such activity that was supremely suited to Celtic society was the cattle raid. Along with gold jewellery and iron swords, cattle were one of the most useful and prized forms of wealth among the early Celts. Riding through the night to capture a neighbour's cattle – i.e. rustling – was the perfect means to demonstrate courage, cleverness and general one-upmanship.

Although the wealth represented by the stolen cattle was undoubtedly an important factor, material gain was not the whole of it. The scoring of 'points' was probably equally important, and there were no doubt many conventions, such as the degree of allowable force, or severity of casualties, which influenced the overall 'score'. The finer points of the 'game' aside, the popularity of cattle-raiding may in some places have reduced Celtic society to a state of permanent low-level localised warfare.

Overpopulation

The economic success of the La Tène Celts, which is evidenced by the volume and exuberance of their art and craft output, also had another inevitable effect – an increase in population. Celtic society, for all its mobility and flexibility, could only absorb limited numbers of surplus population. The most volatile elements of this surplus (able-bodied but underemployed males aged 18–40) posed a danger to all levels of the established order, threatening to disrupt the traditional patterns of loyalty, allegiance and raiding.

Greek communities of the early classical period, particularly those situated on coasts and islands, had eased similar population pressures by sending off boat-loads of young people to make new lives on distant shores. In the 5th century BC, the Celtic societies of Europe lacked any such communal traditions, and had not yet developed the mechanisms for reaching such decisions as a matter of routine. Among the Celts, young males who could not find a legitimate place in society usually departed individually and

▼ **Gallic chief** by Eugene Grasset (1841–1917). The illustration contains several symbols that we have come to associate with the Celts: the crested boar on top of the battle standard and the warrior's waxed moustache, for example. The bird wing-feathers on the helmet carry faint echoes of the spectacular helmet found in Romania (see opposite page). A horsehair crest sprouts from the top-knot of the helmet.

◄ **Bronze bird of prey** crest on an iron helmet found at Çiumeşti, north-west Romania. This sophisticated armour was created using the finest technological and artistic skills available. The wings of the bird are cleverly modelled so that they would have flapped as the warrior rode full-tilt towards the enemy. It is a perfect example of barbaric splendour and the Celtic warrior's obsession with personal display and adornment. The raven or crow may have been a magical deity whose protection was sought in battle. The helmet dates from the 3rd century BC, and is 25 centimetres (9.8 inches) high.

▼ **Raids and migrations** *c.*400–260 BC Historically attested, the great migrations of the middle La Tène period, dispersed large numbers of Celtic settlers across northern Italy and south-eastern Europe, and into the fringes of Asia.

lived an 'outlaw' existence on the fringes. Some joined together to form *gaesatae* (bands of warriors) and used their strength of numbers to increase their negotiating power with those that they encountered. A growth in the numbers of *gaesatae* in the late 5th century BC may have hastened the crisis in Celtic society which first impacted on north Italy. However, while the warrior class was important, it should be remembered that entire tribes migrated to north Italy for "land and for plunder".

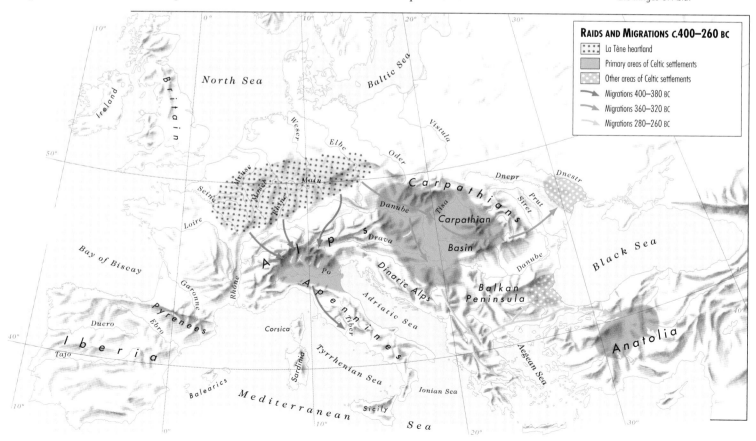

RAIDS AND MIGRATIONS c.400–260 BC
- La Tène heartland
- Primary areas of Celtic settlements
- Other areas of Celtic settlements
- Migrations 400–380 BC
- Migrations 360–320 BC
- Migrations 280–260 BC

INVASION OF ITALY

In the years around 400 BC, large numbers of Celts from various parts of south-central Europe streamed across Alpine passes into northern Italy and settled in the broad valley of the River Po. According to Roman historians, the first to arrive were the Insubres, who remained in the western part of the region, and established a centre at Mediolanum (now Milan). Other tribes followed the Insubres, including the Boii and Cenomani, who settled further west, and the Senones who pushed down the east coast of the Adriatic Sea.

According to ancient tradition there were Celts living in northern Italy at an earlier date, perhaps as early as 600 BC, and there is some evidence to support this (see pages 50–51). These earlier Celtic settlers (if that is what they were) arrived in too few numbers to have any great impact on the societies developing in Italy. This was not the case, however, with the migrations that occurred around 400 BC, which amounted to nothing less than a full-scale invasion.

▶ **Italo-Celtic bronze helmet** from the 3rd century BC. This 'jockey cap' helmet is 15 centimetres (5.9 inches) high. The border of the cap features repoussé spirals and dots.

▼ **Celts in north Italy** Celtic settlement in Italy was concentrated around the Po Valley and parts of the north-east coastline. Both the Etruscans and the Romans succeeded in repelling occasional Celtic raids, ensuring that the Celts were remained on the other side of the Dolomites.

Etruscan losses

The arrival of the Celts was a major blow to the beleaguered but still-vigorous Etruscan civilisation. To the south and in the western Mediterranean region, the Etruscans were threatened economically by competition from the Greek cities of southern Italy. In response, the Etruscans expanded their influence to the north-east, establishing ports at Adria and Spina (near present-day Venice). The growing political power of Rome placed further pressure on the Etruscans, who were forced to surrender the city of Veii (now Veio) to the Romans in 396 BC.

The Etruscan settlements in the north-east were lost in the first invasion of the Celts – the Boii took over the city of Felsina (now Bologna) – and the Etruscans were pushed back behind the Apennine mountains. Even the Etruscan heartland was not safe from raids by Celtic warriors in search of plunder. In 391 BC, a warrior-band of the Senones (who already controlled Ancona) laid siege to the Etruscan city of Clusium (now Chiusi). In a grand gesture, the Romans sent ambassadors to arbitrate between the two sides. Unfortunately, the ambassadors failed to maintain diplomatic neutrality and joined the defenders of Clusium in battle against the barbarian invaders. The Senones were deeply offended by this breach of military etiquette and, after the Romans refused to make recompense, they marched on Rome.

Defeat of Rome

In 387 BC, the Celts destroyed the Roman army in battle at the River Allia (a tributary of the Tiber), c.16 kilometres (10 miles) from Rome. They then sacked the city, with the possible exception of the Capitol – which is supposed to have stubbornly resisted while the rest of the city burned.

According to later Roman historians, the Celtic forces occupying Rome were soon afflicted by malaria and other diseases. So many died, that the corpses were piled up and burned at a place that became known as the 'Gallic Pyres'. Weakened, the Senones were eventually persuaded to return across the Apennines after receiving a massive payment of gold. When the gold was being weighed out, Roman senators are said to have complained loudly at the expense. On hearing them, the Senones' chieftain Brennus is supposed to have added his sword to the weight to be balanced with gold, silencing further complaint with the remark, "Woe to the conquered".

This humiliating defeat at the hands of 'uncivilised' barbarians had a profound effect upon the Romans. The popular myth of the invincibility of Roman armies was shattered, and Rome's confidence was severely shaken. One immediate consequence was the construction of the first defensive rampart to encircle the city of Rome – the

CELTS IN NORTH ITALY

- La Tène 'heartland'
- La Tène 'mainland'
- Area of Celtic settlement
- BOII Celtic tribes
- Golaseccan culture
- Etruscan territory
- Roman territory
- Celtic movements
- Senones' attack
- Celtic centres
- Towns
- Battles

remains of these fortifications are now incorrectly referred to as the 'Wall of Servius Tullius'.

Military defeat also brought a temporary halt to Roman expansion in central Italy, and a more conciliatory approach was adopted in Rome's dealings with neighbouring Latin settlements. This more peaceful policy was largely successful, but within 50 years Rome had returned to an aggressive strategy in order to expand its influence. The humiliation of the Celtic sack of Rome was, however, never forgotten. When Rome finally felt strong enough to mount an offensive against the Celts, after the Battle of Sentinum (295 BC), the Celts were pursued and exterminated with a ferocity that the Romans reserved for only their bitterest of foes.

Celtic raiders

Before Sentinum, the uncertain political situation in Italy was highly profitable for the Celts. Bands of warriors continually made raids into Etruscan and Roman territory in search of loot, and during the 360s BC, they once more threatened Rome itself. There is some evidence (a warrior's grave in Puglia) that the Celts may even have settled south of the city.

Some of those who raided deep into southern Italy took up employment as mercenaries with Greek rulers and fought against the Etruscans. By the beginning of the 3rd century BC, however, the Celts of Italy were making common cause with the Etruscans and other Italian allies, against the rapidly growing power of Rome.

◄ **Celtic warrior with loot**, part of a terracotta frieze in a temple at Civita Alba, near Sassoferrato, north-east Italy. The sculpture, 45 centimetres (17.7 inches) high, dates from the early 2nd century BC. The image of a Celt running off with stolen goods would have conformed both to local prejudice and Roman propaganda.

▼ *Gauls in Sight of Rome* by Evariste-Vital Luminais (1822–96). This oil painting, 122 × 177 centimetres (48 × 69.7 inches), captures something of the cultural drama behind the Celtic attack on Rome – the 'eternal city' lies at the mercy of barbarian warriors.

BALKAN EXPANSION

According to the Roman historian Livy (writing some three centuries after the event), the great Celtic migrations resulted from the twin drives of overpopulation and greed for the products of the more developed Mediterranean economies. In Livy's version, Ambigatus, king of the Gauls, divided the surplus Celtic population into two groups: one band he sent southwards into Italy under his nephew Bellovesus, while the other was sent eastwards led by another nephew, Segovesus.

If we accept Livy's account, we might conclude that of the two nephews their uncle favoured Bellovesus. Compared with the great treks to the east the invasion of northern Italy was little more than a tricky hike across the Alps. However, the account of this journey to the east remains largely unwritten because the Celts in the Balkans are only sporadically mentioned in contemporary histories as a result of their occasional and glancing impacts with more developed societies. This contrasts strongly with the situation in the melting pot of northern Italy, where face-to-face confrontation between Celts and 'civilisation' was inevitable.

▲ **Bronze boar** with crest from Bata, Hungary, dating from the 5th or 4th century BC. The boar was probably a source of meat for the ancient Celts, but its belligerent nature may have lead to symbolic identification with the warrior.

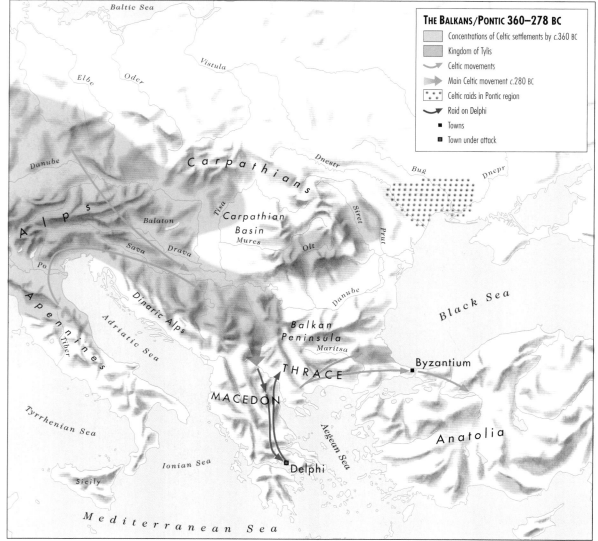

THE BALKANS/PONTIC 360–278 BC
- Concentrations of Celtic settlements by c.360 BC
- Kingdom of Tylis
- Celtic movements
- Main Celtic movement c.280 BC
- Celtic raids in Pontic region
- Raid on Delphi
- ■ Towns
- ■ Town under attack

▶ **Alexander the Great's** death in 323 BC considerably weakened the power of Macedon, which had become the protector of Greece. Taking advantage of this weakness, Celtic war parties began raiding the Balkan peninsula.

Moves to the east

Broadly following the course of the Danube, Celtic war parties and their families, reinforced by latecomers who could find no place in an overcrowded Italy, travelled more than 1500 kilometres (1000 miles) eastwards across Europe. Progress was slow and, we may suppose, completely disorganised.

Nor were pickings particularly bountiful. Loot was scarce because the easterly migrating Celts were overrunning not urban city-states such as in Italy, but diffuse societies where wealth and population were less concentrated. There can be little doubt, however, that Celtic expansion to the east was essentially motivated by greed: one group that emerged during this process was the Tectosages, whose name literally means "migrant seekers after wealth".

Through a combination of sheer weight of numbers and fighting prowess (the equal of any army in the Mediterranean region), the Celts were able to subdue native populations along their line of advance, including the Illyrians and Pannonians, leaving some of their number behind as a ruling or tribute-extracting élite.

The vanguard reached the Balkan region in c.350 BC. Behind them, stretched and scattered across eastern Europe, were assortments of Celtic groups whose size and composition must have varied considerably. The degree of 'Celticisation' in eastern Europe is open to question. There is little doubt that, locally, Celts 'ruled' from Bohemia to the Black Sea. What is equally certain, however, is that Celts never achieved numerical majority in the region, and that 'Celtic' populations in the Balkans were culturally mixed.

Some groups of Celts, presumably the most adventurous and optimistic, travelled from the middle Danube westwards to the northern shores of the Black Sea, deep into the realm of the nomadic Scythians and Cimmerians. A Celtic presence here is attested by a considerable amount of archaeological evidence, including a La Tène sword made in Italy and equestrian objects from Bohemia. Some local warrior graves have been found containing Etruscan helmets, dating from the migration period, which were probably brought into the region by marauding Celts, and subsequently lost through battle or trade. Some of the easternmost Celtic bands may have ventured as far as the Crimea and the Sea of Azov.

Further expansion into Anatolia

In c.300 BC, there was a second surge of expansion in the Celtic 'far east'. War bands gathered and coalesced in the south, and descended on Thrace and Macedonia in 298 BC. The Macedonian army commanded by Cassander (c.358–297 BC) – who had fought alongside Alexander the Great (c.356–323 BC) – repulsed this first assault, but a second attempt (281 BC) succeeded and the Macedonians were decisively defeated in battle.

Internal disputes now divided the Celtic forces. One group, said to number c.20,000, broke away and was soon lured across the Hellespont (now Dardanelles) to serve as mercenaries in Anatolia (Asia Minor). Thereafter, known as the Galatians, they carved out their own place in history. The main party of Celts, however, made an abortive raid on the temples and treasuries at Delphi in 279 BC, and after heavy losses were forced to retreat back to Thrace in disarray.

In 277 BC, a resurgent Macedonian army defeated another Celtic army, led by Cerethrios, and thousands of Celts were captured and sold as slaves. Some Celtic tribes retained sufficient cohesion to negotiate terms of service as mercenaries with the Macedonians, and one group established the kingdom of Tylis in south-east Thrace, from where they briefly made a living by piracy. The remainder, which if Greek accounts of slaughter are to believed must have been a fraction of the original numbers, disappeared back into the middle Danube region, from where some undoubtedly returned to their heartland in the west.

▲ **Stone head** found at Mšecké-Žehrovice, central Czech Republic. Perhaps the most famous of all Early Celtic sculptures, this torque-wearing male head with twirled moustache and backcombed hair dates from 2nd–1st century BC. It is 25 centimetres (9.8 inches) high.

◀ ▲ **Bronze ankle rings**, dating from the late 3rd or early 2nd century BC, found at Batina (formerly Kis-Köszeg), north-east Croatia. Each of the rings, eight centimetres (3.1 inches) high, was made from three hollow balls.

CELTIC MERCENARIES

The 4th and 3rd centuries BC marked the height in power of the Celtic warriors. In addition to the battles they won on their own account, Celtic fighting-skills (especially in cavalry) were employed by many of the major armies in the Mediterranean region. Consequently, Celtic warriors found themselves plying their trade with spear and sword far beyond the boundaries of the newly expanded Celtic world.

In Greek service

While the Romans were still reeling from the sack of their city, the martial flair of the Celts and their battlefield effectiveness against classically trained armies, was noticed by some of the Greek rulers of southern Italy, among them Dionysius the Elder (c.430–367 BC), the tyrant of Syracuse. Dionysius established a colony at Ancona, on the north-east coast of Italy, in what was fast becoming Celtic territory, and in 385 BC he formed a military alliance with some of the Senones' warlords.

In 383 BC, Celts fought alongside Greeks in a raid on the Etruscan port of Pyrgi. During the middle decades of the 4th century BC, Celtic mercenaries fought all over south and central Italy in the pay of Dionysius and, after his death in 367 BC, his son Dionysius the Younger (active 368–344 BC). At least one contingent was sent to the Greek mainland in c.368 BC to assist in the defence of Sparta against the rising power of Thebes. A few decades later, the prestige of the northern

Italian Celts was sufficiently great for them to be part of the delegation that 'greeted' Alexander the Great (c.356–323 BC) on the River Danube in 335 BC. In view of subsequent events, and the Celtic invasion of Macedonia (see page 63), the Celtic greeting may also have contained a gentle warning, enhanced by the presence of such fearsome warriors.

Following the disastrous raid on Delphi, many Celts stayed on as mercenaries in Macedonian service, from where they either eventually travelled home in sporadic fashion or became involved in the internecine struggles between the Diodochi (successors to Alexander the Great). A group of Celtic mercenaries, recruited by Nicomedes of Bithynia (r. 281–245 BC), ravaged Anatolia (Asia Minor), before carving out their own state in northern Phrygia (see pages 76–77).

In 277 BC, some Celtic mercenaries were diverted from Anatolia to serve Ptolemy II (308–246 BC), the Greek ruler of Egypt and builder of the Pharos lighthouse at Alexandria. After success on the battlefield, some of the Celts reverted to raiding and looting, and 4000 of them were driven onto a barren island in the Nile delta where they either committed suicide or died of starvation. Others must have remained loyal and completed active service, because they and their descendants formed a military reserve beside the Fayoum oasis. Their presence there, deep in the Western Desert of Egypt, has been confirmed by archæologists.

► **Damaged bronze helmet** found at the Kandija necropolis, Novo Mesto, south-east Slovenia. Blows from a heavy axe caused the dents and holes in the helmet. The helmet, which is of the so-called 'Negauer' type, dates from the 5th century BC. It is 19.5 centimetres (7.7 inches) high.

◄ **Alexander the Great** (c.356–323 BC) This detail from a mosaic in the House of the Faun, Pompeii, south Italy, dates from the 2nd or early 1st century BC. The Romans greatly admired and imitated Alexander's imperial ambitions. In 335 BC, Alexander and his Macedonian army set up camp beside the River Danube, where they received a delegation of Celts from the upper Danube. According to Ptolemy Soter (c.366–c.283 BC), a young Celtic chief was invited to a personal audience with Alexander who asked him what the Celts feared the most, expecting to hear his own name as the answer. Instead, the Celt replied that his people "feared nothing so much as the possibility that the heavens might fall on their heads".

◀ **Mercenaries in the Greek World** Celtic warriors, who had a fundamentally different attitude to war than 'civilised' citizen-soldiers, found ready employment as shock troops on Mediterranean battlefields.

In 217 BC, Celts formed part of the Egyptian forces mobilised to defeat a Seleucid invasion at the battle of Raphia, near Giza, north Egypt. In 187 BC, Celtic troops were used to suppress a rebellion at Abydos in south Egypt. Some 50 years later, there were still Celts in Egyptian service, among the garrison at the town of Hermopolis Magna, north Egypt.

Celtiberian mercenaries

In their Sicilian wars against Greeks such as Dionysius the Elder, the Carthaginians relied heavily on Celtiberian mercenaries. Subsequently these mercenaries would earn the grudging respect of the Roman legions who conquered Sicily in the First Punic War (264–241 BC).

During the Second Punic War (218–202 BC), both Rome and Carthage used Celtiberian and Celtic mercenaries. Hannibal (247–c.181 BC) marched from Spain with c.10,000 Celtiberians from the south-east and, although en route to Italy he had to fight his way through the territory of the Celtic Allobroges in southern Gaul, the Celts of the Po Valley flocked to his cause. Even those, such as the Boii, who initially sided against him, soon deserted their Roman paymasters, in one case taking their paymasters' heads with them.

About half of Hannibal's army that crushed the Roman legions at Lake Trasimene (217 BC) and Cannae (216 BC) was composed of Celtic mercenaries. Although they fought for pay, many of them were motivated by revenge for the Celtic defeat at Telamon in 225 BC (*see* pages 72–73). However, by the time the Romans launched a counter invasion of Spain in 202 BC, many of the Italian Celts had already deserted the Carthaginian cause. In Spain, the Celtiberian mercenaries proved equally faithless, and showed themselves content (at least initially) to fight for Roman pay.

By the middle of the 1st century BC, the Roman army (overhauled by Marius) was much less reliant on mercenaries. Instead they preferred to be assisted by 'allies' – a term which covered both compulsory service by subject peoples, and voluntary co-operation by peoples and groups who perceived that their self-interest was best served through alliance with Rome. During Julius Caesar's (100–44 BC) conquest of Gaul in the 50s BC, for example, Celtic tribes such as the Aedui and Remi were perfectly happy to assist the Roman legions in the defeat of their Celtic neighbours (*see* pages 82–83). Only when Gallic opposition to the Romans coalesced under Vercingetorix (d.46 BC) did they change sides and align themselves with the nascent cause of Celtic nationalism.

▼ **Bronze Italo-Celtic helmet** dating from the 3rd century BC. The helmet bears incised decoration of s-shaped tongues, pearls and dots. The rim features a pattern of swastika-like designs.

RAID ON DELPHI

During the classical and early Hellenistic periods, mainland Greeks had some dealings with Celts – trade in the far west, two diplomatic missions, and the acquisition of battlefield paraphernalia from Italy – but not much in the way of direct contact. Then, suddenly, in 279 BC, something quite shocking happened – as it had to the Romans a little more than a century earlier. Celts flooding into the middle Danube region spilled over southwards into Thrace. In 281 BC, they defeated a Macedonian army and beheaded the king. Two years later, the Celts invaded Macedonia itself. Although one group of Celts was diverted eastwards into Anatolia (Asia Minor), towards the end of 279 BC, the main band, led by Brennus and Acichorius, continued southwards into Greece with the intention of sacking the temple and treasuries at Delphi. Incidentally (and resonantly convenient for the Greek historians) the Celtic chief Brennus had the same name as the leader of the war party that had sacked Rome.

'Navel of the world'

Today, one of the most picturesque archaeological sights in Greece, in 279 BC, Delphi was still the *omphalos* – the 'navel of the world', the site of the umbilical cord that joined this world to the next. The sacred

cliff-top sanctuary in central Greece had been recognised and revered by Greeks from the 8th century BC, and may have been the site of earlier snake- or spring- cults whose origins stretched back to the Neolithic period. The sanctuary was dedicated to the god Apollo. The oracle at Delphi (the 'voice' of Apollo), like the Olympic Games and the Greek language itself, was part of a common cultural heritage that united the communities of the Greek world – although politically they were often bitterly divided and at war with each other.

After the enforced unification of Greece under Philip II of Macedon (382–336 BC), and the explosive eastward expansion of Greek culture under his son Alexander the Great (356–323 BC), Delphi (along with Athens) became culturally enshrined as a symbol of the Greeks' European heritage. Many cities continued to maintain their individual treasuries at Delphi, containing gold and silver offerings dedicated to Apollo, along with piles of tarnished trophies – helmets and shields carried triumphantly from the field of battle. The temple and its precincts were also adorned with thousands of statues; many decorated with precious metals.

Although Delphi was a sacred sanctuary, it was not sacrosanct, and throughout its history had been under the 'protection' of various cities. One Greek

▼ **Tholos** temple in the sanctuary of Athena Pronaia on the slopes of Mount Parnassós, Delphi, south Greece. Athena Pronaia was the gateway to the sacred home of the Delphic oracle. Built in *c.*380 BC, the temple has an unusual circular shape. Leaf motifs on the capitals of its Corinthian columns are symbolically associated with Athena, the Greek Earth-Goddess.

protector or another had already melted down many of its greatest treasures. There was, however, still more than enough precious metal at Delphi to be worth marching through a Greek winter.

Celtic defeat in Macedonia

According to Greek historians, who may have been flattering both the Celts and themselves by their comparisons with the last 'barbarian' threat to the Greek homeland (the Persian invasion), the Greeks made their initial stand against the Celts at the Pass of Thermopylae. Coincidentally, a cunning enemy again outflanked the Greeks.

The Celts continued their advance, but were finally checked by a Greek army on the outskirts of Delphi. The following day, the Greeks attempted to seize the offensive but, despite desperate hand-to-hand fighting during which Brennus was severely wounded, they were unable to drive the Celts back. That night, according to Greek legend, the gods spread panic among the sleeping Celts who fell into disorderly retreat, harassed by the Greeks as they struggled northwards through winter storms. Many of the Celtic wounded were supposedly slaughtered by their comrades rather than let them be captured, and Brennus himself is reported to have committed suicide. In total, the Celts lost about half their fighting force because of the expedition to Delphi. In early 278 BC, the survivors reached Macedonia.

No sooner had the Celts regrouped in Macedonia, than they were lured into an ambush (277 BC) near Lysimacheia by the new Macedonian king, Antigonus II Gonatas (c.319–239 BC). The Celts fought their way out, but again suffered heavy casualties. Soon the only Celts remaining in Macedonia were either slaves or mercenaries.

Sack of Delphi – fact or fiction?

That is the Greek version of events – but a persistent ancient legend relates that the Celts did indeed sack Delphi, and Brennus is supposed to have mortally offended the Greeks by laughing at their humanistic gods. Some of the gold and silver looted by the Romans from the Celtic sacred lake at Tolosa (now Toulouse) in south-east Gaul, was widely believed to have been treasure that the Celts themselves had taken from Delphi. While this is plausible, it is very unlikely. Some of the objects thrown into the lake may indeed have been 'Greek antiquities', even to the Romans, but the workshops of southern Italy and the port of Massilia (now Marseilles) are more likely sources than Delphi.

Although we have no reason to doubt the basic facts of a Celtic raid on Delphi, no archaeological evidence has been found, either at Delphi or along the probable lines of attack. This is not in itself a problem – a fast-moving band of warriors is unlikely to have had time to carry out any of the elaborate funerals that have yielded most of the La Tène material. Indeed, Greek propaganda relates that the Celts were so barbaric that they did not bury their dead. Something undoubtedly happened at Delphi during the winter of 279–278 BC but Greek accounts, with their neat 'historical' parallels and supernatural interventions, read more like well-orchestrated tragedy than reliable history.

▲ **Decree** of the town of Kos in the Dodecanese. The inscription describes the sack of Delphi (March 278) by a Celtic army, led by Brennus, and their subsequent expulsion by the Greeks.

▼ **Treasury** of Athens at Delphi, on the slopes of Mount Parnassós, south Greece. The treasuries of the Greek city-states were the target of the Celtic raid on Delphi in 278 BC. The reconstructed marble building, which measures 6.89 × 10 metres (22.6 × 32.8 feet), was originally built to hold the spoils of victory over the Persians at the Battle of Marathon (490 BC).

CELTIC EUROPE IN 200 BC

In 200 BC, the Celtic world was in many ways quite different from that of two centuries earlier. Chiefly, the differences were ones of scale. The frontiers of this world had moved southwards and eastwards with the flow of war-bands and settler families. By 200 BC, however, this Celtic tide had long-since reached its high-point and was slowly ebbing back. The easternmost Celtic communities around the shores of Black Sea had been overrun, northern Italy was all but lost to the Romans – the process being having been temporarily halted by Hannibal's invasion – and the Celtiberians were already defending their homeland against the legions. Despite these setbacks, the Celtic world of 200 BC was still territorially larger than that of 400 BC, and the distinctive La Tène art style flourished across a broad swathe of Europe from the Shannon to the Middle Danube.

The Celtic world was not only larger, it was economically stronger and more complex than in the Early La Tène period (500–400 BC). Iron production had increased, and iron tools were now commonplace throughout most of Europe. With improved tools and techniques – iron-tipped ploughs, scythes for harvesting grain and cutting fodder, rotary querns (hand mills) – farmers had become prosperous. During the 2nd century BC, *oppida* (towns) emerged as the focal points of Celtic societies (*see* pages 88–89).

The emergence of *oppida* coincided with, but was not dependent upon, the re-establishment of trade links with the central Mediterranean region – although now it was Romans instead of Greeks and Etruscans who traded with the Celts. Compared with the previous century, the 2nd century BC witnessed a dramatic increase in the number of Mediterranean objects imported into Gaul.

The 'developed' Celtic society

Despite the beginnings of urbanisation, Celtic society remained strongly aristocratic in structure and agrarian in character. There is evidence, however, provided by Roman historians from both Gaul and the eponymous state of Galatia, that, among the élite, elected councils and magistrates were beginning to temper executive power.

In central Gaul, social relations within and between Celtic tribes became sufficiently organised – in terms of diplomacy, the hiring of foreign mercenaries, an independent judiciary and military command, and the use of coinage – for these societies to be described as proto-states, fully capable of developing into nations.

With hindsight, it is fair to say that Roman expansion shortened the life of the developed Celtic world by a couple of centuries or so. However, it is also equally fair to say that even a very developed (but non-

▲ **Enamelled bronze plaque** that probably formed part of a horse's harness. This fretted plaque dates from the 1st century AD, and was probably made in Britain. It was discovered at Paillart, near Breteuil, north France.

▶ **The Gundestrup cauldron** was found at Gundestrup, West Himmerland, north Jutland, Denmark. It is made of silver and measures 70 centimetres (27.5 inches) in diameter. The elaborate styling of head and facial hair on the god is typical of Celtic art. The Celts' attention to grooming is mentioned by several Roman writers. The cauldron features motifs, such as elephants and griffons, common in Asian art of the period.

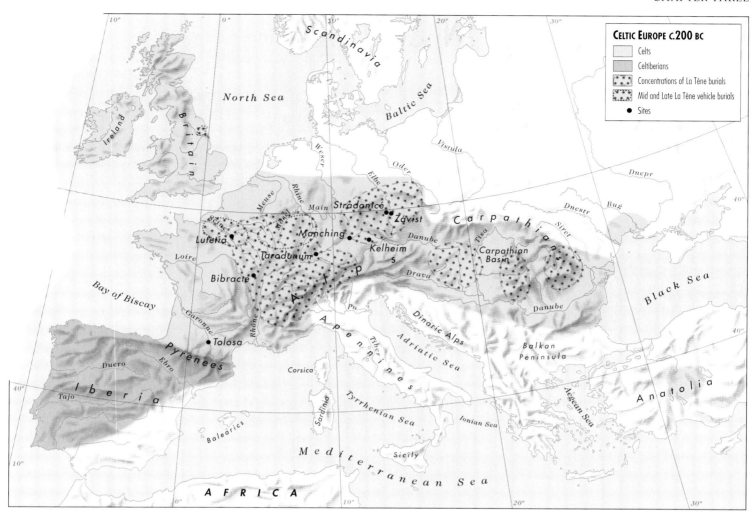

Romanised) Celtic world is unlikely to have long survived the sustained onslaught from the east. Julius Caesar's (100–44 BC) self-justifying remark – that it was necessary to Romanise Gaul to prevent it from being Germanised – has more than a faint ring of truth.

Celtic identity

Back in the 2nd century BC, within the developed Celtic world, we can be almost certain that those who would have recognised the term 'Celt' were in the minority; and, even within this minority, it would have different meanings.

None of them would have understood the all-embracing term 'Celt'. Family lineage, tribal status and local territory – this was the extent of their self-awareness. Terms such as 'Celt' came only to the lips of 'significant others' gazing in from outside. In the presence of foreigners, some groups would have admitted to being Gauls, but only if they came from somewhere they understood to be Gaul. To understand the term Celt, they would have had to be so thoroughly immersed in Graeco-Roman culture, as to be on the edge of becoming non-Celtic. However, it should also be stressed that some sense of a shared Celtic identity may have been imparted through recognition of common cultural practices. This recognition may have been achieved through links established by migrations and/or trade. An example of this sense of shared identity is the help that the British Celts gave to their continental cousins in the struggle against Julius Caesar.

Languages that are now considered to belong to the Celtic language family were widely spoken across much of western and central Europe, but that is no guarantee of mutual intelligibility or shared ethnic identity. Concepts of ethnic purity are even more absurd. The previous two centuries had involved prolonged settlement in 'non-Celtic' areas such as northern Italy and the Lower Danube, and co-existence with Germans along an unstable and shifting border. Culturally mixed marriages may have been common during the migration period, and many of the offspring may have swelled the ranks of Celtic society. Among the adult population, we know nothing of the rules and regulations by which outsiders might become members of a 'tribe'. We may reasonably assume that Celtic society was fairly open, not least because its beliefs and customs were firmly rooted in a common European heritage.

Classical historians present us with a confusingly large number of named groups of Celts, and these are generally equated with tribes. However, it is important to bear in mind that classical histories are very largely written by war correspondents. Their contact with the enemy was fleeting, and their explanations superficial and one-sided. Some of the groups, such as the Boii in Bohemia, may have originated through local agglomeration and development in a particular region. Others, perhaps the Tectosages of Galatia, may represent opportunistic recruitments that became forged into permanence through the shared experiences of migration, settlement and the confrontation with Rome.

▲ **Celtic Europe in *c*.200 BC**
La Tène culture was established across a broad band of central and eastern Europe by the end of the 3rd century BC, as demonstrated by concentrations of burials. In the west, however, the picture is much less clear.

CELTIC COINAGE

Greek commercial enterprise at the mouth of the River Rhône had introduced the Celts to wine-making, and may have shifted the focus of prosperity within the Hallstatt culture decisively westwards. Greek influence led to a change of direction in trade – from within Europe to between Europe and the Mediterranean. A consequence of trade contacts with the Greeks was that some Celtic peoples (individuals at this stage, rather than communities) were exposed to one of the great Iron Age innovations – coinage.

Following a recently established Greek tradition, Massilia (now Marseilles) began striking its own silver coins in *c.*520 BC. Although these coins were produced for use within the Massilians own peer-group (i.e. the Greek world), some inevitably found their way into the hinterland, and into the hands of Celts. During and after the great migrations, the Celts became more familiar with coinage – both as booty and as payments made to Celtic mercenaries.

By the middle of the 3rd century BC, some Celtic groups recognised the benefits of coinage enough to begin producing their own. By the 1st century BC, coinage was widespread throughout the Celtic world. Many of the earliest coinages produced in mainland Europe were designed and produced by Celtic craftworkers at the behest of Celtic kings and princes. The adoption of coinage – instead of its acquisition as quantities of valuable metal – implies profound economic and political changes in the Celtic world.

From cattle to coins

Coinage was not the first medium of exchange to be used by the Celts, and in light of all other evidence, we may safely assume that cattle had a long-established position as a useful form of exchangeable wealth. Non-precious

(but nonetheless valuable) metals were also used. In Germany, 'double-pyramid' iron ingots were distributed and hoarded. In Britain, iron bars were used. The most popular Greek denomination – the silver *drachm* (now *drachma*) – is supposed to have represented the same value as a handful (Gk. *drachm*) of iron rods.

When Celtic groups began striking their own coins (for use as gifts, as payment to mercenaries, or just copying southern systems), they were mainly based on the abundant examples of coins from the reigns of Philip II of Macedon (382–336 BC) and his successors. However, other prototypes were also used. In southern France and the Po Valley, for instance, the issues of Massilia were copied, and in north-east Spain, those of the Greek city of Emporion (Ampurias).

In the southern part of the Celtic region – from the mouth of the Danube to southern France – silver was the chief metal used for coins. To the north, gold was preferred. Bronze and other base alloys were only introduced in the 2nd or 1st centuries BC, although they had been used in the Greek world since the end of the 5th century BC. Most coins were cast as blanks and then struck between engraved dies, although some base-metal coins were cast in strips in clay moulds bearing simple designs. The use of base metals reflects the new function for coins as currency for everyday exchange.

For the most part, the designs on Celtic coins were well conceived and executed. Over time there is a discernible trend away from the simple copying of typical Hellenistic designs, such as the portrait/horseman combination used on the silver coins of Philip II, towards abstract flights of fancy incorporating many elements of Celtic symbolism, including wheels, trumpets and elements of the horse. However fanciful

▶ **Human-headed horse** coin made of low-alloy and dating from the first half of the 1st century BC. The creature, guided by a person waving a torque, is leaping over a boar. It probably belonged to the Veneti of Armorica (now Brittany), north-west France.

▼ **Celtic coinage** This map shows the tribal locations of the coins illustrated on these pages, a small sampling of the hundreds of different coins that were issued by Celtic peoples across Europe.

LOCATION OF CELTIC COINS
- Tribal locations
- Greek city

▼ **Gold coin** of the Ambiani in north Gaul. It depicts the Greek god Apollo with laurelled hair.

▲ **Gold coin** (1st century BC) with human head, from the first coinings of the Parisii, north Gaul.

the design, the execution was invariably carefully controlled. One British coin, measuring only 9 millimetres (0.35 inches) across, carries a detailed image of an eagle with outstretched wings, the painstaking work of a master die-engraver. After *c*.100 BC, Celtic coinage became increasingly modelled on that of Rome, often incorporating Latin inscriptions.

Although the archaeological discoveries of Celtic coins provide solid evidence of a great many Celtic tribes and rulers, there is nothing inherently Celtic about their coins, apart from the identifying designs on their surface. In all other respects, the growth and spread of Celtic coinage charts the progressive absorption of the Celtic world into the mainstream Mediterranean economy.

◀ **Norici silver coin** from Hungary, made in the 1st century BC. The face, shown here, features a male head with ornamental wreath and hair. The Norici were a Celtic tribe who lived near the Danube, and to whom is ascribed the art of converting iron into steel. The Norici supplied the Romans with iron weapons. Once subsumed into the Roman Empire, their territory became the province of Noricum.

◀ **Celtic and Roman silver coins** found at Eriswell, Suffolk, east England. The selection includes coins of the Iceni tribe, led by Boudicca, and a newly minted denarius (bottom right corner) of Roman Emperor Nero (AD 54–68).

ROMAN CONQUEST OF ITALY

As we have already seen, only two generations after the Celtic sack of Rome, the city had regained its composure and was once more engaged in the conquest of the Italian peninsula. Initially Roman energies were directed against the Etruscans and other native cultures of central Italy. From the Celtic point of view, the decisive turning point was the Battle of Sentinum (295 BC). At Sentinum, which ended the lengthy Samnite Wars, the Roman legions smashed a coalition of Samnites, Etruscans and Italian Celts.

A few years later, the Senones seized the opportunity to bloody Rome's nose when they massacred a Roman army sent to the north. Unhindered now by central Italian preoccupations, the Romans finally were free to crush the Senones. In 283 BC, the Senones were driven from Italy by Roman legions, and the Roman colony of Sena Gallica was established as a military strongpoint between Ravenna and Ancona. The Boii rallied to their expelled comrades, but were easily defeated in their attempts to drive off the Romans, and forced to sign a peace treaty with Rome.

Celtic unity counts for nought

In the middle of the 3rd century BC, Rome was diverted by the First Punic War (264–241 BC) with Carthage. After a decisive naval victory, the Romans once more turned their attention to sources of insecurity closer to home and, in 232 BC, Rome formally annexed the territory of the Senones.

This clear statement of intent provoked the Italian Celts into something approaching united action. In 225 BC, the warriors of the Boii and Insubres, supported by *gaesatae* (bands of non-aligned warriors) from across the Alps, marched on Rome. In the intervening years, Roman generals had accumulated considerable experience in fighting against the Celts and, in a daring manœuvre, they were able to trap the Celtic forces in a pincer movement at Telamon near the west coast. Despite a brave rearguard action the Celts were finally overwhelmed. Celtic casualties were high and the combined forces lost more than half their men, with many of the remainder taken prisoner.

In the aftermath of Telamon, the Boii were obliged to supply troops to fight alongside Roman legions, and Rome extended its control northwards. In 222 and 218 BC, the Romans established colonies at Cremona and Placentia (now Piacenza) in the territory of the Cenomani, who had chosen to remain neutral during

▼ **Roman conquest of north Italy** Celtic Italy was systematically reduced by a series of Roman campaigns between 232 and 180 BC. The process would have been completed much more rapidly if Hannibal (and the Second Punic War) had not intervened.

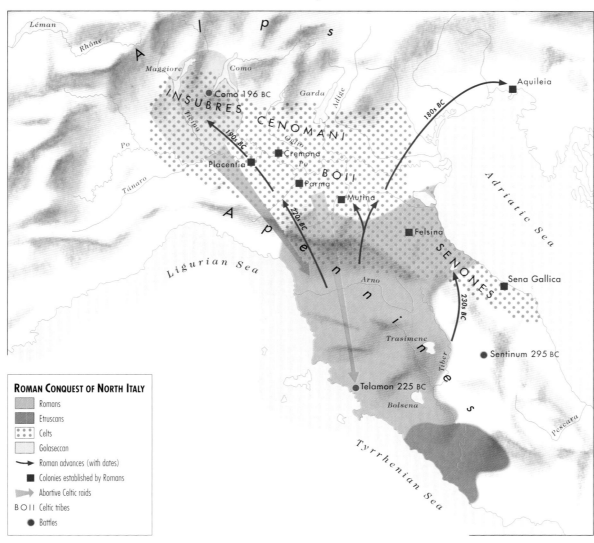

▼ **Celtic chief on a chariot**, part of a terracotta frieze from the temple of Civita Alba, near Sassoferrato, north Italy. The sculpture, which is 45 centimetres (17.7 inches) high, dates from the 2nd century BC.

ROMAN CONQUEST OF NORTH ITALY

- Romans
- Etruscans
- Celts
- Golaseccan
- Roman advances (with dates)
- ■ Colonies established by Romans
- Abortive Celtic raids
- BOII Celtic tribes
- ● Battles

the Telamon campaign, but were now compelled to accept a Roman presence.

Hannibal and the Celts

The situation in northern Italy was dramatically transformed at the start of the Second Punic War (218–202 BC), when Hannibal (247–c.181 BC) emerged from the Alps at the head of an army of Celtiberian and North African warriors. He defeated the Roman army on the banks of the River Trebbia (218 BC), and the Italian Celts flocked to join him – even those allied to Rome and serving with the legions deserted to a man. His forces greatly strengthened by the Celts, Hannibal ambushed and destroyed a Roman army at Lake Trasimene (217 BC) and, in 216 BC, he crushed two more Roman armies at the Battle of Cannae. However, by the time Hannibal captured the port of Tarentum (now Tarento) in 212 BC, the Carthaginian armies in Spain were fully committed against a Roman counter-invasion and Hannibal's brother, Hasdrubal Barca, was defeated and killed by the Romans in 207 BC. Hannibal failed to launch a decisive attack against Rome and was pushed into southern Italy by the guerrilla tactics of Fabius and Marcellus. When Hannibal did not receive reinforcements from Gaul as had been expected, his Italian allies gradually drifted back home to prepare for an expected backlash by the Romans.

In 203 BC, Hannibal was recalled to North Africa to organise the last-ditch defence of Carthage. The following year, he was defeated at Zama and forced to conclude peace on Roman terms. The Carthaginians were stripped of their overseas possessions, and many Celtiberians came under nominal Roman rule. The Celts in north Italy, however, had gambled and lost everything. If they had remained steadfastly loyal to Rome, or at least stayed neutral, they might have had a bright future as Roman allies, perhaps even as citizens. However, they had joined Hannibal, and their fate was sealed.

Celts' expulsion from Italy

Roman retribution was swift and uncompromising: within 20 years, the Celts had been swept out of Italy. In 196 BC, a strong Roman thrust to the north-west captured Como, the stronghold of the Insubres, who surrendered unconditionally. In 191 BC, the Boii were driven from the Po Valley, and a Roman colony was founded at the Boii's former chief centre of Bologna. In 183 BC, Parma and Modena were established as colonies to consolidate the Roman hold on the north, and in 181 BC the fortress town of Aquileia was founded at the head of the Adriatic. Large numbers of Roman settlers, including many veterans, were encouraged to settle in the Po Valley, and although there is some evidence of continued Celtic presence it was on a small scale and at subsistence level. Northern Italy became the Roman province of *Cisalpine Gaul* ("Gaul on this side of the Alps"), and was later renamed *Gallia Togata* ("Gaul where the toga must be worn") – an indication of the intense Romanisation that was imposed throughout the newly occupied region. The era of Celtic Italy, with its innovative metalwork shops and fierce mercenary warriors, was over.

Yet, in 73 BC, the Celts caused the good citizens of Rome one last frisson of fear, when Spartacus (d.71 BC) led the great slave rebellion. Many of the warriors in Spartacus' army were Celts (although few of them will have been of Italian descent), and at least one of his generals, Cenomaros, had a Celtic name. Despite intial successes, the so-called 'Gladitorial War' (73–71 BC) ended in defeat and death for Spartacus, and many of his Celtic supporters were slaughtered.

▼ **Battle in the Punic War** between the Romans and the Carthaginians, manuscript illumination (c.1470–75) by Jean Fouquet. The parchment probably depicts the Battle of Cannae (August 2, 216 BC), where Hannibal encircled the Roman army in Puglia, south-east Italy, killing c.56,000 Roman soldiers. The parchment is 44.8 × 33.4 centimetres (17.6 × 13.2 inches).

THE ROMANS IN SPAIN

▼ **The Fall of Numantia** (1880) by Alejo Vera y Estaca (1834–1923). Numantia is a symbol of Celtiberian resistance to Roman rule. For 14 years the city (near to present-day Soria, Castile León, north-east Spain), successfully resisted Roman attempts to capture it. In 133 BC, after a long siege by Roman forces led by Scipio Aemilianus, and a failed attempt to breach the Roman ramparts surrounding the city, the Celtiberians decided to commit suicide rather than surrender to the Romans. The inhabitants torched their city before stabbing or poisoning themselves. In the 19th century, Spanish historians interpreted this as an expression of national pride and courage.

Although the Iberian Peninsula was rich in metals, and possessed both landscape and climate ideally suited to Italian methods of cultivation, the initial Roman conquest was not undertaken as part of some greedy expansionist policy. It was rather a tactical move that sprang from the grim exigencies of war.

Iberia was Carthaginian territory. After losing Sicily, Sardinia and Corsica to the Romans at the end of the First Punic War (264–241 BC), the Carthaginians massively reinforced their garrisons in southern and eastern Iberia in the 230s BC, and recruited Celtiberian mercenaries. The resurgence of Carthage was signalled by Hannibal's (247–*c*.181 BC) invasion of Italy in 218 BC.

The battle for Iberia

Although ultimately fruitless, the Carthaginian invasion terrified the Roman populace and created a serious security problem. In 210 BC, while Hannibal was still in Italy, a counter-invasion of Iberia was launched by Scipio Africanus the Elder (*c*.185–129 BC), and the following year a surprise Roman attack captured the city of Carthago Nova (now Cartagena, south-east Spain) – the main Carthaginian base.

The Romans followed up this military success with a diplomatic offensive among the local Iberian and Celtiberian peoples. Although not hailed with quite the same vigour as the Italian Celts had greeted Hannibal, the Romans found many that were eager to turn against

their Carthaginian oppressors. Reinforced by local warriors, the Romans continued southward along the coast, and then marched inland. At a battle near present-day Seville, south-west Spain, they destroyed what remained of the Carthaginian forces in Iberia. By 206 BC, although the whole of southern Spain was under nominal Roman control, the situation was far from secure.

In 197 BC, a revolt broke out among Iberian tribes in the south. The rebel forces were defeated, but the leaders hired Celtiberian mercenaries to continue the fight against the Romans. In 195 BC, the Romans bribed the mercenaries to change sides, and occupied the gold and silver mines that funded the rebellion. Two years later, the Celtiberians rose in revolt and were decisively defeated near Toledo, central Spain, and their king, Hilernus, was captured. Within ten years, however, the Celtiberians were again threatening the stability of Roman Iberia. In 181 BC, Roman legions defeated a Celtiberian army at Talavera de la Reina, central Spain, and then captured the stronghold of Botorrita (now Zaragoza, north Spain). The Romans routed a Celtiberian relief force, and advanced into the Sistema Ibérico Mountains.

During a spring season of campaigning (179–178 BC), the Roman general Tiberius Sempronius Gracchus systematically razed some 300 Celtiberian towns and hillforts, including Certina, Alcázar and Ergavica. The Celtiberian chieftain Thurrus, one of the main leaders of

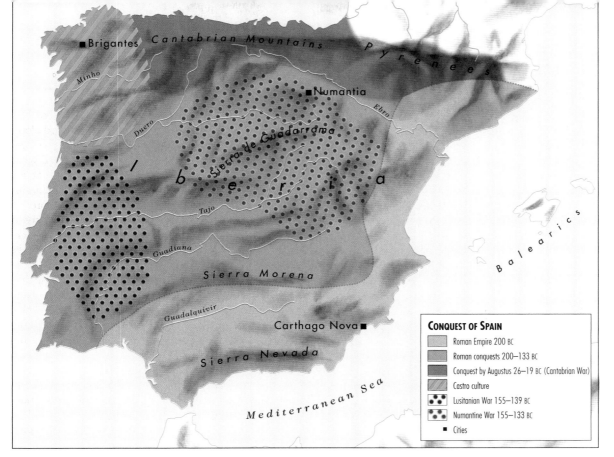

CONQUEST OF SPAIN

◼ Brigantes — Cantabrian Mountains — Pyrenees — Minho — Duero — Numantia — Ebro — Sierra de Guadarrama — Iberia — Tajo — Guadiana — Sierra Morena — Guadalquivir — Carthago Nova ◼ — Sierra Nevada — Mediterranean Sea — Balearics

	Roman Empire 200 BC
	Roman conquests 200–133 BC
	Conquest by Augustus 26–19 BC (Cantabrian War)
	Castro culture
	Lusitanian War 155–139 BC
	Numantine War 155–133 BC
◼	Cities

◀ **Conquest of Spain** Rome gained southern and eastern Spain by virtue of defeating the colonial Carthaginians. In a series of campaigns which extended over two centuries, the Roman armies finally subdued the native inhabitants in the rest of Iberia.

the revolt, was captured, and subsequently became an officer in the Roman army. Resistance was finally extinguished by a Roman victory near Complegna. Among the loot Gracchus took back to Rome was *c*.20 tonnes of silver, enough to mint eight million *denarii* (silver coins). A treaty imposed on the Celtiberians brought 20 years of superficial peace to the Peninsula.

Renewed resistance

By the mid-2nd century BC, native opposition to Roman rule again flared into open revolt. The Roman suppression of this rising is conventionally divided into two separate conflicts: the Lusitanian War (155–139 BC) which subdued the far west, and the Numantine War (143–133 BC) which ended Celtiberian resistance. However, the actual fighting was much less clear cut. Betrayal and treachery on both sides marked the campaigns, and reprisals were often brutal. After capturing the town of Cauca, central Spain, for example, the Romans massacred all 20,000 male inhabitants; when they took Numantia, north-east Spain, the victorious Roman general sold all but 50 of the inhabitants into slavery.

The Lusitanian leader Salendicos, who carried a symbolic silver spear, fomented open revolt in the west. Salendicos fortified the town of Seges, contrary to the peace treaty, and in 153 BC, Roman legions destroyed the town. The survivors fled to the Celtiberian stronghold of Numantia, which successfully withstood an attempted Roman siege. In 151 BC, the Lusitanians were defeated on the battlefield and most of those who surrendered were massacred by Roman troops. One of the survivors of the massacre, Viriathus, assumed leadership of the anti-Roman forces and in the course of the next few years scored a number of military successes, and attracted increasing Celtiberian support.

In 143 BC, the Romans captured the Celtiberian towns of Nertobriga and Ricla, but they again failed to take Numantia. After Viriathus was assassinated by Roman agents in 140 BC, resistance began to crumble although Numantia withstood another attempted siege in 138 BC. Five years later, the Romans eventually succeeded, and the fall of Numantia (133 BC) marked an end to organised opposition in Iberia, most of which was now under Roman military control. The occupation of Iberia could be completed in leisurely fashion.

In the mid-130s BC, General Decimus Brutus made the first inroads into the Castro culture region of the far north-west, and in 61 BC Julius Caesar captured the rebellious Celtiberian town of Brigantium (now La Coruña, north-west Spain). The conquest of the entire Peninsula was eventually completed with Augustus' successful conclusion of the Cantabrian War (26–19 BC).

▼ **Restored Iron-Age hut** on Monte Santa Tecla, Pontevedra, north-west Spain. The hut was originally built in the 1st century BC, and is part of a large village of the Castro culture (discovered 1913). A 'castro' is a settlement situated on a mountain or cliff, and protected by ditches and solid walls. Castro houses were circular and made of stone. They had straw roofs and wooden doors. The Castro culture was one of the last pockets of resistance to Roman rule in Spain.

THE GALATIANS

Although they were hired to fight for Nicomedes of Bithynia against his rival the king of Pontus, the Celts who crossed the Hellespont (now Dardanelles) soon entertained other ideas. Indeed, the fact that about half of the Galatian force were non-combatants suggest that long-term settlement was always intended. The Celts' martial skills were soon in great demand, and the long coastline, populated by many rich cities, provided fertile ground for pillage.

The antics of these Celtic newcomers infuriated Antiochus I of Syria (324–c.262 BC), the greatest single power in the region. Antiochus assembled a mighty army (including war elephants) that ended the Celts' first surge of freebooting activity in c.275 BC. For his troubles, Antiochus earned the title 'Soter' (saviour), while the Celts were forced to assume a more settled lifestyle in central Anatolia.

The Celts continued, however, to pursue a warrior ethos, either serving as mercenaries or reverting to raiding. They extracted bribes by menace from rulers of cities such as Pergamum (Pergamon), and in 261 BC, they killed Antiochus II of Syria (c.287–246 BC). In 246 BC, engaged as mercenaries in a dynastic dispute, the Celts defeated Seleucus II outside Ancyra (now Ankara).

Attalus I (269–197 BC), king of Pergamum, tired of paying tribute to the Celts, now organised resistance to their raids, defeating the Celts in 240 BC, and again in 232 BC, at the Battle of Kaikos. In return for peaceful coexistence, Attalus formally recognised Celtic rights to lands around the River Halys (now River Kizilirmak), thus giving international recognition to the Galatian state. Attalus celebrated the concord by commissioning statues for his palace.

The State of Galatia

According to Greek historians, the Celts who settled in Anatolia (Asia Minor) comprised three tribes: the Tolistobogii, the Trocmi and the Tectosages. The Galatian state was ruled by a council led by 12 tetrarchs (four from each tribe). The council met at Drunemeton, which literally means 'sacred oak-grove'. Some commentators have interpreted this as evidence that druids mediated the Galatian council, but there is no direct evidence of druidic activity in Anatolia, and the Romans did not note it.

The main settlements were the towns of Ancyra, Tavium and Pessinus, which served initially as fortresses/markets but, by 200 BC, emerged as tribal capitals. Celtic immigration from Europe may well have continued on a small-scale, but it was not encouraged by the other powers in the region. Precious few examples of La Tène style material have

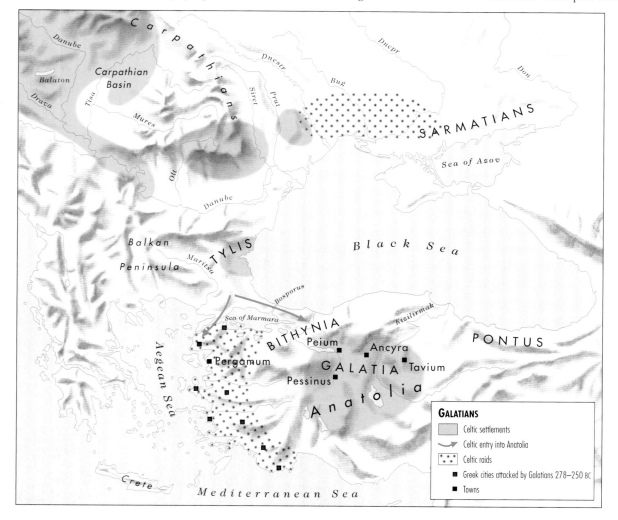

GALATIANS

▢	Celtic settlements
⤳	Celtic entry into Anatolia
⋯	Celtic raids
■	Greek cities attacked by Galatians 278–250 BC
■	Towns

◄ **Galatians** Rich cities along the Mediterranean and Aegean coast were the initial attraction for the Celts recruited into Anatolia. Later, they were 'persuaded' to move eastwards into the highlands of Anatolia where they established Galatia.

been found in Anatolia, which may indicate that the Galatians adopted local styles of ornament and manufacture, but retained their language and social structure. This may serve as a timely reminder of how artistic form is often only loosely attached to ethnicity.

Celtic alliance with Syria

In the 2nd century BC, the Romans began to make their presence felt in the region. In 190 BC, the Galatians allied themselves with Antiochus III of Syria (242–187 BC) against the Romans, but their joint forces were defeated at the Battle of Magnesia (now Manisa) in ancient Lydia. The following year, the Romans mounted a punitive expedition into Anatolia and defeated the Galatians at Mount Olympus, west of Ancyra, and again at Mount Magaba. Some 40,000 Celts were taken as slaves, the rest were left under the rule of Pergamum, which was allied to Rome.

The Tolistobogii chieftain Ortagio, keen to make alliances against Pergamum, forged diplomatic links with Pontus and Bithynia, and thus reunited the Celts. In 165 BC, they felt strong enough to launch a war against Eumenes II of Pergamum (d. *c.*159 BC), son of Attalus I, but although they met with some initial success, they were soon defeated.

Any hopes of a Celtic recovery were dashed in 88 BC, when King Mithradates VI (d. 63 BC,) of Pontus invited 60 Galatian officials to a meeting and then treacherously had them and their families massacred. A survivor of the massacre, one Deiotarus, was

◀ **War elephant** trampling on a Galatian soldier. This Hellenistic terracotta statuette, which measures 11.3 centimetres (4.5 inches) high, was found at Myrina, on the island of Lemnos. It dates from the mid-2nd century BC. The statuette graphically conveys the force with which the Celts were crushed in Anatolia.

recognised as king of Galatia by the Roman general Pompey (106–48 BC), who defeated Mithradates. Mark Antony (*c.*82–30 BC) later confirmed this title but unfortunately for the Celts, he then lost the struggle to rule the Roman Empire. In 25 BC, Emperor Augustus (63 BC–AD 14), formally annexed Galatia to the Empire.

IMAGES OF DEFEAT

Attalus I celebrated his victory over the Galatians by adding a frieze of the conflict to the altar of Zeus at Pergamum. He also commissioned a number of bronze statues for a sanctuary

at his palace. The bronze originals, long-since melted down, were evidently popular because we know two of them from marble copies made in Roman workshops. Unlike the crudely victorious propagandising of Roman

sculpture, these images of defeated enemies are more Hellenistic and humanistic meditations on life and mortality. On the left is the famous Dying Gaul, *while on the right is the lesser known* Suicidal Gaul.

ROMAN CONQUEST OF SOUTHERN GAUL

With the fall of Numantia, north-east Spain, Rome was poised to enjoy the peaceful exploitation of Iberia. The sea routes of the western Mediterranean were firmly under Roman control but, along the overland route, Roman Italy and Roman Spain were separated by a distinctly hostile stretch of coast.

Centrally situated, and nominally controlling most of the coastline, was the city of Massilia (now Marseilles), once the main calling point for coastal traders and the entrepôt for southern and central Gaul. Trade, however, especially northwards up the River Rhône, had more or less dried up – very few Mediterranean articles were imported into Gaul during the Celtic migration period (400–200 BC). The Massilians had developed into a small territorial power, sandwiched between the sea and barbarian tribes. Although still largely Greek, or of Greek descent, in culture and population, Massilia was no longer an outpost of the Greek social and economic commonwealth. Greece itself had been subjugated, first by the Macedonians, and subsequently twice by the Romans. Only the city of Athens, given special status because of its ancestral achievements, retained any degree of political autonomy.

In 154 BC, when Massilia was threatened by the Saluvi, a people of mixed Celtic and Ligurian affinities who lived on the eastern borders of Massilian territory,

it greatly suited Rome to assume the mantle of the city's protector and dispatch legions into southern Gaul to reinforce Massilia. When the Saluvi again attacked, in 125 BC, the Romans assumed control of all Massilian territory – the conquest of southern Gaul had begun.

Roman capture of Entremont

The immediate Roman objective was the siege and destruction of Entremont (near present-day Aix-en-Provence), the Greek-inspired hilltop capital of the Saluvi. This task was quickly accomplished in 124–123 BC. The Romans then established a military strongpoint called Aquae Sextiae at Aix. After the fall of Entremont, the Saluvian leader fled northwards and sought refuge with the Celtic Allobroges. The Romans demanded his surrender, but the Allobroges were as little inclined to help Rome as they had been to help Hannibal almost a century earlier.

In 122 BC, Rome went to war with the Allobroges, who were supported by the more powerful Arverni from west of the Rhône. The involvement of the Arverni provoked the Aedui, their bitterest rivals, to ally themselves with Rome. This alliance was to prove enduring and to have important consequences in the next century.

► **Roman denarius coin** struck at Narbo (now Narbonne), south-east France, in 118 BC. This bronze coin was made in commemoration of the victory for the Roman legions over the Gauls, led by Bituitus. The Romans named Narbo as the capital of Gallia Transalpina, the first Roman province beyond the Alps. The reverse side of the coin (shown right) depicts a Celtic war chariot, driven by a single, naked warrior. The warrior is armed with a spear and shield. In the background can be seen a carnyx (war trumpet) with a bell in the shape of a boar's head.

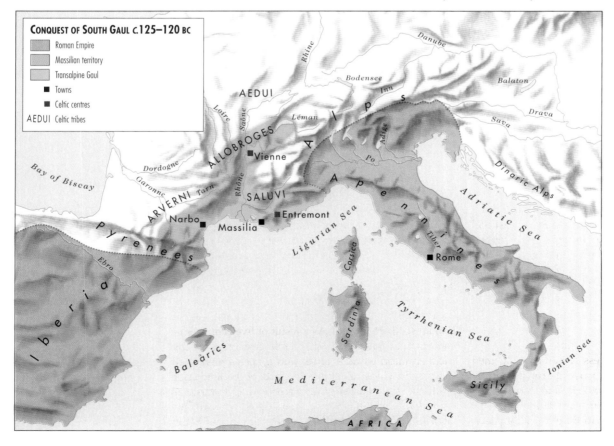

CONQUEST OF SOUTH GAUL c.125–120 BC
- Roman Empire
- Massilian territory
- Transalpine Gaul
- ■ Towns
- ■ Celtic centres
- AEDUI Celtic tribes

◄ **Conquest of South Gaul** *c.*125–120 BC Rome had already annexed the Greek cities in Italy, Anatolia and Greece by *c.*125–120 BC. The annexation of Massilia (now Marseilles) enabled Rome to establish a strategic route between Spain and Italy, which was safeguarded by incorporating the territory of local Gallic tribes into the Empire.

◄ **Arc de Triomphe** at Carpentras, south-east France. The triumphal arch shows Gallic prisoners in chains. It was built in the 1st century AD. A Memini *oppidum*, located at La Lègue, about four kilometres (2.5 miles) south-east of town, was occupied from at least the 6th century BC. In 125 BC, the inhabitants of Massilia appealed to the Romans for help against a coalition of Celts and Ligurians. The Romans defeated the coalition but remained in occupation of the region. The arch celebrates the subjugation of southern Gaul.

Bituitus, King of the Arverni

In 121 BC, the Arvernian King Bituitus, an ostentatious individual who is said to have ridden in a silver chariot, assumed a leading role in Gallo-Roman relations. He sent ambassadors to negotiate with the Romans, and when his overtures were rebuffed, he led his men into battle against the legions on the banks of the Rhône. The Celts were defeated, and the territory of the Allobroges was annexed and pillaged.

The Arverni escaped incorporation into the Empire, although Bituitus was imprisoned when he later visited Rome and attempted to deal with the Senate on an equal footing. The ease of the Roman success intimidated other Gallic tribes, such as the Helvetii in the east and the Volcae (Volcae Tectosages) in the west, into accepting 'alliances' with Rome. By 118 BC, when the colony of Narbo (now Narbonne) was established in south-east France, Roman control stretched along the coastline as far north as Geneva, and work had begun on the Via Domita road that would link Italy with Spain.

Crushing of resistance

In *c*.110 BC, the tranquil progress of the newly formed province of Transalpine Gaul was interrupted by the violent incursions of the Teutones and the Cimbri, armed hordes of broadly Germanic origins who had been roaming around the Roman Empire for the previous dozen years or so. Having inflicted crushing defeats on the legions, the Cimbri rampaged through southern Gaul where their presence steeled the Volcae to repudiate their involuntary 'alliance' with Rome and rise in revolt. Four years later, after the Cimbri had been moved on, a punitive Roman expedition sacked Tolosa (now Toulouse), the Volcae capital, and looted the precious offerings from its sacred lake. The territory of the Volcae was incorporated into Transalpine Gaul.

The Roman presence in southern Gaul stimulated a rapid increase of trade in what remained of the Celtic world, and wine once more became an available luxury in central and northern Gaul. The difference was that it was now packaged in Roman rather than Greek amphorae. In the occupied zone, Romanisation proceeded rapidly and smoothly. Towns were established, and endowed with temples, forums and amphitheatres. These towns swelled in size and importance as their amenities attracted more of the native population. More by virtue of climate and geography, than by reason of early conquest, the south became the most thoroughly Romanised part of Gaul. As a result of five centuries of contact with the Greeks, the staple cash-crops of the Mediterranean world – olives and grapes – were well established. Under Roman rule, parts of the landscape gradually acquired the same manicured appearance as equivalent areas in northern Italy. By 60 BC, southern Gaul had become markedly different from the rest of the country, and in some ways has remained so to this day.

EARLY CELTIC RELIGION

Statements about pre-Christian Celtic religion(s) must be made with a great deal of caution. Our own patterns of thinking about such matters are themselves the products of more than two millennia of sophisticated, literate development. Since the Celts left behind no catechisms or detailed pantheons, our interpretation of Celtic religious belief is heavily reliant on the anthropological study of contemporary 'primitive' societies and groups.

It is now virtually impossible for us to discard our own beliefs and journey into the spiritual mindscape of the ancient Celts. What seems very probable is that the physical landscape they inhabited was charged with a much greater and overtly relevant significance than most of us acknowledge today.

Water, stone and wood

Our main point of contact with the religion(s) of the ancient Celts is through the most tangible and best-preserved aspect of their belief systems – their religious sites. Celtic religious architecture may be divided into

▲ **Severed head** from Entremont, south France. It originally sat in front of a stone Celtic warrior, seated in a Buddha-like pose. The warrior's hand rests on the head. It dates from the 3rd or 2nd century BC.

three broad categories, each involving progressively more manipulation and enhancement of the natural landscape – watery places and groves (lakes, rivers and the like), enclosures with wooden structures, and stone temples.

Stone temples were a comparatively late development (2nd–1st centuries BC) and occur only in southern Gaul, close to the Greek colony of Massilia (now Marseilles). These Celtic temples combine Greek elements, such as stone columns and lintels, with distinctly non-Greek elements such as the display of severed heads. At Entremont (near present-day Aix-en-Provence, southern France), piles of heads are sculpted in stone, and at Roquepertuse (also near Aix-en-Provence), some columns contain niches for the display of heads or skulls. It is probable that the heads represent war-dead rather than human sacrifices, although the lives of defeated enemies were often offered to the gods.

Shrines and *Viereckschanzen*

Away from the Mediterranean region, Celtic religious sites maintained much stronger links with Bronze Age traditions. A number of open-air shrines,

dating from the 4th to 1st centuries BC, have been investigated by archaeologists. These ditched enclosures surround a central structure that was approached through a gateway. Some idea of the activities that took place at these shrines can be obtained from the objects that have been recovered. At the sacrificial shrine of Gournay-sur-Aronde, north-east France, thousands of ritually 'killed' iron weapons were found, along with the bones of sacrificed animals neatly stacked in pits. At Ribemont-sur-Ancre, also in north-east France, an 800 metres (2500 feet) -long complex contained the remains of at least 1000 human sacrifices. Similar enclosure shrines have been discovered at Libenice in central Bohemia and at Monte Bibele in northern Italy.

The *Viereckschanze* (rectangular enclosures), a related group of religious structures, are fairly common across southern Germany and central France. Mainly dating from the 2nd to 1st centuries BC, but with much older traditions, these are rectangular banked enclosures with sides of *c*.50 to 100 metres (165 to 330 feet). Most *Viereckschanzen* have the remains of a wooden structure and/or filled shaft in one corner. The shafts often contain animal and human bones, along with crude wooden carvings and pieces of pottery; and may have developed from the habit of ritually 'killing' a storage pit at the end of its useful life and filling it with refuse. Some of the shafts are up to 40 metres (130 feet) deep, and were probably dug as wells.

Archaeologists have discovered no architectural evidence of sacred groves, and we can only surmise that such groves were 'constructed' and maintained through skilful arboriculture; some locations, however, that have no other physical remains do display evidence of ritual activity. At Snettisham, east England, for instance, eight separate hoards of precious metal have been found buried close to each other – the largest hoard containing *c*.35 kilograms (77 pounds) of debased gold and silver alloys. One likely explanation is that the hoards were buried within some kind of sacred precinct.

Water had a special significance for the ancient Celts. Shrines at springs and at the sources of rivers preserved an ancient practice that probably predates farming and which, suitably Christianised, continues in many parts of modern Europe. The Celts may have thought of bodies of water, both still and running, as portals to a world beyond. Like their Bronze Age predecessors, the Celts 'sacrificed' valuable metal objects by casting them into rivers, lakes and bogs. The Romans recovered numerous precious objects from a sacred lake at the *oppidum* (town) of Tolosa (now Toulouse) in southwest France; and British archaeologists appear to have discovered a similar 'votive deposit' at Llyn Cerrig Bach (literally 'Lake of the small stones') in Ynys Môn (Anglesey), north-west Wales. The larger rivers, such as the Seine and the Thames, also provided offering sites, particularly for weapons and armour.

▲ **Wooden pilgrim** statues from the Gallo-Roman cult site at the source of the River Seine, St-Germain-Source-Seine, east France. The statues, which date from the 1st century BC, were votive offerings.

◄ **Two stone heads** joined by their occiput from the Salluvian shrine at Roquepertuse, southern France. The sculptures, which measure 20 centimetres (7.9 inches) high, date from the 4th or 3rd century BC. The Janus-like heads were originally painted.

► **Human skulls** set into the portico of the temple at Roquepertuse, southern France. The doorway was crowned with a stone sculpture of a demonic bird. The portico was built in the 3rd or 2nd century BC.

CAESAR'S INVASION OF GAUL

▼ **Julius Caesar** (*c*.100–44 BC) was a great military commander and brilliant politician who defeated formidable rivals to become dictator of Rome. He shared power with Pompey and Crassus in the so-called First Triumverate. After conquering Gaul, Julius Caesar refused to obey the Roman Senate's demand to disband his army and crossed the River Rubicon. Caesar emerged victorious from the ensuing civil war, and was proclaimed 'dictator for life' in 45 BC. He was murdered on March 15 (the Ides of March) in a conspiracy led by Cassius and Brutus.

In the middle of the 1st century BC, the remaining western portion of Celtic Europe collided head-on with the political ambition and military skill of Julius Caesar (*c*.100–44 BC).

During the first half of the 1st century BC, the rest of Gaul attained an uneasy accommodation with the Roman occupation of the south. Celtic Gaul was generally a prosperous and peaceful region where farms flourished and *oppida* (towns), stimulated by Roman trade, grew ever larger. In central Gaul, societies became sufficiently complex and well organised to be on the brink of independent statehood, and left to their own devices they might well have achieved this within a generation or two.

Caesar, however, had an alternative agenda. He was already a powerful man of great reputation, and had recently been allocated defence of the land approaches to Italy. However, he needed to score a great propaganda victory in the west, if he was to match the exploits of his rival Pompey (106–48 BC), who had

acquired territory for Rome in the east. Gaul was the obvious target. The conquest of Gaul would arouse great admiration among Roman politicians, citizen voters and the mob. Besides the accumulated lore of Celt-fighting that he inherited from his predecessors in southern Gaul, Caesar had his own recent experience of fighting against Celts in northern Iberia.

A suitable pretext for military intervention arose in 58 BC, when the Helvetii, who lived beyond the eastern borders of Gaul, began massing for a planned migration in the face of Germanic pressure. On the pretext of defending the stability of Gaul, Caesar led his legions northwards, intercepted the Helvetii near the *oppidum* of Bibracte (now Mont Beuvray in France) and forced them back across the border. Meanwhile, Gaulish allies of the Arverni had engaged a large contingent of German mercenaries led by one Ariovistus, to attack the Aedui, long-standing supporters of Rome.

Caesar manoeuvred Ariovistus into battle and defeated the German army. Some other Gaulish tribes,

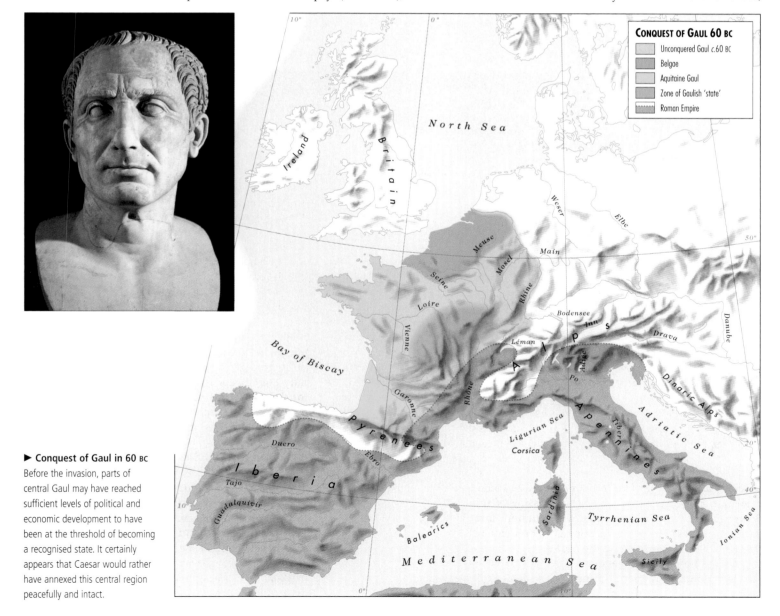

▶ **Conquest of Gaul in 60 BC**
Before the invasion, parts of central Gaul may have reached sufficient levels of political and economic development to have been at the threshold of becoming a recognised state. It certainly appears that Caesar would rather have annexed this central region peacefully and intact.

CONQUEST OF GAUL 60 BC

- Unconquered Gaul *c*.60 BC
- Belgae
- Aquitaine Gaul
- Zone of Gaulish 'state'
- Roman Empire

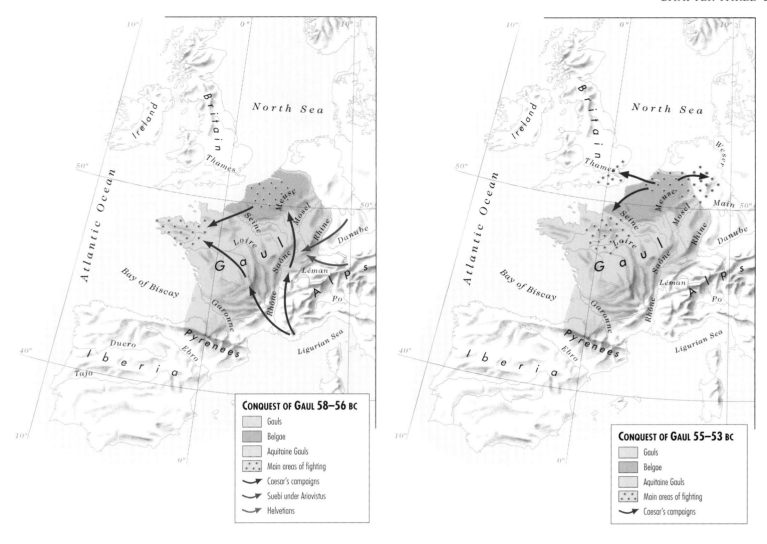

CONQUEST OF GAUL 58–56 BC
- Gauls
- Belgae
- Aquitaine Gauls
- Main areas of fighting
- Caesar's campaigns
- Suebi under Ariovistus
- Helvetians

CONQUEST OF GAUL 55–53 BC
- Gauls
- Belgae
- Aquitaine Gauls
- Main areas of fighting
- Caesar's campaigns

such as the Remi, now forged alliances with Caesar, but most prepared themselves to resist, or submit to, what was now obviously a full-scale Roman invasion.

Caesar's advance

In 57 BC, Caesar divided his forces: Caesar marched north into the territory of the Belgae, while his lieutenant, Publius Licinius Crassus, sought the submission of Brittany. Caesar's legions destroyed the Nervii at the Battle of Sambre in the north-east, capturing (according to Roman records) more than 50,000 Celts. The Romans immediately sold their Celtic prisoners into slavery. The following year, the Veneti, engaged mainly in the Atlantic sea-trade, led a revolt aginst Roman rule in Brittany. The battle-hardened Roman legions made short work of Celtic warriors who lacked the ruthless military discipline of the Roman soldiers. The Romans executed the Veneti elders, and sold the rest into slavery. Caesar then returned to the north-east, where he defeated the Morini and Menapii.

In 55 BC, with Gaul seemingly secured, Caesar decided to push beyond its frontiers. He made a technically superb, but purely symbolic, crossing of the River Rhine. During his 18-day excursion into Germany, Caesar accepted the nominal submission of some of those who lived on the eastern bank of the Rhine, but both combatants knew that the reckoning was far from complete. Later that year, Caesar took two legions on a brief and unexpectedly hazardous

▲ **Conquest of Gaul in 58–56 BC** After defeating Aristovarus and turning back the Helvetii, Caesar advanced against the Belgae, while other Roman forces invaded the north-west.

▲ ▶ **Conquest of Gaul in 55–53 BC** Success against the Belgae provided a springboard for brief (and mainly symbolic of future intentions) excursions into Germany and Britain. Continuing Gallic resistance brought the fighting to the Seine-Loire area at the edge of the central region.

crossing of the English Channel to Britain. The journey was both for reconnaissance purposes and to further Caesar's prestige. It also established a symbolic precedent. After defeating some of the local British tribes, and obtaining promises of hostages and tribute, Caesar returned to Gaul.

In 54 BC, having assembled an invasion fleet of c.600 transport ships and warships, Caesar returned to Britain with five legions. Forewarned by the previous year's experience, the Britons in the south-east had elected a war leader, Cassivellaunus (active 1st century BC), who co-ordinated resistance to the Roman invasion. Although he employed all his by now well-honed tactics of intrigue, bribery and military muscle, Caesar was unable to achieve a decisive, or defensible, advantage and withdrew from Britain to contain a revolt among the Belgae led by King Ambiorix of the Eburones. Ambiorix's forces mounted staunch resistance and inflicted heavy losses, but the Romans ultimately dispersed and routed the Eburones to the brink of annihilation.

So far, either through luck or strategic judgement, Caesar had been able to restrict the destructive activities of his legions to the outer regions of Gaul. Central Gaul, the best developed and economically successful part, had largely escaped the ravages of war. However, the final stages of Caesar's conquest, prompted by a widespread Gaulish revolt at the beginning of 53 BC, was to wreak devastation across this prosperous region.

VERCINGETORIX AND ALESIA

Towards the end of 53 BC, the whole of Gaul erupted in almost simultaneous revolt, sparked by the massacre of Roman settlers at Cenabum (now Orléans), the main *oppidum* (town) of the Carnutes. Such was the speed of the revolt that the Roman authorities were taken by surprise, and most of the legions in Gaul were trapped inside their camps. Caesar, who was wintering in north Italy, was also taken aback by the rising.

In 52 BC, a young Arverni chieftain, Vercingetorix (d.46 BC), was appointed as supreme military commander of the Gauls, and he immediately seized the initiative. Vercingetorix launched a daring invasion of the Roman-occupied south, aiming to seize the strategically important town of Narbonne (now in southeast France). With a hastily assembled force of Roman troops, augmented by Germanic mercenaries, Caesar marched to intercept the Gaulish army, and forced them to retreat.

Resistance in Gaul

The prosperous *oppida* of central Gaul now became pawns, to be taken, defended or sacrificed according to the necessities of war. Caesar besieged and burned Cenabum, massacring its inhabitants as punishment for the murder of Roman citizens. He also captured Avaricum (now Bourges, central France) but failed to take the Arverni capital of Gergovia (Gergovie).

The Gaulish leaders held a great council at Bibracte (now Mont Beuvray) to draw up fresh plans for war. Such was the strength of anti-Roman feeling, that even the Aedui were persuaded to put aside their long-established friendship with Rome, and defect to the Gaulish cause. Vercingetorix urged a scorched-earth policy against the Romans, and encouraged Gauls to strip their fields and even burn their own towns and granaries, in order to deny supplies to the Roman legions.

Although effective, this type of passive resistance was contrary to the martial spirit of the Gauls, and soon Vercingetorix was tempted into a cavalry battle and was defeated. He was forced to withdraw his army to the hilltop *oppidum* of Alesia (now Alise-Sainte-Reine, east France), the capital of the Mandubii, where he was besieged by the Romans.

The siege of Alesia

Faced with the sudden influx of the Gallic army, Alesia had enough supplies to last about a month. Vercingetorix called for reinforcements from all corners of Gaul, while the Romans fortified their siegeworks. They constructed twin lines of earthen ramparts and ditches. The outer rampart measured 22 kilometres (14 miles) in length, and the inner rampart was topped with a continuous wooden wall, strengthened by numerous

▼ **Vercingetorix throws down his arms at the feet of Julius Caesar** (1899) by Lionel Noel Royer (1852–1926) depicts the moment of Vercingetorix's surrender after the siege of Alesia. Vercingetorix was an unlikely choice as supreme leader of the Gaulish armies. His father, Celtillus, had been executed on the orders of the democratrically elected magistracy for plotting to install himself as king of the Arverni. Vercingetorix proved a first-rate general, but he was outclassed by the tactical brilliance of Caesar, and the superior discipline and organisation of the Roman military machine.

forts. Pits, lined with sharpened stakes, honeycombed the ground in front of the ramparts, and spiked iron caltrops were scattered to inhibit further the movement of Gaulish cavalry.

The well-practised skills of Roman military engineers, who had nearly two centuries of experience in besieging Celtic hillforts, enabled Caesar's army not only to contain a numerically superior force inside Alesia, but also to delay the encroachment of reinforcements.

Gaul and Vercingetorix submit to Caesar

By the time the relief column arrived (supposedly with more than 200,000 warriors from at least 40 Celtic tribes), the defenders of Alesia were at the edge of starvation. Despite several days of desperate fighting, during which the Romans withstood simultaneous attacks on both ramparts, the Gauls were unable to breach the Roman lines. Having suffered massive casualties to no avail, the relief column withdrew. All hope of rescue now having vanished, Vercingetorix rode up to the Roman lines and surrendered. Caesar was not magnanimous in victory; the survivors of the siege were made slaves to be distributed among his legionnaires. In northern Gaul, some Gallic leaders attempted to continue the revolt, but were easily defeated. A few were captured, to be flogged and then beheaded as public examples, while others managed to escape across the Rhine into Germanic territory.

With the crushing of the revolt, the whole of Gaul was now Roman territory, and further resistance was dealt with severely. In Aquitania and Uxellodunum (perhaps the Puy d'Issolu on the Dordogne), where some tribes continued to fight, any Celts captured had their right hands amputated as a warning to others.

As a result of Caesar's conquest, Gaul had lost about two million people – one million killed, and another million sold into slavery. Vercingetorix himself was kept prisoner until 46 BC, when he was marched in chains through Rome as part of Caesar's formal victory-parade. He was then executed according to Roman ritual.

Romanisation of Gaul

The Celtic threat in Gaul having ended, and the economy devastated by the campaigns of 53 BC, the Romans began rebuilding and transforming the landscape in their own image. Most of the *oppida* were abandoned and their surviving populations moved to new Roman towns that were established nearby.

In 12 BC, the political process of the Romanisation of Gaul was symbolically completed when a new national shrine to Rome and the Emperor Augustus (63 BC–AD 14) was inaugurated at Lugdunum (now Lyon, south-east France), an *oppidum* of the Aedui that was allowed to keep its Celtic name. Having previously wielded an iron hand, the Romans now extended the velvet glove, and did much to promote trade, farming and industry within Gaul.

The Romanisation of Celtic society, especially among the élite, was extremely rapid – even before the conquest, many Gauls had already adopted some of the customs and trappings of their sworn enemies. Within a generation, some Gaulish aristocrats had become not merely citizens of the Roman Empire, but members of the high-ranking equestrian order.

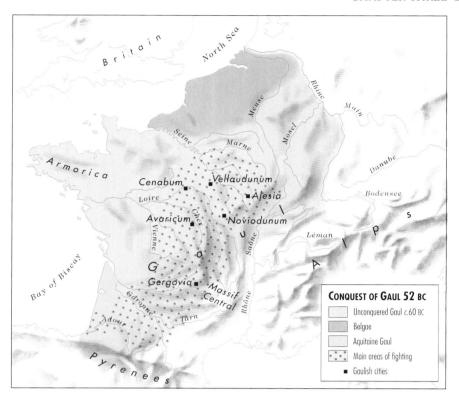

▲ **Conquest of Gaul in 52 BC** Revolt and massacre compelled Caesar to wage war in the wealthy heartland of Gaul. The devastation caused by the Romans, and the Gauls' own 'scorched earth' policy, may have reduced the immediate economic value of his victory, but did not detract from its prestige or political significance.

▼ **Protective goddess** of the town of Alesia. This Gallo-Roman statue dates from the 2nd or 3rd century AD. It is often identified as the goddess Tyche (Tutela).

LATER LA TÈNE ART

The La Tène style became much more widespread with the onset of the historic migration period (*c*.400 BC), but this was not always the result of large-scale population movements. Although the La Tène style is considered a fairly reliable indicator, it was by no means co-extensive with the distribution of Celtic-speaking peoples, and its presence (or absence) is not conclusive. The vast majority of La Tène artefacts have been recovered from burial sites, but uncertainty over the dating of some burials (particularly in the eastern-most regions) makes it unclear whether the occupants of graves obtained their La Tène artefacts directly, or at several removes from Celtic populations.

From the middle of the 4th century BC, La Tène began to develop numerous stylistic 'schools', the local and regional development of which is almost impossible to trace. There is some evidence that the Po Valley may have become a centre of Celtic innovation, relaying developments in Italy back to Bohemia and Gaul.

La Tène C

The artistic developments of this period (often called Middle La Tène, La Tène II, or La Tène C) were once known as the Waldalgesheim style (after a burial site in central Germany that contained a female skeleton and exquisite gold jewellery), but may be more accurately described as the 'wave-tendril' or 'vegetal' style.

The most characteristic motif is the wave tendril, a curvilinear, running design that flows across surfaces. The tendrils sometimes suggest vaguely human facial features that disappear into the design under a steady gaze, and this is known among English-speaking scholars as the 'Cheshire cat' style. Celtic artisans continued to make imaginative use of classical motifs, such as lyres, palmettes and half-palmettes, as well as traditional symbols like triskeles (literally three-limbs). Wave tendrils were ideal for decorating the iron and

bronze scabbards of the long La Tène swords, and apart from gold jewellery, the La Tène style remained the province of iron- and bronze-smiths.

La Tène D

The later developments of the La Tène style in continental Europe (often summarised as La Tène III or La Tène D) may have begun when ironsmiths became directly involved in the decoration of bronze scabbards early in the 2nd century BC. The new style that emerged was used exclusively for flat, engraved decoration on scabbards, and is known as the 'sword style', or the 'free graphic style'. The essential element is a pair of entwined beasts (resembling dragons or birds) that form a continuous design along the length of the scabbard. Scholars believe that the design was derived from the classical lyre motif, and many regional variants developed.

Slightly later in time, and perhaps in response, the goldsmiths and bronze-casters developed the so-called 'free plastic style', which was (from conception) a fully three-dimensional form. The 'free plastic style' was heavier and more static than the somewhat austere and restrained 'sword style', and many artefacts, such as chariot fittings and bracelets display a tendency towards the grotesque.

None of these later developments had any impact in Spain, where the La Tène style was applied only to a very limited range of artefacts. In *c*.300 BC, the La Tène style was transmitted to Britain, although not, apparently, as the result of regular trade. The 'sword style' was adopted and further developed in Britain, but very few 'free plastic style' objects have been found. Some time after 300 BC, the La Tène style first appeared in Ireland.

Pottery and sculpture

Pottery remained a minor art, although the introduction of the fast-wheel did lead to the development of a

▼ **Wooden carved head** from the Gallo-Roman cult site at the source of the River Seine, St-Germain-Source-Seine, east France. The sculpture dates from the 1st century BC, and was deposited in the river as a votive offering. It shows that La Tène artists not only produced works in metal, stone and ceramic, but were also adept at woodcarving.

► **The Waldalgesheim style** is distinguished by the use of spiralling tendrils, joined here in a pattern reminiscent of a triskele (top). This marks a development from Early La Tène art, which placed a greater emphasis on symmetry and the representation of animals. The predominance of vegetal or comma shapes (middle) is another defining feature of the Waldalgesheim style. These shapes are often composed of tiny dots (pointillism). The wave pattern (bottom) is found on pieces such as a 'jockey cap' helmet from Amfreville, north France. La Tène art was first classified by Paul Jacobsthal (1880–1957), professor of classical archæology at Marburg University, central Germany.

limited trade in prestige forms, such as flasks with wide, flaring bases and tall necks (sometimes inscribed with animal motifs) that were popular in central Europe. In Brittany, designs that had earlier been made by compass on metal were now transferred to fine, wheel-made pots.

A reasonable amount of Celtic sculpture exists, and what survives is very striking. While much of the detail on wood carvings has perished, the animal figures from Fellbach-Schmieden, south-west Germany, and the human figures on the Genevan cult pole give some idea of the woodworkers' skill. Most notable of the stone sculptures are the 'Tarasque' of Noves, south-east France, and the 'Janus' heads from Roquepertuse, southern France. Most dramatic of all, however, is the near life-sized stone-carving of a warrior with leaf-crown discovered at Glauberg, central Germany.

▲ **Ornate terminals** of a torque from Snettisham, Norfolk, east England. They are beautifully decorated with low relief work, and matted hatching made with a round-ended punch. The decoration was modelled in wax. The 'grotesque' torque, which is 20 centimetres (7.9 inches) in diameter, is one of the finest examples of Later La Tène art found (1950) in England. It comes from the territory controlled by the Iceni, and probably probably dates from the mid-1st century BC. The torque is made of electrum – an alloy of about three parts gold to two parts silver. Unusually for Insular La Tène artefacts, the maker was strongly influenced by the so-called 'plastic style' in continental Europe.

◄ **Cremation urn** from Armorica (now Brittany, north-west France). The ceramic urn dates from the 4th century BC. The pattern is made of a continuous series of intertwined S's. These spirals are characteristic of the 'Waldalgesheim' or La Tène C style. Such ornamentation is more commonly found on metalwork or stone sculpture. The central feature of La Tène C style is the use of patterns derived from nature.

OPPIDA

During the 2nd century BC, a period of prosperity and relative stability in Celtic Europe, the first *oppida* (towns) emerged north of the Alps. Like the cities of the Mediterranean region, the *oppida* served as commercial, administrative, manufacturing and distribution centres. Two factors are linked with the rise of the *oppida*: a dramatic increase in ironworking, and a resumption of trade with the civilisations of the south, which, by 200 BC, effectively meant the Roman world.

Each *oppidum* was, however, an essentially local phenomenon, arising from regional conditions. In Gaul, some *oppida* show evidence of foreign trade (in the shape of Roman wine amphorae) from their birth, while in Germany and the east, *oppida* emerged as sizeable centres independently of any Mediterranean contact.

Oppidum is a Latin word, and Julius Caesar used it with reference to some of the Celtic centres in Gaul. Caesar's usage, however, is not wholly consistent. He makes it clear that *oppidum* does not refer to all hillforts, and some of the larger centres he calls *civatates* or *urbs*.

There have been many debates about which Celtic centres can be called 'oppida'. Even today, usage of the term is loose, and varies from region to region. In Spain, it is applied to settlements such as Los Cogotas near Ávilia, with an area of 15 hectares (37 acres), as well as much larger centres such as the 'town' of Numantia.

Broadly speaking, an *oppidum* was a sizeable, defended nucleated settlement with urban characteristics. Most *oppida* were population centres – typically 1000 to 4000 people – and contained areas that were densely packed with houses and workshops. However, even in the most 'industrialised' *oppida*, most of the inhabitants worked in agriculture.

About 40 major *oppida* have so far been identified across a broad zone from southern England to Hungary. Many of the sites could also be described as large hillforts. Fortification was common practice in ancient Europe – there was a long tradition stretching back to the Neolithic period. This does not necessarily mean, however, that fortifications were kept in a permanent state of high repair and preparedness, or even that actual fortifications existed; but at all times, certain aspects of location and architecture were oriented towards defence.

Defensive walls

With most *oppida*, defence was paramount and any natural advantages of a site were reinforced with great ramparts, which were not just simple extended mounds of earth, but represent sophisticated military engineering. They probably also served as a display of wealth and power. In Western Europe, *oppida* were generally enclosed by the so-called *murus gallicus* (Gallic wall) constructions– a sloping rampart of rubble and packed earth, perhaps eight metres (26 foot) high, and held together by an internal framework of stout timbers fastened with iron nails. In Eastern Europe, ramparts

▼ ***Oppidum* wall** at Třísov, situated above the valley of the River Vlatava, south Bohemia. Třísov was a Celtic settlement from the 6th to 1st century AD. It was an important source of clay with a high graphite content. This clay was used in almost all of the pottery produced in Celtic Europe. Třísov thus appears to have one of the first such economic centres

were built with a sheer, outer face of timbers and dry-stone walls. Both types were remarkably effective against conventional attack, and most *oppida* eventually fell to siege or surrender rather than outright assault.

Bibracte and Manching

One of the largest *oppida* was Manching, southern Germany, covering 380 hectares (940 acres) enclosed by seven kilometres (4.5 miles) of ramparts. The size of Manching contrasts with the Hallstatt D princely centre of Heuneburg, which covered just 3.2 hectares (eight acres). Manching developed from a farming hamlet, established in the 3rd century BC, that occupied a low terrace alongside the River Danube. Late in the 2nd century BC, Manching was sacked by the Cimbri, but was rebuilt and continued to flourish for another century.

Further east, the *oppidum* of Závist (near modern-day Prague) covered 150 hectares (370 acres) and possessed nine kilometres (5.5 miles) of ramparts. It developed on the site of a 5th-century BC riverside hillfort that was reoccupied after 300 years of disuse. In the 1st century BC, Závist experienced rapid growth, but was sacked when Germanic tribes overran Bohemia in *c.*20 BC.

In Gaul, one of the most important *oppida* was Bibracte (now Mont Beuvray, near Glux-en-Glenne, east France), a 135-hectares (334-acres) site with ramparts five kilometres (three miles) long. Bibracte was founded by the Aedui in the early 2nd century BC, and hosted a Gallic council during the resistance to Caesar's invasion.

Oppida were a hallmark of the economically developed Celtic world, and by the start of the 1st century BC, a few Gallic examples can almost be considered cities within states. Inside the *oppida*, the major industries were the manufacture of iron weapons and agricultural tools, pottery, bronze casting, glassmaking, woven textiles, jewellery and minting coinage. Iron, often of high quality, was a major export to the Roman world.

By the beginning of the 1st century AD, *oppida* had disappeared from mainland Europe, forcibly Romanised or Germanised. In southern Britain, new *oppida* emerged as a result of trade with Romanised Gaul, until these too were eventually conquered.

▲ ***Oppidum* of Bod da Loz**, near St Moritz, east Switzerland. In the Hallstatt period (*c.*1200–480 BC), Bod da Loz was a fortified settlement north of the Julier Pass, on an important trade route north from the Mediterranean to the interior of Europe.

▲ **Major *oppida* in Europe** emerged in the last two centuries BC across mainland Europe. Their location was often dictated by tactical requirements of defence.

▼ **Heuneberg** in Upper Swabia, south-west Germany, was one of the main 'princely centres' in the West Hallstatt culture. The majority of 'princely centres' were hillforts, whereas *oppida* included a wider range of locations and fortifications. The hillfort at Heuneburg marked a decisive transition in Celtic defensive structures. In imitation of Mediterranean models, the first sun-dried mudbrick enclosure wall north of the Alps was built here in the 6th century BC.

COLLAPSE IN THE EAST

The abortive raid on Delphi (279 BC) represented the high-water mark of Celtic expansion in the east; thereafter the story of the Celts in the east is one of rapid decline and disappearance as a cohesive group. Their individual fates varied. Many were killed or captured, some hired into foreign service, some returned west, while others were simply absorbed into the societies of rival groups that shared a similar warrior ethos.

Loss of Galatia

The Celts near the north coast of the Black Sea were probably the first to be overrun – by the Sarmatians, who at times raided deep into central Europe. Some suggest that the Celts co-operated to some extent with the Sarmatians, and that a lengthy period of assimilation, rather than annihilation, followed the Sarmatians' arrival. The Celtic enclave of Tylis, south-east Thrace, lasted longer, preying on the trade going to and from the city of Byzantium (now Istanbul) – a main focus for shipping between Greece and the grain-producing Crimea region. Finally, in 212 BC, the Celtic lords of Tylis were overthrown by their subject Thracian population and their power extinguished.

With the effective loss of Galatian independence in 189 BC, the Balkan mountains became the south-east frontier of the Celtic world. Political turmoil and the activities of less literate peoples than the Romans, such as the Dacians and Thracians, obscure the subsequent fate of the Celts behind this frontier. In the medium term,

most of what had been Celtic eastern Europe ended up within the Roman Empire, the remainder (those parts the Romans were unable to 'protect') became Germanic. Ultimately, the Romans merely delayed the Germanising process by 500 years or so, apart from Galatia, which remained within a 'Roman' (Byzantine) context until conquered by the Ottoman Turks.

Rise and fall of Dacia

During the 170s BC, the Dacians emerged as a coherent force, resisting Sarmatian incursions from the Black Sea coast. Between c.85 and c.65 BC, King Burebista welded the various Dacian tribes into a state with the approximate extent of present-day Romania. He then instigated a westward expansion to regain 'ancient' Dacian territory that had been 'stolen' by the Celts. His ambitions extended to present-day Slovakia.

Burebista then felt strong enough to enter Roman power politics, supporting Pompey (106–48 BC) in the struggle against Julius Caesar (c.100–44 BC). He did not live long enough, however, to face punishment for picking the losing side, and died in obscure circumstances at about the same time as the all-conquering Caesar. After Burebista's death, the Dacian state evaporated into small petty kingdoms, but irreparable damage had already been inflicted on the Celtic world – most of the eastern *oppida* (towns) had been sacked and burned. Between AD 105 and 107, Dacia was conquered by Rome, an event commemorated on Trajan's Column, Rome.

▲ **Rider fighting a bear** on a silver and gilt ornamental fitting, found at Letnica, north Bulgaria. A splendid example of Thracian art, the piece, which is five centimetres (two inches) high, dates from c.400–350 BC. Below the horse's hoofs is a boar that the hunter has killed.

◀ **Scene from Trajan's Column** (AD 113) in Trajan's Forum, Rome. The Column is a celebration of Emperor Trajan's triumphant campaigns against the Dacians in AD 101–102 and AD 105–106. The scene here shows the Roman legionaries crossing the River Danube near Dobreta Turnu Severin, south-west Romania, by means of a pontoon bridge.

▶ **Eastern Celtic world in 120–60 BC** Squeezed by the expansionist tendencies of Dacians, Romans and Germans, the Celtic communities of eastern Europe were overrun during the 2nd and 1st centuries BC. Some Celts may then have travelled to Gaul, either as refugees or as members of 'German' raiding parties.

The State of Noricum

Further west, the Celts living in what is now Austria had coalesced into a state, perhaps in response to the Roman occupation of north Italy. In 186 BC, this kingdom of Noricum (as the Romans referred to it) established friendly relations with Rome. Noricum became famous throughout the Roman world as a producer of the finest-quality steel, and, because of its close proximity to the new Roman town of Aquileia, north-east Italy, trade flourished. A considerable number of Roman merchants settled in the capital, Noreia (now Magdalensberg, south Austria) which became thoroughly Romanised, even building its own forum in the 1st century BC. Politically, Noricum maintained nominal independence until 15 BC, when it was absorbed (almost painlessly) into the Roman Empire, under the pretext of 'saving' it from the Germans who had overrun neighbouring Bohemia. The Romans then renamed the capital Virunum.

Along the north-east flank of the Celtic world, a region of which the Romans had little direct knowledge, the distinctions between Celts and Germans were already becoming blurred by the 2nd century BC. The evidence of archæology suggests that – linguistic variations aside – there was little material difference between the two cultures, and that ethnic distinctions may have had little local significance. It is quite possible that the ethnic labels 'Belgae' or 'German', allocated by the Romans to the

▲ **Woman with three-headed snake** on a silver and gilt harness plate found in a grave at Letnica, north Bulgaria. The woman is also holding a mirror. A fine example of Thracian art, the piece, which is five centimetres (two inches) high, dates from c.400–350 BC.

peoples of this region, in fact reflected the difference between 'conquered' and 'unconquered'.

The Cimbri hordes

A good example of the ethnic uncertainty in the north-east is provided by the phenomenon of the Cimbri. Depending on one's point of view, the Cimbri's erratic progress across Europe, in the late 2nd century BC, may be seen either as reprising the Celtic population movements of the migration period, or prefiguring the later Germanic migrations.

The origin of the Cimbri has been hotly debated. To the Romans, they were unequivocally Germans, but there is no reason to suppose that the armed horde who fought southwards from the North Sea coast in the early 120s BC, was not a mix of Celtic and Germanic elements. Furthermore, such hordes generally have a fairly flexible and non-exclusive membership, and it is likely that the Cimbri were continuously losing and recruiting 'members' throughout their journey.

For 20 years, the Cimbri roamed the Roman Empire. In 120 BC, they attacked Noricum and defeated a Roman army sent to the town's defence, but then veered eastwards. In 114 BC, the Cimbri were expelled from Hungary by the Boii, and then meandered and fought their way into France, where they twice defeated Roman armies – at Bordeaux in 107 BC, and Orange in 105 BC. After a brief excursion into Spain, the Cimbri returned to France, where they were annihilated by the Roman legions between 102 and 101 BC.

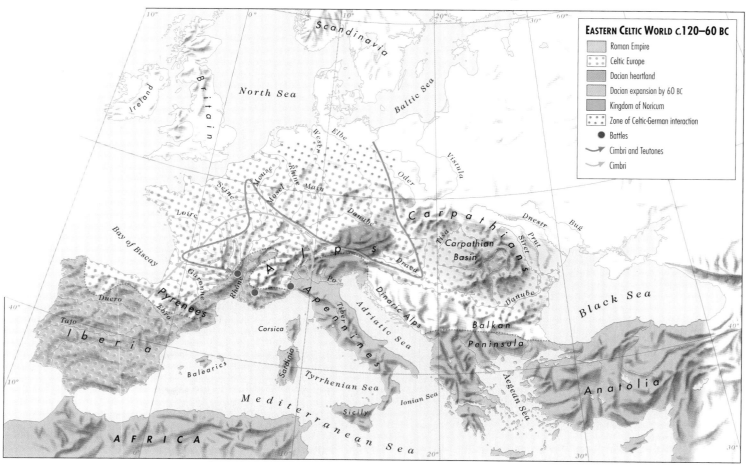

IRON-AGE BRITAIN

It has been argued that the population of Britain (and Ireland) during the last few centuries before the Roman occupation can broadly be described as 'Celtic'. However, the existence in Britain at this time of other languages, such as Pictish (which may not have been Indo-European), has suggested that Celtic was not the language of the original ancient Britons.

Origins and settlements of British Celts

The first iron objects (weapons of continental style) arrived in Britain during the Hallstatt C period (c.750–600 BC), and this has been interpreted as marking the beginnings of a Celtic invasion of Britain. In the mid-20th century, an elaborate theory of successive waves (A, B and C) of Celtic invaders was put forward to account for the varied evidence presented by burial mounds and pottery discovered by archaeologists.

Subsequently, the notion of large-scale Celtic migrations and 'invasions' has fallen into disrepute, and British (and Irish) scholars are currently keen to stress the continuities between the Bronze Age and Iron Age societies.

Celtic seems to have been widely spoken in Britain by the time of the first Roman contact in 55 BC, but it is very unlikely that linguistic uniformity was ever the rule. It is probable that Celtic was gradually adopted as the language associated with élite warrior groups, and with cultural (technical and artistic) innovation. However, what remains unclear is when Celtic was first spoken in Britain.

La Tène art was perhaps first produced in Britain in c.300 BC, and rotary querns (stone hand-mills) – a less reliable indicator of Celtic culture – may have been in use a century earlier, but this evidence reveals nothing about the language or ethnicity of the societies that used them.

Many of the so-called 'Celtic fields' (first identified in Britain and subsequently applied to similar relics in parts of north-west Europe), have been subsequently discovered to have Bronze Age or Neolithic origins.

The ethnic identity of the inhabitants of the British Isles during the pre-Roman Iron Age is open to question; and the supposed 'myth' of the Atlantic Celts has been widely reported. However, as no satisfactory alternative ethnic grouping (accompanied by a coherent historical explanation) has been suggested, we may still refer to the natives of the British Isles in pre-Roman and Roman times as Celts, unless we believe that they spoke a significantly different language, as was the case with the Picts of western Scotland.

Early settlements in Britain

Archaeological surveys of settlement patterns have shown that, in the 5th century BC, Britain was divided into three main zones. While these zones partly reflect the physical geography of the island, they may also reflect differences between the societies that produced them.

In the east, the ancient Britons lived in scattered hamlets and villages, usually with no more than 50 inhabitants. Most of these were open settlements, although in the north of the zone, a majority was enclosed with wooden palisades.

To the west, stretching from north Wales to the south-east tip of Britain, was a zone dominated by hundreds of hillforts. Most of these were built during the 6th century BC, although many were later abandoned after 400 BC, while a few developed into local power centres. An extension of this zone ran across southern and eastern Scotland.

In the far south-west, west Wales, and northern and western Scotland was a zone characterised by small, defended settlements. These sites usually

▲ ► **Bronze boars** from Hounslow, London, probably dating from the 1st century BC. The boar was one of the most popular animal figures in Celtic art. They were probably crafted as votive offerings.

◄ **Gold torques** found at Snettisham, Norfolk, Ipswich, Suffolk, and Needwood Forest, Staffordshire. These three torques date from the second half of the 1st century BC. The Snettisham torque (top) was part of possibly the largest hoard of gold and silver treasure discovered (1990) in Britain this century. More than 11 kilograms (24 pounds) of gold and 16 kilograms (35 pounds) of silver jewellery were unearthed. Snettisham lay in the East Anglian territory of Queen Boudicca of the Iceni tribe.

▼ **Horse's head**, a bronze mount possibly from a war chariot, discovered at Stanwick St Johns, North Yorkshire, north-east England. The piece, which dates from the 1st century AD, is one of the finest achievements of the Brigantes, a tribe in north England that strongly resisted Roman occupation. The artist has beautifully rendered the horse's mournful expression.

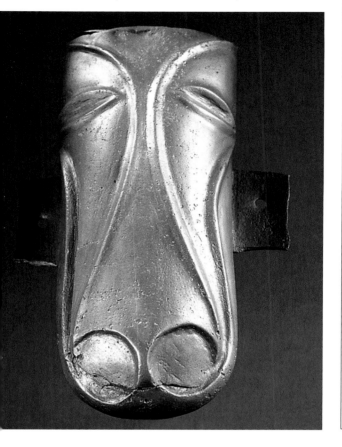

IRON-AGE BRITAIN

ICENI British tribes reported by Romans 1st century AD

☐ Arras culture

☐ Open settlement zone

☐ Hillfort zone

☐ Small, defended settlement zone

▲ **Iron-Age Britain** Continental influences on Iron-Age British societies are certain, but elusive. Some of the earliest evidence (early 3rd-century BC) comes from the Arras culture on the north-east coast. Subsequently, the south coast port of Hengistbury Head became the centre for continental trade. At an even later date, the focus of continental influence shifted to the east coast once more, with Camulodunum (now Colchester) being the most prominent centre in the immediate pre-Roman period.

consisted of no more than fortified farmsteads with a few houses, although some of the coastal forts were considerably larger. While this zone possessed considerable metal resources of gold, tin and copper, their exploitation did not stimulate large settlements, as salt had at Hallstatt, west-central Austria.

All three of these settlement types – open villages, hillforts and defended farmsteads – were once identified as authentically Celtic.

The Arras culture and La Tène style

Supporters of the notion of Celtic immigration point to a large but isolated group of graves in Yorkshire (known as the Arras culture), which date from c.300–250 BC. Some of the graves display strong similarities to burial in northern Gaul – beneath rectangular mounds are disassembled chariots, and weapons and jewellery decorated in La Tène style. However, all these artefacts seem to be of local manufacture rather than imports. Therefore, although the best explanation is that an élite warrior group moved here from Gaul, there is a possibility that a local group adopted continental methods without any actual migration.

By the middle of the 2nd century BC, La Tène artefacts were widely produced in southern Britain. At the site of Gussage All Saints, Dorset, archæologists discovered the clay moulds used in making matched sets of elegant harness decorations. Direct trade with Europe at this time was concentrated on the route through Hengistbury Head, Dorset, to Brittany, north-west France, although a group of possibly 'foreign' burials in the south-east dating from c.150 BC, shows that some communities may already have been using a shorter route across the English Channel.

Caesar's invasions of Britain

Julius Caesar's (100–44 BC) expeditions to Britain provided the first clear picture of Iron-Age Britain. He may also have provoked, through the necessity of tribes unifying under Cassivellaunus (active 1st century BC) to fight the Romans, the first glimmerings of a national consciousness (at least in the south-east). Before Caesar's invasions, the Britons, isolated on their small island, had largely not needed to build tribal coalitions or seek continental assistance. From this time on (coincident with Britain and Ireland's involvement in Roman history), we have evidence of kings who issued coins with Latin inscriptions and made overseas alliances.

After Julius Caesar, the focus of trade to and from Britain shifted to the south-east, and *oppida* (towns) such as Camulodunum (now Colchester) and Verulamium (now St Albans) developed. Through contact with Roman-occupied Gaul, the successful élites in this region began adopting elements of Roman culture, just as their predecessors had adopted La Tène-style designs.

HILLFORTS

In some parts of Europe, there are features discernible in today's landscape that might be identified as Iron-Age Celtic hillforts; however, this label by no means applies to all hillforts. Structures described as hillforts (that have not been altered beyond recognition by incorporation into later buildings) have, upon archæological investigation, not always turned out to be Celtic, nor Iron Age, nor even 'forts' in the accepted military sense of the word.

The Celts certainly had hillforts – the Roman conquests of Spain, Gaul and Britain, largely entailed overcoming hillforts. For every single pitched battle, dozens of hillforts were quickly and efficiently reduced and few were able to resist the well-organised Roman legions for more than a few days. However, many hillfort sites bear no indication of significant military activity.

What is a hillfort?

A hillfort (an elevated site with defensive structures such as ramparts and ditches) is a very convenient 'catch-all' concept for archæologists, and was an equally convenient and intuitive physical structure for the early inhabitants of Europe. It is worth stating the obvious – that hillforts require hills or some approximation thereof. In regions with a predominantly flat landscape, such as northern Poland, equivalent structures (fortified villages) were constructed on artificial islands made of felled trees.

While fortified settlements were established in the Neolithic and Early Bronze Age periods, hillforts are largely Late Bronze Age and Early Iron Age phenomena. Furthermore, there is no continuous tradition of settlement – for example, the hilltop settlement of Hambledon, south England, was settled in the Neolithic period but abandoned until the Iron Age.

Hillforts are often associated with the transition of farming from a subsistence to a profitable activity, and with the exploitation of metals. The number of hillforts increased during the 1st millennium BC (roughly coinciding with the beginning of the Iron Age) and peaked in c.400 BC. At this time, the population associated with each hillfort averaged c.150–200 persons. Thereafter, hillforts declined in number as they were progressively abandoned.

Iron-Age hillforts are most numerous in Britain, and this is where they have received most attention. Burials, apart from those of the Arras culture in Yorkshire, are almost entirely absent from the British Isles during the Iron Age, and archæologists have been forced to concentrate on landscape features. Their counterparts in continental Europe, on the other hand, have had a much greater variety of Iron Age material (such as burials) to study.

Hillforts can be divided into a number of subtypes based either upon the number of concentric ramparts forming the defences – univallate or multivallate (with between 10 and 150 metres [33 to 490 feet] between rings) – or their geographical situation – inland or coastal promontory (although an actual promontory is not a necessity, a cliff-edge is sufficient). These differences are, however, largely architectural, and may merely reflect differing building traditions dictated by the landscape and substrate; the subdivisions say little about the function of the structures they describe.

The purpose of hillforts

Hillforts are usually interpreted as defensive structures, but a fortified hilltop can also be an offensive structure in terms of the display of power. Nor do the defensive capabilities of a site tell us anything about the nature of the perceived threat: was it peer groups in control of rival hillforts, violent risings by subject peoples, or foreign invaders?

Archæologists sometimes find evidence of violence at hillfort sites, however this is usually confined to signs of generalised destruction or caches of projectiles. Skeletons bearing war wounds are found occasionally, but it is difficult to conclusively differentiate defenders from attackers.

Many hillforts show signs of year-round occupation. Those that appear to have been periodically occupied may have had a mainly ritual function,

▼ **Dún Aonghasa** hillfort on Inishmore (*Inis Mór*), Aran Islands, off the west coast of Ireland, is perched spectacularly on the top of a cliff that plunges 91 metres (300 foot) to the sea. The fort consists of four sets of dry-stone walls and a defensive feature known as a *cheveaux de frise* – bands of upright stones. According to legend, the fort was built by the Fir Bolg (a prehistoric tribe), led by Aéngus.

while also serving as a refuge in times of crisis. Whatever their other functions, hillforts probably served as communal granaries and storage areas, although membership of the 'community' may not have been open to all of the local population. At every level, from small residences to the largest population centres, hillforts probably served as hubs of trade and redistribution. Both the princely centres of Hallstatt D (*see* pages 36–37) and the Celtic *oppida* (*see* pages 88–89) included sites that could reasonably also be described as hillforts, but whereas the princely centres are mainly hillforts, the *oppida* (towns) include a much wider range of locations and types of fortification.

Maiden Castle, Dún Aonghasa and Danebury

The fort of Danebury, Hampshire, south-west England, is, in many ways, typical of the larger British Iron-Age hillforts. It was established shortly after 580 BC, with an earthen rampart surrounding a few dozen houses. About 200 years later, an outer rampart was added and the entrances elaborated. The fort at nearby Maiden Castle had a similar appearance, but was in essence much older. The first hilltop enclosure at Maiden Castle was in use throughout much of the third millennium BC, but was abandoned between *c.*2250 and 600 BC.

In the west of Ireland, and especially in the Aran Islands, there are spectacular stone forts that some people have linked with the forts of northern Iberia

◄ **Danebury** hillfort in Hampshire, south-west England. Danebury, which covers more than 5.3 hectares (13 acres) is perhaps the most intensively studied site associated with the Iron Age in Britain. The hillfort was defended by a great timber and chalk rampart and ditches up to 19 metres (62 feet) deep. Inside the fort were 500 storage buildings and 70 houses. The fort was probably a stronghold of the Belgae tribe.

because of similarities in defensive engineering. While the dating of these Irish forts is uncertain, recent excavation at Dún Aonghasa, Inishmore (Inis Mór), has yielded evidence of activity on the site from the Late Bronze Age (1000–700 BC) until Early Christian times (around the 5th century AD).

► **Maiden Castle**, near Dorchester, Dorset, south-west England. The name of the castle derives from the Celtic words *Mai Dun* (Great Hill). This vast earth-work, ringed by entrenchments and ramparts, occupies more than 50 hectares (120 acres). Excavations (1934–37) by the Scottish archaeologist Sir Mortimer Wheeler (1890–1976) uncovered evidence of a settlement dating back to *c.*3500 BC. Later, a bank barrow, 546 metres (1800 feet) long, was added. In *c.*350 BC, further fortifications were added that made it a fully fledged hillfort. Maiden Castle was the major stronghold for the Durotriges, the predominant tribe of Dorset and Somerset. In AD 44, the hillfort finally fell to a Roman army, probably led by Vespasian. This photograph shows the western entrance to Maiden Castle.

LA TÈNE ART IN BRITAIN AND IRELAND

The La Tène art style was well established in Britain by c.300 BC, and first appeared in Ireland during the course of the 3rd century BC. While some continental manufactures have been found in the British Isles, most insular La Tène artefacts appear to have been locally made, although the artistic development initially followed the European pattern. Around 200 BC, and perhaps somewhat earlier, contact between Britain and the rest of Europe seems to have declined – the later 'free plastic style' is found only on a single torque from Snettisham, east England – and British and Irish craftworkers were able to develop their own ideas and designs.

Early La Tène art in Britain

In Britain, the insular development of La Tène can be divided into earlier and later phases. During the earlier phase, the main influences were the contemporary continental 'sword style' and the half-palmette of the La Tène I period. A number of local schools of scabbard decoration developed, such as the Witham-Wandsworth and Yorkshire styles. One common feature of these styles is that the overall design, although containing repetitive elements, is fundamentally asymmetric. Insular metalworkers also developed improved skills of engraving and produced some innovative decorated accessories, such as the so-called 'bean-box' found in a grave in Yorkshire, north England. The use of tightly coiled spirals as a decorative motif is another insular innovation dating to the earlier phase.

The British 'mirror'-style

The later phase saw the development of the 'mirror' style, so-called because it is most frequently found on the backs of bronze mirrors. This style is peculiarly

▲ **Bronze shield** decorated with studs in red glass plate, found in the River Thames at Battersea, south-west London. The shield probably dates from the 1st or 2nd century BC. Its rich ornamentation suggests that it was either a ceremonial or votive piece.

British, and possibly originated in east England. The most distinctive motif is the 'trumpet-void' – an abstract shape formed by intersecting curves, perhaps ultimately derived from the half-palmette. 'Mirror' style designs were usually engraved, but were also executed in *repoussé* (relief) and as *cire-perdue* (lost-wax) castings. Other later developments include a revival of symmetrical designs, and the use of basketry-style infill patterns to cover metal surfaces.

Enamel and shields

La Tène metalworkers had, from the outset, incorporated red glass studs and insets as a substitute for Mediterranean coral. Later, and particularly in Britain, they perfected true enamel, fusing powdered and pigmented glass into engraved panels on copper-alloy artefacts, and producing fields of bright and permanent colour.

The most spectacular examples of insular metalworking skills are the bronze shields (early and late) that have been found, as well as swords, scabbards and other artefacts, in some British and Irish rivers and lakes. The beautifully decorated shields are obviously impractical and show no obvious signs of wear or use. We can only speculate as to the circumstances of their manufacture or their function before they were ritually deposited in water.

From 150 BC, the power and influence of Rome was increasingly evident in southern Britain, largely because of the trade between Hengistbury Head and the western seaboard of Europe. After 100 BC, British tribes began to imitate continental art and coinage. After Caesar's conquest of Gaul and expeditions to Britain, Roman-style objects began to be imported into Britain, and became fashionable status symbols for the Celtic élites.

▼ **Bronze trumpet bell** found at Loghnashade, County Armagh, Ireland, and probably dating from the 1st century BC. It formed part of a large, horn-shaped instrument.

◄ **Horned bronze helmet** found in the River Thames, near Waterloo Bridge, London. The helmet may have been designed for ceremonial use, transforming its wearer into a horned god. It dates from the 1st century BC, and is 24.2 centimetres (9.5 inches) high.

La Tène art in Ireland

Although the La Tène style probably arrived later in Ireland than in Britain, it remained in use much longer – at least until the 4th century AD. While very few La Tène objects may have been imported into Ireland before the 2nd century BC, the style was not adopted by native craft-workers. When it was finally appropriated, the style followed both British and continental developments. The distribution of La Tène artefacts in Ireland is confined almost entirely to the northern half of the island.

The arrival of La Tène in Ireland has been linked to the arrival of the Celts in Ireland, but the archæo-logical evidence does not support this. Although large-scale immigration at this time can be discount-ed, the gradual infiltration and expansion of élite-warrior groups cannot be dismissed so easily.

Ornamental compass-work became very popular in Ireland, both for marking out open-work designs and for filling in backgrounds – even on curved surfaces such as the torque found at Broighter, County Derry. A distinc-tive Irish school of 'scabbard style' decoration emerged and curvilinear La Tène designs were used to decorate beehive-shaped querns and some standing stones.

Irish La Tène metalworkers produced some unique bronze artefacts. The elegant *repoussé* decoration of Monasterevin-type discs is executed with consummate skill, and we may presume that the discs had some ritu-al or social significance. The enigmatic 'Y-shaped' arte-facts are finely crafted and fairly numerous, but no con-vincing explanation for their existence has been offered. The overall size and shape suggests that they may have been a component of a particular type of bridle.

▼ **Bronze disc** from Monasterevin, east Ireland. The disc, which is 28 centimetres (11 inches) in diameter, dates from the 1st century AD. The circular hollow is bordered by deep-relief scrolls. It has been suggested that food offerings to the gods were placed in the hollow. The style of the disc places it in the final phase of insular La Tène art.

◀ **Bronze mirror** found at Desborough, Northamptonshire, central England. The flamboyant engravings on its back were probably drawn with a compass. The highly complex, symmetrical design is characteristic of insular La Tène art. If one looks closely at the design, one can make out several 'Cheshire cat' faces. The mirror, which is 26 centimetres (10.2 inches) in length, dates from the beginning of the 1st century AD.

ROMAN CONQUEST OF BRITAIN

For nearly a century after Caesar's expeditions, Britain eluded Roman grasp, despite being a target both as a rich and prestigious acquisition and as a way of securing the north-west boundaries of the Empire. Like so much of official Roman policy (rather than the whims of individual emperors), the conquest of Britain was at least partially motivated by the obsessive needs of forward defence.

In reality, the continuation of a 'Celtic' threat from Britain was almost wholly illusory. Although unrest smouldered in Gaul, the Celtic rulers of Britain were sufficiently familiar with the Romans to have little interest in provoking them.

Two rival power blocs dominated south-east England. North of the River Thames, the Catuvellauni were in control; south of the Thames, the rival Atrebates had supremacy. During the final decades of the 1st century BC, the Catuvellauni, led by Cunobelinus (d. c.AD 42), bullied and intrigued themselves into the ascendancy. In 6 BC, the rulers deposed by the Catuvellauni sent appeals to Rome requesting assistance for their restoration.

▲ Gold coin of Cunobelinus, King of the Catuvellauni, which bears his name. The coin was probably struck at Camulodunum (now Colchester, Essex), capital of the Catuvellauni, in the 1st century AD. After Cunobelinus' death (c.AD 42), his sons and successors, Caratacus and Togodumnus, pursued an expansionist and anti-Roman agenda that provided Emperor Claudius with the perfect pretext to invade Britain.

Claudius colonises Britain

In AD 43, Emperor Claudius (10 BC–AD 54) launched the long-anticipated Roman invasion of Britain. His pretext, to satisfy the dictates of Roman law, was the restoration of King Verica of the Atrebates, ousted by the Catuvellauni.

An invasion force of three legions sailed from Gesoriacum (now Boulogne) on the north coast of Gaul, and landed at Rutupiae (now Richborough, Kent). The legions fought their way to the River Thames, which they bridged at the site of their future capital, Londinium (now London). Claudius himself now joined the army, complete with a contingent of war elephants, and he personally supervised the attack and rapid capture of Camulodunum (now Colchester, Essex), the largest *oppidum* (town) in Britain and capital of the Catuvellauni. With victory assured, Claudius returned to Rome.

The legions fanned out across England, quickly reviving their somewhat rusty skills of subduing Celtic hillforts. Archaeological excavations at Maiden Castle, Dorset, for example, yielded evidence of the British defenders' desperate final attempts to reinforce the gates, and of their subsequent fate – a skeleton with a Roman projectile embedded in his vertebra. By AD 50, Rome controlled much of south and central England.

The betrayal (AD 52) of Caratacus, son of Cunobelinus and a leader of the British resistance, to the Romans by Queen Cartimandua of the Brigantes reveals much of the divided nature of tribal society in Britain, and the pursuit of tribal self-interest rather than uniting against a common enemy.

Boudicca's revolt

Strategic advances to the Severn and Mersey estuaries enabled the Romans to divide the British forces into three geographical areas (the south-west, Wales, and the north) that could be attacked and subdued in turn. Firstly, the Romans drove back the Silures into the far west. Then, they turned their attention on Wales. Led by Suetonius Paulinus (governor AD 59–61), the Romans were concentrating for an attack on the island of Mona (now Anglesey), the last stronghold of the British druids, when they were surprised by the outbreak of a violent rebellion in eastern Britain.

◄ 'Cupid on a dolphin' mosaic in the Roman palace at Fishbourne (near modern-day Chichester, West Sussex). It has been suggested that the palace was built (c.AD 43–75) by the Romans to reward the loyalty of the local king, Tiberius Claudius Cogidubnus, The mosaic dates from the mid-2nd century AD. The shiny red cubes are made from pieces of red gloss pottery (samian ware), imported from Gaul.

BOUDICCA

Aquatint (1815) of Boudicca, Queen of the Iceni (a tribe in modern Suffolk and Norfolk), by Richard Havell the Elder. In AD 60, Boudicca launched a revolt against Roman rule in East Anglia. She formed an alliance with the Trinovantes, who initially had fought with the Romans against the Catuvellauni. The joint army sacked Camulodunum (Colchester), Verulamium (St Albans) and the market of Londinium (London). According to Tacitus, Boudicca's army massacred more than 70,000 Romans and their allies, including the wholesale slaughter of the 9th Legion. Led by Suetonius Paulinus, the Romans recovered their composure and East Anglia, inflicting a decisive blow against Boudicca on Watling Street, near present-day Fenny Stratford.

When Prasutagus, client-king of the Iceni, died in AD 60 with no male heir, he left his wealth to his two daughters and to Emperor Nero (AD 37–68), seeking to gain imperial protection for his family. The Romans seized the chance to annexe his kingdom, rape his daughters and plunder the Iceni chiefs. Incensed, Prasutagus' wife, Queen Boudicca (d. AD 60), became the passionate and persuasive leader of a full-scale revolt.

Britons flocked to her cause and the army swept southwards, with Boudicca at their head, slaughtering all Romans in their path, and sacking the towns of Camulodunum and Verulamium (now St Albans). Unable to mount an adequate defence, the Romans evacuated Londinium, and the rebels pillaged the empty town. Boudicca then advanced to meet the Roman legions hurriedly recalled from Wales. At a battle to the west of Londinium, the Romans defeated Boudicca, who probably later killed herself with poison.

Building of Roman Britain

The restoration of order enabled Roman expansion to resume its earlier rapid pace. During the AD 70s, they established Eburacum (now York), Deva (now Chester) and Isca (now Caerleon) as permanent strategic bases that marked the perimeter of what was to become the most intensively Romanised region of Britain.

The palace at Fishbourne of the British client-king Cogidubnus (made a Roman citizen by Claudius) provides a good example of the pace of Romanisation within the core south-east region. The palace boasted the material benefits, such as splendid mosaics and under-floor heating, gained through co-operation with Rome

In c.AD 84, Agricola advanced across the Forth, and defeated the assembled Caledonians and Britons at Mons Graupius (probably near modern-day Inverness, north Scotland) – the last time that legions faced chariots in the field. The Romans now occupied the whole of Britain, excluding the Scottish Highlands.

▼ **Britain – Conquest and Revolt** Within two decades, the Roman legions had conquered all of south-east Britain, and were actively campaigning in the north and west. Boudicca's rebellion (AD 60) proved no more than a temporary setback.

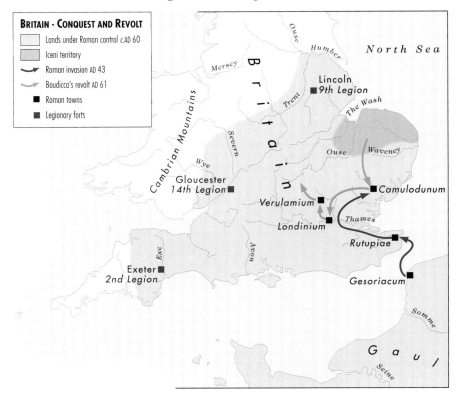

BRITAIN - CONQUEST AND REVOLT

- Lands under Roman control c.AD 60
- Iceni territory
- Roman invasion AD 43
- Boudicca's revolt AD 61
- ■ Roman towns
- ■ Legionary forts

ROMAN BRITAIN

▼ **Portchester Castle** in Fareham, overlooking Portsmouth Harbour, south-east England. The castle was built in the later stages of the Roman occupation (late 3rd century) to fend off attacks by Saxons and pirates. The outer walls are the most intact Roman fortifications in northern Europe. The walls are 5.5 metres (18 feet) high, and up to 3 metres (10 feet) thick. Carausias, a Belgic sailor who led a successful rebellion against Roman rule and styled himself Emperor of Britain (286–93), made Portchester his capital and naval base. The Norman king Henry I (1068–1135) added the keep, and the Norman Church of St Mary's (top left) was built in the 12th century. Portchester Castle was the assembly point for Henry V's expedition to Agincourt (1415).

The Roman occupation of Britain established the approximate boundaries of Celtic cultural regions that endure to the present-day. Throughout the occupation, Roman settlement (and associated economic development) was almost entirely confined to the area that had been subdued by AD 80. Wales and northern Britain formed a peripheral zone, essentially under military occupation, but with no civil development. In the far south-west of England, Roman troops were withdrawn sometime before AD 100, and the natives were left very much to their own devices. Despite Agricola's boast that he could conquer Ireland with a single legion, the Romans almost completely ignored the Irish, although Agricola did build forts along stretches of the west coast of Britain to protect against Irish sea-raiders.

Throughout central and southern Britain, Romanisation (which included the imposition of Latin as the official language) gradually eroded Celtic culture (apart from in the far south-west). While archæology has shown that Celtic personal names (and we may presume the language of the hearth) remained in use until the 3rd and 4th centuries AD, widespread and public use of the Celtic languages was confined to the peripheral zone.

Roman towns in Britain

The native *oppidum* of Camulodunum (now Colchester) served as the first capital of Britain, but was soon replaced by Londinium (now London) which was more centrally located. Other *oppida* in the south-east developed into Roman towns, such as Verulamium (now St Albans), in contrast with central Gaul where the Romans depopulated the native centres and established Roman towns on new sites.

In the rest of the inner zone, where previously there had been very few population centres, Roman organisation was essentially military. The most important centres, such as Deva (now Chester) and Eburacum (now York), developed from legionary bases established during the conquest. Other centres developed at strategic points on the roads that were constructed to allow the legions rapid access to potential trouble spots.

Despite the many towns that developed during the Roman period, the population of Britain remained predominantly rural and scattered: only about 5 per cent can be considered urban citizens, and they were concentrated in the south-east.

Legions and villas

The legions were one of the most efficient instruments of Roman cultural colonialism. In addition to stimulating the various civilian activities that inevitably accumulate around large garrisons, the legions also built roads, organized many types of industry and introduced new techniques. The legions also absorbed the martial activities of young Britons, who were forbidden

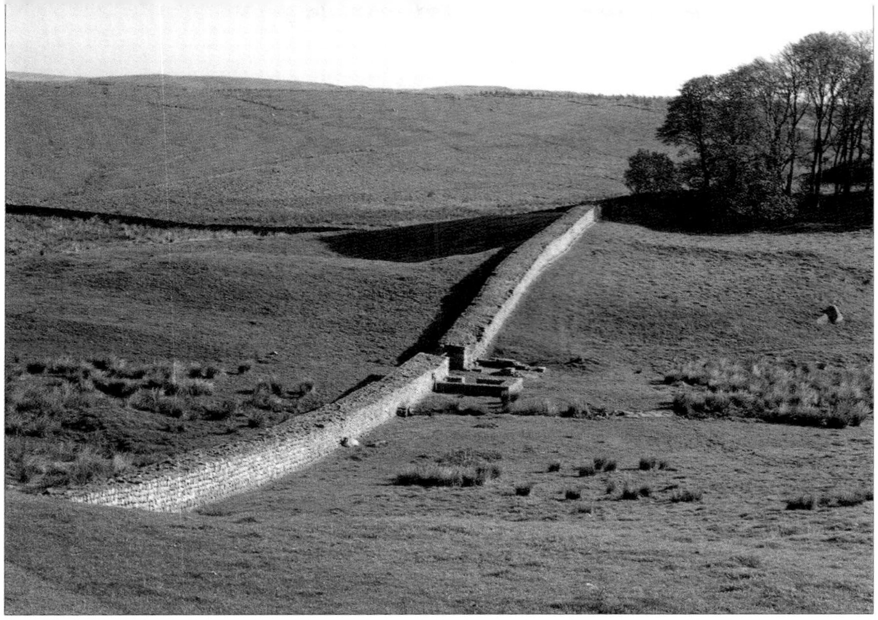

◀ **Hadrian's Wall** at Housesteads, north England. This section of the wall is adjacent to the ruins of a Roman garrison town built into the wall itself. The wall was built in the 1st century AD.

▼ **Roman Britain in AD 100–300** Roman occupation provided Britain with an infrastructure of roads, towns and internal frontiers that remains fundamentally still in place. The modern road from London to York is designated the A1, and the A2 runs between London and Canterbury.

to wage private wars. Amenable local notables were made auxiliary officers, and encouraged to adopt the culture of their Roman peers.

Outside the towns, with their temples and baths, the other main instruments of Romanisation were the villas. Although they were centres of food production and processing, the villas were more than just large commercial farms. They often had extensive workshops producing pottery and other items, and served as local outposts for the administration of justice and the collection of taxes. Some villas also became centres for the worship of various imported religions, including Christianity.

By the 4th century AD, there were more than 1000 villas in Britain, almost exclusively inside the inner zone conquered by AD 80. However, even in the south-east there were *c.*100 native-style small farmsteads for every Romanised villa.

Defence and decline

In AD 119, the garrison at Eburacum was massacred during a raid by the Brigantes. After the ensuing repression, Emperor Hadrian, who was visiting Britain, ordered the construction of a fortified wall across northern Britain. In the AD 140s, the northern border was further advanced by the construction of a wooden palisade barrier between the firths of Forth and Clyde. The maintenance of this forward defence required the presence in Britain of *c.*50,000 Roman soldiers, *c.*10 per cent of the Empire's total military force. The Forth-Clyde barrier was abandoned in the AD 160s, and Hadrian's Wall remained the northern frontier of the Empire until the 5th century.

In *c.*AD 365, when the Roman Empire was in steady decline, Eburacum was sacked during a series of raids on Britain that contemporary commentators called the 'Great Conspiracy' – a supposed alliance of the Irish, Western Islanders, Picts and Germans. Although these attacks may have been almost simultaneous, they are unlikely to have been co-ordinated and were a sign of the weakening of Roman power in Britain. In *c.*AD 410, Emperor Honorius refused to defend Britain against increasing attacks and withdrew the legions. Some communities in south-east Britain hired German mercenaries to defend their shores and the distinctions between defenders and invaders soon became less clear-cut.

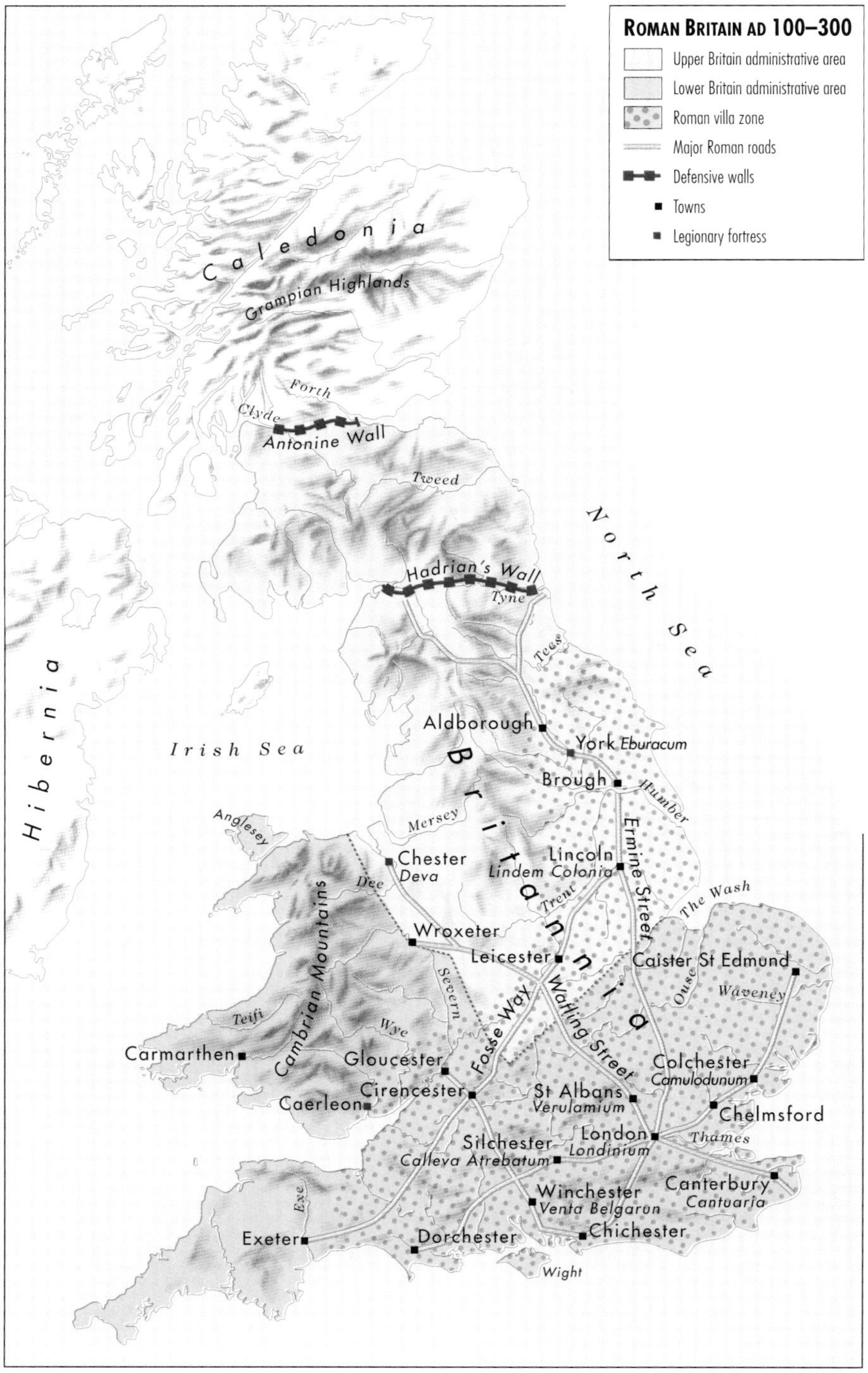

IRON-AGE IRELAND

During the Middle and Later Bronze Age, Ireland was an integral part of the Atlantic trade in metals. Ireland's period of most intensive European links was c.900–800 BC. Trade was conducted with southern Scandinavia, western France, northern and southern Britain, and possibly Spain and the Eastern Mediterranean. It has even been suggested, albeit unconvincingly, that the Celts arrived in Ireland from Spain. A decline appears to have set in after c.700 BC, giving rise to as yet an inexplicable 'dark age' (c.600–300 BC).

▶ **Death of Cuchulain** (c.1940) by J. Junge-Bateman (active 1946–59). Cuchulain (*Cú Chulainn*) is the warrior-hero of the Ulster cycle of stories. The *Cattle Raid of Cooley* (*Táin Bó Cuailnge*) – the longest story in the cycle – tells how Cuchulain single-handedly held off the forces of Queen Medb of Connaught, and defeated Fer Díad, his friend and foster brother. The cycle greatly influenced the development of Arthurian literature.

▼ **Mound of the Hostages** (*Dumha na nGiall*) at Tara, County Meath. This small passage-grave is the earliest (early 3rd millennium BC) of the remains at Tara. According to legend, the coronation stone (*Lía Fáil*) of the kings of Tara once stood on this burial mound.

Land of bronze?

In c.600 BC, the Iron Age began in Ireland, possibly with objects imported from Britain. Native ironworking is presumed to have started soon afterwards, although there is very little, if any, direct evidence of this. One of the conundrums of Irish history is that the arrival of iron-making technology, which many believe synchronous with the advent of the Celts, also coincided with the start of a general social and economic depression which was to last for more than 300 years. Arable and pastoral farming and bronzemaking declined, while pottery-making skills were either lost or fell into disuse.

The use of the term 'Iron Age' with reference to Ireland has more to do with chronology than social or economic reality. The problem is that we simply do not know what was happening, and what was the nature of society in Ireland in the formative centuries of the 'Early Iron Age'. While bronze probably remained the most popular material, iron was smelted and fabricated locally. Iron was mainly used for weapons, but iron horsebits, Y-shaped objects and an iron-sickle have also been found from the pre-Christian era. The appearance and development of the Irish 'scabbard style' in the latter 3rd century BC, marks the introduction of La Tène art in Ireland. This 'scabbard style' was based on British and continental models.

Irish isolation

The Romans chose not to invade Ireland (although one Roman general believed it a task for a single legion), and throughout their occupation of Britain, Ireland remained isolated from the rest of Europe. There was some trade with Britain and, although evidence of Roman sites in Ireland has proved illusory, it appears

that Romanised tourists did visit the megalithic site at Newgrange, County Meath. The Roman artefacts discovered at Newgrange are thought to be votive offerings. Burials provide further evidence of a Roman presence, but the material recovered could represent loot captured by Irish sea-raiders.

Ireland lay largely beyond the scope of Roman geographers, although Ptolemy mapped out the coast, some rivers and reported some tribal names. Thus, we have only two main sources of information about Iron-Age Ireland – archæology, which has its own limitations, and the Ulster myth-cycle, which presents a distorted, and often inaccurate, picture of pagan Celtic Ireland.

The sagas, of which *The Cattle Raid of Cooley* is perhaps best known, make much of such Celtic archetypes as cattle raids, feasting and single combat. They represent an oral tradition which was not written down until the medieval period, and consequently they appear to contain many serious anachronisms. For instance, there is no archæological evidence to support the fearsome and stereotypically Celtic chariots that are described in the sagas – indeed the evidence for wheels of any kind in Iron-Age Ireland is scanty. While they may be valued as ripping good yarns, the Ulster myths make for very unreliable history.

Iron Age sites in Ireland

Archæology has revealed that some groups in Iron-Age Irish society, particularly after *c*.200 BC, were well organised and capable of mobilising a considerable workforce to produce specialised structures. While there is no reason to doubt that Irish society was organised on a tribal basis, no archæological finds can be confidently ascribed to any of the groups named by Roman commentators. Nor, at present, can we be certain that we fully understand the role and function of these structures.

At Navan Fort, County Armagh, on a site occupied since the Bronze Age, a large, circular timber structure

◄ Tubular gold torque found (1896) by a ploughman at Broighter, County Derry. The exquisite decoation of this neck-ring has been created by hammering, and is based on insular-style compass decoration. The elaborate clasp mechanism at the front functions by inserting a key-shaped bar on one side into a corresponding rectangular opening on the other. It dates to *c*.100 BC.

was erected shortly after 100 BC. Measuring 37 metres (121 feet) in diameter and with a single entrance, the structure is usually described as a meeting-place or temple, and may well have been roofed. Shortly after completion, it was filled with stone blocks to a depth of 2.5 metres (8.2 feet), and then set on fire to leave a massive cairn. There is no doubt that this cycle of construction and destruction had enormous significance to the local inhabitants, but we cannot yet explain why.

In 148 BC, according to dendrochronology, a very different kind of structure was built – a two kilometre (1.25 mile) -long roadway across empty wetland – at Corlea, County Longford. With a width of three to four metres (ten to 13 feet), the roadway was much more substantial than similar Bronze-Age timber tracks, and was more massive than contemporary German roads which were intended for wheeled transport. The width of the Corlea roadway does suggest use by at least one vehicle, but no conclusive evidence has so far been found. It is probable that the roadway served some vital ceremonial function, but its exact purpose, and the reason for its abandonment soon after completion, remain a mystery.

► **The Turoe Stone**, found near a small ringfort in Feerwore, County Galway, is one of five decorated monoliths discovered in Ireland. The low-relief designs, more commonly found on metal-work, are characteristic of Irish La Tène art. The carvings include a profusion of triskeles, floral, and trumpet motifs with spirals, palmettes and tendrils predominate. The granite stone, which is 168 centimetres (66.1 inches) high, dates from between the 1st century BC and the 1st century AD. Some experts believe that the piece is an *omphalos* stone, like the one at Delphi, Greece, and that it had some religious significance.

CHAPTER
FOUR

▲ Carpet page to the Gospel of St Matthew from the *Book of Kells* (c.800)

THE DARK AGES

The Dark Ages in Europe (c.AD 450–c.1000) seem doubly dark. During the 5th century, the 'shining light' of Roman civilisation was swept away by barbarian, often pagan, hordes. The Roman Empire – the first unified European super-state – was torn apart and replaced by a patchwork of emergent territories. These events remain obscure because the collapse of the Roman Empire also meant the loss of Roman histories.

Instead of the well-informed and wide-ranging accounts available to their counterparts studying the Romans, modern historians of the Dark Ages have only fragmentary chronicles and annals compiled from much more restricted viewpoints, and often with a marked tendency to embroider fact with fiction. These accounts were, however, generally well intentioned, and the Dark Ages were not completely bereft of historical skills. For instance, in the middle of the 6th century, Italian monks introduced the system of dating years from the birth of Christ (*anno domini*, AD).

A recent theory proposes that the Dark Ages were literally dark, as the result of an environmental disaster, perhaps of global proportions, caused either by a volcanic eruption or meteorite impact in the 6th century. In addition to a few contemporary reports, there is some archaeological evidence of climate change at about this time, and this has been linked to a variety of historical events from epidemics to migrations.

New warriors in Europe

The Germanic migrations had reached equilibrium by the end of the 6th century, and in their wake, Slavs began settling and establishing kingdoms in the Balkans. Other arrivals made even greater journeys. For instance, the Avars, displaced from central Asia by the Turks, migrated westwards and eventually settled in what is now Hungary.

In the 7th century, Arabs, inspired by the new religion of Islam, burst out of their peninsula and swept along the coast of North Africa and, at the beginning of the 8th century, across into Europe. Islamic armies quickly conquered Iberia, but were decisively defeated at the Battle of Tours (732) in west-central France, and confined south of the Pyrenees. Despite this setback against the Franks, Islamic rule continued in parts of Spain until 1492. From the beginning of the 9th century, Scandinavian Vikings raided and settled from Greenland to Constantinople (now Istanbul), and their successor states emerged in the medieval world.

The rise of papal power

The disintegration of the Roman Empire in western Europe enabled the development of a new geopolitical superstructure, broadly similar to that of today. However, much of the underlying social infrastructure of the Empire survived, or was soon re-established.

Despite the imposition of foreign control and culture – Germanic, Islamic or Slav – it was the Romance languages of Spanish, French, Italian and Romanian (all derived from the same dog-Latin) that emerged as the native tongues in those regions. This underlying continuity was strengthened in the west by the gradual extension and consolidation of a 'shadow' Roman Empire – that of the papacy, which claimed absolute control over the minutiae of Christian worship and belief, and, at times, aspired to an equivalent level of political authority. By the beginning of the medieval period, the papacy, wielding the ultimate spiritual sanction of excommunication, had become a secular power increasingly engaged in the rough and tumble of power politics.

Christianity remained a unifying force in Europe throughout the Middle Ages, and was, in many respects, the defining characteristic of a region that became known as 'Western Christendom'. From Christian Europe, Crusades were launched to the Holy Land for prestige and pilgrimage. These energies were soon diverted, however, to the forceful spreading of the word among the Baltic peoples, and the suppression of heresy in southern France. Within Iberia, an internal crusade (the *Reconquista*) gradually pushed Islam southwards

▼ *Pope Gregory I (the Great)* by Carlo Saraceni (c.1580–1620). Pontiff (590–604) in the midst of the Dark Ages, Gregory was the last of the Latin Fathers of the Church. He initiated the conversion of the Lombards in north Italy, and sent Saint Augustine of Canterbury to England convert the Anglo-Saxons. Gregory encouraged monasticism, and his doctrinal writings were influential in the development of scholasticism.

◄ **Battle of Tours** (732). This manuscript illustration depicts Charles Martel's (*c*.688–741) victory over Muslim invaders from Spain. According to legend, the Muslim attack was repelled by Charles' cavalry near Tours, west-central France. The Arab leader Abd-ar-Rahman was killed in the battle, and the Arab forces retreated behind the Pyrenees. Charles' victory is seen as crucial in preventing an Islamic conquest of Frankish lands.

and allowed the kingdoms of Portugal and Spain to emerge. The process was completed in 1492, with the fall of the Islamic enclave of Granada. Western Europe was now entirely under the rule of Christian princes.

Challenges to the papacy

During the 15th century, an explosion of artistic and cultural development in Italy – the Renaissance – was accompanied by a revival of interest in the pre-Christian writings of Greek and Roman authors, especially philosophers. The Renaissance soon spread to other parts of Europe where, armed with new ideas about the role of priests and the Church, some thinkers began to challenge papal authority.

The Catholic Church was in dire need of reform at this time – many of the clergy were corrupt, and the pope was one of the richest princes in Europe. Once inspired by the preaching of Martin Luther (1483–1546), the Reformation swept much of Europe introducing a new, northern brand of Christianity – Protestantism. These events – the Reformation and the rise of Protestantism – mark the end of the medieval period and the beginning of the early modern era.

◄ **Court of Lions** at the heart of the Alhambra palace, Granada, southern Spain. Built between 1238 and 1358, the Alhambra is a masterpiece of Islamic architecture and the chief surviving glory of the Moorish culture in Spain. The Court of Lions, with its delicate columns and marble fountain supported by a circle of carved stone lions, is believed to represent the Islamic idea of paradise. In 1492, the palace was captured by Ferdinand and Isabella of Spain.

GERMANIC INVASIONS

The Romans' failure to conquer Germany was a cause in the downfall of its Empire. Despite the best efforts of Julius Caesar (100–44 BC), Augustus (63 BC–AD 14), Tiberius (42 BC–AD 37), and later emperors, the Romans never controlled more than a small part of southern Germany and a foothold in the north. Although adjacent Germans had been 'tamed' to a considerable extent, beyond their frontiers lay largely unknown territory, within which population accumulated and agglomerated into warrior-bands and confederations. Tension on the borders of Germanic peoples began the process of collapse within the Empire itself.

Population pressures, and the lure of Roman wealth, created a very unstable society in which many groups adopted a semi-permanent state of migration. These groups constantly moved around the perimeter of the Roman world, probing for points of weakness.

Germanic threats

Even in the 2nd century AD, during Rome's 'golden age', the German threat was real and ever present. In the 170s, large numbers of Germanic peoples crossed the middle Danube and penetrated deep into the Empire. One group crossed the Alps and besieged the city of Aquileia on the borders of Italy. Another group attacked the sanctuary of Eleusis in Greece with considerably more success than the Celts at Delphi some 450 years earlier.

The situation deteriorated further in the middle of the 3rd century, when many German groups breached the Danube frontier. In 251, Emperor Decius (c.AD 201–51) was killed in battle against the Goths, who had migrated from southern Scandinavia to the northern Black Sea region. In 268, a concerted Gothic attack was defeated at Niš, Serbia, and other Germanic groups, such as the Alemanni, were driven out of north Italy in the next two years. During this state of emergency, the western part of the Empire came under the control of a short-lived dynasty of 'Gallic' emperors, and Queen Zenobia (d.275?) briefly separated Syria and Egypt from Rome. After 274, the Empire was reunified by Aurelian (c.212–75) and his successors, albeit with the permanent loss of Dacia (now part of Romania).

Goths and Huns

In c.370, the final collapse of the Roman Empire was precipitated by the arrival in southern Russia of large numbers of Huns, warrior equestrians from the eastern steppes near the borders of China. Other peoples were pushed westwards, and both branches of the Goths – Visigoths and Ostrogoths – spilled across the Danube and killed Emperor Valens at the Battle of Adrianople (now Edirne, north-west Turkey) in 378. Faced with this *fait accompli*, the Romans 'permitted' the Goths to settle within the Empire.

In 395, the Roman Empire was separated into western and eastern empires, formally acknowledging

▶ **Hun cauldron** dating from the 4th or 5th century. This bronze vessel was found at Toertel, Hungary. The nomadic lifestyle of the Huns necessitated the making of easily portable cooking vessels such as this cauldron. The Huns were excellent equestrians and the finest examples of their art are items associated with the horse, such as saddles and rugs.

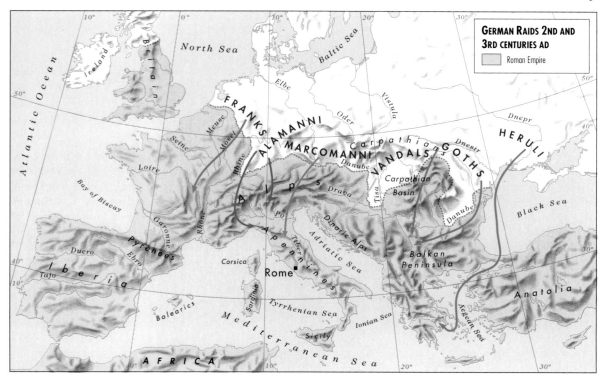

GERMAN RAIDS 2ND AND 3RD CENTURIES AD

☐ Roman Empire

◀ **German invasions** Germanic raids were a constant threat to the Empire during the 3rd and 4th centuries. The northern frontier was breached many times, and some raids penetrated deep into Roman territory before being turned back by a combination of force and bribery.

▶ **German invasions 5th century AD** The distances travelled by the Germanic invaders varied greatly. For instance, the Franks had a relatively short journey, while the Vandals migrated to the opposite shores of the Meditterranean.

a situation that had existed for most of the 4th century. The Eastern (Byzantine) Roman Empire survived and endured for another millennium, but the Western Empire was doomed. In 406, the Rhine frontier was breached and thousands of Germanic warriors flooded into Roman territory. Within 70 years, the city of Rome was sacked three times and the whole of western Europe, with the exception of the extreme western fringes, came under the control of Germanic groups.

The fall of the Roman Empire

During the first decade of the 5th century, the Burgundians established control of central France and the Vandals conquered Spain. In 408–09, the Visigoths, under Alaric (c.370–410), invaded Italy and sacked Rome in 410. Bribed by Pope Innocent I (d.417) to depart, they established a kingdom in southern France, which they used as a platform to invade Spain. The Vandals, led by Gaiseric (d.477), were forced to evacuate to north Africa, where they quickly established control, seizing the city of Carthage in 439. Meanwhile, north-east Gaul came under the control of the Franks, who settled in large numbers. The peasant leader Bagaudae held northwest Gaul, while much of central Gaul was ruled by the Roman General Flavius Aetius (d.454).

During the 440s, the Huns, under their elected leader Attila (d.453), ravaged the Balkans, but were eventually bribed by the Eastern Roman Emperor Theodosius II (410–50) to turn westwards into France. In 451, Attila was defeated by a combined army of Roman and Visigoths under Aetius at the Battle of the Catalaunian Plains, near present-day Châlons-sur-Marne, north-east France. The Huns were deflected into northern Italy, which they continued to plunder until forced to withdraw by Attila's death.

In 455, Vandal raiders sacked Rome and captured Emperor Avitus' (d.456) wife and daughters. In 476, the Empire itself was overthrown when the German mercenary-general Odoacer (c.433–93) seized power from Emperor Romulus Augustulus and declared himself king of Rome. In 493, Odoacer was 'replaced' by the Ostrogoths, who established the kingdom of Italy.

Meanwhile, the Franks had conquered most of Gaul. In 481, Clovis I (c.466–511) established the Merovingian dynasty, which was to conquer the Burgundians and form the basis of the medieval French state. The other newly gained Germanic territories proved less enduring. In 533, the Eastern Roman (Byzantine) Empire crushed the Vandals in north Africa. In the 7th century, the Byzantines themselves were driven out of north Africa by Islamic Arab and Berber armies, who went onto conquer Spain from the Visigoths.

Other groups arrived in the 6th century, causing further disruption. Between 530 and 550, Slavs moved into the Balkans and established territorial kingdoms; and the Avars occupied Carpathia. In 568, the Germanic tribe of Lombards invaded Italy and established a kingdom in the north. By this time, Roman political power was well and truly extinct. Roman political influence was, however, somewhat maintained through conversion of the German rulers to Christianity and the creation of a spiritual 'Roman empire' by the early popes.

▲ *Attila the Hun* by Cristofano dell'Altissimo (1530–c.1605). Above this portrait of Attila appear the words *Flagellum Dei* (Latin, 'scourge of God'). Attila built an empire in the southern Balkans and Greece, before attacking the Western Roman Empire in its heartlands in Italy and Gaul. He reached as far as modern-day Orléans, central France, before being forced to withdraw from Gaul by an army led by the Roman General Aetius and the Visigothic King Theodoric I.

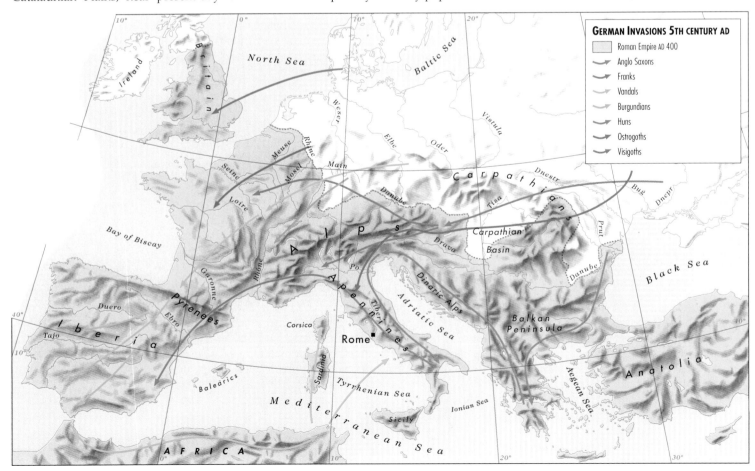

POST-ROMAN BRITAIN

▼ Kingston Brooch dating from the early 7th century. This round fibula is a fine example of the Anglo-Saxon mastery of the craft of *cloisonné*. It is decorated with cuttlefish shells, garnets and lapis lazuli. The brooch was discovered (1771) on Barham Downs, near Kingston, Kent, south-east England.

It was during the Dark Ages, after the Romans had withdrawn, that the Welsh and Scottish nations were created. The birth of these nations took place at the same time as, and was largely contingent upon, the emergence of a larger and more populous nation on their borders – that of the English.

As part of the Roman Empire, Britain had been little affected by the movements of Germanic peoples that had plagued a succession of emperors from the middle of the 2nd century onwards. A well-organised fleet stationed in Britain was sufficiently powerful to protect the coast from invasion; and it was the loss of this fleet, as much as the withdrawal of the Romans legions, that laid the island open to invasion.

In the early 5th century, Germanic peoples, having stormed the rest of the Western Roman Empire, invaded Britain. Those arriving in Britain came across the North Sea from Germany and Denmark. Their numbers included peoples identified as Angles, Saxons and Jutes; and there were undoubtedly smaller numbers of other affiliation, such as Frisians and Franks. Although their origins and areas of settlement were somewhat distinctive, they are most conveniently described as a homogeneous entity – the Anglo-Saxons.

Who were the Anglo-Saxons?

There were already some Germans (mercenaries and perhaps merchants) settled in southern Britain by the

▶ Post-Roman Britain AD **600–700** Anglo-Saxons changed the political map of Britain. In the south-east, new frontiers emerged, as separate kingdoms were established by members of the invading elite. In the rest of mainland Britain, similar 'kingdom-making' processes were at work, in part stimulated by internal population displacements.

BRITAIN AD 600–700
Celtic areas
Angle and Saxon areas

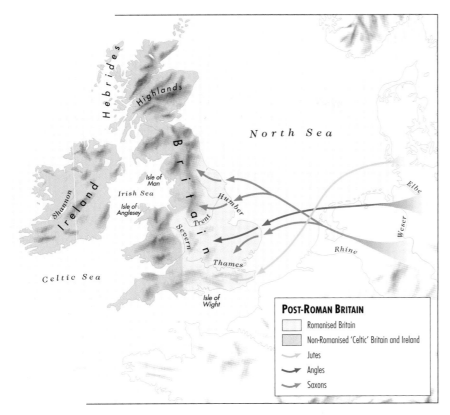

POST-ROMAN BRITAIN

☐ Romanised Britain

▨ Non-Romanised 'Celtic' Britain and Ireland

➤ Jutes

➤ Angles

➤ Saxons

end of the Roman period, but they were there by mutual consent. According to tradition, the first post-Roman settlers were mercenaries invited by Vortigern (active 425–50), king of the Britons, in *c*.449. Soon afterwards, the Anglo-Saxons began forcibly establishing themselves in the Roman heartland of south-east England. In *c*.500, King Arthur supposedly halted their advance at the Battle of Mount Badon (*see* pages 128–129). By *c*.650, Anglo-Saxon expansion had reached the borders of Wales and Scotland. Not withstanding political differences, the Germanic invaders were ethnically mixed bands of adventurers, whose group name often came from their leader.

The invaders' society was hierarchical and strongly competitive. By the end of the 6th century, some of the profligate numbers of small kingdoms were issuing their own coinage. The more powerful of these kingdoms gradually absorbed their neighbours. The Anglo-Saxon kings ruled with the (not always unanimous) consent of a land-owning aristocracy, who in turn exercised authority over free peasants. Outside south-east England, the bulk of the population was British, but the Saxons still dominated. Even in south-east England, there were substantial numbers of British landowners as well as peasants. Although they remained politically divided for some time, the Anglo-Saxon kingdoms soon achieved a cultural unity, and an English nation emerged, speaking a Germanic Anglo-Saxon (Old English) language.

Saint Augustine of Canterbury

The 'creation' of the English was greatly assisted by the reconversion of Britain to Christianity. When the Romans departed, they left behind a nominally Christianised society that was a part of the greater European Church. In the 4th century, for instance, a bishop of London visited an Episcopalian meeting in southern France. Despite the severing of links with Rome by the Anglo-Saxon

▲ **Post-Roman Britain** Farmers from the plain of north Germany found the landscape of eastern Britain (manicured by more than three centuries of Roman activity) greatly to their liking, but they did not initially extend their occupation beyond the Romanised zone.

invasion, Christianity survived in north and west Britain, and even made some Saxon converts.

In 597, Pope Gregory I sent a mission, led by Augustine (d.604?), to convert the population of Britain. Augustine's task was part of a consistent papal policy that, a century earlier, had resulted in the conversion of the Frankish king Clovis I (*c*.466–511).

Augustine landed on the Isle of Thanet, south-east England, effected the conversion of the local king and established Canterbury, Kent, as the enduring centre of British Christianity. Further conversions were attempted along the eastern coast, but success was limited and temporary; Essex soon reverted to Germanic religion and the mission to Northumbria was withdrawn. The Roman mission having faltered, the emergent and largely independent Celtic Church seized the initiative. Between 630 and 660 most of the rest of England was converted by Celtic missionaries and by *c*.680, with the conversion of the last heathens in Sussex, the English were a Christian nation. Latin was once again widely written and spoken, but only within a religious context.

King Offa of Mercia

In 700, England was roughly coterminous with the so-called 'villa zone' established under Roman occupation. Wales and Scotland were developing independently, and the far south-west, although nominally under English control, remained relatively autonomous.

England was by now divided into less than a dozen kingdoms, of which Northumbria and Mercia were the two most important. By the middle of the 8th century, King Offa (d.796) of Mercia was, in effect, king of all England (with the exception of Northumbria). On his authority, a great earthwork (Offa's Dyke) was erected to protect the border with Wales. Such was the extent of Offa's power that Charlemagne, king of the Franks and emperor of the West, treated him as an equal.

ANGLO-SAXON ART

The art styles that the Anglo-Saxons brought to Britain were those of the Germanic migration period. Cloisonné (gold with coloured inlays) was very popular. The richest pieces, such as this shoulder-clasp in gold, garnet and millefiore glass from the Sutton Hoo burial (c.625–30), were inlaid with semi-precious stones. Surfaces were often covered with abstract patterns made from interlocking geometric shapes, such as stepped crosses. The most *distinctive feature was the use of stylised and greatly distorted animal motifs. Sometimes just an animal's face was used for decorative purposes, but usually the whole beast was employed, often in repetitive interlaced patterns, especially around borders.*

LATER CELTIC MIGRATIONS

The Germanic invasion of Britain effectively completed the erasure of Celtic culture that had begun with the Roman occupation, and it was only in those areas where Roman control was ineffectual that Celtic culture survived. However, it would be wrong to think that the surviving Celtic societies were 'frozen' remnants of pre-Roman (or even immediately post-Roman) populations. Significant population transfer within the remaining Celtic fringe accompanied the German invasions.

Most of the movement was from Ireland to the west coast of Britain. Although the numbers involved were insufficient to give the invaders anything more than a local advantage, those who made the journey were often well organised and ambitious.

Gwynedd, Dalriada and Brittany

During the fifth century, the Déisi from south-east Ireland settled on the peninsulas of south-west Wales, and the Féni tried to establish a kingdom on Ynys Môn (Anglesey) and the Lleyn Peninsula in north Wales. According to legend, the Féni were opposed to and defeated by Cunedda, who came from the Firth of Forth area of Scotland. According to tradition, Cunedda and his sons founded the Welsh royal house of Gwynedd.

According to the traditional view, by far the most important of these Irish invasions was that of the Scotti, who migrated from Ulster into western Scotland where they established the enclave of Dalriada as an extension of their Irish kingdom. However, recent studies argue that the Scotti were natives of Dalriada, but were culturally and linguistically closer to Ireland than Scotland. Whatever their origins, in the succeeding centuries the Scotti would, through military prowess and diplomatic skills, establish supremacy over the northern British tribes and make Scotland their own.

The other main movement of Celtic peoples at this time, however, had very little Irish involvement. This was the migration of people from south-west Britain (mainly) and south Wales (to a lesser degree) to

▶ **Baptism of Clovis I**
(c.466–511) from the 15th-century manuscript *Great Chronicle of France*. Our knowlege of Clovis is almost wholly derived from the writings of Bishop Gregory of Tours. According to Gregory, Clovis' converted to Catholicism in c.496, when faced with defeat in his campaign against the Alemanni at Zürich; and defeat turned into victory. In c.498, Clovis was baptised by Saint Remigus of Reims. In his efforts to found a united Merovingian Frankish kingdom, Clovis battled against the Celtic Armoricans of western Gaul, capturing the town of Blois in 491.

◀ **Conan, Duke of Brittany**, on a panel of the Bayeux Tapestry (c.1080). Panicked by news of the approaching Normans, Conan slithers down a rope from Dol Castle. Wearing helmets with nose-pieces and knee-length hauberks of chain mail, the Norman knights give chase past the city of Rennes, north-west France. Conan eventually surrenders at the Castle of Dinan According to the tapestry, William of Normandy defeated Conan before conquering England.

Brittany, north-west France. According to traditional accounts, this was a migration of British peoples fleeing from the Anglo-Saxon advance, but it may have started on a small-scale during the final stages of the Roman Empire. The motives for the migration remain unclear; it may have been shortage of fertile land caused by population increases, opportunism bred by the breakdown in Roman authority, but there may also have been a spiritual element. Christian missionaries from Britain and Ireland were certainly active in Brittany during the post-Roman period, and they may have had druidic predecessors.

Although there is some material evidence of the British invasion, the firmest traces are found in British-style place names, which are concentrated in the north and west of the Breton peninsula. There is considerable debate concerning the nature of the British contribution to the Celtic language in Brittany. Some authorities hold that the British arrival reinforced a Celtic tongue that had survived since before the Roman occupation; others maintain that the British reintroduced a Celtic language to the region.

A further migration has been postulated, perhaps with Irish involvement, from Brittany to north-west Spain. However, while there is some evidence of links between these regions, such as the overtly Celtic monastery of Santa María de Bretona near Mondoñedo, Galicia, north-west Spain, it is unclear whether they represent anything other than Dark-Age missionary activity.

Breton independence

The people of Brittany, known by their language as Bretons, managed to retain some degree of political independence from the French State throughout the Dark Ages and medieval period; and they have retained their spirit of independence until the present day.

Clovis I (c.466–511) defeated the Bretons during his creation of the Frankish state, but the Bretons were never subject to Merovingian taxes or government. Brittany was eventually conquered at the end of the 8th century by Charlemagne (then king of France and soon to be emperor of the West), but it did not long remain under Carolingian control.

In 841, Nomenoë (d.851), duke of Brittany, rebelled against Emperor Charles II (823–77) and, after winning the battle of Ballon (845), forced Charles to recognise the independence of Brittany. Five years later, Nomenoë conquered the towns of Rennes and Nantes and incorporated them into his dukedom.

In the 10th century, the formation of Normandy by the Vikings placed a new threat on Brittany's borders, and Duke Alain Barbetorte (d.952) repulsed an initial Norman invasion. Thereafter, the two states were sometimes at war and sometimes in alliance against rebellious French nobles.

In the early 13th century, a dynastic marriage resulted in an English claim on Brittany, but during the Hundred Years' War (1337–1453) between England and France, the dukes of Brittany maintained an uneasy neutrality. In the 16th century, Brittany became joined to France through marriage and treaty, but was able to maintain a measure of autonomy from the French crown.

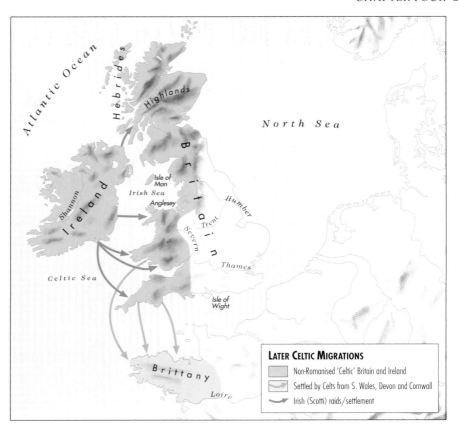

LATER CELTIC MIGRATIONS
Non-Romanised 'Celtic' Britain and Ireland
Settled by Celts from S. Wales, Devon and Cornwall
Irish (Scotti) raids/settlement

▲ **In the post-Roman period**, Irish raiders formed settlements on the west coast of Britain. A small number of Irish may also have migrated from Britain to Brittany.

▼ **Omphalos stone** from Kermaria, near Pont-l'Abbé, Finistère, Brittany (ancient Armorica), north-west France. The granite stone, which dates from the 4th century BC, is decorated with panels of swastikas and meanders, typical of La Tène art. Removed from its original position, the stone's spiritual meaning is unclear.

SCRIPTED STONES

Ogham stones – monoliths bearing simple dedications carved in a unique script – are one of the most unambiguous indications of Celtic culture during the post-Roman period. About 375 ogham stones have so far been identified, mainly in Ireland but also in western Britain and Scotland, and they are all believed to date from the 4th to 8th centuries AD. The ogham script and the phenomenon of the stones are usually considered to be of Irish origin, but this is not certain because the stones straddle the period during which Ireland was Christianised by missionaries from overseas.

The stones and their inscriptions have been familiar to scholars since the medieval period; the earliest key to the translation of the ogham script is found in the 14th-century *Book of Ballymote*.

Location of ogham stones

Of the *c*.300 ogham stones in Ireland, the vast majority (*c*.250) are concentrated in the far south and southwest of the country. In Wales, *c*.40 ogham stones have been found, mainly near the north and south coasts, and there are ten on the Isle of Man; the rest are scattered across Scotland (especially along the west coast), with a few in south-west England. When transcribed, the language of the ogham script is revealed to be Celtic. Many of the Welsh stones carry the same inscription in Latin, although there is only a single instance of a bilingual stone in Ireland.

Inspired by Latin or by sign-language?

There can be little doubt that the ogham script arose through contact with Latin writing (which used a

▶ **Ogham stones** found near Coláiste Íde, Dingle, County Kerry. Ogham script takes its name from Ogma, a Celtic god associated with the magic power of the word. Ogham was probably first used in Ireland in the fourth century AD.

► **Runes** Runic writing, as used by Anglo-Saxons and Scandinavians, was once thought to be a possible source for the ogham script, but this now seems unlikely. Runes are derived from a northern Etruscan script, and were adopted by some Germanic peoples near Europe's North Sea coast about 200 BC. During the early Dark Ages the use of runic alphabets spread to Britain and Scandinavia, where they were widely used for secular inscriptions and magical writing. This inscription on the Rök rune stone in Östergötland, Sweden, uses both the traditional 24-character runic alphabet and a later 16-character version.

modified Greek alphabet) and Roman numerals (which the Romans had devised for themselves). It is reasonable to assume that a single individual or 'school', already literate in Latin, devised the ogham script in order to write simple, standardised formulae in the Celtic tongue. The basic ogham alphabet has 20 letters (including z, which is not used in Celtic), arranged in four groups (*aicme*) of five. This grouping in fives may have been inspired by the five vowels, which come at the beginning of the ogham alphabet, although in a different order to that of Latin.

The letters of the basic alphabet consist of straight line cut across, or at angles to, a baseline that is usually vertical, i.e. the edge of an upright stone. The style of the letters is strongly reminiscent of tally-sticks – small pieces of wood with notches cut across one face representing agreed amounts. An alternative suggestion is that the alphabet derived from some more ancient method of communicating (perhaps secretly or ritualistically) by means of signing.

Subsequently, five more symbols, known as the *forfeda*, were introduced to represent additional sounds. These symbols deviate from the spare elegance of the basic alphabet and do not show any consistent pattern. It seems likely that they were *ad hoc* inventions, collated later.

Reading ogham

Ogham inscriptions are read in a straight line, usually starting at the bottom of a stone, and going up, over, and down the other side if required. The contents of the inscriptions are short, formulaic declarations, usually recording kinship. The most common form is *x* son of *y*, for instance "*Moinena Maqi Olacon*" (Moinena, son of Olacon) or "*Maqi Cairatini Avi Ineqaglasi*" (MacCairthinn, grandson of Enechglass). Some inscriptions record a tribal affiliation, such as "*Bir Maqi Mucoi Rottais*" (Bir, son of the tribe of Rottais). Other inscriptions imply that the

stone has additional significance in representing the spirit (or relics) of the named individual.

The function of ogham stones remains unclear and unproven. The nature of the inscriptions has led to the general belief that they were grave-markers, although not one ogham-inscribed stone has been found in direct association with a burial; but in any case, few if any remain in the original position. There is some evidence that the stones served as boundary markers, but whether this was the original intention is unknown. It is quite likely that the stones were multifunctional, because burial implies a strong territorial connection; although whether the burial site represents heartland or frontier is open to question.

The other great uncertainty about ogham stones is whether they originated among pagan or Christian societies. About one in six of the ogham stones in Ireland carries an inscribed cross – some inscriptions refer directly to the Christian priesthood – and at least one in three of the stones are associated with early Christian sites. The earliest of the cross-marked stones probably constitutes the first physical evidence of Christianity in Ireland.

Some stones, however, show evidence that the crosses were a later addition, and in a few cases, tribal affiliations appear to have been deliberately defaced. This may represent the Christianisation of earlier pagan memorials, or it may simply be the result of the over-enthusiastic rededication of Christian sites. According to early Irish literature, such as the *Cattle Raid of Cooley* ('Tain Bo Cuailnge'), the ogham script was also used to carve messages into pieces of wood.

► **Ogham alphabet** Ogham inscriptions were carved on the edges of graves or memorial stones. The black vertical line on the chart represents the edge of a stone. Five characters (*forfeda*) were added to the basic 20 letter alphabet. Its strange alphabetic order suggests a link with Latin. Each character has a name: for instance, 'b' is *beithe* (birch) and 'd' is *dair* (oak).

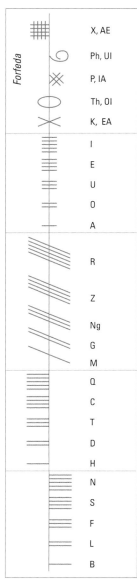

Forfeda		X, AE
		Ph, UI
		P, IA
		Th, OI
		K, EA
		I
		E
		U
		O
		A
		R
		Z
		Ng
		G
		M
		Q
		C
		T
		D
		H
		N
		S
		F
		L
		B

CHRISTIAN IRELAND

The rapid conversion of Ireland to Christianity in the 5th century is usually attributed to the divinely inspired mission of Patrick the Briton, beginning in either 432 (the traditional date) or 455 (a date preferred by some modern historians). However, the *Chronicle* of Prosper of Acquitaine (*c.*390–*c.*463) clearly states that Pope Celestine I (d. 432) sent Palladius as the "first bishop of the Irish believers in Christ" in 431.

At the beginning of the 5th century, it is certain, therefore, that there were sufficient numbers of Christians living in Ireland to attract the pope's attention and to make a mission viable. Most of these Christians were slaves captured, like Patrick himself, in raids on the British coast, while others were converted by missionaries from Roman Gaul and Britain.

The influence of Rome and Christianity

Throughout the Roman period, Ireland remained almost completely isolated. There was some trade with the Roman world, but not of any great importance. Few Roman artefacts have been found, and there is no evidence of Roman settlement. It was only after the collapse of the Roman Empire, when the rest of Western Europe was reeling from 'barbarian' (Germanic) invasions, that Ireland became again subject to foreign influence and reconnected culturally with the rest of the continent.

The arrival of Christianity marked a change in the material, as well as the spiritual, life of the Irish people – a new type of plough and water mill both came into widespread use at about this time. Associated with these technological innovations from the Roman world was an increase in arable and pastoral farming, and a consequent rise in population – the most dramatic signs of which are the tens of thousands of raths (popularly known as ringforts) scattered across the Irish landscape.

Hillforts had been built in Ireland since the Bronze Age (*see* pages 94–95), as strongholds or centres of power. Between *c.*AD 600 and 900, individual farmers constructed smaller – *c.*30m (100ft) in diameter – enclosures with earthen ramparts around their family homestead. Usually these raths were built within sight of a similar, neighbouring ringfort. We poorly understand the reasons for this change in the pattern of settlement, but some suggest a link with the Celtic Irish 'sport' of cattle raiding.

The first churches (more strictly, monasteries) in Ireland followed this new pattern – behind the ramparts lay an enclosure in which stood three wooden buildings: living quarters, a church or oratory, and a kitchen-cum-refectory. These wooden buildings have long-since rotted away, but the earliest stone churches (which probably date from the 7th and 8th century) are, in effect, 'petrified wood' constructions. Their arching shape preserves the form dictated by the curved timbers used in the original construction.

▼ **The hermitage of Skellig Michael** is perhaps the best preserved of all early Irish monasteries. Built in the 6th–9th centuries, it is perched on South Peak, a narrow, windswept ridge on the island of Skellig Michael, off the coast of Kerry, southern Ireland. The monks lived in small, beehive-shaped cells made of piled stones.

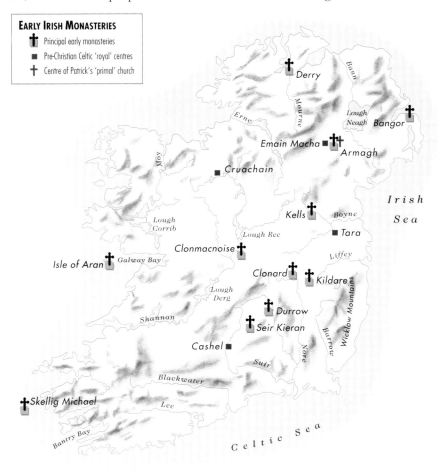

EARLY IRISH MONASTERIES
- ✝ Principal early monasteries
- ■ Pre-Christian Celtic 'royal' centres
- ✝ Centre of Patrick's 'primal' church

▶ **Early Irish monasteries**
Early Christians in Ireland had little enthusiasm for a Church hierarchy organised like the Roman Empire, and monasteries soon became the most important components of Irish religious life. In addition to their missionary work, some monasteries also became centres of artistic and economic activity.

◄ **Church of Saint Benignus** (*Teampall Bheanáin*) on the isle of Inishmore (*Inis Mór*), Aran Islands, off the west coast of Ireland. The church was built in the 6th century. Benignus (d. c.467), the son of Sechnaa, a chief in Meath, was baptised by Saint Patrick and succeeded his mentor as chief bishop of Ireland (461–67). He converted the Irish in Clare, Kerry and Connaught. According to tradition, Benignus assisted in compiling the Irish *Code of Laws* (*Senchus Mór*), and contributed to the *Psalter of Cashel* and the *Book of Rights*.

Foundation of the Church in Ireland

Patrick founded the Church in Ireland along Roman lines, placing power in the hands of bishops. By tradition, he established the first Irish bishopric in 444 at Armagh, near the 'royal' Celtic centre of Emain Macha. Within a decade or two, several other bishoprics had been established, and Armagh was promoted to the primal See. By the end of the century, however, the Irish Church was a Church dominated by monasteries rather than bishops. A monastic church was better suited to the rural settlement pattern of Ireland than church-based bishoprics.

The monastic ideal came not from Rome, but from the Sinai Desert in Egypt, and it spread rapidly through the early Church – despite the opposition of the Fathers of the Church in Rome, who viewed the monastic movement with great suspicion. Even during his lifetime, Patrick was aware of the popularity of monasticism among his newly converted flock, and commented in his journal that, "the sons of the Irish and the daughters of chieftains who were monks and virgins (nuns) of Christ, I am unable to enumerate."

Shortly after Patrick's death (c.461), the ecclesiastical rule of bishops collapsed. By the beginning of the 6th century, Armagh had become a monastic centre, and another important monastery had been founded at Kildare, Leinster, supposedly by Brigit (d. c.524–28). In c.520, Enda founded the island monastery of Aranmore (Inishmore or *Inis Mór*) off the west coast of Ireland, and Finnian, who trained in Wales, founded the great monastery at Clonard, County Meath (of which not a trace remains today). In 548, Enda and Finnian's pupil, St Ciaran (c.516–c.549) founded the great abbey of Clonmacnoise, County Offaly.

The 'golden age' of Irish monasticism had begun, and it would not long be confined to Ireland. In c.563 Columba, who trained at Clonard, sailed to Britain and established the monastery of Iona, off the west coast of Scotland. In the early 6th century, other Irish monasteries were established on the east coast of Britain, while Kevin (d.618) strengthened the monastic tradition in Ireland itself by founding a monastery at Glendalough, County Wicklow. (*For further details on the influence of the Irish Church, see pages 118–125*)

SAINT PATRICK

The Apostle of Ireland was probably born in south Wales of Romanised Christian parents. When a teenager, Patrick was kidnapped by Irish raiders and spent six years as an agricultural slave in Ulster. Inspired by a dream, he escaped by ship to France, and from there journeyed back to Britain. Some years later, another dream inspired him to return to Ireland as a missionary. Scholars can be certain of very little about Patrick's life, and the ancient sources are unreliable. On balance, it seems likely that the tradition holds some elements of historical reality. However, given the abrupt transition from paganism and other profound social changes in Ireland, it would be extremely unlikely if the nature of the conversion had not become embroidered and immeshed with older beliefs and legends.

THE IRISH CHURCH IN BRITAIN

► **Statue of St Aidan** on Lindisfarne, north-east England. In 635, under the protection of King Oswald of Northumbria, Aidan founded a monastery and church on the island. He also established a training centre for church ministers, including Chad (first bishop of Lichfield), his brother Cedd (who converted the East Saxons), and Eata, abbot of Melrose.

▼ **Lindisfarne Abbey** off the coast of Northumberland, north-east England. Lindisfarne's importance as a religious centre dates from AD 635, when St Aidan established a church and monastery there. St Cuthbert (634/5–87), the great evangeliser of Northumbria, was bishop of the Benedictine abbey of Lindisfarne. His body and the fabulous 7th-century Lindisfarne Gospels were both removed to Durham Cathedral to protect them from Viking attack. The monastery was abandoned in 875.

In the 4th century, towards the end of the Roman occupation, Britain became nominally Christianised, and the new religion survived in some areas, such as south Wales. Early missionary work had also established some isolated Christian centres in other remote parts of Britain. In *c*.400, for example, Ninian (*c*.360–*c*.342) is supposed to have founded a church at Whithorn, south-west Scotland. Although these British centres were influential overseas, they had little effect on the vast majority of the population, both British and Anglo-Saxon. Britain became Christianised later, largely through the missionary work of the Irish.

The Celtic Church that was exported from Ireland in the 6th century was monastic in character, although it retained some vestiges of Episcopalian organisation. Monasticism and Christianity circulated around the Celtic fringes before finally reaching a nascent England. The origins of Saint Patrick aside, Ireland acquired monasticism from Wales, which in turn received it from Egypt via Gaul at the end of the Roman period. From Ireland, monasticism spread to Scotland and from there into north-east England.

The monasteries of Iona and Lindisfarne
Columba (*c*.521–97) was a member of the ruling O'Donnell family in Ulster, which was allied to the rulers of Dalriada in western Scotland. After being ordained in

c.551, he founded the Irish monasteries of Daire Calgaich, Derry, and Dair-magh, Durrow. In *c*.563, Columba travelled to Dalriada with a group of followers, and built a monastery and church on the island of Iona, off the west coast of Scotland. The community on Iona soon became the centre for missionary work among the Picts, and several subsidiary communities were established. In *c*.616, Oswald (*c*.603–*c*.642), a claimant to the throne, was exiled from Northumbria, north-east England, and sought refuge on Iona, where he probably received religious instruction and may have been converted.

After he became king in *c*.633, Oswald of Northumbria accepted a mission from the Roman Church via southern England, and formally accepted Christianity. When this mission was withdrawn soon afterwards, Oswald requested that Iona supply him with a new bishop. In 635, Saint Aidan (d.651), a monk at Iona, established a monastery on Lindisfarne (Holy Island) off the coast of Northumbria.

Lindisfarne almost immediately became the centre for a wave of Celtic missionary activity that swept through most of central England during the late 630s, at the same time as Roman missionary work in the south was faltering. In Wessex, the Irish monk Maildubh founded a hermitage at Malmesbury that soon became an abbey. Other Irish monks established communities at Glastonbury, Somerset, and at Burgh Castle, Suffolk. Between *c*.640 and *c*.660, the Celtic

Church reigned supreme north of an imaginary line between the Severn estuary and Essex. Furthermore, large numbers of English Christians travelled to Ireland for the sake of their souls.

Rivalry of the Celtic and Roman Churches

The rivalry between the two branches of Christianity over the rather obscure matter of the date of Easter was finally settled. The Celtic Church, following the example of the early Church, calculated the date of Easter according to astronomical observations performed in a certain manner. The Roman Church had since adopted another, supposedly 'improved', method of calculating the date.

The date of Easter was the subject of intense learned controversy, and the Irish Church, having sent a delegation to Rome to investigate the matter, had officially adopted the revised method in the 630s. The Celtic Church in Britain, however, had not followed this initiative. The matter came to a head when the king of Northumbria found that he and his new wife were celebrating Easter on different days.

At the Synod of Whitby (664), Northumbria chose to side with Rome, and the rest of Britain had little option but to follow. In 669, the English Church imposed fixed bishoprics with clear boundaries and rules against interference in other sees, instead of bishops who assumed a more mobile mandate in the Celtic manner. The clergy in Scotland, however, retained their Celtic organisation until the arrival of the Normans.

Survival of Celtic Christianity

Although spiritual power had passed to Canterbury, the Celtic Church in Britain remained a vital force. Although other English kingdoms, such as Mercia, became politically more powerful, Northumbria remained the intellectual and artistic capital of England, largely because of Lindisfarne, where the influential Hiberno-Saxon art style developed at the beginning of the 8th century (*see* pages 120–121). Other important centres included the monastery at Jarrow, home to the historian Bede (672/3–735), and the school at York where the scholar Alcuin (c.732–804) – teacher of Emperor Charlemagne (c.742–814) at Aachen, northwest Germany – was educated.

▲ **St Martin's Cross** and the Cathedral of St Mary on the island of Iona, off the west coast of Scotland. The granite cross, which is 4.3 metres (14 feet) high, dates from sometime in or before the 10th century. At the bottom of its western shaft there is an Celtic inscription, which reads "OROIT DO GILLACRIST DORINGNE T CHROS SA" ("A prayer for Gillacrist who made this cross'). The Cathedral was founded by St Columba in c.563, but no traces of the original building remain – the present cathedral was built in the 13th century.

LINDISFARNE AND IONA
✝ Monastery

▲ **Lindisfarne and Iona** Irish monastic missionary zeal established two footholds for the early Celtic Church – at Iona (mid-6th century) and Lindisfarne (mid-7th century). These monasteries were central to the early Christianisation of northern Britain, independently of papal influence.

◀ **St Columba** sailing (c.563) with his twelve disciples to the island of Iona off the west coast of Scotland. Columba, known as the Apostle of Caledonia, worked to convert the Picts to Christianity. He also inaugurated Aidan MacGabrain of Dunadd (d. c.608) as king of Dalriada. In c.575, Columba returned to Ireland with Aidan in order to formalise relations between Dalriada and Ireland. Columba's life and work were first outlined by Adamnan (c.628–704), the ninth abbot of Iona.

ILLUMINATED MANUSCRIPTS

During the Dark Ages and Early Middle Ages, the monasteries were the equivalent of today's universities and publishing houses. Literacy was a far rarer phenomenon than Christian belief, and the preservation and increase of both required a constant supply of appropriate reading material – not only the gospels, but also Psalters, missals, hymnals, and lives of the saints. These were painstakingly produced by countless hours of monkish labour, hand-copied word by word, day after day.

Each page of a manuscript – by now they were cut and bound into books, rather than kept as scrolls – represented a considerable investment of time and expense. A sheepskin had to be scraped and cured to provide a sheet or two of vellum (parchment), and a suitable supply of ink obtained. Aside from the skills of the copyists, who may not have been able to read everything that they copied, every page had to be closely compared with the original to check and double-check for errors and omissions.

The monkish tradition of making manuscript copies began in the scriptoria of the first Egyptian monasteries, which themselves followed even older traditions of scholarship. Monasticism facilitated the dissemination of manuscripts across western Europe. It should be emphasised, however, that the material produced was very definitely not for public consumption. Outside of the monasteries, possession of written material was restricted to the ruling élite, or their closest advisers, and usually represented gifts to generous patrons or specific commissions. As such, they were intended to both please the eye and refresh the soul. From the viewpoint of economics, illustrated manuscripts can be seen as resulting from local surpluses of monkish labour that could be mobilised to the production of prestigious objects for a tiny but influential market.

The decoration, or illumination, of manuscripts, with an elaborated initial letter to the first word of each gospel, began during the Late Roman period and was later enhanced and developed in various regional 'schools'. The illuminated manuscripts produced by the Celtic Church are considered among the finest examples of Early Christian art. The continuity of Christian iconography means that we can readily comprehend both the symbolism and overtly higher purpose of this later flowering of Celtic art, while the deeper meaning of La Tène art and artefacts remains shrouded in obscurity.

Celtic manuscripts

During the 6th century, Irish calligraphers developed a distinctive 'Celtic' half-uncial (upper-case cursive) script, and by the beginning of the 7th century they had also developed a distinctive style of illumination. Some of the earliest features of this Celtic style are found in the *Cathach* (Gaelic *"Battler"*, Royal Irish Academy, Dublin) attributed to Saint Columba, where the initial letters are distorted in shape and outlined with contour dotting. Other distinctive elements were the innovation of carpet pages (retrospectively so-described because their intricate, abstract designs resembled Oriental carpets) and the use of the spiral motif.

The *Book of Durrow* (Trinity College Library, Dublin) is the earliest masterpiece of Celtic illumination. The book, which contains the four gospels, was produced (probably in Northumbria) in *c.*AD 650–700. The illuminations – carpet pages, the symbols of the Evangelists, and initial letters – are boldly painted in vivid colours (red, yellow and green) that echo the enamelled metalwork of the period. The decoration around the central motifs of the carpet pages makes imaginative use of interlacing designs. The simple, interlacing ribbon design on some pages follows Celtic traditions, while the animal interlacing on one page probably reflects Anglo-Saxon influences in Northumbrian culture.

The *Lindisfarne Gospels* (British Museum, London), produced in *c.*698, represent the establishment of a new, composite Hiberno-Saxon style of decoration. Here, the interlaced ribbons have metamorphosed into

▼ The *Book of Kells* (*c.*800) is a masterpiece of European art. Shown here is the carpet page to the Gospel of St Matthew (MS 58, fol.32v). The illustration depicts Christ with four angels. It is thought that the manuscript was begun on the island of Iona and completed at the monastery at Kells (now Ceanannus Mór), County Meath. The *Book of Kells* contains 680 pages (all illustrated), and measures 330 × 255 millimetres (13 × 10 inches).

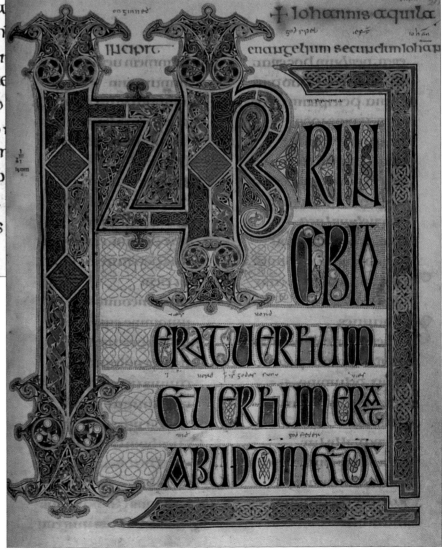

◄ Book of Durrow (c.650–700)
Shown here is the initial page of the Gospel of St Mark (MS 57, fol.86r). This masterpiece of Hiberno-Saxon illumination was produced at the Columban Monastery in Durrow, County Offaly, west Ireland. The interlaced ribbon and spiral pattern draws on the designs of La Tène metalwork and Merovingian and Anglo-Saxon jewellery. The manuscript measures 245 × 145 millimetres (9.6 × 5.7 inches).

▼ Lindisfarne Gospels (c.698)
Shown here is the portrait page to the Gospel of St John (Cott. MS Nero D. iv, f.209v). The Lindisfarne Gospels are an eclectic mix of Irish, classical and Byzantine art styles and, with the *Book of Kells* (c.800), contain the most famous instances of the Insular half-uncial script. The manuscript is thought to have been written and illuminated by Eadfrith, Bishop of Lindisfarne monastery (698–721), and bound by his successor (724–740), Aethelwald. In 875, the *Gospels* accompanied the monks of Lindisfarne on their flight from the Danes, finally finding safe storage at Durham in 996. The manuscript probably lost its original binding during the Dissolution of the Monasteries in the 1530s. The *Gospels* consist of 259 folios, measuring 340 × 250 millimetres (13.5 × 9.75 inches).

narrow threads, and are combined with elaborate spirals and stylised birds and beasts. Small portraits of the Evangelists, as found in contemporary Italian manuscripts, are also included for the first time.

The *Book of Kells* (Trinity College Library, Dublin) was probably begun on Iona in the early 9th century but, before all the illuminations were finished, it was transported to Ireland to preserve it from Viking raids. The illustrations in the *Book of Kells* combine the full range of Hiberno-Saxon semi-abstract designs with large, naturalistic pictures, some populated by groups of saintly figures, within architecturally derived frames. The initial letters are greatly enlarged and form elaborate, sprawling designs that dominate and even obscure the text. Other important sections of text are illuminated and some pages bear small animal illustrations in the margins.

EARLY MEDIEVAL IRELAND

Sagas such as the Ulster myths provide the only documentary evidence of events in Ireland in the early centuries AD. These literary accounts tend to support the notion that the country was slowly coalescing, although full union was not achieved until the very end of the 10th century.

During the Early Medieval period, Ireland was divided into seven primary kingdoms, which together comprised *c*.100 *tuatha* (petty kingdoms/clans). Through marriage, alliance and warfare, two dynasties were able to establish supremacy over the others. In the northern half of the country, the *Uí Néill* (O'Neill's) ruled from Tara, County Meath, and claimed the high-kingship of all Ireland. The *Uí Néill* were, however, unable to subjugate the *Eóghanachta*, who occupied the royal seat at Cashel, County Tipperary, and ruled the south. Both of these rival dynasties claimed descent from Niall Noigiallach (Niall of the Nine Hostages), the quasi-historical Ulster raider-king who supposedly reigned from 379 to 405 – towards the end of the myth-cycle period.

Raths and crannogs

Although the royal courts and the early monasteries provided the basis for a few small settlements, Ireland was a completely rural country at this time, and there were no real towns until the Vikings founded Dublin (*Baile Átha Cliath*) in *c*.831, and refounded it in 917.

The basic unit of settlement was the rath or ringfort, an enclosed farmstead. The rath was the home of a *bóaire* (cow-lord), whose wealth was measured in cattle and *cumals* (bondswomen). The 'cow-lord' owed allegiance to his kin, to the chief of his clan, to his overlord, and, in theory, to the high-king of Ireland. However, such lofty matters will have had little impact on everyday life, and the day-to-day devilment of his neighbours will have been of much greater concern.

Some of the nearly 40,000 raths so far identified have a souterrain, an underground chamber approached through a passage. The function of souterrains, such as those at Loughrea, County Galway, have been widely discussed, and it seems generally agreed that, while their main function was as storage areas, the presence of rear entrances indicates that they also served as human refuges from raiding parties.

Another significant settlement type was the crannog – an artificial lake-island surrounded by a wooden palisade – of which *c*.1200 have so far been discovered. The origin of the Irish crannogs is hotly debated, and some authorities assert that they represent a continuation from similar Bronze Age sites. The latest research suggests that the earlier sites were established on the sides of natural lakes or islands. True crannogs seem to have been built in Ireland only from about the end of the 6th century. It has been suggested that the idea was imported from Scotland, where they seem to have been built since Early Roman times, through contacts with Dalriada. Judging by the quality and quantity of artefacts recovered from many crannogs compared with raths, it seems likely that some crannogs, which required much greater efforts of construction, were the homes of a middle-level élite.

▼ **Cross of the Scriptures** and round towers at Clonmacnoise, County Offaly, west Ireland, engraving (1860s) from *Scenery and Antiquities of Ireland* by George Virtue. In 548/9, St Ciaran founded a monastery at Clonmacnoise. The Cross of the Scriptures (left) was erected in the 9th century, and is one of the finest of all Irish high crosses. It stands 4.6 metres (15 feet) tall. The west face (shown here) depicts scenes from the Passion and Death of Christ, as well as the Crucifixion. The round tower on the right is said to have to have been built by Fergal O'Rourke (d.964). The smaller McCarthy's Tower dates from the 12th century. Clonmacnois was a great centre of learning, and many manuscripts, including the *Book of the Dun Cow* (12th century), were written here.

Monasteries and stonemasons

The monasteries, with their associated farms and workshops, will have provided the closest approximation of urban life, and certainly formed the largest population clusters. A symbolic low rampart (*valla*) enclosed some monasteries, and there are records of monastic disputes over land. The increasing secularisation of the monasteries seems to have provoked an anchorite (seclusive) reform movement during the 8th century.

The fabric of everyday life remained homemade, bronze was used in abundance and many bone items, such as combs and pins, have been discovered. Coins were not used in Ireland until the Vikings introduced them in 997. Local production of pottery, which restarted in the 8th century after a break of more than a millennium, was at first limited to the far north-east. These crude, non-wheel thrown pots are known as souterrain ware.

The one major 'industry' that flourished in Early Medieval Ireland, was stonemasonry. Apart from the monastic buildings and churches (now all in ruins), the stonemasons produced two of the most enduring monuments of Ireland: the high crosses and round towers.

High crosses, monumental stone crosses at monastic sites, are found in Ireland, Iona, Islay and Northumbria. Their distinctive shape is believed to have originated with circular metal reinforcements for wooden processional crosses, and some of the decorative elements carved into the sandstone crosses originated with metalworkers. The earliest crosses, from Ahenny, carry only limited illustration, and do not have a central crucifixion scene. Later high crosses, such as the Cross of the Scriptures at Clonmacnoise, County Offaly, have carved scenes on nearly every surface.

From the early 10th century, round towers were built at monastic sites, and *c*.80 are still extant. Although the earliest towers may have been intended as bell-towers, they were undoubtedly used as watchtowers and places of refuge – most have a single entrance, three to four metres (10 to 13 feet) above ground level.

▲ **Muiredach's Cross** at Monasterboice, Louth, east Ireland. The cross, which is 4.9 metres (16 feet) high, dates from the 8th or 9th century. At the centre of the west face is a depiction of the crucifixion of Christ. The three panels on the shaft show (from the top) Christ as ruler of the world, Doubting Thomas, and Ecce Homo.

▲ **Glendalough Tower** in County Wicklow, east Ireland. The monastery at Glendalough was founded in the 6th century by St Kevin, and was destroyed by English troops in 1398. Construction of the Round Tower was begun in the 10th century. It is *c*.34 metres (112 feet) high, and 16 metres (52 feet) in circumference at the base.

▼ **High crosses and round towers** Surviving crosses and towers reveal the widespread distribution of the material and organisational skills required for their construction in Early Medieval Ireland. Then, as now, these skills were concentrated in the areas of richest farmland in the south-east of Ireland.

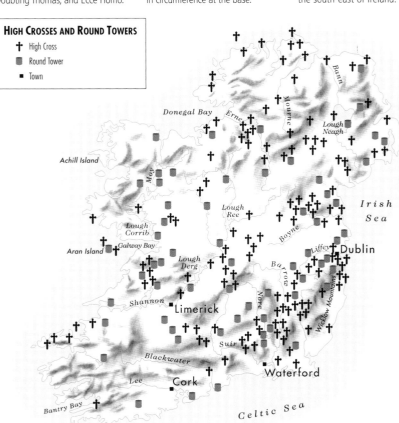

HIGH CROSSES AND ROUND TOWERS
† High Cross
▪ Round Tower
▪ Town

CELTIC CHRISTIANITY IN EUROPE

At the same time as the Celtic Church was spreading across Scotland and England, Irish missionary monks were also active in mainland Europe. Combining scholarship, religious zeal and austerity, they played an important role in the revival of monasticism in western Europe during the 7th century.

Saints Columban, Gallen and Fursey

One of the earliest, and certainly the most celebrated, of the Irish missionaries to Europe was Saint Columban (c.543–615). In 591, Columban left Bangor, County Down, with a group of companions, and travelled to central France where he established a community at Annegray in the Vosges Mountains, and soon founded another monastery at Luxeuil, Burgundy. In 602, he was summoned before an ecclesiastical court because of his adherence to the Irish method of calculating the date of Easter. Eight years later, he was driven out of France because of the Easter controversy, and made his way to Switzerland, where his companion Saint Gallen (c.550–c.645) founded a hermitage (at present-day Sankt Gallen) that later became a monastery. Columban then journeyed to northern Italy and established a monastery at Bobbio, where he died. In the wider context of western Europe, Saint Columban is considered (along with Saint Benedict) to be one of the founders of European monasticism.

Another early Celtic missionary was Saint Fursey (c.567–650), who, in c.633, travelled from Ireland to England and established the monastery of Cnoberesburgh (near present-day Yarmouth,

Norfolk). Fursey then crossed to northern France where he founded a monastery at Lagny, near Paris. Fursey was something of a mystic and a visionary; he became famous even during his lifetime, and the English historian Bede (673–735) later reported his visions. His shrine at Péronne, Picardie, soon became a place of pilgrimage, and the monastery there remained a centre of Irish Christianity until the 8th century.

Dominance of Benedictines

Irish monastic influence slowly declined over the following centuries, as more and more religious communities adopted the rules of Saint Benedict, which carried full papal approval, and which was imposed in France and north Germany by Emperor Charlemagne at the beginning of the 9th century. Irish scholarship, however, remained at the very heart of European affairs, and Irish clerics became the teachers of princes and emperors.

Irish scholars and the Carolingian Renaissance

During the 9th century, when Celtic monasticism was in decline, Europe received a second wave of Irish Christians because of the Viking attacks on the homelands of the Celtic Church. Many Irish scholars travelled to the mainland in order to escape the Viking threat, and congregated at the centres of power and learning, where they made a considerable contribution to the political and intellectual debates of the day.

The Irish scholar Dicuil (active early 9th century) was one of the outstanding figures at the Carolingian

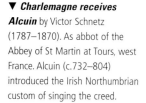

▼ **Charlemagne receives Alcuin** by Victor Schnetz (1787–1870). As abbot of the Abbey of St Martin at Tours, west France. Alcuin (c.732–804) introduced the Irish Northumbrian custom of singing the creed.

▼▶ **Flight into Egypt** (1475) from the Gothic *Schotten* altar in the *Schottenkirche*, Vienna, Austria. The *Schottenkirche* was built (as a monastery) in 1200, by Irish monks from St Jakob's monastery in Regensburg, south-east Germany.

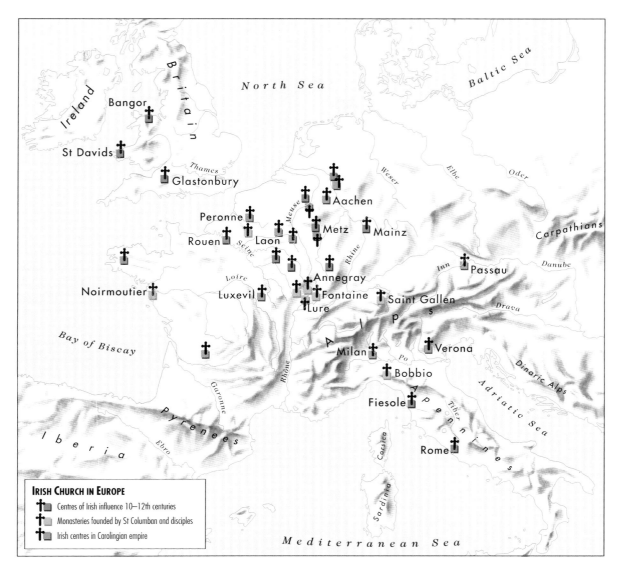

◄ Irish Church in Europe
Monastic revival in mainland Europe was greatly influenced by 7th-century Irish missionaries such as Columban and his companion Gallen. Subsequently, Irish scholars became part of the intellectual élite at the courts of the Carolingian empire, which was formally established by Charlemagne at the beginning of the 9th century.

IRISH CHURCH IN EUROPE

✝ Centres of Irish influence 10–12th centuries

✝ Monasteries founded by St Columban and disciples

✝ Irish centres in Carolingian empire

court during the 820s. By trade an astronomer and mathematician, Dicuil's consuming interest was geography. His great treatise *De mensura orbis terrae* ("Concerning the Measurement of the World") demonstrates familiarity with more than 30 Greek and Roman texts, but also includes the most up-to-date geographical information. Dicuil's work contains, perhaps with patriotic pride, the first European report on the discovery of Iceland (*c*.795) by Irish hermits – holy voyagers in search of perfect spiritual solitude.

By the mid-9th century, Irish scholars were to be found across most of northern France and Germany. At Liège, Belgium, the Irish poet Sedulius Scottus was widely admired for his mastery of Latin metres and ornate, sophisticated language. His elaborate poems mainly sing the praises of Lothair II, king of Lotharingia (*c*.835–69) or his patron, the bishop of Liège. Sedulius was also a grammarian and biblical scholar of some renown and he made comparative studies of Greek texts.

At the court of Charles II (823–77), king of the West Franks and later Emperor of the West, in Laon, Picardie, the Irish theologian and philosopher Johannes Scotus (*c*.810–77), called Erigena ("belonging to the people of Erin'), emerged as one of the most notable thinkers of the early medieval period. Although formally employed as master of the palace

school from *c*.850, his principal task was to translate and provide commentary on the Neoplatonist works of Pseudo-Dionysus the Areopagite (supposedly a disciple of Saint Paul). Like many of his learned contemporaries, Erigena was overwhelmingly concerned with the integration of reason and belief.

Schottenklöster

Along the eastern fringes of the Western Roman Empire, Irish missionaries and monks continued to play an important role as the German peoples consolidated their hold on the region. Travelling south-east from centres such as Bremen on the North Sea coast, Irish Benedictine monks established so-called *Schottenklöster* ('Irish monasteries') into the 12th century. However, these monks were much worldlier than were their Celtic Church predecessors.

By this time, the Church in Ireland had become a hereditary institution, whose members were allowed to marry and divorce, and was in sore need of the Gregorian reforms that began in the mid-12th century. Furthermore, the communities in southern Germany found themselves inextricably involved in the petty wars that accompanied the struggle between the German emperors and the papacy. As Benedictines on German soil, both sides laid claim to their allegiance.

▼ Charles II (1587–88) by Filippo Ariosto. By the Treaty of Verdun (843), Charlemagne's empire was partitioned into three regions, with Charles II receiving Francia Occidentalis. Charles was forced to cede independence to the Bretons, led by Nomenoë.

LATER CELTIC ART

▶ Irish enamelled brooch found in the River Shannon, County Westmeath. Produced in the 6th or 7th century, the brooch owes its shape to Roman influences, but the flow of curves and counter-curves is firmly in the spirit of Celtic craftwork from a thousand years earlier.

▼ The Tara Brooch found at Bettystown, County Meath, east Ireland. Perhaps the most celebrated piece of Celtic Irish jewellery, it was probably produced in the 8th century. The brooch is made of silver, embellished with gold strips, amber, amethyst and enammelled studs. The circle is *c.*8 centimetres (3.1 inches) in diameter, and the pin is 25 centimetres (9.84 inches) in length. Around the jewels on the front of the brooch are fierce beasts designed in delicate filigree of gold wire. The elaborate spiral, interlaced and zoomorphic patterns are similar to those found in the *Lindisfarne Gospels*, while the corner lobes recall the illuminations in the *Book of Durrow*.

The last great phase of Celtic art – which was, for all practical purposes, Irish – flourished at a time when the Church had established a virtual monopoly over artistic output, both intellectually and at a practical level. Ideally, human endeavour was for the greater glory of God, and the most precious resources directed to this most priceless of objectives. Not until the 15th-century Renaissance, would art again become the preserve of princes.

Apart from the illustrated manuscripts and carved crosses, Later Celtic art was, like the La Tène style, essentially the art of metalwork – either objects made entirely of metal or components for composite artefacts. Coloured glass, incorporating *millefiori* (coloured glass rods) in the Roman style, and enamels were widely used to decorate and embellish metalwork, but pottery was not a significant material at this time. In north-east Ireland from *c.*AD 800, the local pottery (souterrain ware) consisted of crude household ware, and only very limited numbers of luxury pots were imported, mainly from France.

Stylistically, Later Celtic art is a fusion of Insular La Tène with some late-Roman and Germanic (Anglo-Saxon) elements, especially the use of animal motifs. There is a continuing obsession with filling surfaces and the decoration of some artefacts approaches almost fractal levels of intricacy. The popularity of ribbon interlacing (on manuscript and metalwork) may reflect the mastery of manipulative crafts, such as fancy ropework and leatherwork, the artefacts of which have not survived. Such designs may also have decorated the numerous horn and wooden utensils that were the mainstay of everyday life.

Religious art

Most of the art objects that survive (and presumably the majority of those made), have a wholly religious context, and range from church plate, such as chalices, to various types of portable reliquaries and shrines. The sacred significance of such artefacts permitted and enjoined the fabricators to a far greater expenditure of time and skill in the decoration of, for example, a chalice as compared to even the most regal of royal drinking cups.

The Ardagh Chalice (National Museum of Ireland, Dublin) is a representative masterpiece of the early 8th century, made of silver and lavishly decorated with gold, gilt-bronze castings, and polychrome enamel studs. The decoration, mainly confined to the handles, rim and base, is mainly abstract interlaces, although some animal motifs also appear. Inscribed on the base is the traditional triskele (three-legged) symbol, although this had probably been Christianised and now represented the Trinity.

Portable reliquaries, carried or worn during religious processions, were often made of, or completely encased in, decorated metal. The Emly Shrine from Ireland is typical of the small, house-

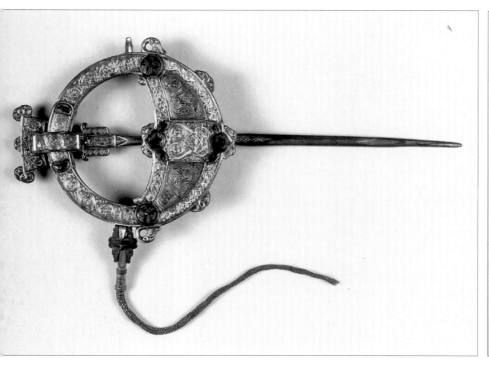

WOODEN HARPS

Among the finest surviving examples of late medieval woodcarving skills are the celebrated Irish, or Celtic, harps that were developed during the early Christian era. The distinctive features of the Irish harp are the huge sound box at the back and the thick, curved front pillar; both of which were usually covered with carved ornament. Although they were soon replaced by slimmer instruments in most of Europe, the reclusive nature of Irish society under English occupation meant that they remained in common use, albeit as treasured heirlooms, until the 18th century.

► **The Ardagh Chalice** was found (1868) in County Limerick. This silver cup dates from the 8th century. It was probably used to dispense wine during Mass. The gold and silver filigree, which combines interlaced zoomorphic forms and spirals with abstract designs, is similar to the decoration on the Tara Brooch. The exterior of the bowl is inscribed with the Latin names of the Apostles.

▼ **Crucifixion plaque** probably dating from the 8th century. It is 21.1 centimetres (8.3 inches) high and made of gilt bronze. The plaque is one of the earliest extant representations of Christ's crucifixion found in Ireland. The plaque may have been the decoration for the front cover of an illuminated manuscript, or part of a large shrine, cross or altar. The Late La Tène style engraving on Christ's breast features semi-circular motifs (*peltae*) and tightly wound spirals. The vast majority of Later Celtic art is religious in inspiration and context. Metalwork, such as this plaque, was produced within the ancient Irish monasteries and was at the service of the church.

shaped shrines that were popular in many parts of northern Europe. The shrine combines elegance of shape with richly coloured abstract designs that cover the entire surface. Belt shrines and crosier (staff) shrines were also very popular in Ireland, and their metal components, decorated in exquisite detail, show a more restrained use or even absence of bright enamels.

Secular art and the Vikings

Within the secular world, artworks were confined to personal ornament, mainly in the form of clothes' fastenings. The most typical form is the penannular (ring-shaped) brooch that evolved from Iron-Age designs, with animal-headed types appearing at the very end of the Roman period. Penannular brooches became progressively larger and more decorated, for example the Ballyspellan Brooch, and reached something of a climax with the spectacular, pseudo-penannular, Tara Brooch (National Museum of Ireland, Dublin) which carries the full decorative repertoire of Late Celtic metalwork.

At the start of the 9th century, Irish art begins to display Viking influence. Two results of the Viking raids were that the overall standard of manufacture declined, and the amount of decoration on (and embellishment of) objects decreased, with large areas being left unadorned. One interpretation of this trend is that the increased threat of pillage and theft disinclined artisans and their patrons to cover artefacts with precious resources. The use of red enamel and *millefiori* glass declined, and soon became unfashionable.

The positive influence of the Vikings was largely confined to their coastal settlements. In the 11th and early 12th centuries, a composite Hiberno-Ringerike and Urnes style evolved around Dublin, that was strongly Scandinavian and had few if any Celtic elements. The Norman invasion put paid to this Scandinavian influence, reconnecting Ireland with artistic developments in western Europe and introducing the new Romanesque style.

ARTHURIAN LEGEND

The romantic legends of King Arthur and the Knights of the Round Table are now familiar to audiences around the world. The 'lady of the lake' was as popular a subject with 19th-century painters as 14th-century French illustrators. The tale of this warrior-king has been told in a myriad of ways, from the heroic odes of bards to feature-length animated films.

Some see Arthur as a fictional Celtic hero and the wizard Merlin as an archetypal druid, while others have searched vainly for some evidence of his historical existence. What can be stated with veracity is that the Arthurian story is a long-running saga, and that each generation has come up with fresh interpretations.

The survival and development of the Arthurian legend must be viewed in context; not only against a multitude of local and regional folk-heroes across the ages, but also against the long-term evolution of 'world' legends such as Alexander the Great (356–323 BC) or some of the early Christian saints.

Arthur – historical figure or literary character?

The earliest report, that of Gildas in the middle of the 6th century, locates Arthur in southern Britain during the darkest part of the Dark Ages. In *c*.500, according to Gildas, Arthur led a British army that defeated the invading Anglo-Saxons at the battle of Mons Badonicus (Mount Badon). A subsequent 'historical' source,

Nennius' 9th-century *History of Britain*, describes 12 of Arthur's battles against the Anglo-Saxons, although we may question whether this detail comes from reliable information or a vivid imagination.

An early 20th-century view of Arthur placed him slightly earlier in time, as a Romano-British cavalry commander engaged in the defence of Britain against German attack. However, there is no mention of Arthur in Roman records, and this interpretation is partly reliant on Nennius' use of the phrase *dux bellorum* (a late-Roman military title) to describe Arthur. There are tiny snippets of late 5th- and early 6th-century information that would seem to confirm the core of the legend – that he defeated a Saxon attack.

We have no way of judging Arthur's popularity among the British in what was soon to become England, because only Anglo-Saxon writings have survived. He was, however, popular in Wales during the post-Roman twilight, and a 7th-century Welsh poem, the *Book of Aneirin*, acknowledges Arthur as a great warrior. It is noteworthy that Arthur was, at this time, confined entirely to the secular realm, and the early Christian centres in southern Wales laid no claim upon him. Subsequent Welsh poetry transformed Arthur into a magnificent king who slew monsters and performed marvels; and the Arthurian legend has become mainly associated with Wales and south-west Britain.

◄ *Le Morte D'Arthur* (*c*.1861) by James Archer (1823–1904). In Sir Thomas Malory's (d.1471?) medieval prose-romance *Le Morte D'Arthur* (1469–70), Arthur's discovery of Guinevere's adultery with Lancelot leads to war between Arthur and Lancelot. Mordred, Arthur's son by his half-sister Morgan le Fay, leads a revolt against the king. After Arthur's death in battle against Mordred, his body is borne away in a ship with three queens (Morgan le Fay, Queen of Northgalis and Queen of the Waste Lands). The ghostly figure bearing a goblet in the left of the painting is probably Nimue, the 'lady of the lake'.

◄ *Lancelot at the Chapel of the Holy Grail* (*c*.1896) by Sir Edward Burne-Jones (1833–98). Arthurian legend was a favourite source of inspiration for Burne-Jones and his associates in the the Pre-Raphaelite Brotherhood (PRB). The angel that stands guard at the door of the chapel informs the sleeping Lancelot that he will never attain the Holy Grail because of his adultery with Queen Guinevere. Burne-Jones has painted himself as Lancelot. The painting, which measures 138 × 170 centimetres (54.5 × 67 inches), was probably inspired by Sir Thomas Malory's *Le Morte D'Arthur* (1469–70).

Building of a legend

Most of the detail about the life of King Arthur comes from the largely fictional *History of British Kings* produced by the Welsh priest, Geoffrey of Monmouth (*c*.1100–54). Writing in Latin, Geoffrey claimed his book was a translation of an older text "in the British tongue", and this dubious statement has been held to 'prove' Arthur's Celtic affinities.

About one-quarter of the book is devoted to the tale of Arthur and most of the action seems to have been wholly the writer's invention, or based largely on classical (rather than Celtic) sources. Other characters mentioned elsewhere in the book, such as King Lear and his daughters, have also achieved immortality through subsequent elaboration.

Geoffrey's work became extremely popular in England (it boosted his own career and he was promoted to bishop), and was introduced to the royal court of Normandy, where the legend became progressively embroidered. The 12th-century French poet Chrétien de Troyes composed five romances about Arthur which introduced the love-interest between Lancelot and Arthur's Queen Guinevere, and the quest for the Holy Grail, while somewhat relegating Arthur to the background. These new themes dominated medieval renditions of the Arthurian legend, which became inextricably entwined with notions of chivalry and courtly love.

The incorporation of the Grail legend confirmed the Christianisation of Arthur and greatly contributed to his popularity. Several religious centres, including Glastonbury, south-west England, claimed to be the site of the Holy Grail and attracted thousands of pilgrims.

The monks of Glastonbury were not above exploiting their connections with Arthur, and in 1191, they 'exhumed' his body from its supposed resting-place.

Medieval Welsh poets celebrated Arthur, but by then he had become a generic superhero, and his legend had acquired a life of its own. For those so inclined, Arthur can be seen as a Celtic king who battled valiantly against Anglo-Saxon invaders, and certain elements of the tale, such as the casting of his sword Excalibur into a lake, are authentically (but not exclusively) Celtic. The only certainty is that the Arthurian legend remains a gripping story.

◄ **Manuscript illumination** (14th century) of *A Tournament of the Knights of the Round Table Before King Arthur and Queen Guenevere* from Chrétien de Troyes' *Romance of King Arthur*. Writing in the late 12th century, Chrétien provided the first literary description of a tournament. In his five verse romances, Chrétien established many of the central features of Arthurian literature: Lancelot and his love for Guinevere; Gawain, the model knight; and Percival and the quest for the Holy Grail.

THE VIKING ONSLAUGHT

From the end of the 8th century, Scandinavian peoples, collectively known as Vikings (pirates), terrorised the coastline of the British Isles and briefly gained control over parts of England, Scotland and Ireland. Although characterised as bloodthirsty warriors, the Vikings were essentially farmers and traders; and during the 9th and 10th centuries they established themselves as far afield as present-day Iceland, Turkey and even Canada (Newfoundland). Under the guise of the Norseman (Normans), one branch of Vikings who had settled in northern France went on to conquer Britain and Ireland, while another branch freed Sicily from Muslim rule.

British resistance to the Danelaw

In the 790s, Viking raids on Britain began with sporadic attacks on the tempting targets of isolated monasteries, and early in the next century these raids escalated into a full-scale Danish invasion and the colonisation of eastern England. Despite fierce resistance by English kings, the Danes made steady progress and sacked London in 836. By the end of the 860s, the zone of Danish settlement extended into East Anglia, Mercia and Northumbria, and York became a major Viking centre. The Vikings forced the English to cede a large part of eastern and central England (the Danelaw) and to pay a yearly tribute (the Danegeld). Meanwhile, Vikings had captured the Isle of Man and settled the north-west coast of England.

Danish expansion was curtailed finally through the efforts of kings such as Rhodri Mawr (d. 878) of Gwynedd and Alfred the Great (849–99) of Wessex. In 886, Alfred seized London and recaptured some of the Danelaw. Edward the Elder (d. 925) of Wessex completed the reconquest of England when, in 920, he accepted the submission of the remaining Viking territories – although York remained largely under Viking control until 954. Edward's son Athelstan (c.895–939), who took Northumbria in 925, was the first monarch to rule directly over the whole of England. In the 980s, the Danes renewed their attacks on Britain and these raids continued until Canute the Great (c.994–1035) conquered England in 1016 and incorporated it into the Danish empire. The Anglo-Saxons did not re-establish their rule until 1042, by which time the Norman threat was also emerging.

Vikings in Ireland

Viking activity in Ireland followed a pattern similar to that in Britain – raiding followed by settlement; although the Vikings in Ireland never controlled large swathes of territory, and their settlement was restricted to a few fortified ports.

In 795, the first raiders struck at island monasteries on the north coast of Ireland and coastal raids continued intermittently for the next 40 years. Even the remote hermitage of Skellig Michael, off the south-west coast of Ireland, was attacked in 824. Towards the end of the 830s, the Vikings began to penetrate further inland, destroying the great religious centre of Armagh in 838. Two years later, the raiders wintered beside Lough Neagh, Northern Ireland. In 841, they established a permanent camp at Dublin – the first Viking settlement in Ireland. Dublin grew rapidly to become the capital of Viking territory in Ireland, and served as a base for numerous raiding parties, particularly in the south-central region. The newly established port at Dublin also conducted an extensive trade with other Viking centres in Britain and Scandinavia.

◄ *Viking Sea Raiders* by Albert Goodwin (1845–1932). From the late 8th century, the Vikings exploited advances in ship technology (sail design and a stronger, more flexible hull) to undertake extraordinary voyages of exploration. These voyages were made in search of profit. Commerce and plundering were linked: slaves were captured in raids and exchanged for Arab silver. The 860s marked a new era in Viking expansion as the 'Great Armies', mostly composed of Danes, began to conquer and settle in western Europe.

On land, the Irish warriors matched their Viking counterparts and an uneasy co-existence developed. The Irish recruited Viking support to help resolve Irish dynastic disputes, and some Irish kings became involved in pan-Viking power struggles between Danes and Norwegians.

At the beginning of the 10th century, the Irish briefly expelled the Vikings from Dublin, but the town was reoccupied in 914, and in the same year, another Viking centre was established at Waterford. In the next few decades, the Vikings achieved the greatest extent of their power in Ireland. Their territory around Dublin enlarged, and Limerick was established in 920 and grew to rival Dublin. In 939, Vikings from Dublin seized control of York, north England, briefly threatening to revive Viking power in England.

By the middle of the 10th century, however, the Vikings in Ireland were in decline again. Apart from a few fortified towns, their territorial control was soon restricted to the Dublin hinterland. In 1014, Brian Boru's victory at Clontarf, near Dublin, marked the end of Viking power in Ireland, but not the end of their settlement; many chose to remain as traders within their largely self-contained towns, where they continued to enjoy commercial success.

▶ **Viking raids** The coasts and islands of Britain and Ireland bore the brunt of the Scandinavian onslaught until about the middle of the 9th century, when the raiders began arriving in greater numbers and venturing further inland. Eastern Britain was settled mainly by Danes, and Ireland by Norwegians.

◀ **The Gokstad** Viking longship was recovered from a grave mound in Norway. It was built in the 890s, and buried with a chieftain between 900 and 905. The ship measures 23.5 metres (77 feet). It has 32 oar holes and could have carried up to 80 men. The immensely strong keel was hewn from a single oak tree. In 1893, a replica of the Gokstad ship completed the crossing the Atlantic from Bergen, Norway, to Newfoundland, Canada, in just 28 days.

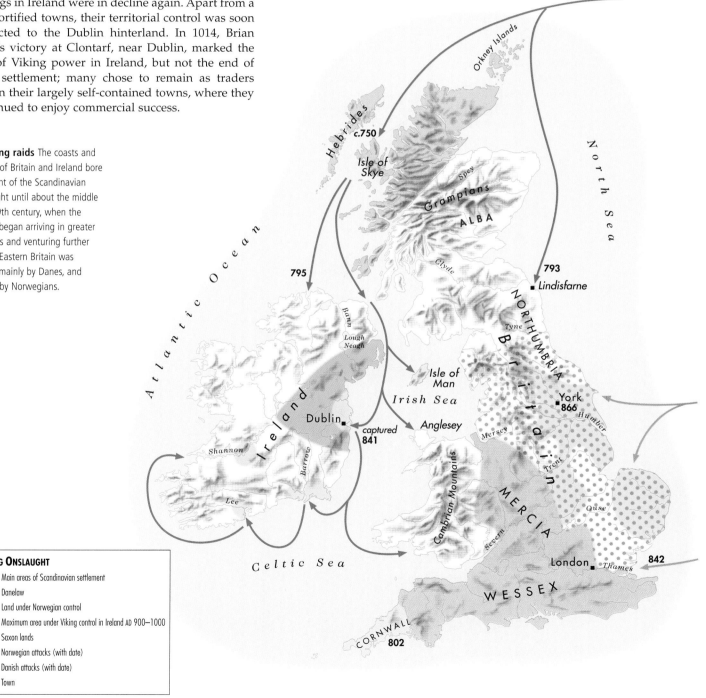

VIKING ONSLAUGHT

- Main areas of Scandinavian settlement
- Danelaw
- Land under Norwegian control
- Maximum area under Viking control in Ireland AD 900–1000
- Saxon lands
- Norwegian attacks (with date)
- Danish attacks (with date)
- ■ Town

FORMATION OF SCOTLAND

▶ The Hunterston Brooch

dates from the late 7th or early 8th century. It was found at West Kilbride, Ayrshire. Made of solid silver with gold and silver filigree and amber studs, each of the eight main panels has an interlaced beast of Pictish design. At the centre of the brooch, two abstract birds face each other and enclose a rectangular panel with a Celtic cross. The brooch is a synthesis of Irish, Pictish and Anglo-Saxon art. The use of amber studs supports the theory that the brooch derived from the Kingdom of Dalriada in Scotland, where amber was very popular.

To the north of Hadrian's Wall, the British people had remained almost completely free of Roman influence and interference. The Antonine Wall, built by the Romans in *c.*AD 142, had not lasted long enough to deposit more than a thin and temporary veneer of Romanisation across parts of the Scottish lowlands. The people of what was to become Scotland were initially known to the Romans as Caledonians, but at the end of the 3rd century a new appellation appears in Roman records – the *Picti* or Picts.

The Picts are one of the more mysterious of the peoples of ancient Europe. One view is that the Picts represent one of the last surviving pockets of a pre-Indo-European population, perhaps with continuous traditions stretching back to the Neolithic period. An opposed opinion holds that the Picts represent a phenomenon that only emerged during the Roman occupation of Britain, resulting from the retreat and consolidation of Celtic peoples in the face of Roman expansion. There are many viewpoints between these two extremes.

The few surviving material relics of Pictish culture show some distinctive features that would seem to set them apart from the Celts, and some scholars discern non-Indo-European elements in fragments of Pictish language. Against this, it should be noted that the forms (metalwork and carved stones) that bear these distinctive features fall entirely within the repertoire of contemporary Celtic, Germanic and Scandinavian craftworkers. Furthermore, the available evidence seems to favour the view that Pictish language is a form of Celtic.

Dalriada and Argyll

During the 7th century, the Picts were the inhabitants of the Scottish Highlands and were strongest in the east. In 685, Bridei, king of the Picts, is reported to have defeated an Anglo-Saxon invasion at the Battle of Nechtansmere in Angus.

THE PICTS

This engraving of male and female 'Pict' warriors is largely a product of the artist's imagination, and in many ways resembles the contemporary (and equally fanciful) illustrations of the native inhabitants of the Americas. The enigmatic nature of the Picts is enhanced by their distinctive art with its limited repertoire of symbolic animals and strange symbols. Pictish animals were usually carved in pairs on the face of standing stones. The most commonanimal depicted is the bull but others, such as wolves, fishes and a variety of birds, were also shown. The animals are portrayed in outline and profile in various static poses, and often incorporate some conventionalised (and presumably significant) anatomical details. The elaborate Pictish symbols, such as the so-called Z-rod and V-rod, are sometimes accompanied by animal symbols, but were often used alone.

To the south of the Picts was a region dominated by native peoples from northern Britain, from whence emerged the kingdom of Strathclyde with its capital at Al Cluith (now Dumbarton), and the smaller kingdom of Gododdin (now Lothian) to the south-east.

Sea-raiders from Ireland had been visiting and settling the islands and peninsulas of the west coast throughout the Roman period. According to tradition, around AD 500, these Scotti (raiders), under the leadership of Fergus Mor MacEirc, formally established the enclave of Dalriada, with its capital at Dunadd, near present-day Crinan, Argyll and Bute. However, recent research suggests that the Scotti had always inhabited Dalriada, but were culturally and linguistically closer to Ireland than Scotland. The west-coast region of Scotland soon became known as Argyll (literally, coastline of the Gaelic [Irish] speakers) and emerged as the most powerful political force in the region. It steadily expanded, mainly at the expense of Strathclyde. From the mid-6th century, Celtic missionaries from Dalriada carried Christianity to the Picts with such success that Pictish society was strongly 'Celticised' (if indeed the Picts were a separate people) long before the Scotti achieved political control.

The Kingdom of Alba

In 843, Kenneth I MacAlpin (d.c.858), king of the Scots, formally acquired the Pictish crown and created the new kingdom of Alba. Meanwhile, Picts in the lands north of the Great Glen had suffered a major defeat (839) at the hands of Viking raiders. However, there was only sparse Viking settlement, and the territory remained largely Pictish but independent from Alba.

According to legend, Kenneth symbolically fused the traditions of the two former kingdoms by placing the so-called *Lia Fáil* ('Stone of Destiny'), originally from Tara in Ireland, at the symbolic heart of the new kingdom, in Scone, a Pictish centre in the east. However, the creation of Alba resulted in the rapid erosion of a distinctive Pict culture from central Scotland.

By the 10th century, Alba was sufficiently powerful to ensure that Strathclyde owed allegiance northwards, rather than to the newly emergent English nation to the south, although the Scots did not immediately establish direct control. In c.1018, Malcolm II of Scotland (c.954–1034) defeated the English at the Battle of Carham and acquired Lothian from the Anglian kingdom of Bernicia. Malcolm also manoeuvred his grandson Duncan into line for the throne of Strathclyde. In 1034, the accession of Duncan I placed all of Scotland under a single ruler, with the exception of a lingering Viking presence on the northern fringes.

In 1040, Macbeth –a rival claimant to the Scottish throne – murdered the unpopular Duncan. Contrary to his literary reputation, Macbeth is thought to have been a well-liked and successful king. His successor Malcolm III Canmore (c.1031–93), had fled to the English court of Edward the Confessor. In 1057, Malcolm, backed by English troops, defeated and killed Macbeth in battle. By the time Malcolm finalised his second marriage (1070), to Margaret, sister of the English Prince Edgar the Aetheling, the English had lost their kingdom to the Normans, while the Scots retained a large measure of independence.

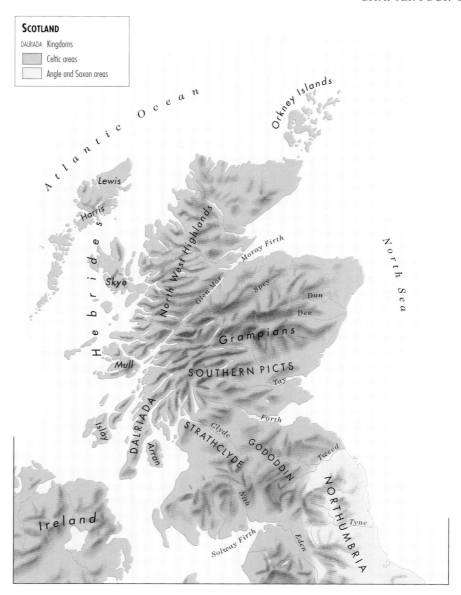

SCOTLAND

DALRIADA Kingdoms

Celtic areas

Angle and Saxon areas

▲ **Highland Picts** were under pressure from all sides during the 8th century. To the west were the Irish-speaking Scotti; to the south were British peoples and Anglo-Saxons; and from the north came Viking raiders. In the 9th century, the kingdom of the Picts ceased to be a separate political entity.

◄ **The Stone of Scone** used to be kept under the throne of Edward I of England (1239–1307). In 1296, Edward seized the stone from Scone Abbey, near Perth, west Scotland, and placed it in Westminster Abbey, London. Since 1996 it has resided at Edinburgh Castle, Edinburgh. Rulers of Scotland, including Elizabeth II, have been crowned on the stone for more than a thousand years

BRIAN BORU

In the early 10th century, the resurgence of Viking power in Ireland considerably diminished the power of the *Eóghanachta*, dynastic overlords of Munster. The establishment of the west-coast port of Limerick, which permitted unhindered access to the River Shannon, created a new power base to rival Cashel (Caiseal) – the traditional centre of power in southern Ireland.

During the latter half of the 10th century, the Irish resistance movement became better organised and forced the Vikings on the defensive. This Irish revival was associated with the emergence of a new dynastic force in Munster, the *Dál Cais*, whose territorial heartland lay along the north bank of the lower Shannon. By the end of the century, the *Dál Cais* had eclipsed both the declining *Eóghanachta* in the south and the *Uí Néill* (O'Neill's) in the north and, for the first time, Ireland was united under a single ruler.

Rise of the *Dál Cais* under Brian Boru

The *Dál Cais* rise to power began during the reign of Mathgamain MacCennetigh, who, in *c.*950, became king of North Munster. In 964, Mathgamain overthrew the *Eóghanachta* and occupied Cashel. In 968, he inflicted a crushing defeat on the Vikings and captured Limerick. In 976, Mathgamain died in mysterious circumstances – some say he was assassinated – and the *Eóghanachta* briefly regained control.

Two years later, Mathgamain's brother, Brian MacCennetigh (941–1014), led the *Dál Cais* against Cashel and killed the king of the *Eóghanachta* at the Battle of Belach Lechta. Secure on the throne of Munster, Brian now laid claim to the high-kingship of Ireland. He became known as Brian Boroimhe (Boru) through the *boroimhe* (cow tax) that was his due as supreme king.

Other Irish dynasties did not recognise Brian's claim to be the legitimate high king of Ireland, and Brian had to impose his authority by force. During the next 20 years, he completely subdued southern Ireland and made raids deep into the north. In 997, for the sake of a temporary peace, Brian acknowledged the *Uí Néill* high-kingship in return for their formal recognition of his rule in the south.

At the Battle of Glenn Mama (999), Brian inflicted a crushing defeat on the kingdom of Leinster, which had allied itself with the east-coast Vikings, and afterwards occupied Dublin. He was now too powerful to be denied and, in 1002, the *Uí Néill* surrendered the high-kingship to him.

In 1005 and 1006, Brian made a grand circuit of the country, styling himself 'emperor of Ireland' – his visit to Armagh confirmed its position as the spiritual centre of Ireland. Late in 1006, Brian had to deal with the first of several rebellions against his rule. The most serious threat came in 1014, when the King of Leinster, in alliance with Vikings from Dublin, the Isle of Man, and the Western Isles, assembled a large army to the north of Dublin. At the Battle of Clontarf, Brian's forces, commanded by his son Murchad, won the day and finally extinguished the Viking threat. Brian, by now an old man, watched the battle from his tent, where he was killed by a stray band of Viking warriors.

Resurgence of the *Uí Néills*

Although his own line did not immediately succeed, Brian's ascendancy had permanently ended the *Uí Néill* monopoly on the high-kingship. The title initially passed to the rulers of Leinster, who greatly enhanced its status when, in 1052, they formally took the kingship of Dublin,

◀ **Rock of Cashel**, County Tipperary, south-east Ireland. Brian Boru was crowned king of Munster at Cashel. In the foreground of this 19th-century engraving stands St Patrick's Cross, which probably dates from the 11th century. Its base may have served as the coronation stone of the Munster kings. Today, the Cross is displayed in the nearby Hall of the Vicars Choral. The Gothic limestone cathedral, with its high-set lancet windows, was built between 1235 and 1270. To the left of the cathedral stand the twin towers of Cormac's Chapel, built in *c.*1127. The Chapel is the earliest and finest Romanesque church in Ireland.

BRIAN BORU

- 10th-century Viking activity
- ULAID The seven kingdoms
- ■ Irish centres
- ■ Viking centres
- ⟶ Early campaigns
- ⟶ Raids into the north
- ⟶ Final campaign against Vikings
- ● Battles

NORTHERN
UÍ NÉILL

Donegal Bay

Achill Island

CONNAUGHT

Atlantic Ocean

Lough Corrib

Galway Bay

Aran Island

Lough Ree

Ireland

SOUTHERN
UÍ NÉILL

Lough Derg

Shannon
Limerick

Cashel

Belach Lechta
978

MUNSTER

Blackwater

Lee

Moy

Erne

Mourne

Bann

Lough Neagh

ULAID

Armagh ■
AIRGIALLA

Boyne

Irish Sea

■ Tara

Glenn Mama
999

Liffey

● Clontarf 1014

■ Dublin

Barrow

Nore

Suir

LAGIN

Wicklow Mountains

■ Waterford

Celtic Sea

▶ **Brian Boru** Years of campaigning across much of Ireland finally won Brian Boru the coveted high-kingship in 1002. As king, his final act was to lead the campaign that inflicted a decisive defeat on the Vikings at Clontarf.

bringing the town under Irish rule for the first time since its foundation. Dublin now began to replace Tara as the symbolic centre of Irish political life, just as Armagh had become the new spiritual centre. However, the brief political unity imposed by Brian was lost, and wars between competing kingdoms again divided Ireland.

Brian's great-grandson, Muirchertach, claimed and held the high-kingship at various times between 1086 and 1119. An aggressive and ambitious ruler, Muirchertach pursued marriage alliances with the emergent powers of Normandy and Norway, but in Ireland his rule was chiefly marked by a series of destructive raids that devastated the lands of his rivals but did little to impose central control. He was eventually forced to surrender his title by a temporary alliance of the other Irish kings.

By the middle of the 12th century, the high-kingship was once again in the hands of the *Uí Néill* in alliance with Leinster; although they were challenged by the rising power of Connaught (Connacht). When the *Uí Néill* king died in 1166, the high-kingship passed to Connaught, and the consequent shift in power resulted in the expulsion from Ireland of Dermot MacMurrough (Diarmaid MacMurchada), King of Leinster (d.1171). Dermot sought assistance from Henry II of England (1133–89), and invited the Norman invasion of Ireland.

◀ *Assassination of Brian Boru*, drawn by H. Warren and engraved by J. Rogers. Brian was killed in the process of securing victory against the Vikings at the Battle of Clontarf (April 23, 1014). A small, breakaway band of Norsemen, fleeing the battlefield, stumbled on the king's tent, overpowered his bodyguard, and hacked the aged king to death.

NORMAN INVASIONS

Towards the end of the 9th century, as the Carolingian dynasty declined, their control over France became progressively weaker. In c.911, Charles III of France (879–929) was forced to concede part of Neustria in north-west France to the Vikings, who had raided as far inland as Paris. In return for accepting Christianity, the Viking leader Rollo (c.860–c.932) was formally recognised as the Duke of Normandy – in effect an independent kingdom. The Normans, the southernmost group of Viking settlers, soon adopted the language and customs of the French aristocracy, and immersed themselves in the mainstream of European politics.

Norman Conquest of England

In 1066, claiming to be the nominated heir of King Edward the Confessor of England (c.1003–66), William, Duke of Normandy, invaded southern England. Although a Viking invasion of northern England had been repelled earlier in the year, William defeated the English armies at the Battle of Hastings and killed King Harold of England.

The Norman Conquest of England proceeded smoothly as the Vikings seized the apparatus of state, adapting it to their own customs. England was divided into shires, and the feudal system was introduced,

▲ **Tomb of Henry II** of England, in Fontevraud l'Abbaye, west France. The first Plantagenet King of England, Henry was supposedly empowered by a papal bull (1155) from Pope Adrian IV to invade Ireland in 1169. In 1171, Henry declared himself 'Lord of Ireland'. In 1174, after the murder (1170) of Thomas à Becket in Canterbury Cathedral, Henry was forced to do public penance.

▶ **Norman invasions** Norman occupation was achieved with astonishing speed. Within six years of the battle of Hastings, they had subdued the whole of England and forced the submission of Scotland. About a century later, much of Ireland was taken with almost equal speed.

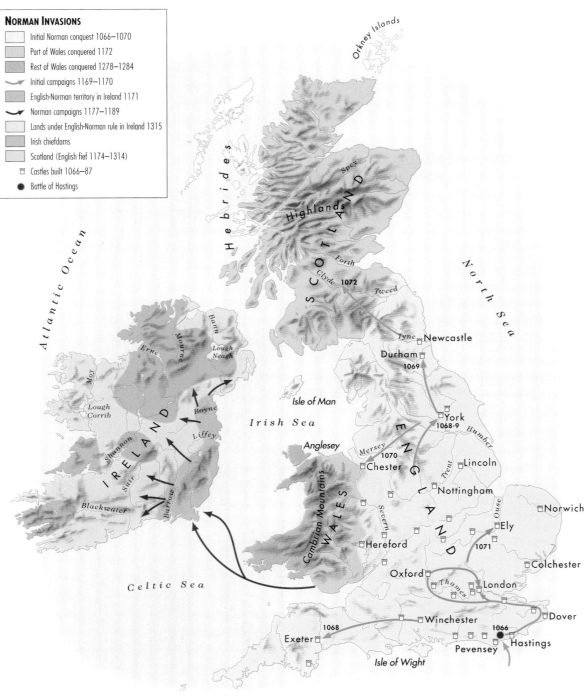

NORMAN INVASIONS

- Initial Norman conquest 1066–1070
- Part of Wales conquered 1172
- Rest of Wales conquered 1278–1284
- Initial campaigns 1169–1170
- English-Norman territory in Ireland 1171
- Norman campaigns 1177–1189
- Lands under English-Norman rule in Ireland 1315
- Irish chiefdoms
- Scotland (English fief 1174–1314)
- Castles built 1066–87
- ● Battle of Hastings

which transformed free peasants into serfs tied to their lord's land. The composition of early Norman England was meticulously recorded in the famous Domesday Book (compiled 1085–87).

In 1072, Norman armies forced the submission of Malcolm III Canmore (c.1031–93) of Scotland. In return for concessions to the Anglo-Norman barons, Scotland was allowed to retain nominal independence and its own king. Along the border with Wales, the Normans established castles at Chester, Shrewsbury and Hereford, and began the initial colonisation of Gwent. After 1093, these border strongholds were used to launch a full-scale invasion of southern and central Wales that resulted in the creation of earldoms in the Welsh Marches, over which Anglo-Norman aristocrats exercised almost sovereign control.

After the death of Henry I (1069–1135) of England, William's grandson, Stephen (c.1097–1154) usurped the throne. A civil war (often called 'The Anarchy') ensued between the supporters of Stephen, and those of the legitimate claimant Matilda (1102–67) and her son, the future King Henry II (1133–89). When Henry II acceded to the throne in 1153, those Norman lords who had sided with Stephen were forced into line.

Norman Ireland

After Dermot MacMurrough (d.1171) formally approached Henry II for assistance in regaining the kingdom of Leinster, he was grudgingly allowed to recruit a small party of disaffected Norman fighters from southern Wales. In 1167, Dermot returned to Ireland and, with Norman aid, regained his kingship.

Three years later, a much larger party of Norman knights, led by Richard FitzGilbert de Clare, 2nd Earl of Pembroke (c.1130–76), arrived to reinforce Dermot, and their combined armies seized the still largely Viking towns of Waterford and Dublin. After the death (1198) of Dermot, Pembroke (now married to Dermot's daughter, and known as Strongbow) routed a counter-attack by Irish kings and Viking mercenaries, led by Roderic, the high king of Ireland, and became King of Leinster. Pembroke faced almost unanimous Irish opposition and, in return for military assistance, he was forced to offer his new territories to Henry II of England.

Henry intervened in person, and travelled to Ireland to accept Pembroke's formal submission. Pembroke was allowed to retain Leinster, but Henry acquired the rest of Ireland for England. The Norman barons fanned out from Dublin, conquering and establishing their own territories. Although they encountered spirited resistance – Pembroke himself was severely defeated in Connaught (Connacht) in 1171 – the Normans' superior military organisation and weaponry generally prevailed. The process continued into the early 13th century, when a second wave of Anglo-Norman expansion successfully subdued and colonised Connaught.

The Norman invasion had a marked effect on the Irish landscape. The first stone castles were built, manors were constructed (with fields organised and husbanded according to Norman tradition), and the feudal system was adopted. The new Norman

◀ **William the Conqueror** depicted in the manuscript *Liber Legum Antiquorum Regum* (c.1321). After defeating and killing Harold at the Battle of Hastings (1066), William rapidly sought to consolidate his power in England. He ruthlessly crushed resistance and repelled a Danish invasion. William rewarded his followers with grants of land, eventually replacing the entire Anglo-Saxon feudal ruling class with Normans, and intimidating potential rebels by the rapid construction of castles.

aristocracy evolved alongside the traditional Irish chieftains, and formed the rootstock for the creation of the Anglo-Irish.

Although bloodlines may have remained distinct, the new aristocracy gradually lost much of its cultural identity. They adopted Irish customs and language – as they did to a lesser degree in England, where Norman French was subsumed into Anglo-Saxon to produce the Middle English mastered by the poet Geoffrey Chaucer (c.1342–1400).

Ultimately, the lasting significance of the Norman Conquest was that it established a direct and forceful political relationship between England and Ireland, and connected these two nations to the mainstream of European political life.

▼ **Death of Harold** depicted on the Bayeux Tapestry (c.1080). The Latin text reads, "HIC HAROLD REX INTERFECTUS EST" ("Here King Harold was killed"). The tapestry (strictly a wool embroidery on linen) depicts the history of the Norman Conquest of England. It shows William's preparations for the invasion of England, the decisive Battle of Hastings, and ends with the retreat of the English. The tapestry is c.51 centimetres (20 inches) high, and 70 metres (230 feet) long.

WALES

The Welsh arguably have the best claim to be the direct descendants of the pre-Roman population of Britain, although it must be admitted that, from the 1st century AD onwards, Wales received a considerable influx of peoples from Ireland as well as from other parts of Britain.

The appellation 'Welsh' comes from the Anglo-Saxon/Old English *wealas*, which means foreigners (in Anglo-Saxon eyes). The Welsh language is considered to represent a survival of the ancient British language (Brythonic), as opposed to the Irish language (Goidelic), which later spread to Scotland. The British seem to have referred to themselves as *Cymry* ('fellow compatriots'), but, as the Anglo-Saxon invasion proceeded, this term became confined to Wales.

Resistance of Welsh kingdoms

Parts of Wales, especially on the north and south coasts, had been effectively Romanised during the period of occupation, and Christianity had become established. Some of the early Irish monastery-builders, such as Finian, the founder of Clonard, received their training at Welsh centres such as St Davids, Pembrokeshire. By the 7th century, four distinct kingdoms had emerged in Wales: Gwynedd, Powys, Gwent and Dyfed. Each had its own royal lineage, and encompassed the territories of numerous sub-kings and princes.

The Welsh kings resisted the Anglo-Saxon invasion, sometimes acting in concert with other British rulers. A disastrous expedition to assist Strathclyde ended in defeat at the Battle of Chester (616). Cadwallon of Gwynedd (d.634) and Penda of Mercia combined to defeat Edwin of Northumbria at the Battle of Heathfield (633), north England. The following year, Cadwallon was killed fighting against Oswald of Bernicia. The strenuous defence of their territory made Welsh independence a *de facto* reality, and this was later acknowledged by Offa (d.796), King of Mercia, who ordered the construction of a massive earthwork (Offa's Dyke) to protect his eastern border.

During the Viking period, the Welsh coastline suffered raids and some settlement, but stubborn resistance by leaders such as Rhodri Mawr (d.878), King of Gwynedd and Powys, prevented any part of Wales from being incorporated into the Danelaw. During the re-establishment of English control in the 10th century, the Welsh rulers traded allegiance to England in return for practical independence and their theoretical subjugation was completed by mid-century. Welsh literature and learning flourished at this time, and the reign of Hywel Dda (d.950) saw the creation of a separate Welsh coinage and the codification of Welsh laws.

Due to the Welsh succession laws, which divided lands among heirs to the throne instead of giving them intact to the eldest son, Welsh rulers often vied for supremacy. In *c.*1055, however, Gruffudd ap Llywelyn briefly united the whole country under his control. After Gruffudd's death in 1063, Wales became fragmented once more and was unable to mount sustained resistance to the Norman invasion, which began in earnest in 1093. Spearheaded in the south by Robert Fitzhamon, Earl of Gloucester, the Normans made rapid progress and established the Welsh Marches. The Norman Marcher lords were virtually independent of the English throne and assumed the same regal status as the native rulers in the unoccupied portions of Wales.

Rise and fall of Gwynedd

In the 13th century, Gwynedd gradually established supremacy over the remnants of the Welsh kingdoms

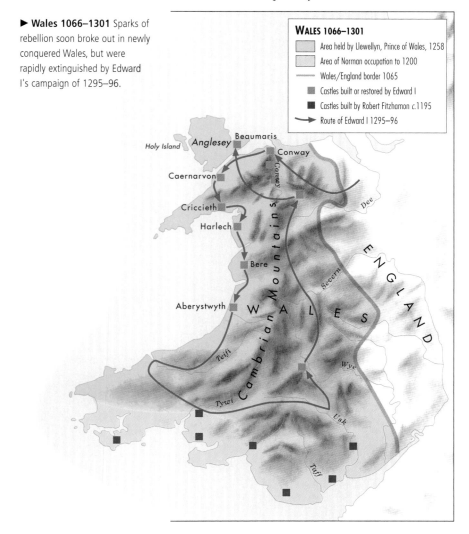

WALES 1066–1301

- Area held by Llewellyn, Prince of Wales, 1258
- Area of Norman occupation to 1200
- Wales/England border 1065
- Castles built or restored by Edward I
- Castles built by Robert Fitzhamon *c.*1195
- Route of Edward I 1295–96

Holy Island · Anglesey · Beaumaris · Conway · Caernarvon · Cricieth · Harlech · Bere · Aberystwyth · Cambrian Mountains · WALES · ENGLAND · Conway · Dee · Severn · Teifi · Tywi · Wye · Usk · Taff

◀ **Harlech Castle**, Gwynedd, north Wales, was the site of the independent Welsh Parliament established by Owain Glyn Dŵr in the early 15th century. In 1283, after his defeat of Llywelyn ap Gruffydd, King Edward I began the construction of Harlech Castle. Harlech was the last Welsh fortress to surrender (1468) to the Yorkists during the Wars of the Roses.

▶ **Llywelyn ap Gruffudd** kneels to be beheaded, watched by Edward I at the window, in this 15th-century Flemish illustration in the English *St Alban's Chronicle*. Llywelyn united the kingdoms of Gwynedd, Powys and Deheubarth, and parts of the Welsh Marches into the Principality of Wales. A year after Llywelyn's defeat and death (1282), the English gained complete control of Wales.

▶ **Glyn Dŵr's Rebellion**
Owain Glyn Dŵr led a highly successful revolt against English rule in Wales. By 1404 he held most of Wales, but Prince Henry of England regained the initiative the following year.

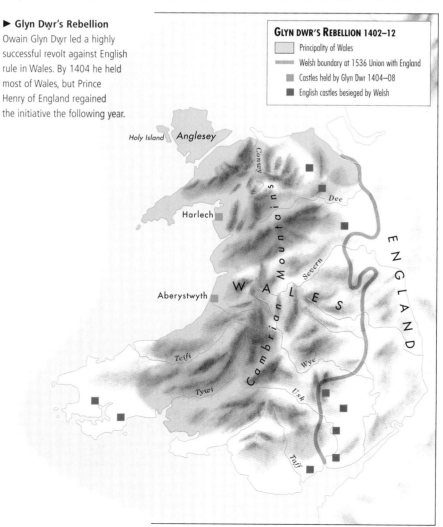

GLYN DWR'S REBELLION 1402–12
Principality of Wales
Welsh boundary at 1536 Union with England
Castles held by Glyn Dwr 1404–08
English castles besieged by Welsh

and, in 1258, Llywelyn ap Gruffudd of Gwynedd (d.1282) began styling himself the 'Prince of Wales'. The bitter conflict between Henry III (1207–72) of England and his barons played into Llywelyn's hands and, by the Treaty of Montgomery (1267), Henry was forced to recognise Llywelyn's rule over the Principality of Wales.

Ten years later, Henry III's son and successor, Edward I (1239–1307), took a less sanguine view on Welsh independence, and imposed his rule over the whole country by military force. In 1282, Llywelyn was killed in battle against Edward near Builth Wells, Powys. The following year, the English conquest of Wales was finally completed. A series of heavily fortified castles was built, mainly along the north coast of Wales, each forming the nucleus for English colonisation. In 1301, the future Edward II (1284–1327) of England was proclaimed Prince of Wales at Caernarfon Castle, Gwynedd, and received the homage of the Welsh rulers. This later became an established pattern, with the heir to the English throne always being invested as Prince of Wales.

In 1399, Henry IV's (1367–1413) overthrow of Richard II (1367–1400) of England allowed a group of Welsh lords, led by Owain Glyn Dŵr (c.1354–c.1416), to rebel against England without breaking their oaths of allegiance. Glyn Dŵr's revolt soon gained popular support in Wales and, by 1404, he captured the castles at Harlech and Aberystwyth. Between 1400 and 1407, Wales was ungovernable by the English. By 1405, however, the tide was turning as Henry IV's son, the future Henry V (1387–1422), assumed control of the English forces. Despite assistance from the French, the rebels were eventually defeated, and English control re-established. Wales was formally joined to England by Acts of the English Parliament in 1536 and 1543.

THE BRUCES

The peaceful coexistence between England and Scotland, established in 1071, lasted for two centuries – long enough for the Norman lords south of the border to become thoroughly English, while their counterparts in the north acquired Scottish sensibilities. In 1290, the peace was shattered by the childhood death of Queen Margaret, who had succeeded her grandfather, Alexander III (1241–86). The throne of Scotland lacked an obvious successor.

With more than a dozen Scottish aristocrats laying claim to the throne, Edward I (1239–1307) of England, whose son, the future Edward II (1284–1327), had been betrothed to Margaret, selected John Balliol (c.1249–1315), whom he judged most amenable to English influence. Balliol was supported by the Comyns – the most powerful Scottish lords. In 1296, Edward marched north to impose English rule. Scottish resistance crystallised around the knight William Wallace (c.1270–1305), who defeated the English army at Stirling in 1297, but was defeated at Falkirk the following year. In 1305, Wallace was captured and executed in London – an act that may have stirred Robert the Bruce (1274–1329) into action.

▶ **Robert the Bruce** and his first wife, the daughter of the Earl of Mar, from *Seton's Armorial Crests* (1306). This manuscript dates from the first year of Robert the Bruce's reign. He was crowned at Scone on March 25.

nobility. In 1306, Bruce killed Comyn and the ever-present hostilites between Scotland and England flared into open warfare, as Prince Edward marched to arrest Bruce. Bruce raised the flag of rebellion at Scone, where he was crowned Robert I of Scotland.

The English quickly defeated the new monarch; Bruce's wife was taken prisoner, and he was forced to hide on the island of Rathlin, off the north coast of Northern Ireland. Shortly before Edward I's death in 1307, Bruce secretly returned to Scotland. Edward II soon proved a far less capable ruler than his father and, by 1308, Bruce's hastily assembled army had gained controlled of much of Scotland. In 1312, Perth fell to Bruce. In 1313, Edward II was finally stung into action by Bruce's raids into northern England. On June 24, 1314, Bruce inflicted a crushing defeat on the English at the Battle of Bannockburn (near present-day Stirling). This victory effectively secured Scotland's independence, which was confirmed by Pope John XXII. Although independence was guaranteed by treaties with England, signed at York (1324, 1327) and Edinburgh (1328), the exact location of the Scottish border and control of the strategic town of Berwick-upon-Tweed remained matters for armed dispute.

Robert the Bruce and Bannockburn

Bruce was a Scottish aristocrat of Norman descent, and his family were members of the inner élite – his grandfather had been one of the unsuccessful royal claimants in the 1290s. In the decade after the defeat at Falkirk, Scottish political life was dominated by the conflict between Bruce and Comyn – a conflict fuelled by political competition and personal animosity. In 1299, Bruce was appointed co-regent of Scotland by the Scottish

Edward the Bruce and Ulster

Events in Scotland were closely watched in Ireland, especially in Ulster, which contained the largest of the Irish chiefdoms that remained free of direct English control. In the aftermath of Bannockburn, the O'Neill family invited Robert the Bruce's brother, Edward (d.1318), to lead a Scottish army into Ireland to drive out the English.

In 1315, Edward the Bruce landed on the north-east coast of Ireland and, gathering considerable Irish support, marched southwards. Not all of the Irish kings supported Edward, however, and some may have preferred their new allegiances and alliances, while others may have chosen to remember older rivalries. During the first two years of fighting, Edward was able to beat the English forces in battle, but the settlers remained united in their opposition to the Scottish invasion.

In 1317, Robert the Bruce led an army that defeated the English at the Battle of Slane and penetrated as far south as Cashel, County Tipperary. Frustratingly, although the pair reached the outskirts of Dublin, the Bruces' combined army was unable to capture what by now had become the capital of Ireland. After a single year in Ireland, Robert was forced to return to Scotland for the siege of Berwick-upon-Tweed, and any gains that he had made in Ireland were not consolidated. Edward proclaimed himself King of Ireland and fought on until his death at the Battle of Fochart, near Dundalk, County Louth, in 1318, when English control was re-established.

▼ **Battle of Bannockburn** (June 23–24, 1314). The 19th century engraving by T. Bolton shows the Abbot of Inchaffray blessing the Scottish army, led by Robert the Bruce, before its famous victory over the English.

◄ **Urquhart Castle, Loch Ness**, Scottish Highlands, was fortified and enlarged by Edward I of England, following his victory at the Battle of Dunbar (1296). William Wallace ('Braveheart') rose up against the English, and Castle Urquhart was attacked and captured by Andrew Moray. A few years later, Sir Alexander Forbes refused to surrender the Castle to the English, but he was eventually defeated and killed. In 1306, Robert the Bruce regained the Castle for Scottish forces. In 1691, the Castle was blown up in order to prevent it being used as a base by the Jacobites.

THE BRUCES IN SCOTLAND AND IRELAND

- Lands controlled by Bruce in 1309
- Irish chiefdoms
- Conquests of Edward I
- Bruce expedition in 1311
- Bruce expedition in 1315
- Bruce expedition in 1319
- Edward I expedition in 1314
- ■ Towns
- ● Battles

▶ **In 1306, Robert the Bruce** was crowned King of Scotland, but his forces were quickly defeated by Prince Edward of England. By 1309, however, Robert I had recovered control of the Highland region of Scotland, and later expeditions brought further gains. Robert secured a decisive victory over the English at the Battle of Bannockburn (1314) and Edward was forced to recognise Scottish independence. Allied with the O'Neill family, Robert and his brother, Edward the Bruce, were less successful in their attempts to expel the English from Ireland.

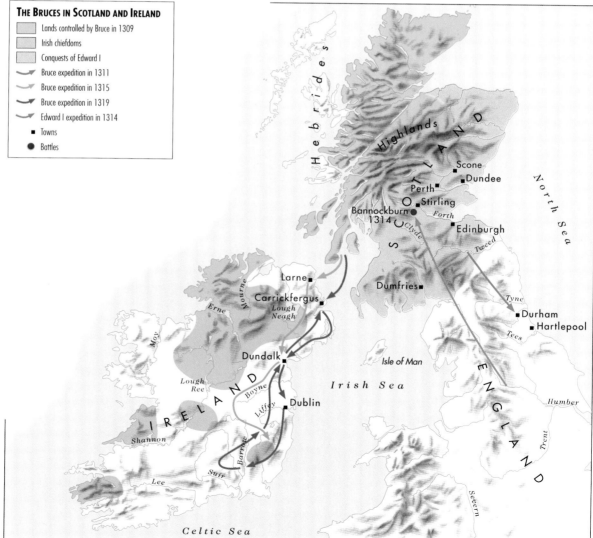

ENGLISH PLANTATIONS IN IRELAND

▲ *James I* by Paul van Somer (c.1577–1622). In 1607, after the failure of peace talks with James, the northern earls of Tyrone (O'Neills) and Tyrconnell (O'Donnells) fled Ireland. The 'flight of the earls' paved the way for the plantation of Ulster by a new influx of settlers, mainly Lowland Scots Presbyterians. The earls' lands were confiscated in 1609, and in 1613 James I granted Derry to the citizens of London.

The first English colonists in Ireland were the Norman lords and their retainers, who settled on conquered lands at the end of the 12th century. Ireland was reorganised into administrative counties, and the manor system of large-scale mixed farming was introduced. This overhaul of Irish agriculture produced something of an economic boom in the 13th century, and the authorities brought in English farmers and artisans in order to sustain the development. Many of these immigrants were attracted by the ready availability of land, which was already scarce in England.

In the middle of the 14th century, Britain and Ireland were devastated by an outbreak of the Black Death that swept across Europe. The mortality rate (30 to 40 percent) produced an economic crisis as farms and manors fell into disuse and disrepair. Land was no longer scarce and some settlers returned to England. Those that remained were considerably weakened in numbers and confidence, and the English authorities felt it necessary to reinforce their separate identity. In 1366, the Statutes of Kilkenny banned the English in Ireland from speaking the Irish language or marrying Irish partners.

English influence, and the use of the English language, became concentrated in the east-coast region between Dublin and Dundalk, and this became known as 'the Pale'. To live 'beyond the Pale' was deemed a misfortune, not least because the Irish were beginning to reassert themselves, particularly in the north-west, where native aristocrats led a revival of Irish scholarship.

The Plantation of Ireland

During the 16th century, Europe was again swept by social upheaval, this time caused by the emergence of Protestantism and the Reformation of the Catholic Church. The Reformation was expediently embraced by Henry VIII of England (1491–1547), and extended as a matter of course to Ireland. The effects of this imposed Reformation were largely material – the confiscation by the state of monastic property – and spiritually the country was little affected. There were few converts to the new branch of Christianity and even the Pale remained staunchly Catholic.

During the brief restoration of Catholicism under Mary I of England (1516–58), the English authorities organised the first large-scale immigration into Ireland for nearly three centuries – the first of the so-called Plantations. The lands of rebellious Irish lords on the borders of the Pale (Laois and Offaly) were seized and distributed, mainly to new English arrivals although some Irish property owners also benefitted. A number of other private plantations were attempted on confiscated lands, but these were unsuccessful.

The accession of Elizabeth I (1533–1603) to the English throne, and the establishment of a unified Church of England, brought conflict with the Catholic powers of Europe. During the 1580s, in the wake of an Irish rebellion led by the 14th Earl of Desmond (c.1538–83) – in which Spanish and Italian troops fought and died – new, official plantations were imposed on his confiscated lands. More than 30 large estates were created and distributed among Elizabethan courtiers, who undertook to recruit sufficient English families to work the land, but only succeeded in attracting about one-third of the required numbers.

Scottish farmers, mainly Protestant, had begun settling in north-east Ireland, but this process was interrupted in 1594 by the O'Neill rebellion in Ulster, which ignited nine years of warfare and again brought Spanish troops to Ireland. By 1600, the rebellion was contained, although it symbolically held out until Elizabeth's death (1603), after which Hugh O'Neill made his peace with the new English king, James I. The peace was soon shaken after the 1605 Gunpowder Plot against James unleashed a fierce anti-Catholic

◄ **Shane O'Neill** (c.1530–67), Earl of Tyrone (1559–67), imagined submitting to Sir Henry Sidney (1529–86), Lord Deputy of Ireland (1565–71, 1575–78) in 1566. The engraving is by Friedrich van Hulsen (c.1580–1660) from *The Image of Ireland* (1581) by John Derricke. Appointed (1569) by Elizabeth I, Sidney pioneered the first systematic attempts to colonise Ireland. In 1559, Shane O'Neill launched a rebellion against English interference in Ireland. O'Neill was murdered by the MacDonnells. In 1598, his successor, Hugh O'Neill (c.1540–1616), inflicted a heavy defeat on the English forces. The English rallied, however, and Hugh O'Neill was one of those involved in the 'flight of the earls'.

backlash. In 1607, O'Neill, together with his family, retainers, and several like-minded Ulster lords, fled Ireland for exile on the European mainland. This pivotal event – the flight of the lords – allowed the English king to confiscate their lands and, to many people, marks the end of the old "Celtic" Ireland.

In 1605, the earlier Scottish settlements had been given official recognition, and, in 1609, most of Ulster was turned into medium-sized estates for Scottish and English property owners and their tenant farmers. The district settled and developed by a group of London companies became known as Londonderry. In 1620, the Stuart plantations were extended southwards to the borders of Laoighis (Laois) and Offaly, which, together with the Elizabethan plantations south of Limerick, created an almost unbroken chain that effectively separated Connaught (Connacht) from the rest of Ireland.

The Stuart plantations were more enduring than earlier schemes, but were not entirely successful. Not all grants of land were taken up and many of the new settlements remained underpopulated while a few, especially Ulster, thrived and became island strongholds of Protestant belief amidst a sea of native Catholic Irish.

◀ *Elizabeth I* (English school, *c.*1600). The Irish staunchly resisted Elizabeth's attempts to establish large plantations for English and Scottish settlers in Ireland. Elizabeth faced three major revolts in Ireland: Shane O'Neill (1559), the Fitzgeralds of Desmond (1568–83), and Hugh O'Neill (Earl of Tyrone) and O'Donnell (1594–1603). Elizabeth crushed the rebellions at great economic cost to the English crown and only temporarily succeeded in subduing Irish resistance.

▼ *Irish types* by Jodocus Hondius (1563–1612), from the *Theatre of the Empire of Great Britain* (1610) by John Speed (1552–1629). These engravings are early examples of colonial stereotyping of the Irish.

ENGLISH SETTLEMENT IN IRELAND

- The Pale 1488
- Scottish settlement (formalised 1605)
- Tudor plantations
- Tudor plantations (Laois and Offaly)
- Jacobean plantations
- ■ Town

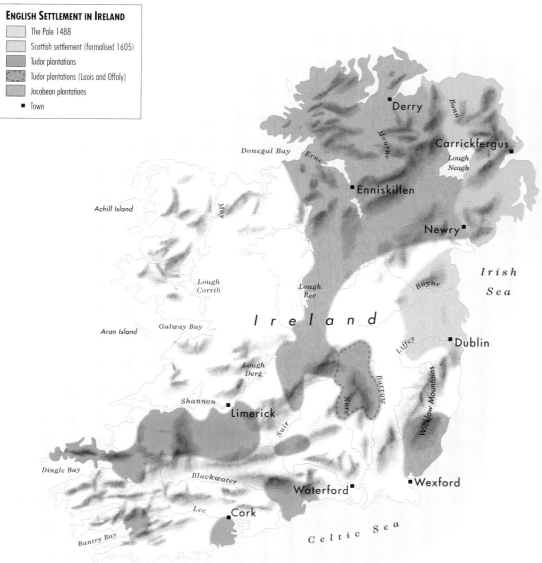

◀ **English settlement** Settlers worked on plantations established on land confiscated from rebellious Irish lords.

OLIVER CROMWELL AND 'KING BILLY'

In the mid-17th century, the Irish became involved in a bitter struggle for control of England that was further complicated by strong religious sympathies on both sides. The peaceful co-existence of Protestantism and Catholicism in Ireland was shattered, and by the end of the century, the Protestants had gained ascendancy.

Confederates in Ireland

In 1640, the Catholic officials who administered Ireland were removed and replaced by Puritan commissioners appointed by the English Parliament. The following year, the Ulster Catholics (again led by an O'Neill) rebelled – not against Charles I of England, but against Parliament. They were joined by other Catholic Irish and became collectively known as the Confederates. Many isolated English farmsteads were destroyed, and the Pale came under heavy attack.

In 1642, the English Civil War broke out between Charles and the Parliamentarians, and a Scottish 'Covenanter' army was sent to Ulster to protect the Protestant settlers. A peace treaty (1643) left the Confederates in control of most of Ireland, and talks for a long-term settlement were opened; the negotiators were, however, overtaken by events. In 1649, the execution of Charles I united the Confederates and the Dublin royalists against the new English regime; Ireland became another battleground of the English Civil War.

Oliver's army occupy Ireland

An English army was sent to Ireland, and the Dublin royalists surrendered to the Parliamentary forces. The Confederates were forced to retreat to Drogheda, County Louth. An English invasion force of 12,000 men, under the command of Oliver Cromwell (1599–1658), swelled the ranks of the Dublin forces. Cromwell's army quickly captured Drogheda, massacring most of the town's inhabitants. Soon afterwards, Cromwell captured Wexford, again slaughtering the defenders. None of the castles or walled towns could sustain resistance to the bombardment by English cannon, and Cromwell's army rapidly gained control of the eastern and southern coasts, before turning inland to seize the Confederate

▲ *William III of England*
(1707) from the studio of Sir Godfrey Kneller (1646?–1723). William III's victory at the Battle of the Boyne (July 11, 1690) forced the former king James II to flee Ireland for France. William's force of *c.*35,000 men included two regiments of French Huguenots, English, and many mercenaries. James commanded *c.*21,000 troops, consisting of Irish cavalry and infantry, and 7000 French infantry. Fearing encirclement by William's cavalry, which crossed the River Boyne at Rosnaree and Oldbridge, James beat a hasty retreat, which enabled the Jacobite army to (vainly) continue the war for a further year.

▶ **Cromwell in Ireland**
Cromwell's excesses on the battlefield were followed by the wholesale appropriation of land by the English Parliament, and the internal exile of Irish landowners to Connaught, where even the coastline was denied them.

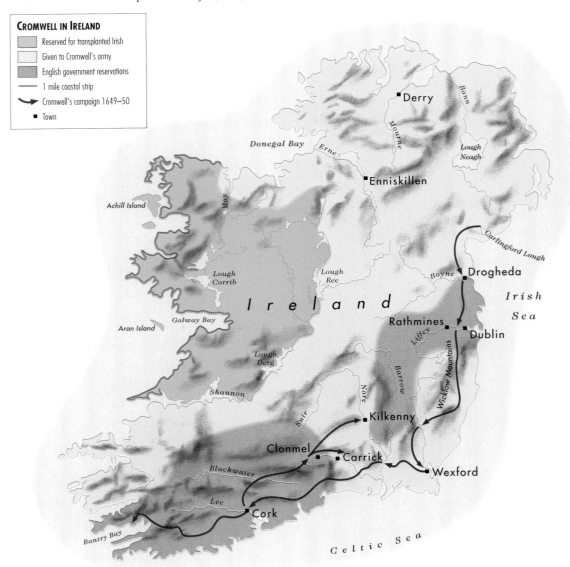

CROMWELL IN IRELAND

- Reserved for transplanted Irish
- Given to Cromwell's army
- English government reservations
- 1 mile coastal strip
- Cromwell's campaign 1649–50
- ■ Town

▶ *Siege of Drogheda* by Marcus Stone (1840–1921). The oil painting, which measures 43 × 68 centimetres (17 × 27 inches) depicts the final night of the siege (September 1649) of the town of Drogheda, east Ireland. The siege, which was laid by Oliver Cromwell, ended in the massacre of the garrison commanded by Sir Arthur Aston. Every able-bodied inhabitant of the town helped build defences, which Cromwell's troops quickly overran. In his announcement to Parliament after the massacre of 3500 Irish soldiers and civilians at Drogheda, east Ireland, Cromwell said, "I am persuaded that this is a righteous judgement of God upon these barbarous wretches, who have imbrued their hands in so much innocent blood."

capital of Kilkenny. In 1650, Cromwell was recalled to Britain in order to subdue the royalists in Scotland, leaving General Henry Ireton (1611–51) to complete the conquest of western Ireland. Limerick was captured in 1651, and within a year, Irish resistance had collapsed.

The settlement imposed on Ireland was far stricter than any previously experienced. Excluding Connaught (Connacht), all remaining Irish lands were confiscated and distributed to creditors or reserved for the English army of occupation. Only those Irish who could prove unstinting support of Parliament were permitted to remain as landowners, and those who were Catholic were required to relocate west of the River Shannon. Inside Connaught itself, the Irish were forbidden to settle within a mile-wide security zone along the coast.

Ireland in the aftermath of the Restoration

In 1660, the situation of the Irish was somewhat mitigated following the restoration of the English monarchy in the person of Charles II (1630–85). Recent English settlers in Ireland were obliged to return some of the confiscated lands, but the continuing strength of Protestant opinion prevented any greater relaxation.

In 1685, the Irish – depending on their branch of faith – viewed the accession of James II (1633–1701) of England, who was a Catholic, with either hope or suspicion. In England, opposition to James II quickly led to his bloodless overthrow in the 'Glorious Revolution' of 1688, and the succession of his daughter, Mary (1662–94), and her Protestant husband, Prince William of Orange (1650–1702), who became William III of England.

In 1689, James II landed in Ireland, accompanied by a contingent of French troops. James was widely acclaimed by the Irish, and in Dublin he summoned the so-called 'Patriot Parliament', which proposed to dismantle the Protestant land settlements. Only the Protestant towns of Londonderry (Derry) and Enniskillen in Ulster held out against his Catholic forces.

Late in 1689, English armies landed in eastern Ulster. In 1690, William III joined his forces and led them southwards. After William's victory at the Battle of the Boyne near Drogheda, James fled Ireland while William continued his march south, capturing Cork and Kinsale, County Cork. In 1691, the last Catholic stronghold, Limerick, was besieged and captured.

By the Treaty of Limerick, supporters of James II were permitted to leave Ireland, and many chose to do so. The departure of the Jacobites to mainland Europe – where many became mercenary soldiers – became known as the 'flight of the wild geese'. Those who remained saw promises of fair treatment evaporate in the face of increasing Protestant domination. By 1700, the exodus of Gaelic and Anglo-Norman aristocracy left less than ten per cent of Irish land in the hands of Catholics.

◀ *Oliver Cromwell* (1708) by Christian Richter (1678–1732). Guided by his Calvininst faith, Cromwell had a fierce prejudice against the Catholic Irish. As commander in chief and lord lieutenant of Ireland, Cromwell waged a ruthless campaign against the Irish, whom he regarded as savages. Cromwell once wrote, "I had rather be overrun by a Cavalierish interest than a Scotch interest, I had rather be overrun by a Scotch interest than an Irish interest, and I think that of all, this the most dangerous.... for all the world knows their barbarism.'

THE UNION OF SCOTLAND AND ENGLAND

The male line of the Stuart dynasty lost the thrones of England and Scotland through fears that James II's (1633–1701) infant son and heir, James Edward Stuart (1688–1766), would be raised a Catholic. The 'Glorious Revolution' of 1688 replaced James with his daughter Mary (1662–94) and her Protestant husband William of Orange (1650–1702), and the couple ruled jointly until Mary's death. William and Mary left no surviving children and, on William's death, the crown passed to Mary's younger sister Anne (1665–1714), who was childless.

It was decided that the Hanoverian descendant of one of James I's daughters would succeed Anne. The succession was formally confirmed by the Act of Settlement of 1701. In order to secure this succession in Scotland, the country was formally joined to England in 1707 by consent of their respective parliaments.

Union of Scotland and England

The union of England (which had included Wales since 1536) and Scotland produced the 'new' nation of Great Britain. It was a recognition of the close links between the two countries, which had become even closer during 70 years of Stuart kingship, and an acknowledgement of the *de facto* economic and political pre-eminence of England, at a time when Scotland's fortunes were on the wane.

During the 16th century, the stubborn defence of Protestantism and competition with Catholic France and Spain had turned England into a maritime superpower. By the end of the century, British merchants had established colonies in the New World and India. In the 17th century, these gains were expanded, both by new English settlements and the conquest of other European colonies, such as the capture (1664) of New Amsterdam (now New York City) from the Dutch. By contrast, Scotland failed to establish a single overseas territory.

▲ **Queen Anne** by Michael Dahl (1656–1743). Anne was the last Stuart monarch and the first monarch of Great Britain. Her reign (1702–14) was dominated by the War of the Spanish Succession (1701–14), which saw the emergence of Britian as a maritime and colonial power. John Churchill, 1st Duke of Marlborough (1650–1722), secured a famous victory over the French at the Battle of Blenheim (1704).

▶ **European empires in c.1770** Colonial empires drove the economies of several European powers during the 18th century, and conflicts between those powers were waged on a global scale. By 1770, victories against the French in India and North America had established British ascendancy.

EUROPEAN EMPIRES c.1770	
	British
	French
	Dutch
	Portugese
	Spanish

In 1700, after only two years of miserable existence, the Scottish colony failed at Darien in Panama, Central America. This event convinced many prudent Scots that an independent Scotland could not by itself mobilise sufficient resources to take proper advantage of the unfolding economic opportunities. Union with England was a prudent course of action, and did not in any case represent complete surrender to the English. Scotland retained its own Church and its own legal and educational systems, although its members of Parliament now sat in Westminster, and it was in other respects a province of the new 'greater England', Great Britain. Active opposition to the union was largely confined to the rural population of the Highlands – a fact that served to reinforce the divide between the Lowlands and Highlands.

The Protestant Ascendancy in Ireland

The union of Scotland and England confirmed Ireland's subordinate position as an 'internal colony', and its inhabitants were treated accordingly. The 18th century is known as the period of the 'Protestant Ascendancy' in Ireland.

◄ **Robert Walpole** by the Irish painter Charles Jervas (1675–1739). Walpole is widely regarded as the first prime minister of Britain (1721–42). His long ascendancy was based on mastery of the House of Commons, and the patronage of George I and George II. His restoration of order after the financial panic in the South Sea Bubble Crisis (1720) sounded the death knell for the Jacobite cause.

From the 1720s to 1793, Protestants maintained a tight grip on power in Ireland, and Catholics, who formed the vast majority of the peasantry, owned little of the land and had even less political power. (The native aristocracy having gone into exile after the defeat of James II.) Although considerable development took place – farming was improved along English lines and the linen-textile industry was overhauled – these were conscientiously Protestant achievements, intended through their commercial success to demonstrate the superiority of their belief system, and their 'right' to rule Ireland. Although Ireland was superficially at peace, the issues of land reform and political representation simmered below the surface, as did the sectarian divide. In Ulster, the Catholic Defenders were organised to oppose unofficial 'disarming raids' by Protestant gangs.

The British Empire

The union of Scotland and England may have further sidelined Ireland, but it greatly strengthened the island of Britain. As well as a fresh national identity, the new nation enjoyed several advantages, not least of which were stable domestic politics and the development of an efficient and centralised administration. These, along with the technological and organisational advances known as the Industrial Revolution, enabled Britain to mobilise and deploy fearsome military power.

Throughout the 18th century and beyond, the British fought a series of wars against France. The Treaty of Paris (1763), which concluded the French and Indian Wars (1689–1763), acknowledged British control of India and a large part of North America.

Thirteen of the American colonies were, however, soon lost in the American Revolution (1775–83), which was won by the colonials with French assistance. In passing, it is worth mentioning that a regiment of the Irish Brigade fought alongside the French in the American Revolution. The British Empire not only survived this tribulation, but also emerged stronger and even more powerful after the French Revolutionary Wars (1792–1802) and the Napoleonic Wars (1803–15).

CHAPTER
FIVE

▲ *The Dream of Ossian* (1813) by Jean-Auguste-Dominique Ingres (1780–1867)

THE 'PROGRESSIVE' CENTURIES

▲ **Who Wants Me?** by Isaac Cruikshank (1756?–1811?). The cartoon depicts Thomas Paine (1737–1809) with his Rights of Man – a defence of the French Revolution. After publication, Paine was accused of treason and fled to France. His pamphlet Common Sense (1776) sought independence for the American colonies.

The Middle Ages ended with momentous events – the Renaissance, the Reformation and the establishment of overseas empires; and most historians date the beginning of the modern period to 1550 or thereabouts. Much has changed since then, and change is a continuous process; but because of their penchant for patterns and compartments, historians have singled out two of the intervening centuries – the 18th and 19th – for particular attention.

It should be noted that the use of centuries is an arbitrariness imposed by the calendar and in some ways the terms are approximate. It has convincingly been argued, for instance, that the 19th century began in 1792, and that the 20th century actually spanned the dates 1914 to 1989. Whatever the 20th century became, and whatever we make of the 21st, the fundamental nature of modern life was forged during the two preceding centuries of 'progress'.

Enlightenment and 'progress'

The idea that history is an inevitable march of progress has long since been discredited, and even the word 'progress' has fallen somewhat into disrepute, but for those wishing to be succinct, there is no suitable alternative.

In Europe, the 18th and 19th centuries have been lauded with a plethora of labels, all seeking to symbolise and capture the spirit of the times, and all suggesting advancement. The 18th century is often described as 'the Age of Reason', 'the Age of Enlightenment', or the time of 'Benevolent Despotism'; while the 19th century is usually referred to as 'the Age of Reform', 'the Age of Revolutions', or 'the Age of Nationalism'.

During the 18th century, the educated élite began to develop a rational approach to the world, along the lines of the ancient Greek philosophers. Scotland played a leading part in this Enlightenment, a result of which was the establishment of the 'scientific method' and the classification of nature. Another consequence was that some of Europe's absolute rulers began, for reasons of State, to take a more keen interest in the welfare of their subjects in matters such as public health, personal freedom and education. Some, such as Frederick II (the Great) of Prussia (1712–86) and Emperor Joseph II (1741–90) who emancipated serfs, became known as benevolent despots.

The clamour for reform intensified and was, in many instances, ignored and some of those who harboured grievances began to take up arms. During the latter part of the 18th century, two political revolutions, in America and in France, would redefine the relationship between rulers and the ruled. The Declaration of Independence (1776) by some of Britain's American colonists established their rights of representation and self-determination, and set a precedent. The overthrow and execution of Louis XVI of France (1754–93) involved

▲ **Otto von Bismarck** (1815–98) laid the foundations of a modern, unified German State. He was the first European statesman to devise a social security system.

▶ **Liberty Leading the People** (1830) by Eugène Delacroix (1798–1863). Delacroix's painting commemorates the July Revolution (July 28, 1830) that overthrew the Bourbon King Charles X. Louis-Philippe, Charles' successor, introduced a liberal constitution.

▶ **Coalbrookdale by Night**
(1801) by Philipp de Loutherbourg (1740–1812). Coalbrookdale in Shropshire, central England, is often called the birthplace of the Industrial Revolution. In 1709, Abraham Darby (c.1678–1717) developed the first coke-fired blast furnace at his ironworks in Coalbrookdale. The relatively cheap and abundant supplies of coke fuelled the Industrial Revolution. In 1779, Darby's grandson, Abraham Darby III (1750–91), built the first cast-iron bridge in the world at Coalbrookdale. The bridge spans the so-called Ironbridge Gorge. The last deep coal-mine at Coalbrookdale closed in 1979.

a further redefinition of citizens' rights, and extended the principle of self-determination to everyone.

During the 19th century, two strands of 'progress' – nationalism and popular democracy – came to dominate politics in Europe. In Britain, it was assumed that nationhood had already been achieved, while democracy was approached through peaceful reform. Across the rest of Europe, however, the two strands became closely intertwined, and provoked numerous violent confrontations. In 1829, following a war of independence, Greece was liberated from the Ottoman Empire, while Belgium gained independence from the Netherlands in 1830. During the latter part of the 19th century, Italy and Germany were welded into nations through *realpolitik* and warfare.

Within established nations, the struggle for political power could be just as fierce. In 1848, while revolution was ringing around the capitals of Europe, Karl Marx (1818–83) and Frederich Engels (1820–95) published the *Communist Manifesto*, a document that was to have profound implications for the 20th century.

The Industrial Revolution

Underlying, bridging and uniting the 18th and 19th centuries is another label, this time economic rather than political – the Industrial Revolution, the process by which machines largely replaced human and animal power and greatly increased people's ability to process materials and manufacture goods. Britain played a pre-eminent role in this Revolution. Initially limited to a few industries, such as cotton textiles and mining, the technological advances of water and steam power became more refined and more widely applied. By the end of the 19th century, there was hardly any aspect of life in Western Europe or North America that was not affected by mechanisation.

Like political progress, this economic advance had two main pillars. Firstly, the manufacturing revolution –

intricate and ingenious machinery, coupled to rotary motion from water-wheels or steam engines – greatly amplified the output of individuals, and encouraged the concentration of workers in mills and factories. Secondly, and slightly later, came the transport revolution – railways and steamboats that permitted distribution of goods and further stimulated trade and production.

In addition, overlying and bridging the two centuries was the spirit of Romanticism, a movement that represented the artistic response to the increasingly rational and scientific world. Expressed in poetry, music and painting, Romanticism was founded on and appealed to emotion, and was particularly sympathetic to nationalism and the aspirations of subject peoples.

◀ **Drafting of the Declaration of Independence** by Jean Leon Jerome Ferris (1863–1930). The Declaration of Independence (1776) was drafted by Thomas Jefferson (standing right) with the assistance of Benjamin Franklin (left) and John Adams (centre). A statement of the aims and principles of the American Revolution, the document was adopted by the Second Continental Congress on July 4, 1776. It states the necessity of government having the consent of the governed, and of government's responsibility to its people. It proclaims that, "We hold these truths to be self-evident, that all men are created equal, that they are endowed by their Creator with certain unalienable Rights, that among these are Life, Liberty and the pursuit of Happiness."

THE 'CELTIC REVIVAL' AND NATIONALISM

The Renaissance revival of the classical authors reacquainted educated Europeans with their own heritage (as depicted by Roman historians) and stimulated a new interest in ancient history. By the end of the 16th century, antiquarians such as John Leland (c.1506–52) in England, Jean Le Fèvre (active 1530s) in France, and George Buchanan (1506–82) in Scotland, had helped produce a composite picture of ancient Britons and Gauls, complete with moustaches, torques, body paint, and wielding the severed heads of their enemies. These fearsome people were not generally referred to as Celts – that appellation would not become commonplace until the beginning of the 18th century.

Birth of Celtic studies

In 1703, the Breton scholar Paul-Yves Pezron published *L'Antiquité de la Nation et de la Langue des Celtes, autrement appelez Gaulois* ('History of the Nation and Language of the Celts, otherwise known as Gauls'), which suggested that contemporary Breton and Welsh were both linguistic descendants of the ancient Gaulish or Celtic tongue. Pezron also outlined a complex series of ethnic migrations to explain how the Celts (who were also the Spartans) arrived in Brittany, north-east France. These two themes – mass migration and a common Celtic ethnicity – remain central to Celtic studies although, in other respects, Pezron is now seen as hopelessly wrong. For instance, he proudly claimed the Celts to be the builders of the great megalithic monuments, whereas today the two phenomena are regarded as being separated by more than 2000 years.

Pezron intended his book to promote the status of Brittany within France and, indeed, it led to a mini-revival of the Breton language during the 18th century. Yet, it probably had a greater impact in the new Britain, formed by the union of Scotland and England in 1707. The formation of Great Britain further diminished the status of Wales at a time when Welsh culture was already at a low ebb.

In 1706, Edward Llwyd (1660–1709), a Welsh scholar and keeper of the Ashmolean Museum in Oxford, published a translation of Pezron's work in both English and Welsh, which specifically identified the Celts as the ancient Britons. In the following year, Llwyd published the first volume of his own *Archaeologia Britannica*, in which he linked the surviving and ancient Celtic languages into the language family and subdivisions that we recognise today.

The Celtic identity of the ancient Britons was embraced by the English antiquarian William Stukeley (1687–1765), who catalogued the ancient monuments of Britain in the 1720s, and in 1740 published an illustrated account of a 'Celtic' Stonehenge, complete with druidical ceremonies. By the mid-18th century, ancient British Celts were fixed firmly in the imagination of educated Britons.

Llwyd's affirmation of ethnicity and heritage based on language was even more popular in Wales and Scotland, where it conferred upon the inhabitants an identity of authentic or pure Britons as opposed to the 'mongrel' English, and provided a cultural counter-balance to their political domination by England. In Wales, Llwyd's book had exactly the effect he had hoped for – stimulating a revival of the Welsh language. In 1725, Sion Rhydderch published a definitive Welsh grammar that formed the basis for a steady growth in Welsh for the remainder of the 18th century – although soon the language's Celtic identity was eclipsed, but not completely extinguished, by Nonconformist enthusiasm.

In Scotland, where union was a very recent phenomenon, Celtic heritage provided a much needed boost to national morale, as evidenced by the popular enthusiasm for the 'Celtic' poems of Ossian, published by James Macpherson (1736–96), and the historical novels of Sir Walter Scott (1771–1832). These unequivocally Scottish entertainments were almost equally popular in England, whose inhabitants could claim to share at least a part of the same proud, ancient British heritage.

These literary expressions of cultural and ethnic identity within Britain also struck a wider chord in Europe, and they were completely in tune with their

▼ *Dream of Ossian* (1813) by Jean-Auguste-Dominique Ingres (1780–1867). The painting was commissioned for the Quirnal Palace, the official residence of Napoleon I in Rome. Ossian (*Oisín*) is the Irish warrior-poet in the Fenian cycle of stories. In 1762, James Macpherson created a literary sensation when he announced that he had 'found' the 3rd-century Gaelic poems of Ossian and published them as *Fingal*. The poems aroused the suspicion and ire of many Irish scholars because they conflated Ulster and Fenian myths and made many of the heroes Caledonian. In the 19th century, Macpherson himself was unmasked as the true author.

time. Language, poetry and songs all became rallying cries to the numerous subject peoples of the two empires – the Austro-Hungarian and the Ottoman – that dominated most of central and eastern Europe. The Celtic cultural heritage, as revived by 18th- and 19th-century writers, became a part of the developing Romantic *Zeitgeist*. Stimulated by the success of the American and French Revolutions, the possession and promotion of national and ethnic literatures became a widespread tool in the many liberation struggles that subsequently erupted in various parts of the world.

▲ **William Stukeley** (1687–1765) self-portrait (1735). Stukeley was an antiquarian and physician whose studies of the Neolithic/Bronze Age stone circles at Stonehenge and Avebury, Wiltshire, led him to publish fanciful theories connecting the circles to the Druids. These ideas fed into the Romantic movement and the Celtic Revival. Although his theories were wrong, Stukeley's fieldwork was of lasting value.

▲ **Ancient Briton** holding a severed human head as trophy by John White (active *c.*1570–93). Such fearsome depictions of ancient British warriors were popular in Elizabethan England. The warrior is wearing a torque, sword-belt and waxed moustache.

◄ **Stonehenge**, Wiltshire, by Nathaniel Whittock (1791–1860). The engraving is based on a plan drawn up by William Stukeley (1687–1765), and currently held in the Ashmolean Museum, Oxford. It depicts Druids sacrificing to the Sun. Note the drinking horn (right) and the carnyx-like horns and harp (left).

JACOBITE REBELLIONS

Although the Scottish did not universally admire the Stuart succession and the union with England, only the Jacobites formed an active opposition. The Jacobites were the supporters of James II (1633–1701) and his male descendants – royal pretenders who, during the first half of the 18th century, pursued an active and sometimes violent claim to the thrones of Scotland and England. Principally due to the clan structure, the Jacobite cause was strongest in the Scottish Highlands, but there was limited support from the Catholic gentry in northern England.

Some of the Highlanders had chosen to follow the last of the Stuart kings into exile, but many of those who remained openly voiced their opposition to the Act of Settlement (1701) and the Act of Union (1707). These Highlanders sided with Catholic France and Spain rather than the Protestant Electorate of Hanover. During the reign (1702–14) of Anne, the Jacobites were content to remain in the Highlands and confine themselves to vocal opposition, but a more dynamic campaign ensued after her death.

The Fifteen Rebellion

In 1715, a year after the accession of the Hanoverian George I (1660–1727) as King of Great Britain and Ireland, the Earl of Mar raised the Highlanders to fight in the name of the would-be James VIII of Scotland (and James III of England), James Edward Stuart (1688–1766). Mar and the Jacobite army marched south to Perth, central Scotland, gaining further support en route. The government hastily assembled a defence force, which prevented the Jacobites from capturing the town at the inconclusive Battle of Sheriffmuir. Meanwhile, magistrates in Edinburgh had ordered the arrest of known Jacobites, and suppressed a sympathetic rising in the city.

In northern England, the Jacobite cause had greater initial success and a small army marched as far south as Preston, Lancashire, although it did meet sporadic

▼ **Jacobite rebellions** Despite their bravery and enthusiasm, the Jacobites were overwhelmed by British forces. In both major rebellions, the British government was able to count on loyalist Scots support.

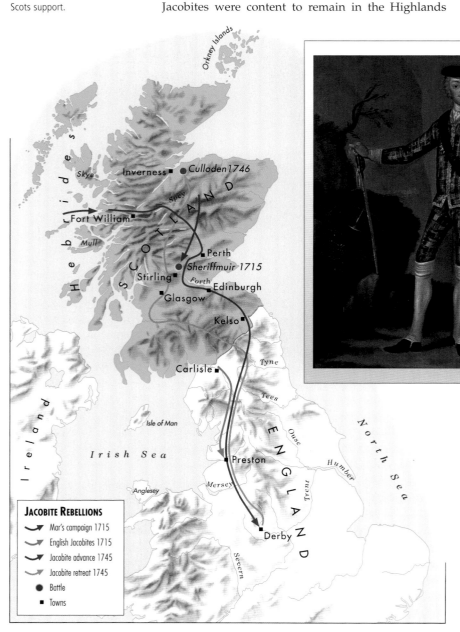

JACOBITE REBELLIONS

- ↝ Mar's campaign 1715
- ↝ English Jacobites 1715
- ↝ Jacobite advance 1745
- ↝ Jacobite retreat 1745
- ● Battle
- ■ Towns

THE 'BONNIE PRINCE'

After his defeat at the Battle of Culloden (April 16, 1746), Prince Charles Edward Stuart (1720–88) became a fugitive, hounded by British troops and sheltered by Jacobite supporters. While taking refuge in the Hebrides, Charles was aided in his flight from Britain by Flora Macdonald (1722–90). Disguised as Betty Burke, an Irish spinning-maid, Charles accompanied Flora on a voyage to Skye, Inner Hebrides. In September 1746, Charles completed his escape by sailing to France. Disowned by Catholic Europe, Charles became a dipsomaniac.

opposition. By this time, however, Highlanders that remained loyal to George I had recaptured the town of Inverness, north-east Scotland, and soon the government had regained control of all Scotland. Active support for the Jacobites melted away. James, who became known as the 'Old Pretender', briefly landed on the Scottish coast before fleeing back to France.

After the British government restored order, the clampdown was severe but hardly excessive by the standards of the day. The government executed a few leaders and condemened hundreds of prisoners to a life of servitude on plantations in the Tropics. Many Jacobite noble families had their titles rescinded, and an attempt was made to confiscate Highlanders' weapons. In 1717, the government issued a general pardon to

those involved in the '15 Rebellion, although there were exceptions and some remained condemned.

The Forty-five Rebellion

The Stuart cause remained a potent threat to the British government, and an abortive Spanish landing in 1719 provoked a more systematic wave of repression. The government enforced a new Disarming Act more rigorously than the earlier confiscations, and recruited loyal Highlanders into special police units that eventually amalgamated into the Black Watch regiment. From 1725 to 1735, the British military commander, General George Wade, constructed a network of highways across the Highlands that, like Roman roads, was intended for the rapid movement of troops.

In July 1745, with the government and most of the army preoccupied with the War of the Austrian Succession (1740–48) in Europe, James Stuart's son, Charles Edward Stuart (1720–88) – the 'Young Pretender' – landed with a small band of supporters on the west coast of Scotland. Highlanders again flocked to the Jacobite standard, although in smaller numbers than in the Fifteen Rebellion. Within a few weeks, 'Bonnie Prince Charlie' had gained control of most of Scotland, and in September 1745 he marched into Edinburgh and proclaimed his father as King James VIII.

Realising that it was only a matter of time before the government called up reinforcements, Charles made a rapid advance to the south, reaching Derby, central England, without meeting serious opposition. The presence of a Jacobite army less than 200 kilometres (125 miles) from London caused panic in the capital,

but Charles was unable to exploit the situation and retreated north to overwinter in the Highlands.

In the spring of 1746, Charles deployed his army in a set-piece battle, at Culloden, near Inverness, against a combined force of regulars and loyal Highlanders, commanded by the Duke of Cumberland (1721–65), son of George II (1683–1760) of Great Britain and Ireland. Cumberland crushed the Jacobite army and showed little mercy to prisoners or the wounded, many of whom were slaughtered.

The immediate aftermath of Culloden was equally brutal and bloody, with both sides claiming betrayal and much settling of old scores and rivalries. In the medium-term, government policy was equally unforgiving – Jacobite lands were confiscated, the inhabitants displaced and their traditional Highland dress prohibited by law.

▲ *Battle of Glenshiel* (1719) by Peter Tillemans (1684–1734). After the failure of the '15 Rebellion, a further rising in the Scottish Highlands, aided by Spain and led by the Earl of Seaforth, was defeated by General Joseph Wightman.

▼ *Execution of the Jacobite Lords*, engraving after George Budd (active 1745–52). On August 18, 1746, Arthur Elpinstone, 6th Baron of Balmerino, and William Boyd, 4th Earl of Kilmarnock, were beheaded for treason at Tower Hill, London.

HIGHLAND CLANS

Although in political union with England, Scotland itself was far from being a united country at the beginning of the 18th century. In many respects, Scotland was divided into two nations – the Lowlands and the Highlands. The Lowlanders (the ancient British territories of Strathclyde and Lothian) were mainly Protestant and had become strongly Anglicised, although they spoke Scots dialect rather than English. The Highlanders, by contrast, were predominantly Catholic and spoke Gaelic. North of an imaginary line drawn roughly between Dumbarton on the Firth of Clyde and Stonehaven, Aberdeenshire, governments and laws had little authority, and real power lay with hereditary clan chiefs.

The clan was the traditional unit of the Highland population, which in 1700 numbered *c.*200,000. The clan chief 'owned' the clan's territory and had absolute powers over land usage. Centuries of absorbing foreign invaders (and they were originally invaders themselves) meant that few Scottish clan chiefs could claim Celtic descent, although others were just as proud of less ancient lineages.

For example, the MacNeils claimed descent from Niall of the Nine Hostages (*see* page 122) and the Lamonts from an 11th-century Irish king. The MacLeod and Gunn clan chieftains had Viking ancestors; and the Sinclairs and Menzies were Norman and Anglo-Norman respectively. While ancestral seniority may still have held some influence in the Highlands, by the 18th century what really mattered was how many warriors a chieftain could muster. Wool was the only cash crop produced, and that was largely

women's work. One of the main occupations for Highland men, when not otherwise engaged in neighbourly disputes, was raiding the Lowlands for loot or protection money, known as 'blackmail'.

Clans and dress codes

The basic organisation of the Scottish clan was along military lines, with the chief as supreme commander. Beneath the chief were the 'gentlemen' of the clan – his relatives and henchmen – who served as officers, and from whom the chief selected members of the clan's advisory council.

The Scottish Highlands are not good cavalry country, and Highland armies mainly consisted of foot soldiers, whose preferred weapon was the sword. Besides his personal bodyguards, a piper and a bard accompanied the chief into battle. When fighting other Highlanders, warriors identified themselves with their clan's traditional plant badge and did not, contrary to popular opinion, wear distinctive 'clan' tartans at this time.

Traditional Highland dress consisted of a shirt over which was a *breacbhrait*, a single piece of plaid, woollen worsted cloth measuring *c.*4.9 × 1.5 metres (*c.*16 × 5 feet). One end of the *breacbhrait* wrapped and tucked around the waist, and was held in place with a belt, while the remaining length draped around the shoulders as a cloak. Many of the wealthier Highlanders, such as the clan gentlemen, disdained the *breacbhrait* and instead wore tailored trews (trousers).

'Tartanes', rectangular patterns (setts) of woven colour, have existed in Scotland since the 15th century

▼ *A Highland Glen* by Richard Ansdell (1815–85). The Gaelic-speaking clans of the Scottish Highlands were the staunchest supporters of Jacobitism. In the 18th century, the traditional clan structure began to erode as the barren landscape proved incapable of sustaining the population. The military and legislative repression that followed the failure of the Jacobite rebellions, coupled with the clan chiefs' attempts to copy the Lowland system of land ownership, brought mass emigration and the disappearance of traditional Highland culture.

or earlier. Although some particular sets may have been associated with certain clans before the 18th century, it seems likely that the main distinction between tartans was that gentlemen wore trews and cloaks of bright tartans, while ordinary clansfolk wore plaids of drabber colours.

Collapse of Highland culture

The failure of the Jacobite rebellions marked the beginning of the demise of the Highland way of life. After the Forty-five Rebellion, the British government banned the wearing of traditional dress and the playing of the bagpipes, which were considered an "instrument of war". New military roads gave the government easy access to the heart of the Highlands and enabled the authorities to enforce the prohibitions and conduct searches for arms.

The final blow to the Highlands was not political or cultural, but economic. In the 1790s, many landowners – both newcomers and traditional chieftains – began to evict their tenants and enclose large areas of land for commercial sheep farming. These Highland clearances caused considerable hardship; many people emigrated while others sought work in Lowland cities.

Highland dress and the bagpipes remained prohibited to civilians until 1782, and they did not become fully respectable until the early 19th century,

when George IV (1762–1830) visited Scotland, fully attired in tartan for the occasion. It was only after this royally sponsored rehabilitation that various self-appointed 'authorities' developed a whole complex heraldry of tartans.

(*For further discussion on the history of tartan, see pages 168–69*)

▼ **Bagpipes** are traditionally associated with Celtic music, but probably originated in south-east Asia. The chanter usually has a double reed. Somewhat limited by its short range (commonly one octave), bagpipes are heard mainly in folk or military music. The instrument shown here is a Scottish Highlands bagpipe, which is mouth-blown and in the key of D Major.

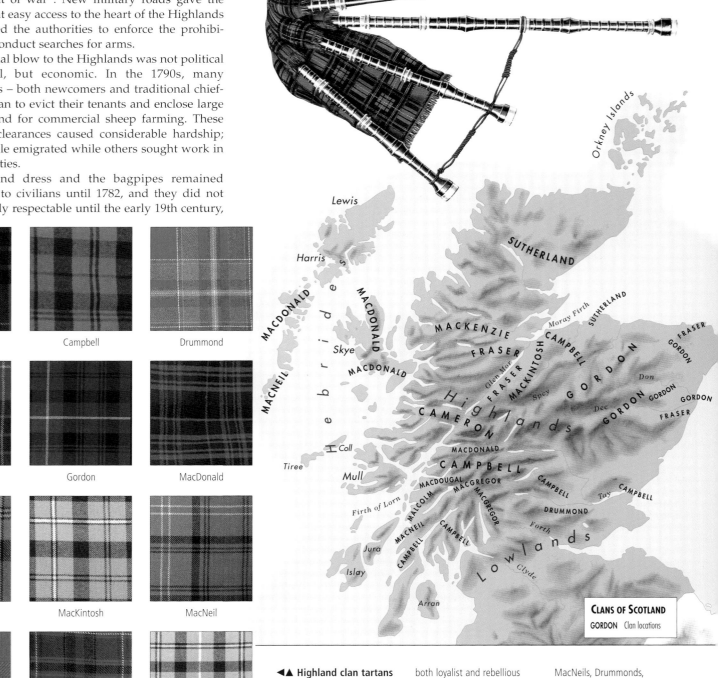

Cameron

Campbell

Drummond

Frazer

Gordon

MacDonald

MacKenzie

MacKintosh

MacNeil

Malcolm

McGregor

Sutherland

CLANS OF SCOTLAND
GORDON Clan locations

◀▲ **Highland clan tartans**
The distinctive patterns of the clan tartans have become a central part of Scottish tradition, and are worn with equal pride by descendants of both loyalist and rebellious Highland clans. The Campbell and Sutherland clans remained loyal to the British government during both the '15 and the '45 Rebellions; while the MacNeils, Drummonds, MacKenzies and Camerons were in the Jacobite camp. Among the Gordons and the Frasers, however, there were divided loyalties.

SCOTTISH POETS

In Scotland the use of the English language and the adoption of educated English pronunciation became much more widespread during the period of Stuart rule. Even before the rebellions of 1715 and 1745, Scottish Gaelic was a minority Highlands language, and in the Lowlands, most people spoke a ver-nacular dialect of English known as Scots. The Jacobite failures, and the strenuous government repression that followed, further marginalised Gaelic because most of those who replaced the dispossessed Highland leaders spoke the educated English of the ruling élite.

During the latter part of the 18th- and the early 19th-centuries, three pop-ular Scottish poets – James Macpherson (1736–96), Robert Burns (1759–96) and Sir Walter Scott (1771–1832) – highlighted and celebrated the diversity of language in Scotland. Although their circumstances and personal agendas varied greatly, all three were part of the Europe-wide Romantic movement, which emphasised emotion over reason in the arts. Macpherson exploited the romantic appeal of the ancient and mysterious Celts; Burns wrote in the 'ordinary' language later advocat-ed by the English Romantic poet William Wordsworth (1770–1850); and Scott developed a new art form – the historical romantic novel.

► **Robert Burns** (1787) by Alexander Nasmyth (1758–1840). Burns spent much of the early part of his life working as a farm labourer. After the publication of his *Poems Chiefly in the Scottish Dialect*, Burns was hailed by Henry Mackenzie (1745–1831).

► **Sir Walter Scott** (1822) by Sir Henry Raeburn (1756–1823). The success of Scott's first novel, *Waverley* (1814), encouraged him to concentrate on the form. *Waverley* is set during the period of the 1745 Jacobite Rebellion in Scotland. *Rob Roy* (1818), perhaps Scott's most popular novel, is loosely based on the exploits of the Highland outlaw Robert MacGregor (1671–1734).

Macpherson and Ossian

In 1760, James Macpherson published *Fragments of Ancient Poetry collected in the Highlands of Scotland*, supposedly translated from Gaelic, although Macpherson would never show anyone the original fragments. The following year, he obtained subscriptions to pay for a trip to the Scottish islands to find the story of the 3rd-century King Fingal as related by his son, the blind bard Ossian. Macpherson succeeded in his quest and announced his 'discovery' to the literary world. Other works by Ossian soon appeared, including *Temora* (1765) and the *Poems of Ossian* (1773).

Ossian's translated poetry became extremely popular, both in Britain and elsewhere and spawned many imitations. Although not overtly nationalist, this 'ancient' poetry had widespread influence among many ethnic groups in Europe, and inspired poets to articulate their own national struggles.

Most of Macpherson's contemporaries were only too happy to believe in the existence of Ossian; but there were some sceptics, among them was Dr Samuel Johnson (1709–84), who, in 1775, accused Macpherson of inventing most of what he ascribed to Ossian. In 1805, a committee concluded that the poet-ry was by Macpherson, while the current view is that Macpherson embellished a core of genuine frag-ments. The uncertainty of authenticity, however, did not diminish Ossian's appeal to those wanting to assert their own heritage.

Rabbie Burns – bard of Scotland

Robert Burns was the son of a poor tenant farmer in Alloway, Ayrshire. The poverty of his family meant that Burns spent most of his youth working on the farm, but his father encouraged him to read widely. Like many people at that time, he kept a commonplace book for writing down household tips, mottos, edifying thoughts, and, in Burns' case, his own poetry. Before he wrote his first poem in 1783, Burns noted in the book, "I never had the least thought or inclination of turning poet till I once got heartily in love, and then rhyme and song were a spontaneous language of my heart."

Burns was, however, no ordinary lovestruck poet, but a conscientious craftsman who carefully studied both Scots and English styles of versification. In 1786, he published a collection of his work, *Poems,*

Chiefly in the Scottish Dialect, which was an immediate and overwhelming success in Scotland. These poems, often known as the 'Kilmarnock Poems' for the town where the book was printed, formed the basis for Burns' fame in his lifetime. The first edition contained 44 poems, including "To a Mouse", with its famous line, "Wee, sleekit, cow'rin' tim'rous beestie," and "The Death and Dying Words of Poor Mallie", the ironic and humorous 'testament' of a dying sheep. Subsequent editions during his lifetime added a further 41 poems, although some of his best poems, such as "The Jolly Beggars" and "Holy Willie's Prayer" were only published posthumously.

Burns moved to Edinburgh where, lionised by the literary establishment, he began working with musicologists, editing and composing lyrics for traditional Scottish tunes. It is chiefly for these songs – most famously "Auld Lang Syne" – that Burns is remembered today, even though his contributions were often anonymous. In 1788, Burns returned to Ayrshire.

After his death, Burns became acknowledged as the national poet of Scotland, and few poets command such a long-lasting reputation. Furthermore, few poets are so well loved. Each year on his birthday (25 January), Scots gather to celebrate Burns' Night.

Walter Scott – Romanticism and history

As a teenager, Walter Scott had learned to read French ballads and the works of Dante in their original languages. In 1802, when Ossian was still very popular, Scott began writing his own imitations of ancient ballads. In 1805, he published *The Lay of the Last Minstrel* and five years later, *The Lady of the Lake*. Although the literary critics acclaimed Scott's poems, they did not attract a wide audience.

In 1814, economic necessity prompted Scott to turn his hand to writing novels, an increasingly popular literary form. He completed *Waverley* in just four weeks, and in the following year he published "Lord of the Isles'. Scott's combination of dashing history and chivalrous romance met with widespread critical and popular acclaim.

Despite being plagued by illness, Scott completed more than a dozen historical novels – including *Rob Roy* (1818), *Ivanhoe* (1819) and *Redgauntlet* (1824) – that mined the same rich vein of Romanticism. Although Scott wrote in English, he used Scots dialect to great effect in passages of dialogue, and his heroic portrayal of Scottish history contributed in large part to the cultural background from which emerged the sanitised Victorian view of Scotland.

▼ **Anonymous illustration** of the Battle of Otterburn (August 19, 1388). Despite the death of their leader, James Douglas, 2nd Earl of Douglas (*c.*1358–88), the Scots gained a famous victory over the English at Otterburn. The Scots captured and held for ransom the English leader Sir Henry Percy (1364–1403). The battle is celebrated in Scottish balladry by among others Sir Walter Scott (1802). In English balladry, the battle is commemorated as "Chevy Chase".

EXODUS TO NORTH AMERICA

Before the start of the American Revolution (1775–83), perhaps as many as 500,000 people from 'Celtic' Britain and Ireland crossed the Atlantic in the hope of building new lives in North America. Few if any of them would have had any sense of a shared Celtic identity – they would have been far more aware of the differences between them. Their internal perspectives dominated by the political, economic and religious realities of their age. Chief among these was the transformation of England into Great Britain and its emergence as a major world power, riding the crest of mercantile capitalism. The one thing that united these 'Celtic' emigrants was a strong desire to escape English oppression.

Emigration to colonies founded and governed by the English may not, in retrospect, seem the best way of escaping English oppression, but there was little alternative. For most, the choice was stark – remain in the British Isles and endure the self-confident and increasingly intolerant English, or get to America by any means possible. The propaganda circulated by the colonial governments (desperately needing to increase their labour force) and the offers of 'free' passage by commercial shipping agents made the alternative seem sufficiently attractive as to be worth taking the considerable risks.

Irish Catholic migration

The first people to arrive in significant numbers were Irish Catholics, who made the voyage to the British sugar plantations in the West Indies as indentured servants. Indenture was a system by which a person contracted to be a low-paid servant, in return for passage across the Atlantic and a small bonus or grant of land on completion of the term of the contract, usually five or seven years.

Servitude in the Tropics, where the mortality rate from 'fever' annually decimated Europeans and the colonial culture openly tolerated the physical abuse of servants, ws an attractive proposition in light of the grinding and hopeless poverty in rural Ireland.

Many of the servants that survived their term in the 'Fever Islands' opted to move to the colony of Maryland (now in the eastern United States), which in 1649 had passed the so-called Toleration Act, permitting Catholic worship. Their numbers gradually swelled until Catholic immigration was restricted later in the 17th century; thereafter, the Irish settled where they could. After 1700, they were joined by some wealthy Irish settlers, 'Castle Catholics', who gravitated to Boston (now in Massachusetts) and other major ports.

Scots migration

At the close of the 17th century, a second group began to arrive – the Scots-Irish, descendants of Presbyterian farmers from the Scottish Lowlands, transplanted into

▲ **Bog-trotters cabin** at Ballintober Bog, Roscommon (19th-century engraving, English school). In the 17th century, the English confiscation of lands owned by Irish Catholics, the barring of Catholics from public office, and the hand-to-mouth existence for much of the Irish peasantry encouraged large-scale emigration to the Americas. The pace of migration increased further after the famine of the 1840s, the majority of migrants settling in the United States.

▶ **The Last of the Clan** (1865) by Thomas Faed (1826–1900). In the 18th and 19th centuries, the Highland clearances all but destroyed an entire culture in Scotland. The clearances entailed the forced eviction and migration of many Highlanders, and the wholesale introduction of sheep-farming. The majority of migrants, both voluntary and involuntary, settled either in the United States or Canada.

Ulster by the English as a counterbalance to the native Irish Catholics. During the 1690s, two factors combined to undermine the Scots in Ireland. Firstly, the ascendancy of the Anglican Church meant that they became effectively second-class citizens, and secondly there was a series of bad harvests. The Scots-Irish began emigrating in large numbers – from 1710 to 1770, as many as 250,000 arrived in North America. Many went as indentured servants, especially to the colonies of Pennsylvania and New Jersey.

The bad harvests of the 1690s also affected Scotland, and some Lowland Scots joined their former compatriots in immigrating to America. After c.1740, their numbers increased as many merchants and traders joined the exodus. As Protestants, but without any hint of 'Irishness', these Lowlanders were closest to the English socially, and they dispersed widely throughout the colonies.

The fourth group to arrive in America were the Highland Scots, who emigrated in direct response to the savage reprisals and land-clearances carried out by English troops after the failure of the Jacobite rebellions. Highlanders often travelled and settled separately from other colonists, such as the 5000 families from the island of Skye who immigrated en masse to Cape Fear in Carolina.

Expansion of the Frontier
Whatever their origins and motives for leaving their homelands, many of these immigrants ended up in the same part of the American colonies – along the western borders where the colonial authorities used them as 'frontier fodder'.

By the early 1700s, prime agricultural land with good access by river was already at a premium in the English-speaking American colonies. The earliest

settlers claimed the best land, and those who followed soon accounted for the rest. There was no room on the flat, easily worked Tidewater region of the eastern seaboard for land grants to newcomers, especially former servants.

Unless they had the resources to dictate otherwise (as few did), these immigrants tended to be pushed inland where the landscape was rougher and nature was wilder. Their enthusiasm, their hardiness and, above all, their non-Englishness made them ideal 'troops' to break trail, clear land and blunt the edge of Native American resistance.

CELTIC MIGRATION TO NORTH AMERICA
- Highland Scots
- Irish
- Scots Irish
- Lowland Scots
- Area settled by 1770
- Towns

▲ **Celtic migration to North America** Atlantic winds, a desire for freedom and a hunger for opportunity carried hundreds of thousands of people from the poorer parts of British Isles to colonies in North America.

▶ **Penn's Treaty with the Indians** (1772) by Benjamin West (1738–1820). In March 1681, Charles II of England (1630–85) granted William Penn (1644–1718) a large province on the west bank of the Delaware River, which was named Pennsylvania after his father (to whom Charles II owed a large amount of money). Penn founded a commonwealth with absolute freedom of worship, which became a refuge for Quakers and other religious minorities in Europe. He established good relations with the Native American nation of Lenni Lenape through a series of treaties. Despite Penn's enlightened approach, the 18th-century expansion of Pennsylvania placed the region at the heart of the French and Indian War (1754–63).

LANGUAGE AND RELIGION IN WALES

Union with England in 1536 meant that English became the official language of Wales and its ruling families became increasingly Anglicised, although the majority of the population remained Welsh-speaking. The emergence of the Protestant Church of England (and therefore of Wales too) imposed on the ecclesiastical authorities the duty of translating the bible and prayer books into Welsh and, by implication, a duty of promoting literacy in Welsh. A Welsh bible was printed and distributed in 1588, and prayer books appeared soon afterwards, but educational policy lagged behind.

In the 17th century, Christian organisations established some charity schools but formal education remained very much the prerogative of the Anglicised élite. During the middle part of the 18th century, this position changed, largely through the efforts of an Anglican churchman, Griffith Jones, who to promote bible study, founded a system of circulating schools in 1737. Jones recruited and organised teachers to travel around the Welsh countryside, spending between three and six months in a village before moving on to the next. While the teacher was in residence, inhabitants received free daily lessons.

By the time Jones died in 1761, his travelling schools had taught some 160,000 people – about one-third of the population of Wales – to read and write in Welsh. Although the promotion of Welsh literacy was undertaken for steadfastly Anglican purposes, during the latter part of the 18th century, the Welsh language was progressively appropriated by the Methodists.

Calvinist Methodism in Wales

The revival of popular religious enthusiasm that characterised Methodism was the result of people's spontaneous reaction to the inspired sermons of a few charismatic preachers, but underlying the rapid growth of the movement was the increasingly officious and dispassionate approach to worship adopted by the Anglican Church. In religious terms, Wales had been a largely conforming country. At the beginning of the 18th century, despite the promotion of Puritan ideals during the Commonwealth period, only about five per cent of the Welsh population dissented from the established Anglican Church. In return, the Church served Wales rather badly, with religious affairs being under the control of largely absentee English bishops.

Welsh Methodism was founded, following the visionary experiences of Howel Harris (1714–73) and Daniel Rowland (1713–90), in 1737 – coincidentally

▼ **John Wesley** (1703–91) preaching to Native Americans in Georgia (engraving *c.*1736). John and his brother Charles (1707–88) founded the Methodist movement in the Church of England. In 1735, the brothers were invited to Georgia to act as missionaries to the Native Americans, but their mission proved unsuccessful. The Methodist movement was led initially by George Whitefield (1714–70), but the movement split over doctrinal differences between Whitefield and Wesley. Whitfield believed in the Calvinist notion of predestination, while Wesley supported the Arminian doctrine that grace is freely available to all.

the same year that Griffith Jones founded his circulating schools. Initially, the Welsh Methodists worked closely with the English Methodists led by John and Charles Wesley, but in the years around 1740, the movement split as a result of doctrinal differences between John Wesley (1703–91) and George Whitefield (1714–70). The Welsh Methodists sided with Whitefield, and became known as the Calvinist Methodists.

Evangelical enthusiasm and the simultaneous promotion of Welsh literacy produced a synergy that was undoubtedly fuelled by lingering nationalist, anti-English, sentiment. After c.1775, Methodism grew rapidly in Wales, and by the end of the century, Welsh Methodists overwhelmingly outnumbered Welsh Anglicans. Relations between Anglican clergy and their Methodist congregations became increasingly strained until, in 1811, the Welsh Methodists began ordaining their own ministers, and thus became a separate Nonconformist Church.

Religion and political dissent

Less than 100 years after its foundation, Calvinistic Methodism had in effect become the national Church of Wales; although this was not officially recognised until 1914 when the Anglican Church was disestablished and replaced by the Presbyterian Church in Wales.

Religious nonconformity had become part of the Welsh 'national character'; and the hundreds of Methodist chapels, sometimes in isolated locations, had become the new centres of community life. During the 19th century, encouraged by the emergence of Welsh newspapers, chapel meetings increasingly became the venues for political discussions and, as in previous times, religious nonconformity soon begot political nonconformity, especially in the industrial region of South Wales.

Within Britain, Wales became a stronghold of progressive Radical-Liberal opinions, although the question of Welsh independence was never a real issue. In the late 19th-century, as the effects of universal suffrage began to make themselves felt, Welsh politicians were able to extract a number of concessions from the British government, in particular regarding the Church's role in education, culminating in the eventual disestablishment of the Anglican Church in Wales.

After the end of World War I, massive emigration from England caused considerable disruption to patterns of life in Wales. Welsh soon ceased to be the language of the majority, and subsequently fell into serious decline – despite still being taught in many schools. In 1967, the British government passed the Welsh Language Act, and since then, Wales has been officially bilingual.

EISTEDDFODAU AND DRUIDS

Wales has an international reputation as the 'Land of Song'. The country's reputation rests largely on the tradition of musical competitiveness, which is exemplified by the competition known as the eisteddfod. Supporters of the eisteddfod movement claim that it follows a tradition that dates back at least as far as the medieval period, while detractors are inclined to view the eisteddfod as a 19th-century invention. Whatever their origin, eisteddfodau have become extremely popular and are now held annually in Wales on both a national and international basis, and are regularly staged in countries as far afield as Australia and South Africa.

Bardic beginnings

Among the ancient Celts, the bards – singer-songwriters, entertainers and social commentators – had an honoured place in society, and this continued into the post-Roman world. Bards were particularly valued as eulogists and satirists; by establishing how the dead were remembered and by poking fun at the powerful, bards were a vital part of the social fabric that tied communities together. In Wales, the laws set down by Howel Dda (d. 950) recognised three grades of bard: the chief poet, the poet of the warrior band and the minstrel.

Competitions between bards, for both vocal and harp-playing skills, were popular in the period between 1100 and 1300, and the gathering held in 1176 at Cardigan, south-west Wales, is often cited as the first eisteddfod. In the 15th century, formal rules were agreed for the strict arrangement of metres in Welsh poetry, although the bardic profession seems to have been suffering from declining standards. In 1568, a formal application was made to the government to license and recognise the status of true bards, as opposed to mere minstrels and rhymesters. By the middle of the 17th century, eisteddfodau were already regarded as outdated by some Welsh commentators.

The modern eisteddfod

During the 18th century, the revival of Welsh culture, initially through the promotion of the Welsh language and subsequently through the emergence of a distinct national Church, created an environment in which the eisteddfod could again flourish. The first modern eisteddfod was held in 1789 at Bala, north Wales, with the support of the London Welsh Society, a group of successful businessmen. At the next gathering in 1792, the eisteddfod ode was devised, which now forms the basis for the main prize each year – bards have to compose an ode on a designated subject, specifically for the competition. The Gorsedd of Bards, an association of people who have made a notable contribution to the Welsh nation, was created by the Welsh scholar Iolo Morganwg (1747–1826), who felt that it should be made known that the Welsh were the direct descendants of Celtic culture and heritage. Eisteddfodau were held exclusively in North Wales until the 1819 gathering at Carmarthen, South Wales, which also introduced druidic overtones.

In 1858, the first official, national eisteddfod was held at Llangollen, north-west Wales, and since 1860, the national competition has been held at a different venue

◄ **Princess Elizabeth**, now Elizabeth II (1926–), at the 1946 National Eisteddfod of Wales, held at Mountain Ash, Glamorgan. The photograph shows the Princess' initiation into the Mystic Circle of the Bards by Archdruid Crwys Williams.

► **Druids** holding their annual summer solstice ceremony at Stonehenge, Wiltshire, south-west England. The pagan ceremony is known as *Alban Heruin* ('Light of the Shore'). It is held to celebrate Midsummer's Day, the longest day of the year. At the ceremony, the druids crown Gaia, mother goddess of the Earth, as 'Britannia' – spirit of the land of Britons. A mock battle takes place in which the holly king (symbol of the waning year) slays the oak king (symbol of the waxing year). A tau cross is also burned. Druids were banned from celebrating the summer solstice at Stonehenge from 1986 to 1997.

each year, alternating between North and South Wales. In 1947, the Llangollen International Eisteddfod was established and has developed into a major music festival that attracts entrants from more than 40 countries.

Druids – ancient and modern

The ancient druids and their modern namesakes are two entirely different phenomena and should not be confused. Modern druids preserve no traditions older than the 18th century at the earliest.

The ancient Celtic druids left no information about themselves and they remain enigmatic. Modern views of the ancient druids depend entirely on the images provided by pre-modern commentators, all of whom seem to have projected their own prejudices onto the mysteries of druidism.

The main source of information is Julius Caesar (*c*.100–44 BC) who, in a single passage in *The Gallic War*, ascribes great influence to the druids in Gaul, but otherwise his account of the conquest completely ignores them. It is likely that Caesar got most of his information from the writings of the Greek author Poseidonius (*c*.135–51 BC) who, according to one modern interpretation, idealised the druids as Hellenistic-style philosophers. Irish writers of the early medieval period portrayed druids, retrospectively, as evil magicians and fierce opponents of the spread of Christianity. In AD 60, the Romans finally eliminated druidic influence in Britain, when they destroyed the druids' stronghold on the island of Anglesey (Ynys Môn).

The close association of druids and Britain was a Roman idea that was enthusiastically revived in the 18th century by William Stukeley (1687–1765), who populated ancient Stonehenge with druids (*see* pages 152–53). In 1792, a Welsh scholar devised and enacted the *Maen Gorsedd* equinoctial ceremony complete with an archdruid and a specially constructed mini-

Stonehenge. In 1819, the new druids appended themselves to the eisteddfod movement, and still preside over the 'chairing of the Bard' ceremony.

The invention of the Welsh druids undoubtedly had strong nationalist and Celtic overtones, but must also be seen in context with the widespread popularity of secret and revelatory societies during the decades preceding the French Revolution (1789–99).

◄ **Archdruid** receiving the Hirlas Horn at the opening of the 1982 National Eisteddfod (*Eisteddfod Genedlaethol Frenhinol Cymru*) held at Swansea, South Wales. A local matron, dressed in a scarlet robe with a gold head-dress, presents the horn to the archdruid, asking him to "drink of the wine of our welcome". The Hirlas Horn is akin to the drinking horn of the Welsh princes. Behind the archdruid is the flag of the Gorsedd of Bards. According to tradition, the first National Eisteddfod was held in 1176 at the castle of Lord Rhys in Cardigan, south-west Wales.

SCOTS IN THE BRITISH EMPIRE

▲ **James Clerk Maxwell**
(1831–79) was born in
Edinburgh. His discovery of the
existence of electromagnetic
radiation, was described by Albert
Einstein as the "most profound
and the most fruitful that physics
has experienced since the time of
Newton." Maxwell's *Treatise on
Electricity and Magnetism* (1873)
developed Michael Faraday's
ideas into a single mathematical
theory. Other contributions to
physics included a demonstration
of colour photography.

After the failure of the Jacobite rebellions in 1715 and 1745, the government transported some Highlanders as prisoners to the American colonies and, in the wake of land clearances, thousands more crossed the Atlantic as voluntary emigrants. Within a generation, many of these emigrants (voluntary and involuntary) had become prosperous farmers and merchants. When the American Revolution broke out in 1775, many Scottish colonists, both Highlanders and Lowlanders, chose to remain loyal to the British monarchy. After American independence was secured in 1783, Scots were prominent among the Loyalists who migrated northwards to British Canada.

The behaviour of these colonists went a long way to rehabilitating the whole of the Scottish nation in official eyes; and although, as the critic Dr Samuel Johnson (1709–84) makes clear, popular prejudice remained on both sides of the border, Scots played an active role in British imperial life.

Empires bring out the best and the worst in peoples. Empires exaggerate; and this is nowhere more noticeable than in expatriate communities where the social status of individual members is paramount. Scots proved particularly enterprising and successful in the building and maintaining of the British Empire and many pre-eminent British expatriates were Scots.

Highland regiments

Nationalism never became a big issue in Scotland: the British Empire was able to appropriate Scottish national pride through a monopolistic hold over forms of national expression, intensified (and sweetened) by royal patronage.

Empires are appropriating forces and, like the Romans before them, the British were keen to acquire and distribute all the resources of their Empire. Subject peoples were repressed or promoted according to their conformity with British (English) expectations.

In an age when battles were won through discipline and drill, the British were especially keen to appropriate and channel fighting prowess. In the same way that the British Empire appropriated the 'martial races' of India (such as the Gurkhas) as élite troops, it also adopted the Scottish Highlanders.

The first Highland regiment in the British Army was the 42nd Foot, formed in 1739 from the loyal Black Watch militia. Other Highland regiments soon appeared, often organised on clan basis. For about 30 years in the middle of the 18th century, Highland soldiers were the only individuals allowed to wear kilts, and they naturally became a focus for national pride.

These 'soldiers in skirts' served the British with honour and distinction all over the world. Highlanders were among the troops that scaled the Heights of Abraham when General James Wolfe (1727–59) took Québec, Canada, in 1759; and Highlanders held 'The Thin Red Line' against Russian cavalry nearly a century later at Balaklava, Crimea (1854). Even in the khaki-clad World Wars of the 20th century, some Highland regiments insisted on marching into battle to the sound of the pipes.

The Industrial Revolution in Scotland

On the home front, the Industrial Revolution harnessed the resources of the Scottish Lowlands. During the last quarter of the 18th century, the production of cotton textiles began, and within 25 years, cotton became

◄ **Black Watch**, 42nd Foot Regiment of the British Army. This photograph, taken in *c.*1912, shows (from left to right) a private, two drummers, a piper and a bugler of the Black Watch. The blue and green tartan uniforms of the independent companies that policed the Highlands for George I inspired the name Black Watch (*Am Freicadan Dubh*). In 1739, the Black Watch were merged to form the 43rd Foot Regiment (renumbered the 42nd Foot in 1749). On May 11, 1745, they fought their first battle at Fontenoy, Flanders, in the War of the Austrian Succession (1740–48). In 1756, the Black Watch were sent to the French and Indian War (1754–63), where they suffered major losses at Fort Ticonderoga. The regiment recovered and, in 1758, King George II honoured them with the title of 'Royal Highland Regiment'.

Scotland's leading industry. The introduction of sheep farming in the Highlands spurred the growth of the long established wool industry. By 1831, Glasgow's population had grown to 200,000 – many of the new inhabitants were Highlanders by origin. The development of coal mining and associated metallurgical industries, such as steel making and shipbuilding, together with the decline of cotton, meant that heavy industry soon dominated the Scottish economy. During the final decades of the British Empire, Scottish workers constructed more than half of all the ships built in Britain.

James Watt and James Maxwell

During the 18th and 19th century, Scotland gave birth to thousands of talented and enterprising individuals who performed sterling service in every field of imperial affairs – government and administration, industry and commerce, science and medicine, and the arts. Two individuals – James Watt (1736–1819) and James Maxwell (1831–79) – symbolise (but not summarise) the contributions made by Scots at this time. Watt and Maxwell were instrumental in the transformation of the horse-drawn world into today's electronic 'global village'.

Although Watt did not invent the steam engine, his improvements – notably a separate condenser in 1765 – transformed steam engines from cumbersome mechanical pumps to versatile power sources that drove the second phase of the Industrial Revolution. The equations devised by Maxwell and presented in 1864, gave the first coherent account of the electro-magnetic spectrum and provided a unified theory of light, electricity and magnetism.

▶ **Double-acting steam engine** built (1784) by James Watt. Born in Greenock, west Scotland, Watt's first and greatest invention (May 1765) was the separate condensor. This modification of the Newcomen steam engine greatly reduced heat loss and thus reduced fuel costs. Watt then went on to develop the rotative engine (shown here) that rotated a shaft instead of providing a simple pumping motion.

▲ **Scots Fusilier Guards** (now Scots Guards) at the Battle of the Alma (September 20, 1854) in the Crimean War. This watercolour by Richard Simkin (1840–1926) shows the Scots Guards leading the assault on the Russian position above the River Alma, near Sevastopol, south-west Crimea.

TARTAN TRADITIONS

▼ *The Royal Magazine* cover (1910) shows Queen Victoria (1819–1901) being sheltered by her Scottish manservant John Brown (1826–83) who worked on the royal estate at Balmoral. Brown proved a great consolation to Victoria after the death of her husband Albert (1819–61) but her reliance on him created gossip, scandal and jealousy at court.

Neither tartans nor men's skirts are exclusively Scottish, but they have been enthusiastically promoted as national emblems of Scotland for nearly two centuries.

Although the British government lifted restrictions on Highland dress in the 1780s, Scottish culture was not totally rehabilitated until the visit of George IV (1762–1830) in 1822. George chose to mark the occasion – the first visit to Scotland by a British monarch – by wearing 'authentic' Highland dress, and was accompanied by the Lord Mayor of London, who wore his 'own' tartan. Since then, successive British monarchs have similarly transformed themselves when visiting Scotland, and today even the Prince of Wales wears a kilt when north of the border.

During the long reign (1837–1901) of Queen Victoria, Scotland became the favourite royal 'playground'. Scottish estates offered peaceful sanctuary from the rigours of the London court, which became increasingly frenetic after the inventions of the telegraph and telephone. Dressing up in tartan clothes became one of the rituals of royal relaxation, and one faithfully copied by aspiratory visitors.

In the Victorian period, which coincided almost exactly with the 'Railway Age', Scotland became a fashionable holiday destination with the public. The massive enthusiasm for souvenirs meant that generically 'Scottish' images, such as tartans and reproductions of Highland landscape paintings, soon became commonplace in all parts of Britain. In the sentimental Victorian imagination, Scotland loomed mistily as one of the last remaining 'wild' places - the realm of the *Monarch of the Glen,* a much-reproduced painting of a Highland stag.

Kilts and clan tartans

The first officially recognised Scottish tartan seems to have been that of the Black Watch regiment, which subsequently became the basis for the first individual clan tartans; with each of the participating clans, the Sutherlands or Campbells for example, adding an identifying coloured stripe to the drab Black Watch sett. During the middle part of the 18th century, when members of Highland regiments were the only people allowed to wear traditional dress, several other 'official' clan tartans were established.

Although the government permitted the Scottish public to wear tartan after 1782, the cloth remained a minority taste until George IV endorsed it. Subsequently, under Victoria, almost every family in Scotland acquired a tartan. Numerous bright 'dress' tartans, and their more muted 'hunting' equivalents, were invented to meet demand, which was ultimately driven by the dictates of royal fashion. There is a cruel irony in the fact that some of the wool used to manufacture the tartan souvenirs for 19th-century visitors came from sheep introduced during the Highland clearances.

Not even that most potent of Scottish symbols, the kilt, has an authentically Scottish origin. Clan historians generally accept that an Englishman, Thomas Rawlinson, who owned an ironworks in the Western

▶ *The Queen of the Swords* (c.1877) by Sir William Quiller Orchardson (1832–1910). The scene here is taken from Sir Walter Scott's description of the Shetland sword dance in his novel *The Pirate* (1822). The 'Queen' is his heroine, Minna Troil, whose courageous character is exemplified by her bold reaction to the arch of sword blades from which her friends recoil in alarm. Many Highland dances originated from martial pageants.

◄ *Harris Highlanders*, engraved (1868) by Vincent Brooks after Kenneth McLeay (1808–78). The original watercolours were commissioned by Queen Victoria, and depict the staff of Balmoral in their clan attire. This engraving shows Kenneth MacSwyde and Donald MacAulay, born on the Earl of Dunmore's estate at Harris, Rúm.

► *Monarch of the Glen* (1851) by Sir Edwin Landseer (1802–73). Landseer was Queen Victoria's favourite painter of animals, and this oil painting is one of the most widely reproduced pieces of Victorian art.

▼ *Highlander soldiers* (*c.*1910). The mounted soldier is a Gordon Highlander. The infantrymen are (from left to right) a Cameronian, King's Own Scottish Highlander, Black Watch and 1st Royal Scots.

Highlands, invented the modern stitch-pleated kilt in the 1720s. Rawlinson hit upon the idea of dividing the traditional plaid worn by his workers into two garments, so that they could wear just the lower half. Even the word 'kilt' appears to be a derivation of a medieval Scandinavian expression meaning 'tucked-up' – a reference to the way men wore the traditional plaid for ease of movement.

Tartan empire

Traditions are often revered most by those furthest from the source, and this was especially the case with expatriate Scots, especially those in Canada. During the latter part of Victoria's reign, before the horrors of World War I (1914–18), there was a craze for amateur, 'volunteer' regiments. In Canada, many of these 'volunteer' units were strongly clan-based and individual members did little more than commission 'authentic' items of Scottish military regalia.

The 19th-century imperial administration encouraged this distillation of the essence of Scotland into a few easily transmitted symbols. Just as Britain had appropriated Scottish martial prowess, the Empire now sought to confer it piecemeal upon others, and kilted pipe-and-drum bands became a feature of the best 'native' regiments. In some countries, this new military 'tradition' persisted into the post-colonial era.

Outside the military, other subsidiary 'tartan traditions' were promoted through a combination of expatriate enthusiasm and imperial propaganda. Scottish dancing and the Highland Games provided safe, cheerful, 'chocolate-box' reflections of a life style that had been hard and often dangerous. The famous Highland Fling was originally danced with the fierce exultation that flows from victory in battle, and the holding of games has long been a sign of peace.

FAMINE IN IRELAND

▲ 'The Herald of Relief from America' cover cartoon from *Harper's Weekly* (February 28, 1880). The cartoon depicts Erin's cry for help, "We are starving", and America's subsequent response. In the decade after 1841, about two million Irish people sailed across the Atlantic to escape poverty and famine.

The Irish famine of 1845–51 – the 'Great Hunger' – was not an entirely natural disaster, but neither was it a deliberate act of genocide. The failure of the potato crop produced famine while misguided governmental forays into socio-economic engineering conditions undoubtedly worsened conditions, but in many ways the famine was a catastrophe waiting to happen.

When the time came, the effects were devastating, heartbreaking and immense. Ireland lost about half its population over a period of less than 70 years; one in five of the deaths occurred as a result of malnutrition, and this in a land that continued to export food to the rest of Britain.

Larders of the east and the 'distressed' west

At fault was the proprietorial attitude of the British towards what had been a 'domestic' colony during the years of the Protestant Ascendancy. Ireland had little industry or other natural resources, and its role in the imperial scheme of things had been to become a larder for the Industrial Revolution. The growing urban concentrations of Britain consumed large quantities of Irish wheat, butter, beef and pork, nearly all of it produced by large farms in the eastern half of the country.

In the less Anglicised west of Ireland, traditional patterns of inheritance kept farms small. Few farmers in the west produced crops or livestock for market – apart from its few towns, the west was almost outside the cash economy – and relied on a subsistence crop of potatoes.

Although Ireland was now a supposedly equal part of the United Kingdom, the early 19th-century administrators of Ireland – mere clerks to the architects of empire – took a dim view of subsistence farming, which to their minds made the land 'stagnant'. Furthermore, the administrators argued that potatoes allowed the population to increase and made the land 'congested'. By 1822, those with an official interest in such matters concluded that most of western Ireland was 'badly distressed'. They can have been little surprised, therefore, that when disaster struck, it struck worst of all in the west.

The role of the potato

The potato is a nutritious tuber that originates from South America and requires no other processing apart from cooking. In the late 16th century, potatoes were introduced into the Cork and Waterford districts of Ireland as a commercial crop for the Dublin market. Storage and transportation problems led to commercial failure, but potatoes survived as a winter food for the poor in Munster. Later improvements in the stock meant that potatoes became an annual staple.

Potatoes, particularly when grown in 'lazy beds' that made the most of poor soils, provided a cheap source of food, and consequently the rural population grew rapidly after 1760, many living as squatters in shanty villages on land hardly fit for cultivation. Indeed, some historians argue that Ireland's curse was that 'the poorer the land, the denser the population'.

By 1830, *c*.3 million people (one third of Ireland's population) relied on the potato for *c*.90 per cent of their calorie intake. The most popular potato variety was the 'Lumper', widely planted because it required little manure – a scarce resource where livestock was being squeezed from the land through poverty and the consuming dominance of the potato.

◀ *The Eviction*: A Scene from Life in Ireland, American engraving published (1871) by J.T. Foley. A verse by O'Donovan Bossa accompanies the picture. It describes how the villagers are forced out of their homes by the "Sheriff with his Black Brigade" because the Earl wants the land for hunting. Among those evicted are a widow with the coffin of her dead child and a dying man. Standing behind the man is his son, recently returned from the Crimean War. The son says "If for thy rights on Irish earth/Thou blighted country of my birth,/Against the robber's flag of red/The blood thy sons at Alma shed/Were vested, how thy veins would glow/With fierce resistance to the foe."

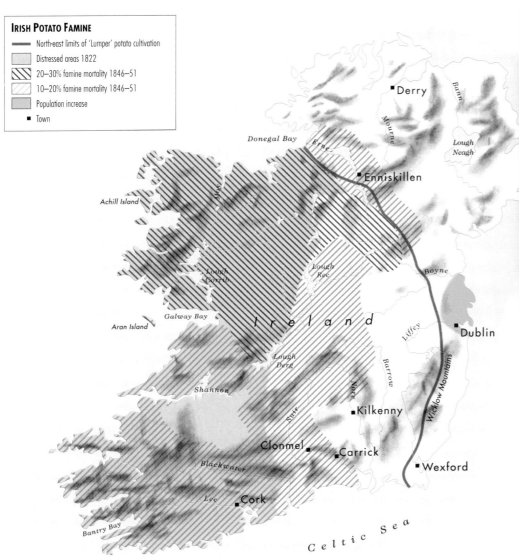

IRISH POTATO FAMINE

— North-east limits of 'Lumper' potato cultivation

▨ Distressed areas 1822

▨ 20–30% famine mortality 1846–51

▨ 10–20% famine mortality 1846–51

▨ Population increase

■ Town

▲ **Irish Emigrants** (1847) by John Joseph Barker (1824–1904). This huge oil painting, 255 × 185.2 centimetres (100.3 × 72.9 inches), shows an Irish family on the road to Bath, south-west England. The picture captures something of the impoverished state of the Irish peasantry, even if the family's health appears to be little affected by the ravages of famine.

◄ **Great Famine** The far west of Ireland was worst affected by the famine. Some places experienced mortality rates of 30%. Here existence had been precarious for decades and was heavily dependent on the 'Lumper' potato crop.

▼ **Great Famine** in Ireland. This cartoon by Smith from the *Illustrated London News* (January 30, 1847) depicts the funeral of a famine victim at Skibbereen, County Cork. An estimated one million people died in the famine.

In 1845, the potato crop (especially the Lumper variety) failed due to infestation by the fungal blight *Phytophthora infestaris*. The following year, the crop failed again and potatoes rotted in their beds while people starved. Despite some localised attempts at charitable relief, hundreds of thousands died of starvation, and as many more from an associated typhus epidemic, dysentery and cholera.

The 1847 harvest was good, but the blight soon recurred and famine conditions prevailed in parts of the country until the late 1850s. Social misery was aggravated by the attitude of many property owners, who used crop failure and non-payment of rents as an excuse to evict tenants and demolish their cottages. The authorities, eager to see the 'stagnant' and 'congested' land cleared and remodelled along English lines, largely condoned this attitude.

The British government's notorious use of maize to relieve the famine was a deliberate attempt to eliminate the 'lowly' potato from the Irish diet, and to impose a regime of 'higher' crops such as cereals. Maize, which will not grow in Ireland, was deliberately chosen because its importation would force the rural Irish to enter the cash economy, rather than relying on the potato crop.

Counting the cost

The 'Great Hunger' cost Ireland dear. The 1841 population of more than 8 million was reduced to *c*.6.5 million by 1851 – *c*.1 million died and the rest emigrated, mainly to the United States and Britain. Continued emigration during the rest of the 19th century was to further reduce Ireland's population, which by 1911 numbered just 4.4 million. After the famine, the Irish economy was to remain debilitated for more than a century.

GAULOIS OR FRANÇAIS?

Insularity conveys several advantages, including the ability to make easier definitions of 'us' and 'them'. In Britain, despite successive Germanic, Scandinavian and Norman invasions, the English had little doubt about who they were; which in many ways was defined by who they were not – the Welsh, Scots and Irish. Inversely, these latter peoples (whether or not they had any sense of mutual affinity) all saw themselves as essentially 'not English'.

Nevertheless, the use of the term English for the dominant language-nation of the British Isles is not always wholly satisfactory. It was England that was conquered by William, Duke of Normandy, but the English nation subsequently flourished. Consequently, it has become convenient for historians to refer to Saxon, rather than English, resistance to the Norman invasion.

Language and national identity

Like England, the nation of France gained its name from 5th-century Germanic invaders (the Franks), although in France the national language evolved from Latin rather than German. Like England, France was essentially defined by its language – the present-day boundaries between French- and German-speaking populations almost exactly matches the Roman borders – and, again like England, France proved intolerant of subsidiary 'nations', and imposed provincial status on once-independent kingdoms such as Brittany and Languedoc.

In the early 18th century, the issue of French identity seemed almost irrelevant. France was the richest country in the world; its language had replaced Latin as the universal language of diplomacy, literature and science, and the court of Louis XIV (1638–1715) was synonymous with the height of civilisation, luxury and fashion. There was little need to dwell on heritage when the present State outshone the Roman Empire in magnificence.

The central role of Louis XIV (*"L'État c'est moi"*), the Sun King, and his successors, concealed a certain diffidence about French national identity. Although the Encyclopædists, the enlightened thinkers who created the intellectual environment for the French Revolution (1789–99), were well aware of the ancient Gauls, they perceived no close affinity with those fierce warriors. When assigning national characters, the Encyclopædists chose "easy-going" for the French, and they claimed no special affinity with the "proud" Scots, or "lazy" Irish, nor with their German cousins, characterised as "drunken".

Celtic studies in France

Napoleon I (1769–1821), who briefly created a French Empire in Europe following the Revolution, was a ruler of contradictory enthusiasms. While building an Empire, Napoleon also encouraged nationalism among subject peoples, and while embracing innovation, he also felt the pull of the past. He took a proprietorial approach to the archæological treasures of

▼ **Louis XIV and family**
(*c.*1715–20). Louis XIV (1638–1715) is seated with his son, the Grand Dauphin behind him. On the right stands the king's eldest grandson, the Duc de Bourgogne. The infant reaching for the king's hand is the Duc de Anjou, later King Louis XV (1710–74), and the lady is his governess, the Duchesse de Ventadour. Louis XIV is the epitome of the absolute monarch of the classical age. Louis built the Palace of Versailles both as a testament to the brilliance of his reign and to display the wealth and power of France. In 1685, Louis' revocation of the Edict of Nantes intensified the persecution of French Protestants and forced many into exile.

(1769–1821). On the archæological front, Napoleon III made great show of excavating the site of Alésia (ironically a place of defeat for the Gauls) in north-east France, and subsequently attempted to revive and promote Vercingetorix (d.46 BC) as a symbol of French resistance to foreign aggression (*see pages 84–85*). Within a few years, however, the Prussians were at the gates of Paris.

In ways that can only be described as typically French, Vercingetorix has mutated into the cartoon character Asterix the Gaul, who combines Celtic fighting prowess with the "easy-going" character of the Encyclopædists. During the latter part of the 20th century, Asterix was the most famous French personality after the war-hero and president General Charles De Gaulle (1890–1970).

France also provides a cautionary tale about national stereotypes and the relationship between material culture and ethnic identity – the familiar figure of the Frenchman in his beret. Until 1923, the Basques in the Pyrenees were the only people in France to wear this type of hat. The beret then rapidly became fashionable throughout France and was soon part of an unofficial national costume. In 1932, French factories manufactured *c*.23 million berets – for a country with a total population of *c*.40 million.

◄ **Vercingetorix**, chief of the Arverni. This beaten copper statue was erected (August 27, 1865) on the orders of Napoleon III at Alise-Sainte-Reine (Alésia), north-east France. The statue is seven metres (23 feet) high. An inscription engraved on the plinth reads, "Gaul unites/Forming one nation, Driven by the same spirit,/Can defy the universe." Napoleon III, who wrote *A History of Julius Caesar* (1862–66), identified Alise as the site of the famous battle between Caesar and Vercingetorix.

▼ **Napoleon III** was President of the Second Republic (1849–52) and Emperor of the French (1852–70). He was provoked by Chancellor Otto von Bismarck (1815–98) into entering the Franco-Prussian War (1870–71). Defeat at the Battle of Sedan was swiftly followed by his deposition and the proclamation of the Third Republic.

Egypt, and brought the *Dying Gaul* (now in the Museo Capitoline, Rome) statue from Italy to France. In 1805, among his many other achievements and foundations, Napoleon established an Académie Celtique.

The one region of France that was still in touch with its Celtic heritage was Brittany where, thanks largely to the efforts of 18th-century writers such as Paul-Yves Pezron, there was an outbreak of literary 'Celtomania' in the early 19th century. The most influential work was the *Barzaz Breiz* ('Breton Bardic Poems'), first published by Théodore Hersart de La Villemarqué in 1839. The Ossianic poems of the previous century undoubtedly empowered the 'Celtomania' that produced the *Barzaz Breiz*, and James Macpherson's (1736–96) own influence may have been even greater (*see pages 152–153*). Although supposedly 'collected' from the villages of Brittany, the poems in the *Barzaz Breiz* appear to have been just as much modern constructs as the poems of Ossian.

One minor manifestation of continuing French diffidence regarding national identity was that no clear self-caricature emerged in 19th-century French journalism; and certainly nothing to match the incisive picture of John Bull – the English colonial bullyboy and smug industrialist.

France – language and nation

During the 1860s, Napoleon III (1808–73) made strenuous efforts to emulate his uncle Napoleon I

THE IRISH IN BRITAIN

Seasonal emigration from Ireland to Britain, mainly for crop-picking and harvest, began before 1700 and has continued ever since, although the number of workers involved each year has never been very great. Few of the early Irish visitors chose to remain permanently in Britain, although this changed dramatically after 1800. Not all 19th-century Irish emigrants made transoceanic voyages to empty lands full of new freedoms and opportunities. Many chose to settle in Britain, or could afford no better alternative.

Increasing immigration

In 1780, there were c.40,000 Irish-born residents in Britain. By 1841, the number had increased to c.420,000, constituting almost two per cent of the population in England, and five per cent in Scotland. Ten years later, after the worst years of the Irish Famine, the Irish-born population totalled c.730,000 (three per cent of England, and seven per cent of Scotland) and was still rising.

The Irish settled mainly in the large industrial towns of Britain, particularly in Liverpool, Manchester, Preston, Newcastle-on-Tyne, Glasgow, London, Swansea and Cardiff, where they tended to form 'ghetto' communities in the poorest areas. Several factors prevented the Irish from assimilating easily into British society. Many Irish had fought honourably for either the French or the British during the Napoleonic Wars (1803–15), and this ambiguity, together with increasingly militant Irish nationalism, made the Irish politically suspect. The main impediment, however, was religion – most of the Irish immigrants to Britain were Catholics, and were subject to vilification and abuse that, until the Act of Catholic Emancipation in 1829, had some degree of official sanction. In the 'pressure-cooker' conditions of 19th-century slum tenements, Irish communities were frequently the victims of popular urban discontent.

Navvies and canals

Many of the immigrants found work in mining and heavy industry, but some became involved in a new labour phenomenon – the navigators (navvies). The navigators were a large, mobile and semi-skilled work-force, upon whose efforts rested the completion of the transport revolution in Britain.

The term 'navigator' originally applied to a worker who improved the navigation of rivers. The new factories of the Industrial Revolution needed fuel and raw materials, and had to transport and distribute their products. A draught-horse could haul two tonnes (4400 pounds) in a wagon or cart; the same horse could haul ten times the load in a barge.

Towards the end of the 18th century, some mine-owners and industrialists began commissioning their own artificial waterways – canals – to improve local

► **Stephenson's 'Rocket'** won trials for steam locomotives to run on the new Liverpool and Manchester Railway in 1829. Its multiple fire-tube boiler enabled it to achieve a speed of 58 kilometres per hour (36 miles per hour). George Stephenson (1781–1848) also built the 64-kilometre (40-mile) railroad line between the two cities, the first fully evolved railway in the world. The railway was the primary force in the spread of the Industrial Revolution.

▼ **Manchester Ship Canal** opened on January 1, 1894. It runs for 58 kilometres (36 miles) from Eastham, Merseyside, to Manchester. The canal gave Manchester its own access to the sea, fuelling the city's industrial growth. This photo (1894) shows the creation of Ellesmere Port.

◀ **Erie Canal** excavation at Lockport, New York (lithograph 1825). The canal is 584 kilometres (363 miles) long, and links New York City with the Great Lakes. It was built solely by horse and man power – no roads existed for supply. The construction of the locks and canal at Lockport was made possible largely by Irish and Irish-American labour.

▼ By 1850, the railway companies in Britain had rapidly created a web of steel track across the length and breadth of Britain. Each mile of track represented thousands of hours of back-breaking manual labour.

transportation. By the 1790s, canal building was booming in Britain, and canal companies flourished on the London Stock Exchange.

Thousands of labourers – navvies – were recruited and organised to carry out the hard work of making canals run across rivers and beneath hills. Construction at this time involved very few machines – just picks, shovels and wheelbarrows. Working conditions were often dangerous, and injuries were commonplace.

The Railway Age

Road haulage companies could not compete with canals, but the improved waterways enjoyed only a short-lived supremacy. By the middle of the 19th century, railways with steam-powered locomotives had largely superseded canals. The new railways had several major advantages: they were quicker and cheaper to build than canals, and they offered a much shorter journey time – a trip from London to York took less than a day.

The Railway Age is generally considered to have begun in 1830, when the 'Rocket' steam locomotive made its first journey along the new Liverpool to Manchester Railway. By 1838, there were 804 kilometres (500 miles) of track in Britain, and by 1843 this had increased to c.3200 kilometres (c.2000 miles). Railways really took off between 1845 and 1847 when 'railway mania' quickly eclipsed 'canal mania' in scale and intensity. More than 400 new railway companies were granted licences to build a further 14,000 kilometres (8700 miles) of track: a task they completed by 1860.

The expansion of the railway system in Britain was a cut-throat and commercial 'free-for-all'. Gangs of navvies trampled across the countryside, clearing a level path for the iron rails. Although we remember the achievements of the architects and engineers who designed the great monuments of the Railway Age, we tend to overlook the work of the navvies who sometimes lost their lives in the transport revolution.

At the height of the railway boom in Britain there were c.50,000 navvies. While not in the majority, Irish navvies were sufficiently prominent for it to be said that, in terms of overall population, the Irish made a disproportionately large contribution to the early development of the British transport system.

RAILWAY NETWORK OF BRITAIN BY 1850
- ■ Town
- —— Major railway

IRISH INDEPENDENCE

▼ **Easter Rising** (April 1916) in Dublin. This photo shows British Regulars sniping from behind a barricade of beer casks near the docks in Dublin. The rising followed the arrest of Sir Roger Casement. On April 24, the rebels seized the Dublin Post Office and Patrick Pearse proclaimed the birth of the Irish republic. British troops reacted swiftly, forcing the rebels' surrender on April 29. However, the British authorities' decision to execute the leaders of the rising outraged Irish public opinion and precipitated an end to British rule.

The Protestant Ascendancy in Ireland was brought to an end by the French Revolution (1789–99). The questions posed by the Revolution to the established order in Britain found particular expression in Ireland, where religious differences were put aside in favour of radical politics. In 1791, Wolfe Tone (1763–98) organised the Society of United Irishmen, an alliance between Catholics and Protestants, to agitate for political and economic reforms. In 1793, mindful of the impending war with France, the British government attempted to relieve the pressure by removing most of the legal basis for the Ascendancy and allowing Catholics to vote and hold civil office. One result of this was to provoke a Protestant backlash: the Orange Order was founded in 1795.

The following year, the United Irishmen, with the help of the French navy, attempted an anti-British rising. Although it met with some local success and persisted for two years, the rising was doomed to failure and provoked a stern reaction. In 1801, with the British government on a war-footing, Ireland was formally joined to Great Britain to form the new United Kingdom, with Irish members of parliament joining the Parliament at Westminster.

Democracy and direct action

Throughout the 19th century, Irish discontent became increasingly vociferous and sometimes erupted in violence. Unlike Wales and Scotland, Ireland became a cradle for nationalist sentiments. Increasingly militant demands for Irish independence (or at the very least Home Rule) became a major political issue in Britain, and one capable of bringing down the government.

During the first half of the century, the main vehicle of protest was the 'Young Ireland' movement, which published its own newspaper – *The Nation*. In the aftermath of the Irish Famine (1845–51), 'Young Ireland' made an abortive attempt at a rising in 1848 – a year of revolutions around Europe. Thereafter, the struggle for independence was to be waged on two fronts: legally through the Westminster Parliament, and illegally by a number of secret organisations known collectively as the Fenians (named after an ancient Irish military force).

The parliamentary struggle focused on the issue of Home Rule and came to a head in the 1880s, when Irish members of Parliament, led by Charles Stewart Parnell (1846–91), held the balance of power betwen the Liberal and Conservative parties. In 1885, after Prime Minister William Gladstone (1809–98) had failed to deliver Home Rule, the Irish voted with the Tories to bring down the Liberal government. In 1886, Gladstone regained power thanks to Irish support and pushed forward his Home Rule proposals. Parnell lost influence after a divorce scandal in 1889 and, although Gladstone twice attempted to introduce limited Home Rule legislation, by the end of the century Ireland remained part of the United Kingdom. One response to this failure of the parliamentary process was the revival of traditional literature in Ireland by the Gaelic League during the 1890s.

Meanwhile, some Irish nationalists had been pursuing a more direct course of action. In 1858, the Irish Republican Brotherhood (IRB) was formed to wage a low-intensity guerrilla campaign against the British, both in Ireland and in England. The IRB and other militant nationalists aroused considerable admiration among Irish communities in the United States, where regular fund-raising was organised.

The Easter Rising and partition

The 19th-century debates on Home Rule had revealed the existence of the 'Ulster Question', where local Protestant majorities were strongly opposed to any weakening of the links with the rest of Britain. By the outbreak of World War I (1914–18), Ireland was on the brink of civil war between groups of armed Loyalist and Nationalist volunteers.

In 1916, at the height of World War I, armed nationalists attempted a rising in Dublin, seized public buildings and declared a provisional government. This 'Easter Rising' was ruthlessly suppressed by a week of bombardment by the British and hand-to-hand fighting between British troops and Irish nationalists. Fifteen of the nationalist leaders, including the politician-poet Patrick Pearse (1879–1916), were executed as traitors.

After the end of World War I, the conflict in Ireland resumed with the nationalists, now organised as the Irish Republican Army (IRA), waging a full-scale guerrilla war against the British, who reinforced a depleted police force with mercenary units, such as the so-called 'Black and Tans'. In 1921, political negotiations produced a treaty in which the British and Irish representatives agreed to a partition of Ireland, with the six counties of Ulster remaining part of the United Kingdom, and the rest of the island becoming the Irish Free State. This settlement, which gave the Irish Free State the same 'Dominion-within-the-Empire' status as Canada or Australia, was not accepted by all nationalists, and a civil war (1921–22) ensued in the Irish Free State.

From Free State to Republic

In 1937, the Irish Free State became the Republic of Ireland, with Eamon de Valera (1882–1975) – a leader of the Gaelic League and survivor of the Easter Rising – as its first prime minister. In 1949, Ireland became completely independent from the United Kingdom, while Ulster remained part of the Union.

Since Ireland joined the European Union in 1973, the Irish economy has developed rapidly, initially in the agricultural sector, and subsequently with the establishment of a thriving electronics industry. At the end of the 20th century, it was fashionable to speak of Ireland's 'Celtic Tiger' economy.

▲ **Division of Ireland in 1922**
Conflict and compromise produced a partition that pleased but a few and satisfied nobody. Extreme attitudes became entrenched on both sides of the partition.

DIVISION OF IRELAND 1922
— Boundary between Northern Ireland and Irish Free State established December 1922
Percentage of Protestants
0–10
10–30
30–50
more than 50

◄ **Patrick Pearse** (1879–1916) was a poet and leader of the Easter Rising (1916) in Dublin. His speech at the funeral (August 1915) of the Fenian leader O'Donovan Rossa is one of the most famous in Irish republicanism: "Life springs from death; and from the graves of patriot men and women spring living nations." When the rising was crushed, Pearse was forced to surrender to the British and was court-martialled and executed.

► **Charles Stewart Parnell** (1846–91) is often referred to as the 'uncrowned king of Ireland'. He disproved allegations of support for the Phoenix Park murders (May 1882), but his career was ruined by revelations of an adulterous affair with Kitty O'Shea (1840–1905).

LANGUAGE AND POLITICS

To American visitors, Europe can seem a bewildering and incomprehensible linguistic minefield, with more than 30 languages crammed into a relatively small area. A journey of just a few hundred miles can pass through several language zones. The linguistic complexity of Europe is the result of more than 2000 years of often violent and bloody history. From a practical point of view, Europe compares unfavourably with America where, as the result of a shorter but no less bloody history, a command of just three languages (English, Spanish and Portuguese) enables a person to converse with virtually all the inhabitants of two continents.

Nation-states and language groups

Creating nation-states in Europe has always been an arduous task, often undertaken without reference to self-determination. Élite groups, in pursuit of grand designs, have generally imposed their conception of nation upon their populations. Because of this sometimes arbitrary imposition of boundaries and borders, linguistic groupings often do not align exactly with national borders, and there are many pockets of language stranded on the 'wrong' side of a frontier.

A strong linguistic identity has never been essential for national survival in Europe, as the example of Switzerland (which has three main language districts: French, German and Italian) shows very clearly. In some ways, the concept of nationality itself has already been reduced to a bureaucratic necessity. A prototype for the future may perhaps be the tiny state of Luxembourg, which now has no economic basis for a separate existence and is in effect an administrative district of the fast-developing northern European 'super-state'.

Ethnic divisions in Europe

Any such supranational trends are, however, taking a long time to establish themselves, and indeed may never do so. At the end of the 20th century, the political scene was more fluid than at any other time of general 'peace' and European unity seemed a distant prospect; the partition of Czechoslovakia and the bloody fragmentation of Yugoslavia counterbalanced the reunification of Germany in 1990.

The history of Yugoslavia provides a salutary lesson in the misuse of linguistic nationalism. The nation was 'created' by the Great Powers at the end of World War I (1914–18). After the successful creation of unified states in Germany and Italy in the 19th century, the Great Powers assumed that a linguistic relationship (Slav languages) between disparate groups emerging from centuries of Islamic rule could provide a stable basis for a new nation-state of Yugoslavia (literally 'South Slavia').

The fragmentation of the Balkans, often referred to as 'Balkanisation', can be traced back more than 2000 years to the days of Celts, Thracians, Macedonians, Dacians and Romans. These complexities have since been overlain with Slavic, Byzantine, Ottoman and Austro-Hungarian factors, and the unifying factor of a shared language-family apparent to the Great Powers concealed deep social divisions, which, in the 1990s, exploded into warfare accompanied by 'ethnic cleansing' that recalled the horrors of the Nazi death-camps.

Basque autonomy

The former Yugoslavia may be an extreme example, but it is not an isolated case. In a seemingly contradictory fashion, Europe's drift towards supranational federation in the guise of the European Union (EU) has been accompanied by a simultaneous resurgence of linguistic regionalism within member-states. From a historical viewpoint, those with the best case for autonomy are the Basques.

The Basque nation straddles the French-Spanish border, but is not internationally recognised. The Basque language is not Indo-European, and the best explanation of this is that the Basques are a 'relic' group of pre-Indo-European peoples. The separateness of the Basques from other Europeans is partly confirmed by the distribution of genetic factors in their blood.

▼ **Bilingual road sign** in Québec, eastern Canada. Québecois have strongly defended their French cultural heritage ever since the Dominion of Canada was created in 1867. In 1980 and 1995, the ruling separatist Parti Québecois held referenda seeking approval for secession from Canada, but lost on both occasions (the second ballot by the narrowest of margins).

▶**Québec** More than twice the area of France, the province of Québec in eastern Canada has a population of about seven million people (eight times smaller than the population of France).

In Spain, Basque separatists have waged a long and sometimes violent campaign for independence, yet the only perceptible differences between Basques and their Spanish neighbours are language and history. Their present-day material cultures are identical and the genetic differences between them are only detectable as averages in large samples, and do not ethnically identify individuals.

Québec – a separate society?

Linguistic and ethnic differences between peoples of European origins have also erupted elsewhere in recent times. In North America, the flashpoint was the Canadian province of Québec, which was originally colonised by French settlers. In the 18th century, when the British gained control of eastern Canada, the Québecois were politically separated from France, but steadfastly maintained their cultural heritage.

The use of the French language became the rallying cry of separatists who sought an independent Québec. In 1970, martial law was imposed in Canada after a campaign of violence by the Front de Libération du Québec. In a referendum in 1995, the mainly English-speaking rural districts narrowly defeated the separatists, who constituted a sizeable majority in urban areas such as Montréal and Québec City. However, the narrowness of the vote effectively left unresolved the issue of Québec's sovereignty.

Language and ethnic identity

The political struggles of the Basques and Québecois are based on claims of separate ethnic identity that are largely signified by language. In the case of the Québecois, language is the only factor that distinguishes them from other Canadians. In both cases, language is a major political issue, not out of necessity – the majority of Basques and Québecois are bilingual – but because language has been deliberately selected as the battle-standard.

▲ **Basques** 5000 years of history have squeezed the Basques into a tiny corner of western Europe.

◄ **Basque nationalist** graffiti in San Sebastián (Donostia), north Spain. The graffiti highlights the armed struggle for 'Basque Freedom' from perceived French and Spanish domination.

▼ **Basque separatist group** ETA detonated a car bomb on April 19, 1995, aimed at killing José Maria Aznar (1953–). Aznar, who later served as Spain's prime minister (1996–), suffered minor injuries in the blast.

ETHNIC IDENTITY IN THE 21ST CENTURY

Towards the end of the ethnically charged 20th-century, the popular usage of the terms 'Celts' and 'Celtic' increasingly came under academic attack, particularly in Britain. Broadly speaking, the objectors put forward three main arguments. First, the relationship between the present-day Celtic languages was only established in the early 18th century, Second, modern archæological research has revealed no compelling evidence for westward Celtic expansion as envisaged by philologists. Third, it is a mistake to consider the Iron Age inhabitants of the British Isles as being of the same 'people' as the *Keltoi* identified by the ancient Greeks.

While these objectors have not yet formulated a convincing 'alternative' explanation for the varied evidence (language, archæology and the opinions of the Romans) that supports the idea of ancient insular Celts, their objections cannot be dismissed. Ethnicity and nationality are, in many ways, the products of propaganda.

Hybrid nations

Aristocrats follow bloodlines (or at least they are supposed to), but the rest of us are 'mongrels' with even less chance of having exclusively 'Celtic' DNA (or any other ethnic 'brand'), and the idea of any such substance existing seems quite fantastic. In even the most untroubled parts of Europe (if any such places ever existed), wanderers, invaders, settlers, immigrants, émigres, refugees, displaced persons, economic migrants, and 1500 years of intermarriage (consensual or otherwise) since the fall of the Roman Empire, have all left their mark on local populations.

By the end of the 20th century, it was becoming clear that ethnicity and nationalism had outgrown each other and, in any case, the two were only ever partially related and became linked through political expediency and convenience. We live in a world of nation-states, and we have been conditioned from birth to think of ourselves in national terms. Today, nationality is very much a matter of paperwork and has little, if anything, to do with ethnicity.

In Britain, the utility and desirability of the all-inclusive term 'British' has also been questioned – what sort of ethnicity does 'British' imply? Citizens of the United States, who are acutely aware of the linguistic differences in their country, might say that 'Britishness' is mostly just a state of mind. However, from a Welsh, Scots or Irish viewpoint, this state of mind has often been seen

► European Union (EU) flag
The flag was adopted in 1986, originally being the emblem of the Council of Europe. The twelve golden stars form a circle, representing the union of the peoples of Europe. A single market was established in 1993, and a single currency (the euro) was launched in 1999. The EU grew out of the Schuman Declaration (May 9, 1950), which proposed that European nations pool their coal and steel resources.

◄ Bagpipe band at the Highland Games in Santa Rosa, California. Americans of Scottish ancestry often are enthusiastic promoters of their cultural heritage. Since 1975, the Santa Rosa (now Plesanton) Highland Games has been the US championships for Highland athletics. The Games are organised by the Caledonian Club of San Francisco, which was established in 1865. In 1964, a Pacific Coast Pipe Band Association (PCPBA) was formed to govern pipe bands in California. Similar bands and games exist throughout the United States and Canada.

as quintessentially 'English'. Within England, 'Englishness' appears to have become concentrated among the opinion-forming, and opinionated, inhabitants of London and its neighbouring counties.

Identity crisis?
At the end of the 19th century, Britishness (which everyone has always understood to mean Englishness) was a world standard for cultural superiority, and Britain was the superpower by which other countries measured themselves. By the mid-20th century, Britain had been replaced by the United States as the leader of the western world, and Britain was largely reduced to a role on the European stage. Furthermore, some commentators argue, the re-establishment of Scottish and Northern Irish parliaments and the creation of a Welsh assembly have further diminished the cohesion of Britain and the 'meaning' of British nationality.

In the late 20th century, as US economic and cultural imperialism approached world domination, an increasing number of its citizens became dissatisfied with being simply labelled 'Americans'. Complicated by issues of prejudice and political correctness, the American search for identity became a linguistic minefield: Black American or Afro American? Amerindian or Native American? The homogeneity of the American melting pot – a mere formula of words – separated out into Hispanic Americans, Italian Americans, Irish Americans, Polish Americans, and many other groups.

Transnational identity
In a world where straightforward national identity

has become increasingly unrepresentative and unsatisfactory, we should not be surprised at the popularity of the Celts, who are widely understood to have a transnational ethnicity. In today's multicultural and globalised culture, so the argument runs, a Celt is a good thing to be – the Celts have a long and proud history. Or do they?

The origins of the Celts lie beyond the illumination of history, in J.R. Tolkien's (1892–1973) "...fabulous Celtic twilight, which is not so much the twilight of the gods as of the reason." Ethnicity is not the product of reason, but of emotions such as pride, fear, anger, grief and love. Ethnicity is what people want to be and agree to be.

▲ **Welsh schoolchildren** celebrating the opening of the Welsh Assembly in Cardiff on May 26, 1999. Today, Wales is a multi-faith, multi-racial and multi-cultural nation. The perceived transnational nature of Celtic ethnicity fits well with this modern, plural conception of nation and national identity.

▲ **The transnational** nature of Celtic identity is well illustrated by this matchbox cover. The matchbox is sold in England and manufactured in the Czech Republic. The brand name of the matches is Hibernia (the ancient Roman name for Ireland) and the design features a Celtic harp and Celtic style lettering.

◄ **Chicago police** march in the Saint Patrick's Day parade (17 March) in Chicago, Illinois. The Illinois Emerald Society (founded 1975) is a social, fraternal and cultural organisation for members of the Illinois law enforcement or criminal justice community who are of Irish descent. It promotes and furthers the culture of Irish-Americans within the state. There are similar Emerald Societies throughout the United States.

CHAPTER
SIX

▲ Bronze, half-moon pendant fibula (6th century BC), found in grave 900 at Hallstatt, west-central Austria.

CLOTHING

Writing at the time, or in the immediate aftermath, of the Roman conquest of Gaul, the Greek historian Diodorus of Sicily (active 1st century BC) gave a full description of Celtic dress-sense in the fifth volume of his *Universal History*:

[The men]...wear striking clothing – shirts that have been dyed and embroidered in various colours; breeches, which they call bracae, *and cloaks fastened with a brooch at the shoulder...*

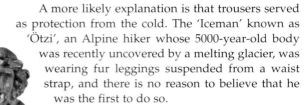

► **Bronze figurine** of a captive Celt, found at Bois-de-Loëze, east France. The Gallo-Roman figurine dates from the 1st–3rd century AD. The bearded man is depicted in long tunic, calf-length trousers and cloak. The figurine is 11 centimetres (4.3 inches) high.

The uncivilised trouser

Diodorus is quite clear that Celtic men wore breeches (trousers) and, despite their subsequent close association with kilts, the Celts are often credited with the invention of trousers. However, this is almost certainly just wishful thinking. The ancient Greeks knew of trouser-wearing Persians and Scythians, but the Greeks considered the garment effeminate, associating it with the concealment of the female body. Greek men, and the Romans who inherited most of their ideas, disapproved of trousers and preferred to keep their legs unencumbered and open to admiration.

Some historians argue that trousers developed as a result of horse-riding but, while this idea is superficially attractive, there is no evidence to support the contention – Greek and Roman cavalry managed quite well without trousers.

A more likely explanation is that trousers served as protection from the cold. The 'Iceman' known as 'Ötzi', an Alpine hiker whose 5000-year-old body was recently uncovered by a melting glacier, was wearing fur leggings suspended from a waist strap, and there is no reason to believe that he was the first to do so.

Trousers were not indicative of 'Celtic' identity, since Germanic tribesmen also wore them, as no doubt did many others. The significance of trousers to Greek and Roman commentators is that they marked out the Celts, like the Persians and Scythians, as uncivilised barbarians who covered their legs.

Wool and the loom

At the close of the Iron Age, which ended in Gaul with the Roman occupation, the range of material available for clothes making was extremely limited. Linen cloth was made from fibres obtained from the flax plant, cultivated especially for this purpose. Linen, however, is not very warm and was mainly used for shirts and tunics. For the wealthy, some imported silk was available, but in quantities far too small to be significant. The mainstay of warm clothing was woollen cloth.

The introduction of the woolly sheep during the Early Bronze Age revolutionised European clothing. The wooly sheep, in contrast to earlier domesticated breeds, had a thick fleece that could be harvested annually

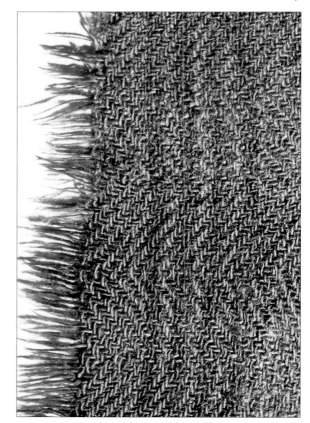

◄ **Reconstruction of a loom** as used during the Hallstatt period (1200–480 BC). The weights at the bottom of the loom are polished stones. Examples of weaved and tailored textiles have been found in the salt-mines of Hallstatt, west-central Austria, and the burial sites at Hohmichele and Hochdorf, south Gemany.

► **Fragment of woollen** cloth found at Hallstatt, west-central Austria. The material, which dates from the 8th–3rd century BC, was probably part of the clothing of a worker in the salt-mines. The fragment clearly contains stripes in brown dye. Woollen clothing provided protection against the harsh environment of the Salzkammergut mountains.

◄ **Scythian horseman**, detail on a felt cloth from the 5th or 4th century BC. The cloth was preserved for c.2000 years in a frozen tomb in the Paryryk Valley of the Altai region of south-west Siberia. Trousers are generally thought to have been invented by the Scythians. One style of Gaulish trousers appears to have been similar to the 'knickerbockers' worn by the Scythians. As this detail shows, the Scythians, like the Celts, wore cloaks and stylised moustaches.

▼ **Funerary stele** of Dupsala, daughter of C. Sorinus, from Les Poussots, near Dijon, east France. This limestone stele, which dates from the start of the Roman occupation of Gaul, shows the type of woollen cloak worn by Gaulish women. It is 62 centimetres (24 inches) high.

without killing the animal. Wool was now woven into cloth to make warm trousers for men, long skirts for women, and cloaks for both sexes.

Making woollen cloth was a two-fold process. First, the wool fibres were spun into continuous threads. Spinning wheels were a medieval innovation in Europe, and the ancient Celts, like the Greeks and Romans, spun the thread by hand using a small rotating weight known as a spindle. Second, the spun threads were woven together at right angles using a loom.

The Celts used upright looms with a wooden framework that held a series of weighted, vertical threads known as the warp. The loom operator wove a series of horizontal threads, the weft, through the warp to produce cloth. Differing weaving techniques could produce different qualities of cloth. The Celts favoured the twill weave, which produced a warm, double-thickness cloth.

Colours and patterns

Woollen cloth also had other advantages that made it desirable even where climate rendered it unnecessary. Wool fibres absorb dye much more readily than flax fibres, and woollen textiles could thus be manufactured in brighter colours than their linen equivalents. Iron Age dyes were mainly extracted from plants, and were not especially colour-fast – any bright colours soon faded when exposed to sunlight and rain.

The availability of colour awakens the mind to the possibility of pattern, and the types of pattern favoured by the Celts, which Diodorus describes as "...stripes in which are set checks of varied hue..." (i.e. plaid or tartan), are inherent in the weaving process. Using pre-dyed thread, the weaver could count and arrange the warp and weft threads to produce the familiar regular patterns. A fragment of Iron Age cloth discovered in the salt mines at Hallstatt has exactly this type of pattern executed in green and brown.

Women's work?

Although there is little direct evidence from either archæology or the classical writers, it seems likely that the production of cloth was an exclusively female occupation in the Celtic world, as it was elsewhere. It is equally likely that many of the facts about ancient Celtic clothing will remain unkown. It is possible that short skirts may have had some ritual or social significance among women, and there may have been equivalent male practises – did boys, for instance, have to earn their trousers?

HOUSING

▲ **Interior** of an Iron Age house at Butser, south-east England. The frame is built from tree trunks, the roof is thatched and the walls are made from wattle and daub.

▼ **Staigue ring fort** in County Kerry was possibly built as early as the 1st century BC. The wall is up to 5.5 metres (18 feet) high.

The Greek statesman Polybius (c.200–c.118 BC) had a varied career before he was sent, as a political detainee, to Rome in c.168 BC. Acknowledging that Rome had eclipsed Greek power, the exiled Polybius compiled and published his *Histories* which detailed Rome's rise to ascendancy, and which contained this snippet of information about the Celts who had invaded northern Italy at the beginning of the 4th century BC.

...They lived in open villages with no permanent buildings...inside, there was little furniture and they slept on beds of leaves...they moved house as they pleased...

Roman palaces and Celtic shacks

By 'permanent', Polybius means enduring in the Graeco-Roman sense – stoutly built of stone or brick bonded by mortar and with a tiled roof – of a building that might last a century or two. By implication, the Celts lived closer to nature, in buildings made of wood and other perishable materials that were definitely 'temporary' by comparison: huts and shacks, not proper houses.

This cursory and dismissive description conveys, as intended, not only comparative construction methods, but also the chasm between the Romans, with their marbled cities, and the Celts with their muddy huts. Although Polybius did not see the world in such terms, the contrast was essentially between urbanised and dispersed populations. At this time, Rome had nearly one million inhabitants, many of them living in multi-storey apartment blocks. The largest Celtic *oppidum* (town) probably had no more than 5000 inhabitants, most of them farmers and their families.

While Polybius' account contains strong elements of truth, it should not be taken at face value. There is evidence that some of the Celts who settled in Italy accommodated themselves in houses and villages of local style and, no doubt, built by local labour.

Materials and form

North of the Alps, where the climate was cool and wet, Europe was still largely a forest realm during the Iron Age. Although agriculture had made considerable inroads, the landscape was much less manicured than in Italy, and much of it was covered with woodland.

Stone was little used for domestic building before the Roman period and, even when readily available, was employed only for low walls. Domestic architecture, like the landscape, was dominated by wood. Timber was the main construction material, with reeds, mud and straw used for weatherproofing.

◄ **Reconstruction** of Early Iron Age dwellings (8th–4th century BC) at Asparn an der Zaya, north-east Austria. The building on the left is a replica of a log-cabin from the Hallstatt period at Roggenbrunn, north-east Austria. On the right is a replica of a bakehouse from Grossweikersdorf, north-east Austria.

Houses were built in a simple pattern that had its origins in the Neolithic period. Upright posts set into the ground and secured with horizontal crossbeams and longer timbers, were used as a framework for a steeply pitched roof. Across most of Europe, houses were rectangular, but in Britain and Ireland, they tended to be circular.

The roof was thickly thatched with reeds, with all the weight being taken by the timbers and uprights. The spaces between the uprights were filled with wooden trellising that was packed tight and covered with a mixture of mud and straw. This type of walling, known as 'wattle and daub', continued to be used in rural areas of northern Europe until fairly recently.

Houses varied in size, with sides and diameters ranging from five to 15 metres (16 to 48 feet) in length. Most houses contained a single, unobstructed space, although larger buildings may have required additional internal uprights to support the roof. Interiors were not usually partitioned, and life revolved around a centrally placed hearth, with smoke escaping (mostly) through an opening in the roof.

Nearly all buildings were farmhouses, and many of these would have had a variety of huts and shacks attached to the house or standing nearby. Farming settlements tended to be small and dispersed, perhaps no more than one or two generations of the same family, although some larger centres, notably the *oppida*, developed after the 3rd century BC.

Celtic forts

Polybius' comment that the Celts lived in "open" (unwalled) villages may be largely true, but it is not especially significant. At this time, most farms across western Europe were undefended, although the Celts were no strangers to defensive fortifications. Since the 6th century BC, some important centres had been fortified with walls, ramparts and timber palisades.

Defended homes and villages were most common in western Britain and this trend continued into the Roman period. In Ireland, there is uncertainty as to the precise nature of domestic settlement during the centuries of the Iron Age but from about the 5th or 6th centuries onwards, tens of thousands of raths were built. Although raths are commonly known as ring forts, they appear, in fact, to have been defended farmsteads with a circular earthen rampart c.30 metres (100 feet) in diameter enclosing the farmyard and farm buildings.

▼ **Replica of a crannog** at Graggaunowen, County Clare, west Ireland. A crannog (from the Gaelic *crann* meaning 'tree') is a dwelling built in parts of Ireland and Scotland from the Bronze Age until the Middle Ages. It consists of palisaded buildings on an artificial island or platform raised on stilts over water.

FARMING

In the first decade of the 1st century AD, Strabo (c.64 BC–c.AD 23), a Greek historian and traveller, published his 17-volume *Geography of the Known World*. Volume Four of the *Geography* describes Gaul.

...[The country] produces grain in large quantities, and millet and nuts and all kinds of livestock...all the land is farmed, except for ground that is too swampy and the forests....

Roman innovation and Celtic productivity

Despite being short on detail, Strabo's assessment draws our attention to one of the less appreciated aspects of Celtic agriculture – its productivity. Modern experiments, using crop varieties and techniques from the La Tène period (c.480–50 BC), have confirmed that Late Iron Age farmers in Britain and Gaul could produce substantial surpluses. The wealth of Celtic society, which 'paid' for the exquisite metal artefacts decorated in La Tène style, was essentially created by the agricultural sector.

By the latter part of the Iron Age, a number of technological innovations – all of which increased output – were available to Celtic farmers. High-yield crop varieties took maximum advantage of the abundant rainfall and shorter growing season. After c.400 BC, iron-tipped ploughs (based on Roman models) were introduced, which enabled better use of heavy soils and soon replaced the traditional wooden ard. Rotary querns, another import from Rome, also appeared in parts of the Celtic world at about this time, and considerably eased the burden of grain processing. The use of long, iron scythes made it practical, for the first time, to harvest large quantities of grasses and other plants for winter fodder, with consequent increases in animal productivity.

Although all of these innovations occurred during the period of the La Tène art style, it is not possible to draw links between the two sets of phenomena. The La Tène style spread much more rapidly than improvements in agricultural technology, some of which did not reach Ireland for more than five centuries after the art style had become established.

Cereal crops and local plants

Crops grew in small fields that were fenced or hedged to keep out large herbivores. Although the expanding Celtic populations undoubtedly cleared many fields for agriculture, they inhabited a landscape that had been farmed for more than three millennia. Many of the so-called 'Celtic fields' ascribed to Iron Age cultivators actually date from earlier periods.

Then, as now, cereals were the staples of existence, and the most important crops were emmer wheat, spelt, bread wheat, barley and millet. Other highly nutritious crops included beans, peas and lentils.

▼ **Iron sickle and adze**, dating from 400–300 BC. The strength of iron made it a useful material for weapons and tools. Agricultural tools made of iron greatly increased the productivity of Celtic farming.

▶ **Experimental farm** at Butser, south-east England. The farm attempts to recreate agricultural conditions in Iron Age Britain in c.300 BC. Wheat fields used to surround Iron Age farms. The crop was part of the staple diet, and in good years provided a surplus that could be traded.

Besides these standard crops, Celtic farmers also made use of local plants, such as bitter vetch and fat hen, which could be gathered from the wild, but may also have been cultivated.

Agricultural technology also included food storage and food processing. Grain was stored in sealed underground pits, where the germination of the outer layer preserved the rest of the grain, or in specially built granaries raised on stilts. The ancient Celts certainly knew how to process grain and water to make alcohol, and may even have developed a distinctive brew – one of the Latin words for beer, *cervisia*, is a loan-word from Celtic!

Celtic pastoralism

Although their society was underpinned by arable farming, the Celts were essentially pastoralists. Properly managed, farm animals provided much greater opportunities for the accumulation of wealth than arable crops and were usually less labour intensive. Moreover, flocks and herds were moveable (by their owners and raiders), in ways that ploughed and hedged fields were not.

The most important animals were cattle, so much so that it is possible to typify Celtic farming as 'cow-and-plough'. Along with meat and leather, cows also produced milk, which could be concentrated and stored as cheese. Cattle were also the main source of heavy traction and did most of the work, yoked in pairs, dragging ploughs and pulling wagons.

Cattle represented the most desirable form of wealth in Celtic society, and the value of other items was often reckoned in terms of numbers of cows. Cattle were also a highly portable form of wealth, and as such were a prime target for thieves and raiders. Cattle raiding (rustling) may well have been the main occupation of some elements of Celtic society, who were to viewed their exploits in heroic terms, as exemplified in the early Irish prose epic, *The Cattle Raid of Cooley*.

Next in economic importance were sheep, which produced a cash commodity as well as meat, dairy and leather products. The third essential component of the livestock triangle was the horse. Although horses were of little use as traction animals at this time (efficient horse collars were not introduced until the medieval period), they were nonetheless high value, high status animals; not least because they gave individuals vastly increased mobility and were fundamental to the extensive management of cattle. The best horses came from south-east Europe, and horse-breeders in Gaul would pay large sums at auction for the finest animals. Other domesticated animals also had a role on the Celtic farm – for instance, pigs scavenged and grew fat on waste material and there were several types of working dog. The religious and mythological status of the pig perhaps reflects its economic importance.

All of these Iron Age animals, with the possible exception of British and Irish hunting dogs, were considerably smaller (by about 10 to 20 per cent) than their modern counterparts. Celtic cattle would look 'miniaturised' compared with most present-day breeds, and the war-horse of a Celtic chieftain would have been no bigger than a modern pony

▲ **Bronze statuette of a farmer** found in the River Saône, east France. The statuette, which dates from the Hallstatt period (*c.*1200–480 BC), shows a farmer with a plough drawn by draught animals.

▶ **Shetland ponies** grazing beside a loch on the Shetland Islands. Queen Victoria's favourite breed of horse, Shetland ponies were heavily used in British coal mines during the Industrial Revolution. Horses like the modern breed of Shetland pony have lived on the islands for more than 2000 years. Animals such as these were surely among the most prized possessions of the ancient Celts. They served as workhorses, means of everyday transport and carried warriors into battle. Their principal use, however, were as pack and saddle animals. The Belgic Treveri tribe were famed for the equestrian skills, and the horse was a favourite figure in Celtic art. The horse goddess Epona was one of the most important goddess in the Celtic pantheon.

TRANSPORTATION

Several of the classical writers comment on the geographic mobility of Celtic society, usually implying a negative contrast with the stable, urbanised societies of Greece and Rome. In his *Geography*, Strabo (*c*.64 BC–*c*.AD 23) analyses this peripatetic tendency and explains that Celtic migration assumed a number of forms:

...they change their abode on the slightest provocation, sometimes migrating in bands in full battle array...more often setting out with their households when displaced by a stronger enemy...

Celtic migrants

This distinction between offensive and defensive mobility, between advance and retreat, is well made. The Celts did not make their living on the move – they were settled ranchers, not nomads – but they were ready and able to move when it was desired or required. Throughout the period of recorded history, the boundaries of the Celtic world have been uncertain and subject to ebb and flow. In order to remain within that world, Celtic populations had to be prepared to pack up and move on when the time was right.

When comparing the migratory nature of Celtic society with the settled existence of Rome, it is interesting to note that the establishment and maintenance of the Roman Empire itself involved a considerable amount of migration, some of it no less permanent than the excursions of the Celts. In the mid-2nd century AD, the temporary northward extension of the Empire's frontiers necessitated the temporary emigration to northern Britain of one in ten Roman legionaries.

Means of transport

The mobility of Celtic society on land was dependent on wheeled vehicles. Warriors can travel light, but moving entire households (even those with little furniture) means transporting cooking vessels and utensils, preserved food and other stores, farm implements and equipment, as well as infants, the elderly and infirm. The Celtic lifestyle was portable, but the Celts had more goods than could possibly be carried by hand; moving house meant loading up the wagons and carts.

Wagons (four wheels) and carts (two wheels) have a long history in Europe; a solid wooden wheel found in Switzerland has been dated to *c*.3000 BC. The earliest wagons were heavy and cumbersome, but by the Late Iron Age, wagon-making had become a highly accomplished craft, producing lightweight yet robust vehicles that were well-suited to long-distance travel. It is tempting, especially in view of the Celtic affinity with horses, to think that this migration was undertaken by horse and cart, but this would be a mistake. Although horses could pull vehicles, the harnessing techniques employed – yokes or chest straps – were too inefficient to make the horse a practical traction animal. Instead, most vehicles were drawn by cattle.

The best vehicles had spoked wheels made of wood, and fitted with iron tyres. Celtic wheelwrights, who were among the best in Europe, developed a method of making the felloe (wooden rim) from a single piece of timber, which made the wheel much stronger. The tyres were hoops of iron that were subjected to fierce heat before being shrunk onto the assembled wheels, to ensure a tight fit when they contracted as they cooled. The number of spokes per wheel varied considerably, and examples have been found with between eight and 12 spokes. Axle width was, however, fairly standard at *c*.135–155 centimetres (53–61 inches).

Not all farmers would have been able to afford the best and most up-to-date vehicles, and not all wheels were spoked. Some of the wagons in use during the Early La Tène period had solid tripartite wheels (made from three pieces of wood) – a design that predated the Bronze Age in Europe.

Celtic seafarers

Overland journeys can be traced and archæologists can sometimes find evidence along the route. Sea voyages,

▶ **Detail of horse's bit** found in a peat bog at Attymon, County Galway, west Ireland. This delicately curved bronze bit was originally part of a chariot harness. It dates from the 1st century AD.

▼ **Gold boat** with oars and mast, found at Broighter, County Derry. This artefact, which dates from the 1st century BC or early 1st century AD, is probably the earliest and best representation of a sea-going vessel in western Europe. It may have been a votive offering to Manannan mac Lir, King of the Ocean.

however, leave fewer unequivocal traces, and Celtic shipbuilding has received far less attention than their wagons and carts. Shipbuilding has been practised in Europe far longer than wagon-making, and nobody doubts that at least some of the ancient Celts were excellent shipwrights and skilled mariners, but we have little direct evidence. An exception is the wreck discovered at Blackfriars, London, which – although of the Roman period – is thought to be constructed according to traditional Celtic shipbuilding design.

At the end of the Iron Age, the best shipwrights were probably the Veneti, who lived on the southern side of the Brittany peninsula in northern France. The Veneti built large, heavy ships, constructed entirely of oak timbers, to withstand the rough conditions of the

Atlantic Ocean, and transported goods to Britain and Spain. According to Caesar, the great size and strength of the Veneti ships initially made it very difficult for the Roman navy, which was used to more lightweight opposition, to engage and defeat them. Most Celtic ships were, however, much more lightly constructed.

Small boats, made from leather stretched over a wooden framework, were widely used on rivers, and it is possible that some of the Irish raiders who settled in Britain crossed the Irish Sea in enlarged versions of these leather boats. According to tradition, St Brendan (c.AD 484–578), an Irish monk, crossed the Atlantic in a leather boat and discovered land on the other side; and it has since been demonstrated that such a feat is at least possible.

▲ **Bronze horse's bit** found at Attymon, County Galway. This two-link horse-bit dates from the 1st century AD. The Celts used chariots, often drawn by a pair of horses, both for travel and war.

◄ **Bronze hub fittings** and a wheel found in the 'Princess' of Vix's tomb in Burgundy, north-east France. The items, which date from the 6th or 5th century BC formed part of a cart. The princess' body was laid on the chassis of the four-wheel cart and then the wheels and hubs were removed and placed separately in the tomb. We do not know if the cart was purely a ceremonial object.

WOMEN

Dio Cassius (c.150–235) was a Roman administrator, politician and amateur historian. During the early 2nd century AD, he published *Romaika*, a history of Rome of which only fragments survive. When describing the conquest of Britain, Dio Cassius sketches a portrait of Boudicca (d.AD 60), Queen of the Iceni, who:

...was tall and of terrifying appearance, with fierce eyes, a harsh voice, and a great mass of long, tawny hair....

At the time Dio Cassius was writing, anybody who might have seen Boudicca at first-hand was long-dead, and we must expect no more than a generic picture of an outraged enemy – angry barbarians tend to have fierce eyes and harsh voices. The 'point' of Boudicca is that she was a woman, and women war-leaders were a shocking prospect to Dio Cassius' Roman readership.

The prominence given by classical authors to Celtic women such as Boudicca and her contemporary Cartimandua, queen of the Brigantes, is sometimes cited as 'evidence' to support the popular belief that women enjoyed a more powerful and 'liberated' position in ancient Celtic society than in the Græco-Roman world. On balance, however, it seems that, apart from a few exceptional women leaders, there was little difference between the societies in terms of gender roles and relative status – so far as we can tell. Most of our knowledge comes from the writings of men about the affairs of men – war, conquest and diplomacy. For most of history, women have had no voice of their own.

A fairer society?

Apart from the words of strangers, there are few other indicators of women's status in Celtic society. Analyses of some Iron Age community cemeteries (as opposed to the mass interments of war dead or sacrifice victims) show an equal sex ratio, with no apparent discrimination in terms of body position or location within the cemetery. The most significant finding is that women appear to have died younger than men did, probably because of complications during childbirth. However, the graves tell us nothing about those who may have been excluded from the cemetery and, in any case, the findings are not necessarily representative of Celtic society as a whole.

The examination of individual graves makes the overall picture no clearer. Undoubtedly some Celtic women, such as the 'Vix princess' in north-east

▲ **Celtic warrioress** on a terracotta frieze from Civita Alba, near Sassoferato, north-east Italy. The frieze dates from the 2nd century BC, and is 45 centimetres (17.7 inches) high. Warrioresses are prominent in Celtic history and legend. For instance, Cuchulain – the warrior-hero of *The Cattle Raid of Cooley* – was taught how to fight by the warrioress Scathach. Scathach is the eponymous goddess of the Isle of Skye.

◀ **Boudicca** This 19th century engraving depicts Boudicca in her chariot rallying the troops of the Iceni to battle against the Romans. Boudicca is the epitome of the Celtic warrioress. Her name in the Brythonic language means 'victor'. She persuaded the Iceni and Trinovantes to unite against the Romans, and led the Celts in a succession of victories over the legions. According to the Roman historian Tacitus, after the Celtic armies sacked London, the Roman women were rounded up and taken to a sacred grove of the Celtic war goddess Andraste, where they were murdered, their breast cut off and and impaled with large skewers. The details of these atrocities may be Roman propaganda, or bloody revenge for the Romans' savage slaughter of Druids at Mona earlier in AD 61. The revolt was eventually crushed by the Romans and, according to legend, Boudicca poisoned herself rather than capture and public execution in Rome. Traditionally, she is buried under platform eight at King's Cross Station, north London.

◄ *La Dama de Baza* This Celtiberian stone statue dates from the 4th century BC. It was discovered (1971) along with weapons and everyday utensils in a grave at Baza, Granada, south Spain. The sculpture shows the influence of 'oriental' and Hellenic art, and these parallels have led scholars to interpret the 'Lady of Baza' as a 'seated goddess' who, like Demeter or Persephone, was worshipped as a divine protector of life. The throne has large wings on the back and is drilled on the right-hand side, perhaps to receive the ashes of the dead.

France (*see* pages 38–39) and the 'Reinheim princess' in south-west Germany (*see* pages 194–195), were accorded prestige burials that signified their high social status, and this would seem to support notions of powerful and wealthy Celtic women. However, it is open to question whether the 'Vix princess' actually owned either the wagon or the krater buried with her, and it is perhaps significant that she took no weapons with her into the next world.

A more representative image of Celtic womanhood might be found in another prestige tomb, at Heuneberg, south-west Germany. The main occupant is a man in his 40s, laid out in full splendour with a panoply of rich grave goods. Sprawled across his body is that of a woman in her 20s; she is finely dressed, but we may question whether she died of natural causes, or willingly by her own hand. One interpretation of this grim scene is that the woman, who may well have been his 'wife', was sacrificed as a 'grave good' to accompany the dead man on his last journey.

A man's world

While scholars may debate whether a woman had greater legal rights under a Roman emperor or an Irish chieftain, there was little basic difference between the cultures – authority was essentially male, and status at all levels of society was determined primarily by paternity and the fighting prowess of warrior-men. The world of the Ulster myths – the earliest surviving Celtic literature – is just as much a man's world as that of the classical writers, with women reduced to roles of drudgery unless they happen to be high-born hostage-wives.

We should, perhaps, not be surprised at the similar lowly status and oppressive experiences of Roman and Celtic women because both societies spoke languages belonging to related branches of the Indo-European family. Among the many achievements with which Indo-Europeans are credited is the destruction (through invasion) of a matriarchal 'Old European' culture that is sometimes called the Goddess culture.

JEWELLERY

The Greek philosopher and traveller, Poseidonius (c.135–c.51 BC), acquired first-hand knowledge of the Celts when he visited southern Gaul early in the 1st century BC. His *Histories* were much cited by some ancient writers, including Strabo (c.64 BC–c.AD 23), and they provided an unaccredited source for others, including Julius Caesar (100–44 BC). When describing the Celts' extravagant taste in jewellery, Poseidonius wrote:

▶ **Gold tubular torque** found at Ardnaglug, County Roscommon, west Ireland. The torque dates from the 3rd century BC, and was probably made in Gaul. The ring is formed by two curved gold tubes soldered together. The nutmeg shaped feature at the front was made in two pieces which were then soldered together and the seam disguised by a meandering wire. The motif is a continuous series of raised S-shapes terminating in round bosses. The cone shaped features either side are decorated with repoussé spirals and round bosses against a dotted background.

.....They accumulate large quantities of gold and use it for personal ornament, men as well as women. They wear bracelets on wrists and arms, and around their necks thick rings of gold...

Discretion, display and status

In Græco-Roman culture – the tone of which was set by high-density urban populations – public behaviour was governed by laws, customs and conventions that tended to minimise the potential for social unrest. The wealthy élite were expected to behave with restraint (at least in public) and the ostentatious display of wealth in personal dress was considered vulgar and 'non-aristocratic'. At the time Poseidonius was writing, Rome was still theoretically a democratic republic, and the élite 'competed' in displays of public austerity – a form of inverse snobbery. A single, discrete finger-ring was typically the only jewellery that well-heeled Roman males would permit themselves; jewellery was strictly for women, and women only wore large pieces on special occasions.

The Celts, whose culture was as much bound by law, custom and convention as its Roman counterpart, had no such inhibitions about jewellery. At all levels of society, the basic rule seems to have been 'if you've got it, flaunt it', although there was undoubtedly more to it than that. Then, just as much as now, the wearing of jewellery carried complex social messages. Among the ancient Celts, we can do no more than interpret some of the most obvious messages.

The male role offered the most opportunities for display, and it should be noted that among the élite, male jewellery extended into the exquisite decoration of utilitarian military items, such as sword grips, scabbards, metal sword-belts and helmets, that surely must have been intended to be worn away from the battlefield. Some of the jewellery worn by men – armlets, bracelets and neck rings – may also have been badges of military rank.

The male body also offered greater potential for adornment, particularly facial hair. Razors have been found in warrior graves dating back to the Bronze Age,

◀ **Jewellery** found (1954) in a wood-lined tomb under a tumulus at Reinheim, Sankt Ingbert, Saarland, south-west Germany. The wood-lined chamber contained more than 200 items of jewellery from the early 4th century BC. The skeleton inside the tomb was completely destroyed, and one of the most spectacular and important of early Celtic burials is defined as female, largely because of the absence of weapons. The hoard included torques, bracelets, finger rings, fibulae, bronze basins and flagons. Imported coral and amber beads are present in large quantities, but they are all incorporated into jewellery of Celtic design. The large gold torque was found to the north of the two gold and the glass and lignite bracelets; gold finger-rings indicate that the hands were placed on the abdomen.

and it seems likely that the full or partial shaving of facial hair was a status symbol. At the time that the two cultures clashed, the Roman élite was clean-shaven, while Gallic aristocrats cultivated flowing moustaches. Celtic portraiture, such as it is, shows that the moustache motif was not confined to Gaul.

Precious metals, coral and glass

Gold – untarnishing, malleable and with a low melting point – was the preferred metal for jewellery. Silver was less popular but, like gold, was available only to the wealthy. Bronze, which today we mainly appreciate with verdigris, oxidised and patinated with age, has an attractive golden hue when freshly worked and was used for the everyday jewellery of ordinary people. As well as items to adorn wrists, necks and ankles, often decorated in the latest styles, bronze was also used for a range of costume jewellery, such as buckles, strap-ends, and various types of pins and brooches to fasten cloaks. One popular type of brooch, found across much of Europe, was the fibula, which fastened like a modern safety-pin. All three metals were sometimes inlaid with red and white coral and red glass; and techniques were developed for enamelling bronze with bright colours. Glass beads – the most prized of which were imports from places such as Phoenicia – were strung into necklaces, and local materials were employed, such as jet for bracelets in Britain.

Torques

The best known, but also the most enigmatic, item of 'Celtic' jewellery is the torque – essentially a single piece of metal (or several thick wires) bent almost into a circle, and worn around the neck with the opposing terminals (ends) at the front. Torques were made in gold, silver, bronze and occasionally iron. They were sometimes plain, but often decorated in some way, from simple twisting of thin torques, to the overall surface decoration of thick torques. The terminals were often enlarged and elaborately shaped. Some were made separately (as cast miniature animals, for example) and attached by the jeweller.

Torques obviously had great significance to the Celts. The horned figure, generally referred to as Cernunnos, on the Gundestrup cauldron wears a torque around his neck, and holds another in his outstretched right hand (*see* page 196). The torque also appears as a symbol on some Celtic coins, and they were prominent as votive offerings. The Romans recognised the 'Celtic' significance of the torque, without fully understanding it. In *c*.367 BC, a prominent Roman citizen, Titus Manlius, defeated a Celtic champion in single combat outside the town of Alba, northwest Italy. Placing his defeated enemy's torque around his own neck earned Titus the appellation 'Torquatus', which was passed down to his descendants.

The wearing of torques cannot have been confined to champions or war leaders, too many have been found and of such varying quality; nor were they an exclusively male item. It is tempting to think of torques as some kind of personal insignia – perhaps indicating status, authority or religious enlightenment – however, it remains probable that we may never fully understand the true significance of torques.

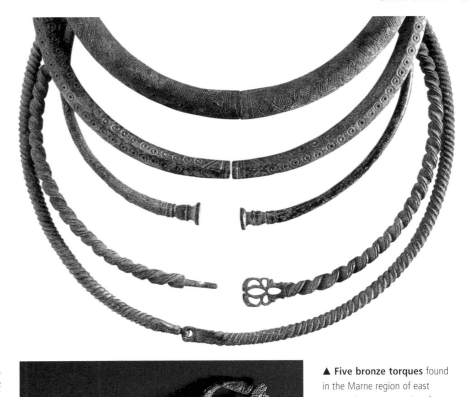

▲ **Five bronze torques** found in the Marne region of east France. These torques date from probably the 4th to 3rd century BC. They show the variety of La Tène bronze neck rings.

◄ **Bronze belt buckle** found in the royal crannog of Lagore, County Meath, north-east Ireland. The item dates from the 8th century AD. The decorated panel consists of three Ultimate La Tène-style 'kerbschnitt' (crystal-cut) spirals. At the narrow end of the panel is a dog-like animal with back-turned head.

▼ **Bronze fibula** found at Clogher, County Tyrone, Northern Ireland. A fibula is a sort of brooch used to pin clothing. They were popular items of Celtic costume jewellery and they were often finely decorated. This fibula dates from the 1st century BC.

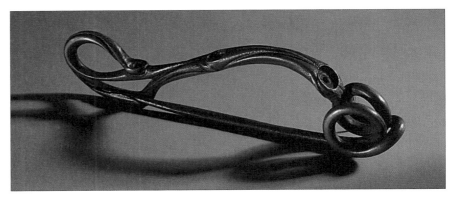

GODS

▶ **Horned figure**, often identified as Cernunnos, with cult beasts on an inside panel of the Gundestrup cauldron. The image of the 'Lord of the Animals' may have been adopted from the Græco-Scythian tradition. Cernunnos is depicted in a Buddha-like pose, wearing a set of antlers, and taming a stag by means of a torque. In his left hand, he holds a ram-horned serpent. The relief plaque was made in copper, which was then plated with silver and gold. Experts usually date the cauldron to the 1st century AD. It was found in moorland at Gundestrup, West Himmerland, north Jutland, Denmark

▶ **Relief of Epona**, Gaulish goddess and protector of horses and riders. This Gallo-Roman relief in clay was produced between c.50 BC and AD 400. It was found at Gannat, Allier, central France. The cult of Epona was widespread thoughout the Celtic world and bears similarities to the Isis cult in ancient Egypt.

L ess than a century after the events occurred, the Roman poet Lucan (AD 39–65) composed an epic poem, usually known as *Pharsalia*, about the civil war between Julius Caesar (100–44 BC) and Pompey (106–48 BC). In the first book of the poem, Lucan describes how, when Caesar led his troops across the Rubicon from newly conquered Gaul in 49 BC, the Gauls (Lucan names the Belgae, the Treveri and the Arverni) were free to revert to their abominable religious practices, and once more:

...pacify with accursed blood savage Teutates, the horrid shrines of Esus, and the cruel altars of Taranis...

The Celtic pantheon

Like the Greeks and the Romans, the Celts had not just one god, but a number of gods and goddesses. However, it seems likely that there was no 'internationally' recognised Celtic pantheon, as had evolved in Greece and Rome, but instead a large number (perhaps thousands) of local gods and goddesses. Although their names probably differed from place to place, there were a few deities whose attributes and significance were the same across the Celtic lands (and who were essentially pan-Indo-European)

making it easy for the Romans to identify local deities with their own.

The names provided by Lucan do not much help our understanding of Celtic deities. *Teutates* means 'god of the tribe', and *Esus* translates as 'Lord'. *Taranis* means 'thunderer' and was presumably a sky god – he may have been the one who could cause the sky to fall on the Celts' heads. According to the Celtic emissaries who visited Alexander the Great (356–323 BC) of Macedonia, Taranis was the deity whom the Celts feared most.

Roman appropriation and Christian relegation

The Romans largely inherited their pantheon from the Greeks, although they gave the deities Roman names. They continued this practice of renaming other peoples' gods when they encountered the Celts. When describing his campaigns in Gaul, Caesar habitually refers to the Celtic deities by what he considered their Roman equivalents, such as Jupiter, Mars and Mercury. This is doubly confusing, because it appears that a cult of Mercury did develop in Gaul after the Roman occupation. Caesar's process of renaming makes it unclear whether or not this cult existed prior to his invasion.

The subsequent Christianisation of Europe relegated Celtic religion to the realm of mythology, and caution must be exercised in making connections with the pre-Christian era. The Irish god *Lugh* ('shining one'), known from 11th- and 12th-century manuscripts, may be the same deity who gave his name to the town of *Lugdunum* ('stronghold of Lug') in Gaul, more than a thousand years earlier. Or this may be an accident of language and the limited repertoire of suitably 'god-like' names and titles.

Anthropomorphism and zoomorphism

In the 3rd century BC, the Celtic warlord Brennus (d.279 BC) is supposed to have humorously derided the Greeks for conceiving of their gods as anthropomorphic (human-shaped) figures – the inference being that Celts believed otherwise. However, as the story was recounted by Greek historians, who also found Brennus' remarks laughable but for different reasons, it may be discounted as propaganda. Although the Celts did not greatly favour human figures, their art is not totally devoid of them and some of the figures depicted are interpreted as deities.

Some of the Greek deities had their own animal totems – Athena had her owl, and Pluto kept a three-headed guard dog – and it is reasonable to expect similar associations among the Celts. Therefore, in the case of Artio – identified as a Celtic 'bear-goddess' in Switzerland – we do not know whether the bear was a permanent or temporary form for Artio; or was the connection merely symbolic? The Gallic 'horse-goddess' Epona was the protectress of horses and riders, and was more generally associated with fertility. Epona is always shown on horseback or with horses (that is how her image is identified), but a horse by itself did not (so far as we know) symbolise Epona.

The figure of Cernunnos depicted on the Gundestrup cauldron is probably the most visually familiar of the Celtic deities, and this horned deity is usually described as 'lord of the animals', but it has been

argued that the figure may be intended to be androgynous – neither lord nor lady. Furthermore, his pose is 'non-Celtic' and decidedly eastern in appearance. Cernunnos' posture is interpreted by some as being yogic (and therefore in someway connected with India), and by others as shamanistic (reflecting contact with the nomad cultures of the steppes). In either case, such influences are more likely to have affected the Thracian artist who made the cauldron, rather than its Celtic owners.

Some inanimate objects were also important in Celtic religious symbolism. The wheel as a religious symbol is as old as the artefact itself, and has been used in Europe since the Bronze Age; as a symbol it is usually linked to the Sun. We do not know how deep or wide the symbolism went; the wheel may have represented not only the shape of the solar disc but also the Sun's daily and annual movement across the sky, and these 'journeys' themselves may have been considered symbolic. Model spoked-wheels are sometimes found in Iron Age graves, and wheels are often incorporated with other symbols in 'religious' contexts.

▲ **Standing stone of Kervadel** Hercules, Mars and Mercury are among the carved decoration. The stone is 2.1 metres (7 feet) high. Caesar argues that Mercury was the most revered of Celtic gods.

◄ **Celtic warrior-goddess**. The bronze sculpture, which dates from the 1st century AD, is inspired by representations of the Roman goddess Minerva. The helmeted goddess with a goose crest was found at Kerguilly-en-Dinéault, Finistère, north-west France (ancient Armorica). The goose with its belligerent nature symbolised the spirit of the warrior. In his book *Gallic Wars*, Julius Caesar writes that the goose was a sacred animal to the Celts.

DRUIDS

Around the middle of the 1st century AD, the Roman scholar, Pliny the Elder (23–79), published his *Natural History*, a wide-ranging compendium of knowledge. In one passage, Pliny describes a Celtic priest – a druid – preparing to sacrifice a pair of bulls:

...clad in a white robe, the priest climbs a tree and with a golden sickle cuts a sprig of mistletoe, which falls onto a white sheet held beneath by attendants.

White robes and mistletoe

In this one short passage, Pliny – who was a master of fiction as well as of history – sketched an enduring image that encompasses the whole panoply of symbolism and mysticism that surrounds the ancient druids.

White has long been held to symbolise purity in Europe (in China, it is the colour of mourning), and

white cloth might have represented a barrier against contamination. There are many beliefs about gold; its incorruptible and untarnishing appearance and the 'royal' connotations it had acquired, made it entirely suitable within a religious context. Mistletoe is an ever-green parasitic plant that remains bright green in dark, north European winters, and is an appropriate symbol of growth and fertility – although its cure-all reputation as an antidote to poisons seems to have been misplaced. The figure linking these disparate symbols, and perhaps through his person giving them potency, was the druid.

Philosophers and priests

Pliny places the druids in a religious context, viewing them simply as priests; and this is the single-word description that is most often used today, although we must not think of the druids as the only religious

◄ **Warrior and druid** from the Roman province of Belgica in Gaul. The 19th-century illustration is based on Julius Caesar's description of the Gauls in his book *On the Gallic Wars* (52–51 BC). According to Caesar, once a year the Druids assembled at a sacred place in the territory of the Carnutes (probably Chartres), where all legal disputes were submitted to a council of druids. Caesar also wrote of the druids' central role in the ritual of human sacrifice, when a human was placed in a wickerwork effigy and burned alive.

leaders among the Celts – there were priestesses, but no female druids. Nor should we see druids solely as priests. Diodorus of Sicily (active 1st century BC), for instance, wrote of druids as philosophers, and emphasised their secular role as teachers and judges.

The word druid is linked linguistically with the Celtic word for 'oak', and this may have conferred even more power upon mistletoe, which grows well on oak trees. The classical writers locate druids only in Britain and Gaul, and identify the island of Anglesey (Ynys Môn), north Wales, as the centre of druidism. While this might be the case, and it is certainly true that the island had a special place in the Celtic spiritual landscape, it may have been that Anglesey (which was not subdued by the Romans until the AD 70s) was merely the last remaining stronghold of druidism. Some modern scholars have, through place names such as Drunemeton (literally 'sacred oak-grove'), inferred the presence of druids in places as far away from Wales as Galatia, central Anatolia.

Human sacrifice and the seers

Like the Greeks and Romans, the Celts believed that their gods could be influenced – pleased or appeased – through the sacrifice of valuable items, and especially through the sacrifice of life. The three cultures also shared the belief that the behaviour of sacrifice victims, or details of their internal anatomy, were among the many signs and omens that could be 'read' by gifted individuals. Where they differed was that, by the 1st century AD, the Greeks and Romans had (with occasional exceptions) abandoned the practice of human sacrifice, whereas the Celts had not.

Although druids were not necessarily the wielders of the sacrificial blade, or the most skilled readers of portents and entrails, their presence was required at such events in order for the actions to be validated, and for the 'messages' to reach the spirit world. The association of druids with human sacrifice was enough to demonise them from a Roman viewpoint as abominations to be eradicated.

Guardians of Celtic culture

Aside from authenticating rituals and ensuring their proper observance, the druids were, in pre-literate Celtic society, the living repositories of lore, law and history. In many respects, they were the very essence of a culture; and this may be the real reason that the druids were so thoroughly suppressed by the Romans, who were usually relatively tolerant of foreign religions that did not directly threaten their political dominance.

Julius Caesar (100–44 BC), without going into any great detail, ascribed the druids considerable influence over tribal politics, and this may have operated at a number of levels. In their role as masters of knowledge, the druids kept the calendar, and may have been able to exercise some control over the occurrence of auspicious and inauspicious days. They were also responsible for the selection and training of their successors from a young age, and it seems that most (if not all) druids were recruited from the ranks of the élite. Far from representing any form of independent spiritual leadership, the druids might better be seen as embodying the spiritual arm of the ruling class.

▲ *Ollamh* **and bard** aquatint (1815) by Robert Havell, Jr. (1793–1878). In Gaelic *ollamh* means 'wise man'. The druids were the source of Celtic traditions. After the coming of Christianity, they survived as bards, historians and judges. The Celtic harp was in use as early as the 10th century, and fragments of a harp were found in the 7th-century Sutton Hoo burial ship found in Suffolk, England.

▼ **Fortress of Tre'r Ceiri**, Gwynedd, north-west Wales. The hillfort was one of the last strongholds of druidism in Roman Britain. It is the best preserved Iron Age town in England and Wales.

WRITING

The *Gallic Wars* – Julius Caesar's (100–44 BC) book about his conquest of Gaul – is a third-person account, a literary style that enabled the great man to appear more objective when describing his own actions. At the beginning of the book, Caesar is most concerned to justify his invasion of Gaul, which he considered necessary to prevent large-scale immigration by the Helvetii. In support of his assessment, Caesar presents information gathered by Roman intelligence officers:

...In the camp of the Helvetii, lists were found, written on tablets in Greek characters, and these were brought to Caesar. The lists were an estimate, name by name, of the number which had gone forth from their country; of those who were able to bear arms, and likewise the boys, the old men, and the women, all listed separately...

Writing in the Greek alphabet

The commentaries on Caesar, and they are lengthy and detailed, make clear exactly what had been discovered. The tablets were slabs of wood coated with wax on one side, onto which writing was scratched with a pointed instrument known as a 'stylus'. The lists were written in Greek letters, but not in the Greek language – if they had been, Caesar would have said so. Although the lists contained numerical information, they would have had no numerals – the Greeks used letters of their alphabet to represent numbers, their numerical significance being made clear by their context.

The actual numbers recorded by Caesar (totalling some 368,000) are not particularly interesting, and may well have been inaccurate. The most interesting piece of 'intelligence' that we can glean from the account, is that (at least some of) the Helvetii were familiar with and employed writing; but they did not have their own writing system, they used Greek letters. The most widely accepted explanation is that the Helvetii learned their letters from Greek merchants based in Massilia (now Marseilles, south France).

Oral culture of druids and bards

Writing is a complex technology that has only been separately invented very few times and usually, it seems, for administrative reasons. Before they encountered the Greeks, Phoenicians, Etruscans and Romans, the Celts inhabited a non-literate world, and seemed content to stay that way long after their initial encounters with the Mediterranean world. This is not to say that the Celts were completely uneducated (the La Tène metalworkers who wielded compasses so effectively must have had some knowledge of formal mathematics), rather that they managed their society

▼ **Gaulish calendar** from Coligny, east France. The Coligny Calendar consists of 150 fragments of a bronze tablet that measured 148 × 90 centimetres (58.3 × 35.4 inches). Written in Roman capitals probably at the end of the 2nd century AD, the five-year calendar is based on a lunar year, adapted from the Julian solar calendar by the addition of two intercalary months to the basic 12 months. A month consisted of either 29 or 30 days. A pin inserted into a hole in the bronze sheet marked the beginning of a new day. A mark next to the name of each month indicates whether the period is thought lucky or unlucky.

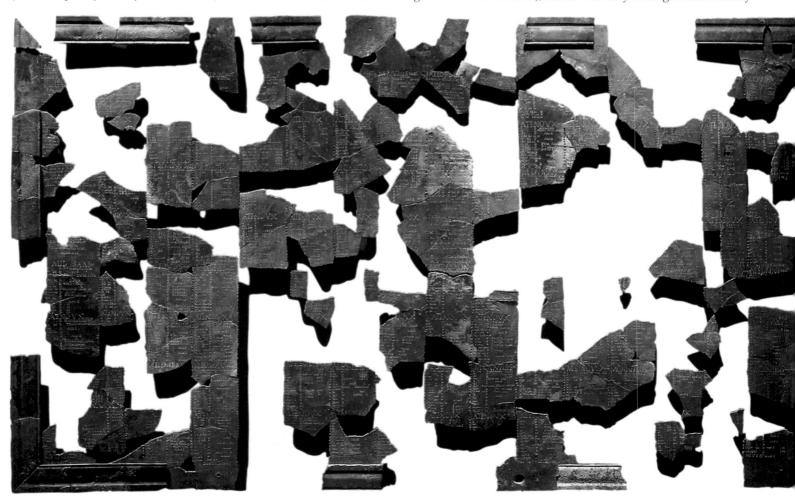

◀ **Celto-Greek** inscription from Vaison-la-Romaine, France, found in 1830. The inscription is a dedication of a temple to Belesamis by Segomaros and reads "S., son of V., citizen of Nîmes, dedicated this sacred place to Belesamis". Made of very fine limestone, the plaque measures 25 × 31 centimetres (10 × 12.5 inches).

without the need for detailed accounts and records. When Celts did take up writing, it was after long association with (usually proximate) literate cultures.

Celtic society stored its information through the mechanism of human memory, and there was a lot to remember – the totality of the beliefs, genealogies, legal precedents, who did what and to whom, first-aid, and the best way to plant beans – in fact, everything that made their culture unique.

The 'official' repositories of Celtic society, as opposed to the vernacular and familial passing on of information, were the druids and the bards. We may imagine that the druids were responsible for the continuance of their own lore, tribal history and laws, and the all-important calendar, while the bards operated more in the province of personal reputation, celebration and eulogy, and perhaps spoke with less authority, but more passion.

Both professions, which must have required long apprenticeships, will have used a variety of mnemonic aids to assist data input and retrieval, including metre, rhyme and the use of catch-phrases. When the Celts did use writing, it seems likely that the scribes were the druids.

Celtic writing

The study of Celtic language is the study of words in the Celtic language written in foreign alphabets. The only script used exclusively for Celtic is Ogham, which shows every sign of having been invented by a scholar, perhaps an early Christian monk, who was familiar with both Latin script and the Celtic language.

In Spain, the Celtiberian language (also known as Hispano-Celtic) was written in a script that the Iberians had adapted from the Phoenician alphabet employed by Carthaginian colonists. Celtiberian inscriptions have been discovered in the region between the present-day Spanish cities of Burgos and Zaragossa, and the script was also used on bronze and silver Celtiberian coins. On the Swiss-Italian border, inscriptions in the Lepontic language used the so-called 'Lugano' alphabet derived from that of the neighbouring Etruscans. If the date of c.600 BC, which has been ascribed to some of these inscriptions, is correct then they constitute the earliest evidence of 'Celtic' writing. In France, where inscriptions are confined mainly to the south, the Gauls used both the Greek and Roman alphabets. In Britain, Caesar's visits seem to have prompted (albeit not immediately) the first use of writing – Latin inscriptions on coins made in southern England. Writing did not reach Ireland until the advent of Christianity.

Writing was rare in Celtic society, and there is no evidence for the labelling of personal possessions, as was the case in Greece and Rome. The name *Korisios* (in Greek letters) stamped into the iron blade of a sword found in Switzerland is likely to represent the maker rather than the owner. The use of writing was confined to 'official' purposes, such as recording legal contracts, or the donation of gifts, and such 'documents' were often bilingual. An engraved bronze plaque found at Coligny, east France, and dating to the Roman occupation, displays the Roman calendar, including market days, written in Latin alongside the traditional Celtic calendar written in Celtic, but using the Latin alphabet.

▲ **Ogham stone** found near Coláiste Íde, Dingle, County Kerry. Ogham evolved in the 4th century AD among Celts in Ireland. According to later Irish legend, it was invented by the god *Ogma*.

ARMOUR

In his account of Rome's rise to greatness, Polybius (*c.*200–*c.*118 BC) describes the Battle of Telamon (225 BC), where the Roman legions halted the Italian Celts' last, desperate assault on the city of Rome. Before the armies clashed, Polybius notes that the Celtic *gaesatae* (bands of warriors), who had crossed the Alps especially for the assault, prepared themselves for battle in an unusual way:

...they threw off their clothes and took a position in the first rank, naked apart from their weapons, believing they would fight better that way...

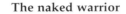

▶ **Celtic warrior**, naked except for his sword-belt, torque and horned helmet. This bronze statuette dates from the 3rd century BC, and comes from Illyria (east coast of the Adriatic).

The naked warrior

Ritual nakedness has its place in many societies – Greek athletes wrestled naked, and the Romans bathed communally – however, for the Greeks and the Romans, the battlefield was not a place for the living to be found naked. Battlefields are like no other places on Earth. For a brief period, normal behaviour is put aside and replaced by extreme violence. It is, therefore, unsurprising that the events of warfare – battles and the like – have always been accompanied by a considerable amount of ritual behaviour. While some of the rituals served to embolden the participants, other rituals, such as that of surrender, sought to mitigate the effects of violence.

It may have been the case that the nakedness of Celtic warriors, particularly the semi-outlaw *gaesatae*, was a ritual expression of their identity on battlefield. Nakedness may also have acknowledged the possibility of death on the field of battle, or may have been a means of invoking magical protection by the gods. Alternatively (or additionally), it is possible that the practise of fighting naked evolved within the fiercely competitive ranks of the Celtic élite. Perhaps 'sporting' contests and duels were fought until blood was drawn, in order to prevent unnecessary loss of life or livelihood. Spectators or judges could best appreciate such wounds if the combatants were naked.

Other classical writers, including Diodorus of Sicily (active 1st century BC), mention naked Celts in battle; however, they all make it clear that the majority of Celtic warriors wore at least one piece of armour. There are three basic categories of armour: shields, helmets and body armour. The wealthiest Celtic warriors would probably have gone into battle with all three.

Shields

The most useful, and ubiquitous, piece of armour was the shield – a large shield could protect the whole body. Unfortunately, a large shield was also heavy, cumbersome and could easily block the user's field of vision. Effective armour has always been a compromise between strength and mobility.

The most famous and impressive Celtic shields are those made from wood covered with beautifully decorated sheet bronze, which have been recovered from rivers in Britain. These shields are too heavy to have been practical, and may have been made specifically for ritual burial in water. Experiments have shown that bronze-covered wooden shields, light enough to be carried on one arm, would soon be cut to shreds by blows from even a bronze sword, let alone the iron blades wielded by Greeks, Celts and Romans. Battle shields were made from wood covered with leather that, weight-for-weight, was much harder and tougher than metal. In the middle of the shield's front there was usually a raised boss, about the size of a saucer and often reinforced with metal, which protected the handgrip located near the point of balance at the back of the shield and also acted as a weapon to punch the enemy. The Celts used a variety of shapes for their shields. One that is considered typically 'La Tène' was ovoid with an elongated boss that aligned with the longer axis.

Helmets

The importance of the human head in Celtic art is underscored by the efforts taken to protect the head in battle. Bronze helmets had been made in Europe since the Urnfield period (1200–750 BC) and continued to be worn by both Celts and Romans until the first century AD or later. Early Celtic helmets were often in the shape of a tall cone with curved sides, but these gradually became more squat as the centuries passed.

The first iron helmets, which offered much greater protection, were made around 400 BC and were essentially close-fitting skullcaps, almost hemispherical in shape. Bronze and iron helmets were enhanced with pieces of armour, such as cheek pieces, nape protectors and peaks. The standard Roman legionary helmet, worn from the 2nd century BC and incorporating all these additions, was based on contemporary Celtic helmets.

Body armour

Metal body armour had also been made since the sheet-metal revolution during the Urnfield period, but was little used by the early Celts. The first chest protectors were bronze discs about 15–25 centimetres (6–8 inches) in diameter, that were held in place on the body by leather straps. These would have been of little practical value in combat, but may have conveyed status or magical potency upon the wearer.

A few chieftains may have commissioned sheet-bronze cuirasses (breast-plates) that were shaped to mimic the contours of the human body. Such cuirasses were popular with Greek and Roman officers, but were more for display than protection.

After about 300 BC, mail (incorrectly called chain-mail) was introduced, and was probably the invention of Celtic smiths. A mail shirt, composed of thousands of interlocking iron rings, was a difficult and costly item to make, and was worn only by the most affluent warriors. In the strongest and most expensive mail shirts, the iron rings, each measuring about 8 millimetres (0.3 inches) in diameter, were fastened together with tiny iron rivets. Most mail shirts were a long tunic design, without sleeves, but with two layers of mail around the shoulders. As individual shirts weighed about 10-15 kilograms (23-35 pounds), they were probably most popular among those who rode, rather than marched, into battle.

▼ **Bronze-faced shield** found (1826) in the River Witham, near Lincoln, east England. Originally the bronze facing was affixed to a wooden frame. At one time, the Witham shield had a mount in the form of a spindly-legged boar – traces of which remain around the central boss. The boss features snail-shell spirals and trumpet motifs with three oval pieces of richly coloured coral. The roundels at each end (only one survives) are supported by a fantastic animal with large eyes, petalled ears and a palmette on its nose. The shield possibly dates from the 3rd century BC.

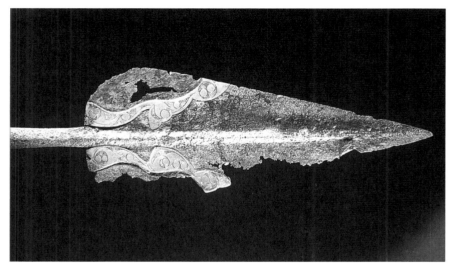

▲ **Iron spearhead** embellished with bronze appliqué, found in the River Thames, London. The bronze openwork decoration is riveted to each side of the wing. The delicacy of the decoration suggests that the weapon was for ceremonial use only. The spearhead is 30.2 centimetres (11.9 inches) long.

◄ **Conical bronze helmet**, dating from c.375 BC. The pointed, slightly curved shape of this piece identifies it as a 'Berru' type helmet – named after a place in north-central France. The earliest form of Celtic helmet, this example has been hammered and engraved in bronze and coral.

CHARIOTS

The Roman general Julius Caesar (100–44 BC), conqueror of the Gauls, provided his readers with this terse military appraisal of British chariot warfare:

...first, they drive wildly in all directions, the warriors hurling javelins...the noise and confusion created by chariots is often enough to disorder the enemy ranks...then the warriors leap off their chariots and fight on foot...

Caesar also praises the skill of the chariot drivers, who could run along the shaft of the chariot to adjust the harness at the yoke, while the vehicle was moving at top speed.

However, what Caesar witnessed in 55 BC – when up to 4000 British chariots took the field against the invading Romans - was a display of rapidly declining battlefield expertise. On the continent of Europe, the last recorded use of massed chariots in battle had been that of the Celts at Telamon in 225 BC. In Britain, which was somewhat backward in terms of military technology, the tradition of chariot warfare was preserved (albeit in diminishing numbers) until the first century AD – they were last used in battle in Scotland in AD 84.

History of the chariot
The chariot – a lightweight, two-wheeled vehicle intended to be drawn by equines (horses or mules) – was developed on the steppe fringes of eastern Anatolia around the beginning of the 2nd millennium BC, probably for prestige and sporting purposes. The use of chariots spread rapidly, reaching both Hungary and China by c.1600 BC, and in the Near East chariots became one of the main weapons of war.

Carrying a crew of two or three (including the non-combatant driver), chariots were at the cutting edge of the armies of the Hittites and the Egyptians during the New Kingdom (c.1567–1085 BC). War chariots are more accurately described as delivery systems for weapons. The weapons that were delivered from the platform of the chariot were projectiles – spears (Hittite) or arrows (Egyptian) – loosed by the fighting members of the crew.

By the beginning of the Iron Age, chariots had largely been supplanted by cavalry (*see* pages 206–207) on battlefields in the Mediterranean region and, among the Greeks and Romans, chariots had reverted to prestige and sporting use. Chariots, drawn by four or six horses, were considered suitable vehicles for deities; and Caesar was neither the first or last military commander to ride in triumph through the streets of Rome in his chariot. Chariot racing remained popular from the early Olympiads of the 8th century BC, to the 'chariot riots' at Constantinople in the 6th century AD.

Celtic chariots
The early Celts seem to have adopted chariots for personal transport, and they quickly became status symbols. The chariot's use in warfare developed out of

▼ **Enamelled bronze terret** found at Lesser Garth, Vale of Glamorgan, south Wales. A terret is a ring mounted on a yoke through which a horse's reins pass. Celtic chariots generally used two terrets for each horse and a fifth, larger ring, at the centre of the yoke. The purpose of this fifth ring is as yet unclear. The enamelled decoration on this example uses the *champlevé* technique (cutting groves into metal and filling with enamel). The terret dates from the 1st century AD.

▼ **Chariot wheel-hub** with bronze fittings and wooden spokes found at Ludwigsburg, Baden-Württemberg, south-west Germany. The pieces date from the 7th century BC.

this initial impetus. Certainly, the administration and tactics of Celtic chariots bore little resemblance to the disciplined manœuvres of charioteers in the Middle East, who were maintained and deployed by a well-organised state machine with centralised production. The production of Celtic chariots was generally on a smaller scale, although ambiguous evidence from Gussage All Saints, Dorset, suggests that local British chieftains commissioned the fabrication of fittings for up to 50 chariots at a time. Nor did the Celts deploy their chariots haphazardly in war. Polybius and other Roman historians attest to the Celts' use of trumpet signals to issue instructions to charioteers in battle and these trumpets are sometimes depicted as Roman trophies along with captured La Tène-style weapons.

In the 2nd century BC, a typical Celtic chariot was a fast, two-horse and two-man vehicle. To make the chariot faster, its wooden frame was pared down to a minimum. The low sides (and possibly the floor) of the chariot were made of basketwork or laths (thin strips of wood) woven together. Apart from iron tyres and the linchpins that held the wheel on the axles, the use of metal was minimal. A few 'royal' chariots may have boasted extensive metalwork – one Gallic king was reputed to ride in a silver chariot – but none have so far been discovered. The most frequently encountered evidence for Celtic chariots are the cast-bronze terrets – rings designed to guide the reins of paired horses.

Among the Celts, the chariot evolved into a means of transporting warriors into the heart of battle – Middle Eastern charioteers were not expected to jump down and fight on foot. The scythed-wheel chariots mentioned by the Roman poet Lucan (d.AD 65), and popularly assigned to Boudicca's (d.AD 60)

army, seem to have been products of the imagination. The Celtic chariot was a carriage, not a tank.

Although their continued use on the battlefield might seem outdated (as it appeared to Roman generals), we must not assume that Celtic chariots were signs of 'backwardness' or underdevelopment. For the Celts, chariots were primarily prestigious vehicles, not battle transport, and this tradition of valuing old vehicles continues to the present-day with classic cars, vintage wedding cars and horse-drawn hearses.

▲ **Chariot parts** in bronze and iron. The pieces formed part of a four-wheeled chariot and were found in a tumulus at Ohnenheim, Alsace, north-east France. They date from the 6th or 5th century BC.

▶ **Hercules in a quadriga** (four-horse chariot). This Attic red-figure vase painting from c.400 BC depicts Hercules driving Nike's team of four horses to the Olympiad, led by Hermes. The vase is 38.1 centimetres (15 inches) high. Introduced in 680 BC, the quadriga race at the Olympiad was the blue-ribbon event in the world of Greek athletics. The running distance for teams of mature stallions was more than nine kilometres (5.6 miles).

CAVALRY

Toward the end of the 2nd century AD, Pausanias (active 143–176), a Greek traveller and geographer, published his famous *Description of Greece* – a guidebook to the antiquities and art treasures of the country. Like any good travel-writer, Pausanias enlivened his descriptions of ruins and temples with digressions into local history. In the section on Delphi, he goes into considerable detail about the defeat of the Celtic raid in 278 BC, making sure that his readers do not underestimate the magnitude of the Greek victory. In particular, Pausanias describes a Celtic cavalry tactic called the 'feat of three horsemen', which effectively multiplied their numbers. Each cavalryman was accompanied by two mounted servants, and:

▶ **Cavalryman** holding a carnyx (war trumpet) on a gold coin (*c*.10 BC) from the reign of Tasciovanus, king of the Catuvellauni of southern Britain. Tasciovanus was the father of Cunobelinus.

▼ *Young Percival* by Walter Crane (1845–1915) from *King Arthur's Knights* (1911) by Henry Gilbert. The illustration shows Percival questioning the page Sir Owen. The medieval relationship between knight and page bears similarities to the hierarchical structure of the Celtic cavalry.

...if a warrior had his horse killed, a servant brought him a fresh mount. If the warrior was killed, a servant mounted his master's horse and fought in his place, and then the other servant in turn. If the warrior was wounded, one servant took his place while the other assisted the casualty back to the rear...

The cavalry élite

If Pausanias' account is to be relied upon, more than 400 years after the events in question, his information is extremely revealing. Significantly, chariots are not mentioned among the Celtic forces, and while the bulk of Celtic army was composed of foot soldiers, there was a sizeable proportion of cavalry – about 25 per cent – who obviously represented the fighting élite. The Celtic cavalry were not just an élite on the battlefield. In terms of military factors such as mobility and shock effect, they were also the élite of society, as evidenced by the elaborate hierarchy of substitution that Pausanias describes – additional horses and two servants were at a cavalryman's disposal, and may well have been his personal 'possessions'.

Similar trends are discernible in the societies of ancient Greece and republican Rome, where the possession of sufficient wealth to maintain a horse for military purposes, was considered a social threshold. The upper-middle class in Rome, who were one rung below the ruling patricians, were known as equites (equestrians). However, by the time the equites were formally recognised in the 2nd century BC, this was a purely symbolic distinction, since the class was far too small to meet Rome's entire requirement for cavalry.

Origins of horse-riding

Horse-riding probably began in southern Russia while the horse was still a food animal, and riding may even predate domestication. It is easy to imagine how mounting and riding a wild horse may have been a test of skill and bravery for young men. It may even have developed a ritual significance beyond rites of passage, possibly akin to Minoan bull-leaping.

Riding skills were needed for hunting and herding, and on the Eurasian steppes, where horses were available in sufficient numbers, they revolutionised society and re-introduced nomadism as a mode of human existence. Among settled peoples, the importance of horses varied considerably depending on the climate and terrain.

Origins of cavalry

The first use of mounted warriors cannot be traced, but a cavalry force first emerged onto the battlefields around 900 BC, and may be considered an essentially Iron Age phenomenon that survived until the Victorian period.

Until recently, it was believed that cavalry did not reach its true potential before the development of the

◄ **Horse's head-plate** in gilded bronze. This horse armour dates from the *c.*3rd century AD. It was part of a hoard found in the country house of a Roman general. Such armour would have provided good protection from spears and arrows aimed at a horse's face.

stirrup, which appears to be of Chinese or Mongolian origin, and which was introduced into Europe by the Avars in the 6th century AD. Several claims for the independent and earlier invention of stirrup-like riding aids have been made, and may indeed be true. However, the importance of stirrups has, perhaps, been overstated. Through the use of saddles with a raised pommel at each corner, horsemen of the Late La Tène period were able to exercise sufficient control, and remain firmly seated, to fight effectively without stirrups.

Away from the steppes, cavalry never dominated warfare, and were only useful during attack or retreat. Their importance further diminished with the rise of citizen armies, comprised of well-drilled infantrymen (the Macedonian phalanxes and Roman legions), that could be equally effective in defence. Increasingly, cavalry became a specialist, often mercenary, force. During the 2nd and 1st centuries BC, among the best mercenary equestrians available to the Romans were Celtiberian and Gallic cavalry. After the conquest of their homelands, many of these warriors continued to serve as Roman auxiliaries.

By the end of the Roman period in Europe, horse soldiers had again come to the fore. Cavalry, some of them heavily armoured, formed the basis for the mobile defence of the Roman Empire against Germanic invaders. Some commentators have seen the figure of King Arthur – a legendary leader of knights – emerge from this late-Roman cavalry.

Armoured knights, encased from head to toe in suits composed of dozens of pieces of carefully shaped sheet steel, dominated the medieval battlefield. Although their military origins can be traced back to late-Roman prototypes, surely the tradition of knight and squire carries more than a faint echo of the Celtic "feat of three riders" as described by Pausanias.

▼ **Cavalry** battle on the Bayeux Tapestry (*c.*1080). This section of the tapestry shows the Breton cavalry floundering in marshy ground having failed to break the Anglo-Saxon infantry line, located on the top of a hillock. Scenting victory, the Anglo-Saxon *fyrd* (militia) break ranks to pursue the retreating Bretons and are cut down. The militia are then encircled by the Breton cavalry.

PLACES TO VISIT

EUROPE

MUSEUMS

Musée des Antiquités Nationales, St-Germain-en-Laye
Château de Saint-Germain-en-Laye
78403 Saint-Germain-en-Laye
Tel: +33 (0)1 34 51 53 65
Opening times:
   Every day (closed Tuesday)
   09.00 to 17.15
Admission: (23 F/16 FF)

Naturhistoriches Museum, Vienna
Burgring 7
A-1014 Wien
Tel: +43 (1) 52 177
Website:
www.nhm-wien.ac.at
Opening times:
   Every day (closed Tuesday)
   09.00 to 18.30,
   except Wednesday 09.00 to 21.00

Musée du Châtillonnais de Châtillon-sur-Seine
Rue du Bourg
21400 Châtillon-sur-Seine
Tel: +33 (0)3 80 91 24 67
Opening times:
   April to June and
   September to November
   09.00–12.00& 14.00–18.00
   June to September
   09.00–12.00& 13.30–18.00,
   closed Tuesday)
Admission: (28 FF/15 FF)

SITES

Delphi (Museum and site)
33054 Delphi
Tel: +30 (0) 265 82312
Opening times:
   SUMMER Monday 12.00 to 19.00
   Tuesday-Sunday 08.00 to 19.00
   WINTER 08.30 to 15.00
Admission: 2000 grd

Hallstatt Salt Mines
Tel: +43 (0)6245 83511
Opening times:
   May to September 09.00 to 16.30
   October 09.00 to 15.00
Admission: 140 (70) Ats

Dürrnberg (Salt mine and Celtic village)
Tel: +43 (0) 6245 83511
Opening times:
   April to October 09.00 to 17.00
   November to March 11.00 to 15.00
Admission: 200 (100) Ats

Bibracte (now Mont Beuvray) Museum and site
Rebout
71990 St.Léger-sous-Beuvray
Tel: +33 (0)3 85 86 52 35
Opening times:
   March to June: 10.00 to 18.00
   (closed Tuesday)
   June to September: 10.00 to 18.00
   (Sat and Sun 10.00 to 17.00)
Admission and guided tour: 60 FF

Entremont (near Aix-en-Provence) *oppida*
Opening times:
   09.00–12.00& 14.00–18.00

Alesia (now Alise-Sainte-Reine)
Musée Alésia d'Alise-Sainte-Reine
rue de l'Hôpital
21150 Alise-Sainte-Reine
Tel: +33 (0)3 80 96 81 03
Opening times:
   April–October 09.00 to 19.00
   July–August 09.00 to 19.00
Admission: 28 FF (18 FF)

Hochdorf Keltenmuseum
D-71735 Eberdingen-Hochdorf
Tel: +43 (0) 7042 78911
Website:
www.keltenmuseum.de
Opening times:
   Tuesday–Sunday
   09.30–12.00/13.30–17.00
   (closed Monday)
Admission: DM7.50 (3.50)

Places to Visit
■ City
■ Museum
● Site

UNITED KINGDOM AND IRELAND

MUSEUMS

British Museum, London
Bloomsbury
London WC1
Tel: +44 (020) 7323 8000
Website:
www.thebritishmuseum.ac.uk
Opening times:
Monday-Wednesday 10.00 to 17.30
Thursday-Friday 10.00 to 20.30
Saturday-Sunday 10.00 to 17.30
Admission: Free

National Museum of Ireland, Dublin
Collins Barracks, Dublin 7
Tel: +353 1 6777444
Opening times:
Tuesday-Saturday 10.00 to 17.00
Sunday 14.00 to 17.00
(closed Monday)
Admission: Free

Butser
Butser Ancient Farm
Nexus House
Gravel Hill
Waterlooville
Hampshire P08 0QE
Tel: +44 (023) 9259 8838
Opening times:
Easter to October 31st
from 10.00 to 17.00
Admission: £3.50 (£1.00)

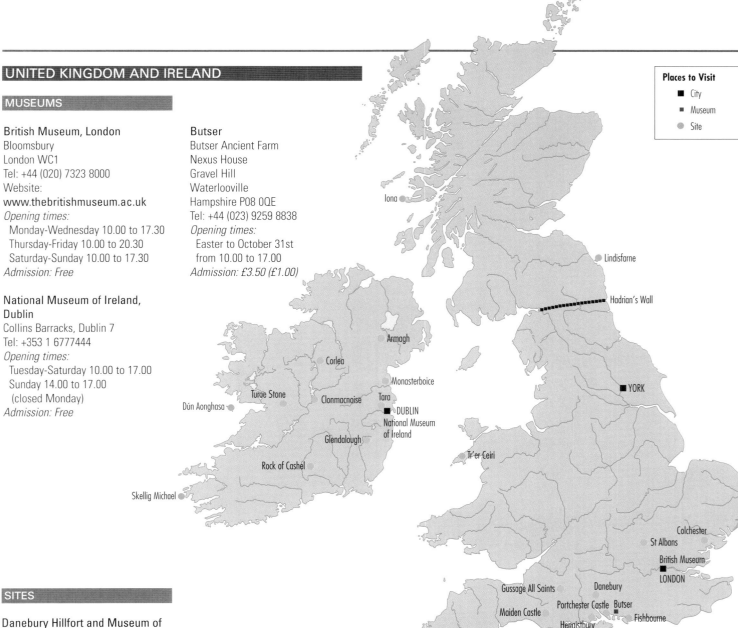

Places to Visit
■ City
■ Museum
● Site

Iona
Lindisfarne
Hadrian's Wall
Armagh
Corlea
Monasterboice
Turoe Stone
Clonmacnoise
Tara
YORK
Dún Aonghasa
DUBLIN
National Museum of Ireland
Glendalough
Tr'er Ceiri
Rock of Cashel
Skellig Michael
Colchester
St Albans
British Museum
LONDON
Gussage All Saints
Danebury
Maiden Castle
Portchester Castle
Butser
Hengistbury Head
Fishbourne

SITES

Danebury Hillfort and Museum of the Iron Age
Museum of the Iron Age
6 Church Close
Andover
Hampshire
Tel: +44 (0) 1264 366283
Opening times:
Tuesday–Saturday 10.00 to 17.00

Lindisfarne
Lindisfarne Priory
Tel: (01289) 389200
Opening times:
April–September 10.00 to 18.00
October 10.00 to 17.00
November–March 10.00 to 16.00

Fishbourne Palace
Salthill Road,
Fishbourne
Chichester
Sussex PO19 3QR
Tel: +44 (0)1243 785859
Opening times:

February, November &
December 10.00 to 16.00
March–July 10.00 to 17.00
August 10.00 to 18.00
September & October 10.00 to 17.00
Admission: UK £4.50 (£2.40)

Portchester Castle
Tel: +44 (0) 1705 378291
Opening times:
April–October 10.00-18.00
November–March 10.00-16.00
Admission: UK £2.50 (£1.30)

Clonmacnoise
Shannonbridge, Offaly
Tel: +353 905 74195
Opening times:
November–March 10.00 to 17.30
Mid-March–Mid-May 10.00 to 18.00
Mid-May–September 09.00 to 19.00
September–October 10.00 to 18.00

Corlea, County Longford
Kenagh
Tel: +353 43 22386
Opening times:
April–May 10.00 to 17.00
June–September 09.30 to 18.30

Dún Aonghasa
Kilmurvey, Inishmore, Aran Islands.
Tel: +353 99 61008
Opening times:
March–October 10.00 to 18.00
November–February 10.00 to 16.00

Glendalough
Glendalough, Bray
Tel: +353 404 45325
Opening times:
October–March 09.30 to 17.00
March–May 09.30 to 18.00
June–August 09.00 to 18.30

September–October 09.30 to 18.00
Admission: IR£2.00 (IR£1.00)

Tara, County Meath
Navan
Tel: +353 46 25903
Opening times:
May–June 10.00 to 17.00
June–September 09.30 to 18.30
September–October 10.00 to 17.00
Admission: IR£1.50 (IR£1.00)

Rock of Cashel
Cashel, County Tipperary
Tel: +353 (0) 62 61437
Opening times:
March–June 09.00 to 17.30
June–Sept 09.00 to 19.30
Sept–March 09.00 to 16.30
Admission: IR £3.50 (IR £1.60)

TIME CHART

METAL AGES & SUBDIVISIONS	EVENTS IN CELTIC HISTORY	EVENTS IN MAINSTREAM HISTORY
800 BC HALLSTATT IRON AGE Hallstatt A: c.1200–1000 BC Hallstatt B: c.1000–750 BC Hallstatt C: c.750–600 BC	Town established near salt and iron ore mines at Hallstatt, Austria. . Iberian city of Gades (now Cádiz) founded.	Assyrians conquer Palestine and Babylon. City of Nineveh built (712), on the River Tigris, Assyria. Phoenicians found Carthage (814), on the east Meditteranean coast of Phoenicia.
700		Assyrians defeat Egypt (c.620). City of Rome founded (c.635/753?).
600 Hallstatt D: c.600–480 BC	Salt mine established at Hallein, near Hallstatt. Growth of Este culture in eastern Europe. Growth of Golaseccan culture around Lake Como.	Persia conquers Assyria (512) Nineveh destroyed (528). Greek colony founded at Massilia (modern Marseilles). Birth of Buddha (c.563). Alalia founded on Corsica (c.560). Birth of Darius the Great, King of Iran (550). Battle of Alalia (c.535). Spina and Adria founded (c.530–520). Birth of Xerxes, King of Iran (519). Birth of Chinese philosopher Confucius (c.551).
500 LA TÈNE IRON AGE La Tène A: c.480–400 BC	Celts invade Po Valley.	Peloponnesian War (431–404 BC). Egypt, Syria and Palestine conquered by Persians. Foundation of Greek city states (Athens 432, Sparta 431).
400 La Tène B: c.400–250 BC	Celtic Gauls sack Rome (390). Celts raid Illyria (380). Celtic embassy to Alexander the Great (335).	Hellenistic Period (323–27). Persian wars with Greece.
300 LA TÈNE TRADITION IN BRITAIN & IRELAND La Tène C: c.250–120 BC	Battle of Sentinum (295). Celts sack Delphi, Greece (279). Romans defeat Celts at Telamon (225).	Alexander the Great conquers Egypt, Persia, Greece and Near East (233–215). Birth of Emperor Shih Huang-ti, Emperor of the first unified Chinese empire (259). First Punic War (264–241). Second Punic War (218–202).
200 La Tène D: c.120–50 BC	Celtic Gauls attack Rome (136). Romans capture Numantia (133). Romans conquer Narbonensis (South of Gaul) (124).	Romans conquer Etruscans (138).
100 ROMANO-CELTIC	Rome captures Alesia from Vercingetorix. Massacre of Galatian chiefs (88). Boudicca's revolt (60). Caesar conquers Gaul (58–50) and invades Britain (54).	Rome conquers Greece and Palestine (39). Rome captures Pannonia (Western Hungary). Jesus Christ born in Palestine (c.4 BC).

METAL AGES & SUBDIVISIONS	EVENTS IN CELTIC HISTORY	EVENTS IN MAINSTREAM HISTORY
AD 0–100 ROMANO-CELTIC	Claudius invades Britain (43). Britain conquered to Scotland by AD 84 Destruction of Jerusalem by Romans (70).	Cleopatra's Egypt conquered by Rome (20, 38).
100	Hadrian's Wall built (120s).	Battle of Lyon (197).
200	Gallic Empire (260–274).	Goths and Germanic tribes sack Athens.
300 EARLY CHRISTIAN (BRITAIN, IRELAND)	Romans withdraw from Britain.	Constantinople becomes Roman capital (330). Eastern Roman Empire founded (395).
400	Saxons invade Britain. St Patrick establishes church at Armagh (444).	Visigoths sack Rome (410). Last Roman emperor in West deposed (476). Clovis founds Frankish kingdom (481). Collapse of Rome's Rhine frontier (406).

500
ANGLO-SAXON (EAST BRITAIN)
	Battle of Mount Badon (c.500).
	St Patrick brings Christianity
	  to Ireland.
	St Columba establishes church on
	  Iona, Scotland (563).
		Franks gain southern Germany from Alemanni.
		Justinian becomes Byzantine Emperor (527).
		Europe is devastated by outbreak of smallpox (541).
		Avars conquer and colonise Hungary (c.557).
		Prophet Muhammad born in Medina (c.570).

700	Death of Venerable Bede, Anglo-Saxon
	theologian, historian (735).
	First Viking attacks on east Britain (790s)
	Vikings invade Ireland (795).
	Work begins at Iona on illumination of *Book
	of Kells* (late 8th century).
		Frankish armies led by Charles Martel (688–741)
		  defeat Islamic forces at Battle of Tours (732).
		In 756, Pepin III (714–68), King of the Franks, donates
		  land in central Italy to the pope (Papal States).
		Abbasids defeat the Umayyads at the Battle of Zab
		  (750), establishing themselves as the dominant
		  power in the Middle East.
		Umayyads establish (756) the independent Emirate of
		  Córdoba in southern Spain.

800
VIKING
	Kingdom of Brittany established (851)
	Scots seize Pictland (843).
	Danes invade south-east England.
	King Alfred of Wessex defeats (849–99)
	  the Danes and confines them to east
	  England (Danelaw).
		Charlemagne crowned in Rome (800).
		Treaty of Verdun (843) divides Carolingian Empire
		  into three kingdoms.
		Magyars migrate into Hungary, replacing the Avars,
		  and begin raiding Europe.

1000	Irish defeat Vikings at Clontarf (1014).	Birth of Ssu-ma Kuang, first Chinese historian (1019). Viking explorers discover New World.

WHO'S WHO IN THE CELTIC WORLD

Agricola, Gnaeus Julius (c.AD 40–c.93) Roman general, conqueror and governor of Britain. As governor (c.78–84), he Romanised Britain without oppression and extended Roman influence to Wales and parts of Scotland. Agricola's enlightened rule was described by Tacitus, his son-in-law.

Aidan, Saint (d. 651) Irish monk from Iona who brought Christianity to north-east England. He became the first Bishop of Lindisfarne, where he established a monastery and sent out missionaries all over north England. His feast day is 31 August.

Alaric I (370–410) King of the Visigoths (395–410). His forces ravaged Thrace, Macedonia and Greece, and occupied Epirus (395–96). In 401, Alaric invaded Italy. Defeated by the Roman General Stilicho, he formed a pact with him. Emperor Honorius executed Stilicho for treason and Alaric besieged (408) and captured Rome (410). He planned an invasion of Sicily and Africa, but his fleet was destroyed in a storm.

Alcuin (c.732–804) English scholar and cleric. While head (778–781) of York cathedral school, Alcuin went on a mission to Rome in 780, where he met CHARLEMAGNE. In 781, he was appointed head of Charlemagne's school at Aachen, north-west Germany, and became a prominent figure in the Carolingian renaissance. He contributed to the development of the Carolingian minuscule, which sped up the tedious process of book-copying and was a forerunner of the modern Roman typeface. In 796, he became abbot of the Abbey of St Martin at Tours, west France, where he introduced the Irish Northumbrian custom of singing the creed.

Alemanni Confederation of Germanic peoples who campaigned against the Roman Empire in the Rhine and Upper Danube area from the 3rd century AD. By the late 5th century, they were established in Alsace and northern Switzerland. They were conquered by the Frankish ruler Clovis I in 496.

Alexander the Great (356–323 BC) King of Macedonia (336–323 BC), son of Philip II. He is considered the greatest conqueror of classical times. As a teenager, Alexander was tutored by Aristotle. He fought alongside his father against Thebes and Athens at the Battle of Chaeronea (338 BC). After Philip's assassination (336 BC), Alexander ruthlessly eliminated all rivals to his succession. He cowed the Greek states into submission by his brutal crushing of Theban opposition (335 BC). Leaving Antipater in control of his European lands, Alexander launched an attack on the Persian Achaemenid empire in 334 BC. According to legend, at Gordium, Phrygia,

Alexander cut the Gordian knot and went on to conquer western Asia Minor, gaining a decisive victory over Darius III at the Battle of Issus (333 BC). Alexander pursued Darius into Phoenicia, storming Tyre in 332 BC. His conquest of the Eastern Mediterranean was completed with the capture of Egypt and the founding (332 BC) of the city of Alexandria. Alexander now turned to Mesopotamia, where victory over Darius at the Battle of Gaugamela (331 BC) led to the occupation of Babylon and Susa and made Alexander master of south-west Asia. In 330 BC, he conquered Media. Alexander continued his relentless march eastwards, subduing Bactria en route to conquering the whole of central Asia by 328 BC. Alexander resorted to increasingly authoritarian measures to ensure the loyalty of his troops, such as the execution of the historian Callisthenes. In 327 BC, Alexander invaded India, founding the city of Bucephala (named after his horse Bucephalus). Alexander was prevented from advancing further into India, however, by the threat of mutiny. He returned to Persia, and his adoption of Persian customs infuriated many Macedonians. Alexander died in Babylon, leaving no appointed heir. He was chiefly responsible for the spread of Greek civilisation in the Mediterranean and western Asia.

Alfred (the Great) (849–99) King of Wessex (871–99), brother and successor of Ethelred I. He saved Wessex from the Danes and laid the foundations of a united English kingdom. After the Danish invasion of 878, Alfred escaped to Athelney, Somerset, returning to defeat the Danes at Edington and recover the kingdom. His pact with the Danish leader, Guthrum (who accepted Christian baptism), roughly divided England in two: the Danelaw occupied the north-east, while Alfred controlled Wessex and part of Mercia. However, after his capture of London (886), Alfred's leadership was widely recognised throughout England. Alfred was a noted scholar, perhaps best known for his translation of the *Soliloquies* of Saint AUGUSTINE. He was succeeded by his son, Edward the Elder.

Angles Germanic tribe from the Angeln district of Schleswig-Holstein, north Germany. In the 5th century, the Angles invaded England with neighbouring tribes, including Jutes and Saxons. They settled mainly in Northumbria and East Anglia. The name England (Angle-land) derives from them.

Ambiorix (active 54 BC) Gallic chieftain of the Eburones. He led the Eburone tribe in resistance to Julius CAESAR's invasion (54 BC). They defeated the Romans at Atuatuca (now Tongeren, central Belgium), but were

subsequently crushed by the Roman forces and forced to retreat across the Rhine.

Anne (1665–1714) Queen of Great Britain and Ireland (1702–14), second daughter of James II. Succeeding William III, Anne was the last Stuart sovereign and, after the Act of Union (1707), the first monarch of the United Kingdom of England and Scotland. Brought up a Protestant, she married Prince George of Denmark (1683). Despite 18 pregnancies, no child survived her. The War of the Spanish Succession (1701–14) dominated her reign and is often called Queen Anne's War. Anne was the last English monarch to exercise the royal veto over legislation (1707), but the rise of parliamentary government was inexorable. The Jacobite cause was crushed when Anne was succeeded by George I. Her reign is notable for the vibrancy that party conflict between Whigs and Tories instilled in contemporary arts and culture.

Antony, Mark (82–30 BC) (Marcus Antonius) Roman general and statesman. He fought with distinction in Julius CAESAR's campaign (54–50 BC) in Gaul. In 49 BC, Antony became tribune. Civil war broke out between Pompey and Caesar, and after the decisive Battle of Pharsalus (48 BC), Antony was made consul. After Caesar's assassination (44 BC), he inspired the mob to drive the conspirators, Brutus and Cassius, from Rome. Octavian (later AUGUSTUS) emerged as Antony's main rival. Octavian and Brutus joined forces and Antony retreated to Transalpine Gaul. He sued for peace. Antony, Octavian and Lepidus formed the so-called Second Triumvirate, which divided up the Roman territories: Antony received Asia. He and Cleopatra, queen of Egypt, became lovers. In 40 BC, Antony married Octavian's sister, Octavia, but continued to live with Cleopatra in Alexandria and became isolated from Rome. In 32 BC, the Senate deprived Antony of his posts. He was defeated at the Battle of Actium (31 BC). Antony and Cleopatra committed suicide.

Arthur Legendary British king featured in the *Matter of Britain*, a medieval cycle of legends surrounding King Arthur and the knights of the Round Table. Two medieval chroniclers, Gildas and Nennius, tell of Arthur's battles against the invading West Saxons and his final defeat of them at Mount Badon (possibly Badbury Hill, Dorset) in the early 6th century. There are trace references to a historical Arthur in the scant records of post-Roman and early medieval Britain. Geoffrey of Monmouth wove some of this detail into his heavily fictionalised *Historia Regum Britanniae*, written for a Norman-Celtic readership in the

1130s. In 1191, the monks of Glastonbury unearthed a double tomb which they believed to be that of Arthur and his Queen Guinevere.

Athelstan (c.895–939) (Aethelstan) King of Wessex (924–39), son and successor of Edward the Elder. He extended the power of the kingdom built up by his grandfather, ALFRED (THE GREAT), by conquest, legislation and marriage alliances. Athelstan's victory at the Battle of Brunanburh (937) established him as king of all England.

Attalus I Soter (Preserver) (269–197 BC) King (241–197 BC) of Pergamum. In c.232 BC, Attalas' refusal to pay tribute to the Celts prompted a Galatian attack on Pergamum, but Attalas' troops secured a crushing victory. In the First Macedonian War (211–205 BC), Attalas joined the Romans and Aetolians against Philip V of Macedonia. He continued to fight Philip V in the Second Macedonian War (200–196 BC), but died before Philip's defeat in 197 BC.

Attila (406–53) King of the Huns (c.439–53), co-ruler with his elder brother until 445. Attila defeated the Eastern Roman Emperor Theodosius II, extorting land and tribute, and invaded Gaul in 451. Although his army suffered heavy losses, he invaded Italy in 452, but disease forced his withdrawal. Attila has a reputation as a fierce warrior but was fair to his subjects and encouraged learning. On his death, the empire fell apart.

Augustine of Canterbury, Saint (d.604) First archbishop of Canterbury. In 596, he was sent from Rome by Pope Gregory I, at the head of a 40-strong mission. Arriving in Kent (597), Augustine converted King Ethelbert and introduced Roman ecclesiastical practices into England. This led to conflict with the Celtic monks of Britain and Ireland, whose traditions had developed in isolation from the Continent. The Synod of Whitby (663) settled disputes in favour of Roman custom. Saint Augustine's feast day is 28 May (26 May in England and Wales).

Augustus (63 BC–AD 14) (Gaius Julius Caesar Octavianus) First Roman emperor (29 BC–AD 14), also called Octavian. Nephew and adopted heir of Julius CAESAR, he formed the so-called Second Triumvirate with Mark ANTONY and Lepidus after Caesar's assassination. They defeated Brutus and Cassius at the Battle of Philippi (42 BC) and divided the Roman territories between them. Rivalry between Antony and Octavian was resolved by the defeat of Antony at the Battle of Actium (31 BC). In 27 BC, Octavian received the title of *augustus* (Lat. reverend). While preserving the form of the republic, Augustus held supreme power. He introduced peace and prosperity after years of civil war. Augustus built up the power and prestige of Rome, encouraging patriotic literature and rebuilding much of the city in marble. He extended the frontiers and fostered colonisation, took general censuses, and tried to make taxation more equitable. Augustus tried to arrange the succession to avoid future conflicts, though had to acknowledge an unloved stepson, Tiberius, as his successor.

Aurelian (c.AD 215–75) Roman emperor. In AD 270, having risen through the army ranks, Aurelian succeeded Claudius II as emperor. His victories against the Goths, reconquest of Palmyra, and recovery of Gaul and Britain earned him the title 'restorer of the world'. He built the Aurelian Wall to protect Rome and was assassinated in a military plot.

Avars Mongolian people who settled near the River Volga in c.AD 460. One group remained there, and another moved to the Danube basin in the 6th century and settled in what is now Hungary. Their domain extended from the Volga to the Baltic Sea, and they exacted huge tributes from the Byzantine Empire during this time. In 796, the Avars were finally crushed by CHARLEMAGNE.

Balliol, John (c.1249–1315) King of Scotland (1292–96). Balliol's claim to the Scottish throne over his rival, ROBERT I (THE BRUCE), was upheld by EDWARD I of England. In return, Edward claimed feudal overlordship of Scotland and Balliol grudgingly acquiesced. In 1295, Balliol formed an alliance with France, which resulted in Edward's invasion (1296) of Scotland. Balliol was defeated and imprisoned (1296–99) in England. He died in exile in Normandy.

Basques Indigenous people of the western Pyrenees in north Spain and south-west France, numbering c.3.9 million. Their language is not related to any other European tongue. Throughout history, the Basques have tenaciously maintained their cultural identity. The kingdom of Navarre, which existed for 350 years, was home to most of the Basques. After its dissolution in 1512, many Spanish Basques enjoyed a degree of political autonomy. This autonomy was removed in 1873, and Basque unrest followed. A Basque separatist organisation, ETA, launched a campaign of terror for an independent state. In 1998, ETA announced a cease-fire and opened negotiations with the Spanish government. The cease-fire was called off in November 1999.

Beaker culture Distinctive culture of the Chalcolithic Age that spread throughout Europe in the late 3rd millennium BC. The Beakers continued the Neolithic tradition of constructing burial chambers with megaliths, but instead of collective tombs, they built single-grave burials in round barrows. Beaker culture was characterised by the bell-shaped beakers that accompanied burials. The Beakers primarily fought as bowmen, but also used daggers and copper-spearheads as weapons. The original Beakers are thought to have originated in Spain and moved into central and western Europe in search of metals. They are credited with introducing copperwork to the British Isles. It is likely that the diffusion of the Beaker culture represented a gradual spread of new ideas to existing groups rather than the migration of large numbers of people.

Bede, Saint (673–735) (Venerable Bede) English monk and scholar. Bede spent his life in the Northumbrian monasteries of Wearmouth and Jarrow. His most important work, *Ecclesiastical History of the English Nation*, is an indispensable primary source for English history from 54 BC to AD 697. His works were profoundly influential in early medieval Europe.

Benedict (of Nursia), Saint (c.480–c.547) Roman founder of Western monasticism and of the Benedictine order. Our knowledge of Benedict is derived from the Dialogues by Saint Gregory I (the Great). Distressed by the decadence of Rome, Benedict went to live as a hermit in a cave above Subiaco. His reputation for sanctity drew a large community of disciples and Benedict founded 12 monasteries. The Rule of St Benedict formed a blueprint for monastic life throughout Europe. His feast day is 11 July.

Boudicca (Boadicea) (d.AD 62) Queen of the Iceni in East Britain. She was the wife of King Prasutagus who, on his death, left his daughters and the Roman emperor as co-heirs. The Romans seized his domain, and Boudicca led a revolt against them. After initial successes, during which her army is thought to have killed as many as 70,000 Roman soldiers, she was defeated and poisoned herself.

Brian Boru (940?–1014) King of Ireland (1002–14). From a power base in Munster, he gained control of the whole of southern Ireland. Brian was killed in the process of securing victory over the Norsemen at the Battle of Clontarf.

Burns, Robert (1759–96) Scottish poet. The success of *Poems, Chiefly in the Scottish Dialect* (1786), which includes "The Holy Fair" and "To a Mouse", enabled him to move to Edinburgh. Although popular, he could not support himself on the revenue from his poetry and so became an excise officer. Scotland's unofficial national poet, his works include

"Tam o'Shanter" (1790) and the song "Auld Lang Syne". An annual Burns night is held on his birthday, 25 January.

Cadwalader (d.1171) Welsh prince, son of King Gruffydd of Gwynedd. After being exiled to Ireland by his brother Owain, he returned, at the request of HENRY II of England, with an army. He was blinded by his own troops for making peace with Owain. In 1165, he and Owain defeated an invasion force led by Henry.

Caesar, Julius (c.100–44 BC) Roman general, dictator and statesman. He was born into a patrician family of limited means, associated with the anti-nobility party of Gaius Marius. After the death of Sulla, Caesar became a military tribune. In 63 BC, as pontifex maximus, he vainly pleaded for mercy in the case of Catiline. Caesar was elected praeter in 62 BC. In 59 BC, he became consul (the highest office in ancient Rome) and secretly formed the so-called first triumvirate with Pompey and Crassus. Caesar's acquisition of Transalpine Gaul and Cisalpine Gaul enabled him to launch the Gallic Wars (58–51 BC) that resulted in the Roman conquest of Gaul and two raids on Britain (55 BC, 54 BC). At home, the Senate demanded (50 BC) that Caesar disband his army. Caesar refused and, by crossing the River Rubicon (January, 49 BC), instigated civil war. He gained a decisive victory over Pompey at the Battle of Pharsalus (48 BC). Caesar pursued Pompey to Egypt, where he became the lover of Cleopatra. He crushed remaining opposition at the battles of Thapsus (46 BC) and Munda (45 BC), and returned to Rome as 'dictator for life'. His dictatorship, however, proved to be short-lived. On 15 March, he was assassinated on the floor of the Senate in a conspiracy led by Cassius and Brutus. His grandnephew, Octavian (later AUGUSTUS), together with Mark ANTONY, later avenged his murder.

Cartimandua (1st century AD) Queen (c.41–60) of the Brigantia tribe in northern England. In 43, Cartimandua signed a treaty with the Romans in order to gain their protection. In 51, she turned the resistance leader, Caratacus (son of CUNOBELINUS), over to the Romans. Roman troops aided her in suppressing an uprising (57) by her husband and co-ruler, Venutius. In 69, she married another warrior, Vellocatus, prompting another rebellion led by Venutius. There are no records after this point, but, in 71, the Romans annexed Brigantia.

Cassivellaunus (1st century BC) British chieftain of the Catuvellauni. He ruled the land north of the River Thames. In 54 BC, Cassivellaunus failed to repel the invasion of Julius Caesar and was forced to pay tribute to the Romans.

Charlemagne (c.742–814) Emperor of the West (800–14) and Carolingian king of the Franks (768–814), eldest son of Pepin III (the Short). On his father's death (768), Charlemagne inherited half the Frankish kingdom and annexed the remainder on the death (771) of his brother Carloman. He disinherited Carloman's two sons, who fled to the court of Desiderius, king of the Lombards. Desiderius then conquered part of the papal lands and tried to assert the sons' claim to the land, but was defeated by Charlemagne. In 773, Charlemagne captured Pavia, northern Italy, and declared himself king of the Lombards. Charlemagne undertook a long and brutal conquest and conversion of the pagan Saxons (772–804), annexed Bavaria (788) and defeated the Avar state of the middle Danube (791–96, 804). His invasion of Spain was less successful and the Basque massacre of his army at the Battle of Roncesvalles (778) is fictionalised into a 'crusading' episode in the epic poem La Chanson de Roland (c.1100). In 800, Charlemagne was crowned as emperor by Pope Leo II, thus reviving the concept of the Roman Empire and confirming the separation of the West from the Eastern, Byzantine Empire. From his court at Aachen (Aix-la-Chapelle), Charlemagne encouraged the spiritual and intellectual awakening of the Carolingian renaissance. He set up a strong central government, and maintained provincial control through court officials. In later life he attempted to learn to read. In 813, Charlemagne crowned his son, Louis I (the Pious), co-emperor and successor. Following his death, Charlemagne attained legendary status. He was widely regarded as a model Christian king and emperor and honoured as a saint in some churches.

Claudius I (10 BC–AD 54) (Tiberius Claudius Drusus Nero Germanicus) Roman emperor (AD 41–54), nephew of Tiberius. As successor to Caligula, Claudius was the first emperor chosen by the army. He had military successes in North Africa (Mauretania) and Asia Minor (Lycia), and reincorporated Thrace and Judaea into the Roman Empire. In AD 43, Claudius conquered Britain. He undertook extensive administrative reforms and built both the harbour of Ostia and the Claudian aqueduct. Agrippina (the Younger), his fourth wife, supposedly poisoned him and made her son Nero emperor.

Columba, Saint (521–97) Irish Christian missionary in Ireland and Scotland. He founded several monasteries in Ireland before leaving (563) to found a monastery on the island of Iona. Iona acted as the base for the conversion of Scotland to Christianity. His feast day is 9 June.

Columban, Saint (543–615) (Columbanus) Irish Christian missionary to the continent of Europe. Accompanied by 12 fellow monks, Columban left (c.590) Ireland for Gaul where he founded three monasteries. Columban's adherence to the very austere Celtic practices led to his expulsion from here in 610. In 612, he founded a fourth abbey at Bobbio, Italy, where he died. His feast day is 23 November.

Cunobelinus (Cunobelinus) (d. c.AD 42) Ancient British king. An ally of the Romans, he was king of the Catuvellauni tribe. After conquering the Trinovantes, he became the most powerful ruler in south Britain. Shakespeare's play Cymbeline (c.1610) was based on the chronicles of Holinshed.

Dermot MacMurrough (Diarmaid MacMurchada) (d. 1171) Irish King of Leinster (1126–1171). Dermot's succession to the throne was fiercely disputed by rival chieftains and continued feuding between them led to his expulsion from Ireland in 1166. He sought the aid of King Edward II of England and returned to Leinster the following year. By 1170, he had regained control of Leinster and on his death he was succeeded by his son in law, the Earl of Pembroke.

Edward I (1239–1307) King of England (1272–1307), son and successor of Henry III. His suppression of the Barons' War (1263–65), led by Simon de Montfort, made him king in all but name. Edward joined the Ninth Crusade (1270) and was crowned on his return (1274). He conquered Wales and incorporated it into England (1272–84). In 1296, Edward captured the Scottish coronation stone from Scone, but William Wallace and ROBERT I (THE BRUCE) led Scottish resistance. His reforms are central to Britain's legal and constitutional history. The Statutes of Westminster codified common law. Edward's foreign ambitions led to the formation of the Model Parliament (1295). His son, Edward II, inherited high taxation and the enmity of Scotland.

Edward the Bruce (d. 1318) Younger brother of ROBERT I (THE BRUCE). In 1315, Edward joined forces with his brother and invaded Ireland in an attempt to drive the English out. Opposition to the invasion from Irish kings allied to the English thwarted their attempts to take the capital, Dublin. Shortly after, Edward was killed in the Battle of Fochart, in which the English were victorious.

Elizabeth I (1533–1603) Queen of England (1558–1603), daughter of Henry VIII and

Anne Boleyn. During the reigns of her half-brother and half-sister, Edward VI and MARY I, she avoided political disputes. Once crowned, she re-established Protestantism. The Elizabethan Settlement, conducted by Matthew Parker, saw the Church of England adopt the Thirty-nine Articles (1571). Various plots to murder Elizabeth and place the Catholic Mary, Queen of Scots, on the throne resulted in Mary's imprisonment and execution (1587), and increasing discrimination against Catholics. Elizabeth relied on a small group of advisers, such as Lord Burghley and Sir Francis Walsingham. For most of her reign, England was at peace, and commerce and industry prospered. Elizabethan drama reflected this 'golden age'. The expansion of the navy saw the development of the first British empire and the defeat of the Spanish Armada (1588). Despite pressure to marry, Elizabeth remained single. Her favourites included Robert Dudley, Earl of Leicester, and Robert Devereux, 2nd Earl of Essex. She was the last of the Tudors, and the throne passed to the James I, a Stuart.

Erigena, Johannes Scotus (810–77) Irish philosopher and theologian. Little is known of his life. His major work, *De Divisione Naturae* (c.862–66), discusses the doctrine of creation.

Finian of Clonard, Saint (c.470–c.549) Irish monk. Finian received his monastic training in Wales, then went to Ireland where he founded several monasteries. The most renowned of these, at Clonard, County Meath, became an important centre for biblical study. Finian died at Clonard of the yellow plague sweeping through Ireland at this time.

Fursey, Saint (c.567–650) Irish monk, abbot of Langny (c.644–650). In 633, Fursey travelled to England and founded the monastery of Cnoberesburgh, Norfolk. He later sailed to Gaul where he established a monastery at Langny, near Paris. After his death, his body was enshrined at Péronne, Picardy, and his tomb became a site of pilgrimage. Fursey's powerful visions were recorded in Saint BEDE's *Ecclesiastical History of the English Nation.* His feast day is 16 January.

Glyn Dŵr, Owain (Owen Glendower) (c.1359–1416) Welsh chief. A member of the house of Powys, he led a rebellion (1401) against Henry IV. Proclaimed Prince of Wales, Glyn Dŵr allied himself with Henry's English enemies, Sir Henry Percy and the Mortimer family. By 1404, he had captured Harlech and Aberystwyth castles. By 1409, Glyn Dŵr had lost both castles and retreated to the hills to maintain guerrilla warfare against the English.

Hannibal (247–183 BC) Carthaginian general in the second of the Punic Wars, son of Hamilcar Barca. One of the greatest generals of ancient times, in 218 BC he invaded northern Italy after crossing the Alps with 40,000 troops and a force of elephants. Hannibal won a series of victories but was unable to capture Rome. Recalled to Carthage to confront the invasion of Scipio Africanus, he was defeated at Zama (202 BC). After the war, as chief magistrate of Carthage, he alienated the nobility by reducing their power. They sought Roman intervention, and Hannibal fled to the Seleucid kingdom of Antiochus III. He fought under Antiochus against the Romans, was defeated, and committed suicide.

Henry II (1133–89) King of England (1154–89), son of Geoffrey of Anjou and Matilda (daughter of Henry I). He inherited the Angevin lands and obtained Aquitaine by marrying Eleanor in 1152. He re-established stable royal government in England, instituting reforms in finance, local government and justice. His efforts to extend royal justice to priests were opposed by Thomas à Becket. His later reign was troubled by the rebellions of his sons, the future kings Richard I and John I.

Howel Dda (Hywel the Good) (d. 950). Welsh chieftain, known as 'King of all Wales'. Howel maintained peace in Wales through a policy of subservience to Edward the Elder of England (d. 942) and the English court. He is credited with the codification of Welsh medieval law.

James I (1566–1625) King of England (1603–25) and, as James VI, king of Scotland (1567–1625). Son of Mary, Queen of Scots, and Lord Darnley, he acceded to the Scottish throne as an infant on his mother's abdication. In 1589, James married Anne of Denmark. In 1603 he inherited the English throne on the death of ELIZABETH I, and thereafter confined his attention to England. James supported the Anglican Church, at the cost of antagonising the Puritans, and sponsored the publication (1611) of the Authorised, or King James, Version of the Bible. The Gunpowder Plot (1605) was foiled and James cracked down heavily on Catholics. In 1607, the first English colony in America (Jamestown) was founded. James' insistence on the divine right of kings brought conflict with Parliament. In 1611, he dissolved Parliament, and (excluding the 1614 Addled Parliament) ruled without one until 1621. The death (1612) of Robert Cecil saw James' increasingly dependent on corrupt favourites such as Robert Carr and George Villiers, 1st Duke of Buckingham. He was succeeded by his son, Charles I.

James II (1633–1701) King of England (1685–88), second son of Charles I. After the second English Civil War (1648) James escaped to Holland. In 1659, he married Anne Hyde, daughter of the Earl of Clarendon, and the couple had two daughters (later Queens Mary II and Anne I). At the Restoration (1660) of his brother Charles II, James was appointed Lord High Admiral. In 1669, he converted to Roman Catholicism and was forced to resign his offices. On his accession, James was confronted by the Duke of Monmouth's Rebellion (1685). His pro-Catholic policies and the birth of a son (James Edward Stuart) to his second wife, Mary of Moderna, provoked the Glorious Revolution (1688–89). Mary and her husband, William of Orange, assumed the crown and James fled to France. With French aid, he invaded Ireland but was defeated by William at the Battle of the Boyne (1690).

Kenneth I (MacAlpin) (d. 858) Kenneth I was the founder of the Scottish dynasty. He defeated the Picts in 846 and moved the seat of government to Scone.

Llywelyn ap Gruffydd (d.1282) (Llywelyn the Last) Prince of Wales, grandson of Llywelyn ap Iorwerth. Allied with the rebellious English barons, he gained control of much territory and was recognised as Prince of Wales by the Treaty of Montgomery (1267). The accession of Edward III brought his ruin. In 1282, he renewed his rebellion and was killed in battle.

Louis XIV (1638–1715) King of France (1643–1715). The first part of his reign was dominated by Cardinal Mazarin. From 1661, Louis ruled personally as the epitome of absolute monarchy and became known as the "Sun King" for the luxury of his court. As ministers, he chose men of low rank or the junior nobility, such as the able Colbert. Louis' wars of aggrandisement in the Low Countries and elsewhere drained the treasury. His revocation of the Edict of Nantes drove Huguenots abroad, weakening the economy. In the War of the Spanish Succession (1701–14), the French armies were decisively defeated.

Mary I (1516–58) (Mary Tudor) Queen of England (1553–58), daughter of Henry VIII and Catherine of Aragon. During the reign of her half-brother, Edward VI, she remained a devout Catholic. On Edward's death, the Duke of Northumberland arranged the brief usurpation of Lady Jane Grey but Mary acceded with popular support. In 1554, a Spanish alliance was secured by her marriage to the future King Philip II of Spain. The marriage provoked a rebellion, led by

Sir Thomas Wyatt, and hostility intensified after England lost Calais to France in 1558. Mary's determination to re-establish papal authority saw the restoration of heresy laws. The resultant execution of *c*.300 Protestants, including Cranmer, Latimer and Ridley, earned her the epithet 'Bloody Mary'. She was succeeded by ELIZABETH I.

Muirchertach (active 1086–1119) Irish king, great-grandson of Brian BORU. Muirchertach held the high-kingship of Ireland sporadically between 1086 and 1119.

Napoleon I (1769–1821) (Napoléon Bonaparte) Emperor of the French (1804–15), b. Corsica. One of the greatest military leaders of modern times, he became a brigadier (1793) after driving the British out of Toulon. In 1796, Napoleon married Joséphine de Beauharnais and was given command in Italy, where he defeated the Austrians and Sardinians. In 1798, he launched an invasion of Egypt, but was defeated by Nelson at the Battle of Aboukir Bay. In 1799, Napoleon returned to Paris, where his coup of 18 Brumaire (9 November) overthrew the Directory and set up the Consulate. As First Consul, he enacted domestic reforms such as the Code Napoléon, while defeating the Austrians at Marengo (1800) and making peace with the British at Amiens (1802). Efforts to extend French power led to the Napoleonic Wars (1803–15). After the Battle of Trafalgar (1805), Britain controlled the seas, but Napoleon's Grand Army continued to score notable land victories at Austerlitz (1805) and Jena (1806). The Continental System attempted to defeat Britain by a commercial blockade that led indirectly to the Peninsular War (1808–14). In 1810, after obtaining a divorce from Joséphine, Napoleon married Marie Louise who bore him a son, the future NAPOLEON II. In 1812, Napoleon invaded Russia with a million-man army. Forced to retreat by hunger, more than 400,000 soldiers perished in the cold Russian winter. In 1813, Napoleon was routed by a new European coalition at Leipzig. In March 1814, Paris was captured and Napoleon was exiled to Elba. In March 1815, he escaped and returned to France, overthrowing the Bourbon king Louis XVIII. The Hundred Days of his return to power ended with defeat at the Battle of Waterloo (June 1815). Napoleon was exiled to St Helena, where he died.

Napoleon III (1808–73) French president (1849–52) and then emperor (1852–70), son of Louis Bonaparte and nephew of NAPOLEON I, b. Louis Napoléon. After the fall of his uncle (1815), he was forced into exile in Switzerland. Louis Napoléon led two failed coups against Louis Philippe of France (1836, 1840). After the first, he was exiled to the United States; after the second, he was sentenced to life imprisonment, but escaped to Britain in 1846. Louis Napoléon returned from exile after the February Revolution (1848) and, trading largely on the basis of his uncle's legend, won a landslide victory in elections for president of the Second Republic. In December 1851, having failed to change the constitution that restricted him to one term in office, Louis Napoléon carried out a successful coup. In 1852, he established the Second Empire, taking the title Napoleon III. His dictatorship restricted the freedom of the press, but promoted public works and improved social-welfare provision for the poor. In foreign affairs, Napoleon joined the coalition against Russia in the Crimean War (1853–56) and defeated the Austrians at the Battle of Solferino (1859), northern Italy. He was awarded Nice and Savoy by the Conte di Cavour. Napoleon also sought to expand the French empire in Indochina, West Africa and the Middle East, but his attempts to establish a Mexican empire under the Archduke Maximilian ended in disaster. In 1860, Napoleon signed a a free-trade agreement with Great Britain and began to relax his restrictions on civil liberties in France, granting freedom of assembly in 1868. Napoleon was provoked by Otto von Bismarck into entering the Franco-Prussian War (1870–71) and defeat at the Battle of Sedan (1870) was swiftly followed by a Republican rising that ended his reign.

Nomenoë (d. 51) Duke of Brittany (826–51). In the 9th century, Nomenoë revolted against Charles the Bald (823–77) and unified Brittany. He seized Nantes and Rennes and created a metropolitan see at Dol which was entirely independent from the Carolingian papacy.

Patrick, Saint (active 5th century AD) Patron saint of Ireland. Facts about his life are confused by legend. What is known of Patrick comes almost entirely from his autobiography, *Confession*. He was born in Britain into a Romanised Christian family. Abducted by marauders at the age of 16, Patrick was carried off to Ireland and sold to a local chief. After six years as a herdsman, during which period he became increasingly reliant on his Christian faith, he escaped back to Britain. In 432, Patrick returned to Ireland as a missionary of Pope Celestine I, and established an episcopal see at Armagh. His missionary work was so successful that Christianity was firmly established in Ireland before he died. By tradition he is also said to have banished snakes from Ireland. His feast day is 17 March.

Rhodri Mawr of Gwynedd (d. 878), leader who became King of Gwynedd (844), Powys (855) and two parts of south-west Wales, previously united as Seisyllwg (872). Spending much of his career fighting the Danes, he was eventually killed by the Saxons.

Robert I (the Bruce) (1274–1329) King of Scotland (1306–29). He was descended from a prominent Anglo-Norman family with a strong claim to the crown. In 1296, Robert swore fealty to EDWARD I of England but in 1297, joined a Scottish revolt against the English. He later renewed his allegiance to Edward, but his divided loyalties made him suspect. After killing a powerful rival, John Comyn, Robert had himself crowned king of Scotland but, defeated at Methven (1306) by the English, he fled the kingdom. Returning on Edward's death (1307), the Bruce renewed the struggle with increasing support. In 1314, he won a famous victory over the English at Bannockburn. The battle secured Scottish independence, which was finally recognised in the Treaty of Northampton (1328).

Seleucus II (r.247–226 BC) Seleucus II spent his reign fighting Ptolemy III of Egypt and Antiochus Hierax, his brother and rival, losing territory to both.

Vercingetorix (d. 46 BC) Leader of the Gauls who united the diverse Gallic tribes against Julius CAESAR's Roman armies in 52 BC. A brilliant strategist, he retreated before Caesar's forces, burning towns to destroy a source of supply for the Romans. He halted at the fortress of Alesia where Caesar encircled him, destroyed his Gallic reinforcements, and captured him. Vercingetorix was displayed in Caesar's triumph (46) and then executed.

William III (of Orange) (1650–1702) King of England, Scotland and Ireland (1689–1702). He was born after the death of his father, William II, Prince of Orange, and succeeded him as ruler in effect of the United Provinces (Netherlands) in 1572. In 1677, he married Mary, daughter of JAMES II of England, and following the Glorious Revolution (1688), he and Mary, strong Protestants, replaced the Catholic James II. William's victory over James at the Battle of the Boyne (1690) confirmed the Protestant succession. William and Mary ruled jointly until her death in 1694. In 1699, he organised the alliance that was to defeat the French in the War of the Spanish Succession. Never popular in England, William approved the Bill of Rights (1689) and other measures that diminished the royal prerogative.

FURTHER READING

Among many, many books, readers may find the following of interest: (in alphabetical order by first named author or editor)

Aalen, F (ed), *Atlas of the Rural Irish Landscape* (Cork University Press, 1997) An excellent and well-illustrated book which emphasises the historical context.

Birkhan, H, *Celts: Images of their Culture* (Verlag der Österreichen Akademie der Wissenschaften 1999) Wide-ranging summary with breathtaking illustrations.

Braudel, F, *A History of Civilizations* (Penguin 1993) A single-volume summary by the 20th century's most influential historian.

Bruneaux, J.-L, *The Celtic Gauls: Gods, Rites and Sanctuaries* (Seaby 1988) Excellent overview of Celtic ritual and religion, including recent French discoveries.

Carman, J (ed), *Ancient Warfare* (Sutton Publishing 1999) Challenges the idea of a peaceful prehistory.

Clutton-Brock, J, *Horse Power* (Harvard University Press 1992) Authoritative historical account of the domestication and use of horses.

Cribb, J (ed), *Money* (British Museum 1986) Excellent and well-illustrated exhibition guide to money and currency from cowrie shells to credit cards.

Cunliffe, B (ed), *Prehistoric Europe* (Oxford University Press 1994) Thought-provoking summaries by acknowledged experts.

Cunliffe, B, *The Ancient Celts* (Oxford University Press 1997) Comprehensive and well-illustrated history of the Celts.

Cunliffe, B, *Iron Age Communities in Britain* (Routledge 1991) **Comprehensive summary of the British Iron Age.**

Crystal, D, *The Cambridge Encyclopedia of Language* (Cambridge University Press 1987) A useful survey of all aspects of language.

Delouche, F (ed), *Illustrated History of Europe* (Weidenfeld and Nicholson 1992) Attempts a euro-view of European history.

Diamond, J, *Guns, Germs and Steel* (Jonathan Cape 1997) An illuminating account of the history of the past 13,000 years.

Edwards, N, *The Archaeology of Early Medieval Ireland* (Routledge 1990) Excellent and well-illustrated guide to the evidence from the early Christian period.

Ellis, P, *Erin's Blood Royal* (Constable 1999) Family histories of Irish aristocracy.

Eluere, C, *The Celts* (Thames and Hudson 1993) Brief, highly illustrated overview.

Fagan, B, *People of the Earth* (Longman 1999) Comprehensive introduction to world prehistory.

Grant, M, *A Short History of Classical Civilisation* (Weidenfeld and Nicholson 1991) Concentrates on the politics and literature of the Greeks and Romans.

Freeman, C, *Egypt, Greece and Rome* (Oxford University Press 1996) Introduction to the great civilisations of the ancient Mediterranean.

Greene, M, *The Gods of the Celts* (Bramley Books 1986) A detailed survey which brings together textual and archæological evidence.

Greene, M (ed), *The Celtic World* (Routledge 1991) Excellent, mutli-authored overview of all aspects of the prehistoric Celts.

James, S, *Exploring the World of the Celts* (Thames and Hudson 1993) Highly illustrated and informative overview.

James, S, *Britain and the Celtic Iron Age* (British Museum Press 1997) A short guide to late prehistoric Britain.

James, S, *The Atlantic Celts* (British Museum Press 1999) Calls into question the idea of Celtic continuity from ancient times.

Litton, H, *The Celts* (Wolfhound Press 1997) An excellent illustrated introduction to the subject.

Mallory, J, *In Search of the Indo-Europeans* (Thames and Hudson 1989) A comprehensive summary of the debates concerning Indo-European origins.

Megaw, R & V, *Celtic Art: From its Beginnings to the Book of Kells* (Thames and Hudson 2001) Standard text on La Tène art.

Paor, M. de, *Early Christian Ireland* (Thames and Hudson 1958) Despite its age, this remains a very useful overview.

Piggott, S, *Wagon, Chariot and Carriage* (Thames and Hudson 1991) Traces the development of vehicles as status symbols over the past 5000 years.

Pounds, N, *A Historical Geography of Europe* (Cambridge University Press 1990) Good overview from 500 BC to the present-day that concentrates on settlement and land use.

Raftery, B, *Pagan Celtic Ireland* (Thames and Hudson 1994) Comprehensive survey of the archæological evidence from Ireland's enigmatic Iron Age.

Raftery, B, Frey, O-H, Kruta, V, Szabó, M, *The Celts* (Thames and Hudson 1991) Massive, lavishly illustrated catalogue of the Celtic exhibition at Venice in 1991.

Renfrew, C, *Archæology* (Thames and Hudson 1991) Well-illustrated exposition of the theories, methods and practice of archæology.

Stringer, C, *African Exodus* (Jonathan Cape 1996) Presents the various evidence for humanity's African origins.

Wells, P, *Farms, Villages, and Cities* (Cornell University Press 1984) Examines the development of towns and commerce in late prehistoric Europe.

INDEX

bold = illustration/map
italic = caption/box text

PICTURE ACKNOWLEDGEMENTS

1 Werner Forman /British Museum, London
2 AKG London /Erich Lessing /Landesmuseum Johanneum, Graz
6 Bridgeman Art Library /National Museum of Ireland, Dublin

CHAPTER ONE
9 Werner Forman /National Museum, Copenhagen
10 Werner Forman /National Museum, Copenhagen
11 Werner Forman /British Museum, London
12 top Bridgeman Art Library /Ashmolean Museum, Oxford
12 bottom Christian Humphries
13 Corbis /Kevin R. Morris
16 AKG London /Erich Lessing /NaturhistorischesMuseum, Vienna
17 AKG London /Erich Lessing /NaturhistorischesMuseum, Vienna
18 top Raymond Turvey
18 bottom Bridgeman Art Library /Private Collection
19 top Wales Tourist Board
19 bottom Corbis /Michael Nicholson

CHAPTER TWO
21 AKG London /Erich Lessing
23 Bridgeman Art Library /Museum of Antiquities, Newcastle upon Tyne
24 AKG London /Erich Lessing /Keltenmuseum, Hallein
25 top Werner Forman Archive /British Museum, London
25 bottom Werner Forman Archive /British Museum, London
26 AKG London /Erich Lessing /Mus. Archéologique, Châtillon-sur-Seine
27 AKG London /Erich Lessing /Musée des Antiquités, St-Germain-en-Laye
28 AKG London /Erich Lessing /Hallstatt Museum
29 top AKG London /Erich Lessing /Hallstatt Museum
29 bottom AKG London /Erich Lessing /Naturhistorische Museum, Vienna
30 AKG London /Erich Lessing /Landesmuseum Johanneum, Graz
30 (inset) AKG London /Erich Lessing / Landesmuseum Johanneum, Graz
31 AKG London /Erich Lessing /Keltenmuseum, Hallein
32 top AKG London /Erich Lessing / Naturhistorisches Museum, Vienna
32 bottom AKG London /Erich Lessing / Naturhistorisches Museum, Vienna
33 top Werner Forman Archive/ British Museum, London
33 bottom AKG London /Erich Lessing /Museum für Urgeschichte, Asparn an der Zaya
34 left Photo RMN /J. Schormans
34 right Werner Forman Archive /National Museum of Ireland, Dublin
35 left AKG London /Erich Lessing /Naturhistorisches Museum, Vienna
35 right Corbis /Gianni Dagli Orti
36 AKG London /Erich Lessing /Naturhistorisches Museum, Vienna
37 top AKG London /Erich Lessing /Naturhistorisches Museum, Vienna
37 btm AKG London /Erich Lessing /Naturhistorisches Museum, Vienna
38 left AKG London /Erich Lessing
38 right AKG London /Erich Lessing /Musée Archaeologique, Chatillon-sur-Seine
39 top AKG London /Erich Lessing /Musée Archaeologique, Chatillon-sur-Seine
39 bottom AKG London /Erich Lessing /Württembergisches Landesmuseum, Stuttgart
40 AKG London /Erich Lessing /Württembergisches Landesmus., Stuttgart
41 top AKG London /Erich Lessing /Musée Archaeologique, Chatillon-sur-Seine
41 middle AKG London /Erich Lessing /Musée Archaeologique, Chatillon-sur-Seine
41 bottom AKG London /Erich Lessing /Musée Archaeologique, Chatillon-sur-Seine
42 AKG London /Erich Lessing /Moravska Museum, Brno
43 top AKG London /Erich Lessing /National Museum, Budapest
43 bottom AKG London /Erich Lessing /Moravska Museum, Brno
44 top AKG London /Erich Lessing /Landesmuseum, Saarbrücken
44 bottom AKG London /Erich Lessing
45 AKG London /Erich Lessing /Landesmuseum, Saarbrücken
46 top AKG London /Erich Lessing /Rheinisches Landesmuseum, Bonn
46 bottom left AKG London /Erich Lessing /Musée des Antiquités, St-Germain-en-Laye
46 bottom right AKG London /Erich Lessing /Museum Carolino Augusteum, Salzburg
47 top Bridgeman Art Library /Staatliche Museum, Berlin
47 bottom AKG London /Erich Lessing / British Museum, London
48 top Museo Arqueológico Nacional, Madrid
48 bottom Corbis /Archivo Iconografico, S.A.
49 AKG London /Erich Lessing /Musée des Antiquités, St-Germain-en-Laye
50 top AKG London /Erich Lessing /State Hermitage, St. Petersburg
50 bottom AKG London /Erich Lessing /Museo Nazionale Atestino, Este
51 AKG London /Erich Lessing /Musée du Louvre, Paris
52 Werner Forman Archive /Musée de Morlaix
53 Bridgeman Art Library /Musée Archeologique et Historique, Angouleme, France

CHAPTER THREE
55 AKG London /Erich Lessing /National Museum, Copenhagen
56 AKG London /Erich Lessing /Musée des Antiquités, St-Germain-en-Laye
57 AKG London /Erich Lessing /National Museum, Budapest
58 Corbis /Gianni Dagli Orti
59 Muzeum de istorie al R.S. Romania, Bukarest
60 Bridgeman Art Library /Ashmolean Museum, Oxford
61 top AKG London /Erich Lessing /Museo Civico, Bologna
61 bottom Musée de Beaux-arts, Nancy /G. Mangin
62 AKG London /Erich Lessing /National Museum, Budapest
63 top AKG London /Erich Lessing /Museo Capitolino, Rome
63 bottom AKG London /Erich Lessing /Naturhistorisches Museum, Vienna
64 top AKG London /Erich Lessing /Museum of Novo Mesto
64 bottom Bridgeman/Museo Nazionali de Capodimonte, Naples/Giraudon
65 Corbis /Gianni Dagli Orti
66 Bridgeman Art Library
67 top AKG London /Erich Lessing
67 bottom, AKG London /Erich Lessing
68 top Werner Forman Archive /Musée Archeologique, Breteuil
68 bottom Werner Forman Archive /National Museum, Copenhagen
70 top Werner Forman Archive /Musée de Rennes
70 bottom left Werner Forman Archive /British Museum, London
70 bottom right AKG London /Erich Lessing /Moravska Museum, Brno
71 top AKG London /Erich Lessing /National Museum, Budapest
71 bottom Bridgeman Art Library /British Museum, London
73 left AKG London /Erich Lessing /Museo Civico, Bologna
73 right AKG London /Erich Lessing /Musée du Louvre, Paris
74 Museo Nacional del Prado, Madrid
75 Corbis /Archivo Iconografico, S.A.
77 top AKG London /Erich Lessing /Musée du Louvre, Paris
77 bottom left AKG London /Erich Lessing /National Museum, Prague
77 bottom right Corbis /Araldo de Luca
78 Werner Forman Archive /British Museum, London
79 AKG London /Erich Lessing
80 top AKG London /Erich Lessing /Musée Granet, Aix-en-Provence
80 bottom AKG London /Erich Lessing /Musée Borely, Marseille
81 top AKG London /Erich Lessing /Musée Archaeologique, Dijon
81 bottom Bridgeman Art Library /Musée Borely, Marseille
82 Bridgeman Art Library /Museo Nazionali de Capodimonte, Naples /Giraudon
84 Bridgeman Art Library /Musée Crozatier, Le Puy-en-Velay, France
85 The Art Archive /Musée Alésia, Alise-Sainte-Reine /Dagli Orti
86 left AKG London /Erich Lessing /Musée Archeologique, Dijon
87 top Werner Forman Archive /British Museum, London
87 bottom Werner Forman Archive /Musée des Antiquités, St-Germain-en-Laye
88 AKG London /Erich Lessing
89 top AKG London /Erich Lessing
89 bottom AKG London /Erich Lessing
90 top AKG London /Erich Lessing /Historisches Bezirkmuseum, Lowetsch
90 bottom AKG London /Erich Lessing /Muzeum de istorie al R.S. Romania, Bukarest
91 AKG London /Erich Lessing /Historisches Bezirkmuseum, Lowetsch
92 top & centre Werner Forman Archive /British Museum, London
92 bottom Werner Forman Archive /British Museum, London
93 Werner Forman Archive /British Museum, London
94 Corbis /Michael St Maur Sheil
95 Corbis /Angelo Hornak
96 top Werner Forman Archive /British Museum, London
96 bottom left Werner Forman Archive /National Museum of Ireland, Dublin
96 bottom right Werner Forman Archive /British Museum, London
97 left Werner Forman Archive /British Museum, London
97 right Werner Forman Archive /British Museum, London
98 top Werner Forman Archive /British Museum, London
98 bottom Christian Humphries
99 Bridgeman Art Library /Private Collection
100 Corbis /Robert Estall
101 Corbis /Eye Ubiquitous
102 top Bridgeman Art Library /Private Collection
102 bottom Werner Forman Archive
103 top Werner Forman Archive /National Museum of Ireland, Dublin
103 bottom Werner Forman Archive

CHAPTER FOUR
105 Bridgeman Art Library /Board of Trinity College, Dublin
106 Bridgeman Art Library /Palazzo Barberini, Rome (detail)
107 top Corbis /Archivo Iconografico, S.A.
107 bottom Christian Humphries
108 AKG London /Erich Lessing /National Museum, Budapest
109 Bridgeman Art Library /Roger-Viollet, Paris
110 Bridgeman Art Library /City of Liverpool Museum, Merseyside
111 Bridgeman Art Library /British Museum, London
112 top Corbis /Archivo Iconografico, S.A.
112 bottom AKG London /Erich Lessing /Musée de la Tapisserie, Bayeux
113 Werner Forman Archive /British Museum, London
114 Werner Forman Archive
115 top Corbis /Macduff Everton
115 bottom Werner Forman Archive
116 Corbis /Michael St Maur Sheil
117 top Corbis /Richard Cummins
117 bottom Gloucester Cathedral/ R. Sheridan
118 top Corbis /Michael Nicolson
118 bottom Corbis /James Murdoch; Cordaiy Photo Library Ltd.
119 top Corbis /Philip Gould
119 bottom Hulton Getty
120 Bridgeman Art Library /Board of Trinity College, Dublin
121 top Bridgeman Art Library /Board of Trinity College, Dublin
121 bottom Bridgeman Art Library British Library, London
122 Bridgeman Art Library /Private Collection
123 left Bridgeman Art Library / Private Collection
123 right Corbis /Felix Zaska
124 left E.T. Archive /Louvre, Paris
124 right Bridgeman Art Library /Schottenkirche, Vienna
125 Corbis /Archivo Iconografico, S.A.
126 top Werner Forman Archive /National Museum of Ireland, Dublin
126 bottom left National Museum of Ireland, Dublin
126 bottom right Lebrecht Collection
127 top Bridgeman Art Library /Schottenkirche, Vienna
127 bottom Bridgeman Art Library /National Museum of Ireland, Dublin
128 Bridgeman Art Library /The Maas Gallery, London
129 top Bridgeman Art Library /Southampton City Art Gallery, Hampshire
129 bottom Corbis /Gianni Dagli Orti
130 Bridgeman Art Library /Christopher Wood Gallery, London
131 Bridgeman Art Library /Viking Ship Museum, Oslo
132 top Bridgeman Art Library /Royal Scottish Museum, Edinburgh
132 bottom Hulton Getty
133 Corbis /Angelo Hornak
134 Bridgeman Art Library /Private Collection
135 Hulton Getty
136 AKG London /Erich Lessing
137 top Bridgeman Art Library /British Library, London
137 bottom Bridgeman Art Library /Musée de la Tapisserie, Bayeux
138 Bridgeman Art Library /Private Collection
139 left Bridgeman Art Library /John Bethell
139 right Bridgeman Art Library /Lambeth Palace Library
140 top Bridgeman Art Library /National Library of Scotland, Edinburgh
140 bottom Bridgeman Art Library /Private Collection
141 Corbis /Robert Holmes
142 top Bridgeman Art Library
142 bottom Bridgeman Art Library /Private Collection
143 top Bridgeman Art Library /Philip Mould, Historical Portraits Ltd, London (detail)
143 bottom Bridgeman Art Library /Private Collection
144 Bridgeman Art Library /The Crown Estate
145 top Bridgeman Art Library /The Fine Arts Society, London
145 bottom Bridgeman Art Library /Wallace Collection, London
146 Bridgeman Art Library /Philip Mould, Historical Portraits Ltd, London
147 Bridgeman Art Library /Private Collection

CHAPTER FIVE
149 Bridgeman Art Library /Musée Ingres, Montauban
150 top Bridgeman Art Library /British Library, London
150 bottom left Bridgeman Art Library /Private Collection (detail)
150 bottom right Bridgeman Art Library /Peter Willi
151 top Bridgeman Art Library /Science Museum, London
151 bottom Bridgeman Art Library /Private Collection (detail)
152 Bridgeman Art Library /Musée Ingres, Montauban
153 left Bridgeman Art Library /Ashmolean Museum, Oxford
153 right Bridgeman Art Library /Private Collection
153 bottom Bridgeman Art Library /Topham Picturepoint
154 Bridgeman Art Library /The Drambuie Collection, Edinburgh
155 top Bridgeman Art Library /Scottish National Portrait Gallery, Edinburgh
155 bottom Bridgeman Art Library /The Drambuie Collection, Edinburgh
156 Bridgeman Art Library /Bonhams, London
157 Blair Urquhart
158 top Bridgeman Art Library /Scottish National Portrait Gallery, Edinburgh
158 bottom Bridgeman Art Library /Scottish National Portrait Gallery, Edinburgh
159 Bridgeman Art Library/The Fine Art Society, London
160 top Bridgeman Art Library /Private Collection
160 bottom Bridgeman Art Library /Robert Fleming Holdings Limited, London
161 Bridgeman Art Library /Private Collection
162 Hulton Getty
163 top Bridgeman Art Library /Guildhall Library, Corporation of London
163 bottom Hulton Getty
164 Hulton Getty
165 top Corbis /Adam Woolfitt
165 bottom Corbis /Farrell Grehan
166 top Science Photo Library
166 bottom Hulton Getty
167 Bridgeman Art Library /Private Collection
168 top Bridgeman Art Library /Private Collection
168 bottom Bridgeman Art Library /Beaton-Brown Fine Paintings, London
169 top left Bridgeman Art Library /Malcom Innes Gallery, London
169 top right Bridgeman Art Library /United Distillers and Vintners
169 bottom Hulton Getty
170 top Hulton Getty
170 bottom Bridgeman Art Library /Library of Congress, Washington D.C.
171 top Bridgeman Art Library /Victoria Art Gallery, Bath and North East Somerset
171 bottom Hulton Getty
172 Hulton Getty/Wallace Collection
173 top Bridgeman Art Library /Alise-Sainte-Reine, Côte d'Or
173 bottom Bridgeman Art Library/Bowes Museum, County Durham
174 Hulton Getty
175 Corbis
176 Hulton Getty
177 left Hulton Getty
177 right Hulton Getty
178 Corbis /Robert Estall
179 top Corbis /Nik Wheeler
179 bottom Rex Features /EFE /Sipa Press
180 Corbis /Dewitt Jones
181 top Photolibrary Wales/David Williams
181 bottom left Corbis /Sandy Felsenthal
181 bottom right Courtesy of Samaco Ltd

CHAPTER SIX
183 AKG London /Erich Lessing /Narodni Muzeum, Prague
184 top AKG London /Erich Lessing /Musée des Antiquités, St-Germain-en-Laye
184 bottom left AKG London /Erich Lessing /Museum Urgesch., Asparn an der Zaya
184 bottom right AKG London /Erich Lessing /Naturhistorisches Museum, Vienna
185 top AKG London /Erich Lessing /State Hermitage, St. Petersburg
185 bottom AKG London /Erich Lessing /Musée des Antiquités, St-Germain-en-Laye
186 top Werner Forman Archive
186 bottom Corbis /Tom Bean
187 top AKG London /Erich Lessing
187 bottom Werner Forman Archive
188 left AKG London /Erich Lessing /Museum für Urgeschichte, Asparn an der Zaya
188 right Werner Forman Archive
189 top AKG London /Erich Lessing /Musée des Antiquités, St-Germain-en-Laye
189 bottom Corbis /Kit Houghton Photography
190 top Werner Forman Archive /National Museum of Ireland, Dublin
190 bottom Werner Forman Archive /National Museum of Ireland, Dublin
191 left AKG London /Erich Lessing /Musée Archeologique, Chatillon-sur-Seine
191 right Werner Forman Archive /National Museum of Ireland, Dublin
192 top AKG London /Erich Lessing /Museo Civico, Bologna
192 bottom Bridgeman Art Library /Private Collection
193 Museo Arqueológico Nacional, Madrid
194 top Werner Forman Archive /National Museum of Ireland, Dublin
194 bottom AKG London /Erich Lessing /Landesmuseum, Saarbrücken
195 top Bridgeman Art Library /Musée des Antiquités, St-Germain-en-Laye
195 centre Werner Forman Archive /National Museum of Ireland, Dublin
195 bottom Werner Forman Archive /National Museum of Ireland, Dublin
196 top Werner Forman Archive /National Museum, Copenhagen
196 bottom Bridgeman Art Library /Musée des Antiquités, St-Germain-en-Laye
197 top Werner Forman Archive /Musée des Antiquités, St-Germain-en-Laye
197 bottom Werner Forman Archive /Musée de Rennes
198 Corbis /Christel Gerstenberg
199 top Corbis /Hulton-Deutsch Collection
199 bottom Werner Forman Archive
200 Bridgeman Art Library /David McCormick, Edinburgh
201 top The Art Archive /Musée Lapidaire, Avignon /Dagli Orti
201 bottom Werner Forman Archive
202 AKG London /Erich Lessing /Antikenmuseum, Berlin
203 top Werner Forman Archive /British Museum, London
203 bottom left Photo RMN /Loïc Hamon
203 bottom right Werner Forman Archive /British Museum, London
204 top Werner Forman Archive /National Museum of Wales
204 bottom AKG London /Erich Lessing /Württembergisches Landesmus., Stuttgart
205 top AKG London /Erich Lessing /Musée Archéologique, Strasbourg
205 bottom AKG London /Erich Lessing /Kunsthistorisches Museum, Vienna
206 top Werner Forman Archive /British Museum, London
206 bottom Bridgeman Art Library /Russell-Cotes Art Gallery, Bournemouth
207 top AKG London /Erich Lessing /Glubodenmuseum, Straubing
207 bottom Bridgeman Art Library /Musée de la Tapisserie, Bayeux with special authorisation of the city of Bayeux /Giraudon